Seeds of Extinction

Bernard W. Sheehan, a former Fellow at the Institute of Early American History and Culture at Williamsburg, is associate professor of history at Indiana University and associate editor of the *Journal of American History*.

Published for the
Institute of Early American History and Culture
at Williamsburg, Virginia

Seeds of Extinction

JEFFERSONIAN PHILANTHROPY
AND THE AMERICAN INDIAN

by Bernard W. Sheehan

W · W · NORTON & COMPANY
New York · London

COPYRIGHT © 1973 BY THE UNIVERSITY OF NORTH CAROLINA PRESS

First published in the Norton Library 1974
by arrangement with The University of North Carolina Press

W. W. Norton & Company, Inc., 500 Fifth Avenue, New York, NY 10110
W. W. Norton & Company Ltd, 10 Coptic Street, London WC1A 1PU

Books That Live
The Norton imprint on a book means that in the publisher's
estimation it is a book not for a single season but for the years.
W. W. Norton & Company, Inc.

Library of Congress Cataloging in Publication Data
Sheehan, Bernard W.
    Seeds of extinction: Jeffersonian philanthropy
and the American Indian.
    (The Norton library)
    Reprint of the ed. published by the University of
North Carolina Press, Chapel Hill.
    Bibliography: p.
    1. Indians of North America—Government relations—
1789–1869. 2. Jefferson, Thomas, Pres. U. S. 1743–1826.
I. Title.
[E93.S54   1974]   970.5   73-19965

ISBN 0-393-00716-2

Printed in the United States of America
          6 7 8 9 0

For Janina

Contents

Preface

Books about Indian-white relations are usually confined to the description of the white man's policy and the Indian's reaction. To be sure, Roy Harvey Pearce has written an account of the Indian's place in American thought; recent works by Robert F. Berkhofer on the Protestant missionaries and Lewis O. Saum on the fur traders have added the themes of ideology and attitude; the writings of Francis Paul Prucha and Reginald Horsman have attempted to place the relationship between white man and native in the context of national development. But no book has yet explained how the white American's conception of himself and his position on the continent formed his perception of the Indian and directed his selection of policy toward the native tribes.

In the discussion of relations between white and Indian, the problem has always been the disparity between the way that the Indian actually was and the way that white men thought he was. It has been difficult to explain government policy without resorting to moral injunctions because writers have seldom taken into account the white man's perception of the Indian as well as the anthropological description of the tribesman. They have assumed that whites saw Indians in the same manner that the modern historian sees them, and hence the treatment of the native population has been judged as reprehensible. The indictment possesses a certain moral appeal, but it explains little about the real relationship between European and native in the New World. The white man dealt with the Indian as he perceived him.

Hence this book presents an account of the way in which certain articulate white men thought of the native peoples in the late eighteenth and early nineteenth centuries and offers an examination of how they translated that conception into a private and government policy to civilize the tribes. It treats the subject from the white man's point of view because it rests on the assumption that the initiative in Indian-white relations remained predominently with the white man. It recognizes, of course, that the native society possessed a culture of its own and that the tribes, despite the considerable influence on them of civilized ways, led a life of their own. But never after the first contact between white man and Indian, and surely not in the Jeffersonian period, could the Indian go about his business without some attention to the presence of European men on the American continent. Moreover, how the white man viewed the Indian became more significant as the two societies became more closely enmeshed in each others' affairs, and the tribal order came more and more to suffer from the strain of that relationship.

Resting as it does on the white man's ideas about himself and the Indian, the story must be seen as a study in the adjustment between intellect and reality. The paucity of native sources for a description of the Indian's part in the meeting with European man only reinforces the need to see it from the white man's side and to stress the importance of ideas. Yet the story can be no more a straight exposition of ideas than it can be a mere description of social conflict. It must take into account the character and resilience of native society, even though described from the white man's view, and it must reveal the way in which European man's ideas were ultimately frustrated in his dealings with the native world. The book is intellectual history, but it is also a history of the meeting and clash of two cultures in the New World.

As its major contribution, this study is designed to bring together the worlds of thought and action in the development of Indian-white relations in the Jeffersonian era. Many of the ideas and their implications for eighteenth- and early nineteenth-century thought will be familiar to intellectual historians, and some of the material on the relations between Indian and white has been discussed previously by western historians. The uniqueness of this volume lies in its juxtaposition of thought and event and in its effort to describe the manner in which the two depend on and are influenced by each other. It is, consequently, an attempt to infuse into the study of Indian-white relations, and into the history of contact between disparate cultures, a deeper perception of the importance of thought and attitude in the making of historical event.

Ultimately, all history seeks to lay bare the sources of human motivation. In the analysis of Indian-white relations, this question becomes particularly relevant. No description of the problem can avoid an attempt to explain why white men behaved as they did when confronted by a new and strange culture on the American continent. Merely noting the opposition of forces cannot interpret the clash of culture in all of its ramifications. Describing how it happened can, but a critical element in the description must be an analysis of the ideas that form so basic a part of the white man's attitude toward the native population of America.

Merrill D. Peterson, at the University of Virginia, opened the question of Jefferson and the American Indian for me. He always gave freely of his knowledge, and under his tolerant but wary eye I expanded the subject to include the Jeffersonian generation and narrowed it to exclude a description of Indian policy. Lester J. Cappon and Stephen G. Kurtz at the Institute of Early American History and Culture provided time and facilities for research and writing and were always available for counsel and criticism. I owe them and the Institute an incalculable debt. My colleagues at the Institute, Thad W. Tate, John E. Selby, Stephen S. Webb, and Sung Bok Kim, and Richard M. Brown and Dale E. Benson of the College of William and Mary invariably listened with patience to my musings and fulminations about Indian-white relations, and they frequently clarified or changed my own ideas. Martin Ridge gave generously of his critical talents at crucial points in the making of the manuscript. And Francis Paul Prucha has graciously allowed his mind to be picked and his work to be poached with never a complaint at what was done with the resultant material. The entire manuscript has benefited from a trenchant appraisal by Robert F. Berkhofer, and the last chapter from the vigorous criticism of Mary E. Young. To Diana Vari I owe thanks for her generosity in sharing her research. The editorial abilities of James H. Hutson and Joy Dickinson Barnes have made it possible to bring the work into print.

I have had the advantage of financial help from the Thomas Jefferson Memorial Foundation, the Institute of Early American History and Culture, and the Office of Research and Advanced Studies, Indiana University, efficient typing from Mrs. Patricia Curtis Blatt and Mrs. Dorothy M. Spencer, and willing service at the following libraries and archives: the Alderman Library and the McGregor Collection at the University of Virginia, the Earl Gregg Swem Library at the College of William and Mary, the Indiana University Library and the Lilly Library, the Departments of Archives and History, Atlanta, Georgia, and Montgomery, Alabama, the New-

York Historical Society, the American Philosophical Society, the Kansas State Historical Society, Topeka. The papers of the American Board of Commissioners are used by permission of the Harvard College Library, and the Yale University Library has granted permission to quote from the Vaill Collection. The editors of the *William and Mary Quarterly* and *American Studies* (formerly *Midcontinent American Studies Journal*) have allowed me to reprint revised versions of material that appeared first in their publications.

My parents, William J. and Margaret C. Sheehan, supplied a precious combination, a profound respect for knowledge and the means to let me seek it in my own way. From my brother, John C. Sheehan, I early obtained a deep regard for ideas. The book is dedicated to my wife, Janina, because she knows most of what can be known about the human things that make books possible. Neil, Manya, and Jessica are happy that it has finally been published and would like to see their names in print.

Seeds of Extinction

When we contemplate the Fortunes of the Aborigines of our Country, the Bosom of Philanthropy must heave with sorrow, and our sympathy be strongly excited—what would not that man, or that Community merit, who reclaims the untutored Indian—opens his mind to sources of happiness unknown, and makes him useful to society? since it would be in effect to save a whole race from extinction. for surely—if this People are not brought to depend for subsistence on their fields instead of their forrests, and to realize Ideas of distinct property, it will be found impossible to correct their present habits, and the seeds of their extinction, already sown, must be matured.

JAMES WILKINSON *to* OWEN BIDDLE, *December 24, 1797*

From whatever angle one regards the destinies of the North American natives, one sees nothing but irremediable ills: if they remain savages, they are driven along before the march of progress; if they try to become civilized, contact with more-civilized people delivers them over to oppression and misery. If they go on wandering in the wilderness, they perish; if they attempt to settle, they perish just the same. They cannot gain enlightenment except with European help, and the approach of the Europeans corrupts them and drives them back toward barbarism. So long as they are left in their solitudes, they refuse to change their mores, and there is no time left to do this, when at last they are constrained to desire it.

ALEXIS DE TOCQUEVILLE, *Democracy in America*

Introduction

    In the late eighteenth century, after the Americans severed the bonds of empire, the problem of Indian-white relations reached a point of crisis. For most Indians, it had always been so. As the white man advanced and gathered strength, the native tribes receded. Some disappeared in the violence of war, some partially adapted to civilized ways and lived a truncated existence on the borderland between the two societies, some disintegrated slowly from disease and social malaise until the remnants joined one of the surviving tribes. Of course, some native peoples endured and even thrived for a time in close association with the white man's society. The Iroquois prospered in the fur trade and during the imperial wars. The southern Indians—called finally the Five Civilized Tribes —because of their remoteness from the main Anglo-American drive into the continent, maintained their social order at varying levels of proficiency until the federal authorities moved them west of the Mississippi in the 1830s. For the northern tribes, immunity from the major consequences of the white man's advance ended in the last quarter of the eighteenth century. The Iroquois chose the wrong side in the Revolution (though in truth it made little difference which side they selected), and as a result the Americans burned their villages and fields, decimated their warriors, and took most of their land. As great numbers of whites in the wake of the Revolution moved over the Alleghenies, the southern natives adjusted their way of life to new incursions. In the Northwest a polyglot mixture of disorganized tribes mingled, some already driven from the East, awaiting the white man's next assault. Determined to make the continent a civilized domain, the new nation was forced to deal with the problem of the Indian.

    From the first formulation of policy in the Washington admin-

istration until the decision in the 1820s to move the tribes beyond
the Mississippi, a basic consistency informed the white man's attitude toward the Indian. He generally believed that savagery would
recede, while civilization spread its influence over the entire continent. In the actual relations between the two societies, this meant
that the government, with the steady application of pressure, obtained new lands from the Indians by treaty. Usually, the acquisition merely ratified what had already taken place: the movement
of frontier population into the Indian territory. Often enough,
when the event proved that more strength than the unorganized
frontier could bring to bear would be required to dislodge the
tribes, the government contributed its military power. The Indian
always retreated, the white man always advanced.

Yet governmental policy, and a substantial portion of civilized
opinion, appraised the situation with more subtle ends in mind
than simply forcing the Indian aside. The elimination of savagery,
many reasoned, could be accomplished in more refined and humanitarian ways. The Indian need not be destroyed; in fact, most men
involved in government Indian affairs, and all those privately interested in the native's welfare, agreed that the white man had a
moral obligation to himself and to his posterity to see that the
tribesman survived. If the Indian were transformed, if he adopted
civilization and lived like a white man, his savage ways would disappear, and he would endure to become a useful member of the
white man's world. Every administration from Washington to John
Quincy Adams and a variety of private philanthropic organizations
supported this policy. When the process of civilizing the native
proved slow of accomplishment, when some foolhardy Indians stubbornly retained their savage habits, or, more important, when the
frontier moved faster than the federal authorities could impress on
the tribes the need to adopt civilization, the government more than
willingly employed force and manipulation to achieve its ends.
Ultimately, however, governmental policy could best be fulfilled
by civilizing the Indian and incorporating him into the white man's
society.

Indian-white relations approached a climax in the decades after
the Revolution. The Indians now had few options. Retreat in the
Northwest meant conflict with other, more hostile tribes. Retreat in
the South meant that more sedentary peoples faced the prospect of
abandoning lands long held and changing the very basis of their
social life. Moreover, the influence of civilization had taken effect.
Many Indians, particularly the mixed bloods among the tribes,

understood the white man's aims. Determined to stand their ground, they used knowledge acquired from civilization to resist him. Some Indians reacted differently; with their social order under severe strain—in places on the verge of disintegration—they showed signs of desperation and malaise. But whether the effect of civilized contact served to strengthen the Indian's capacity to survive or to push him to the point of social collapse, the problem demanded a solution.

From the other side of the dilemma of cultural conflict, American society in the late eighteenth and early nineteenth centuries seemed likely to overwhelm any obstruction to its advance, particularly the comparatively feeble opposition offered by the Indian tribes. Little had changed in the white man's attitude since the first meeting between the two societies. From the beginning, the eventual disappearance of savagery had been accepted, and there had also been a strong missionary impulse to save the Indian from himself by making him a Christian. But by the latter part of the eighteenth century, that long-held mission to subdue the continent and obliterate the last vestiges of the savage world became more than a definition of how things ought to be or even how they would eventually become. Instead it became an immediate imperative that seemed entirely within reach. The generation that threw off British rule and created a new government had few thoughts that its wishes could be denied by some roving bands of savage Indians. On the contrary, the self-esteem and confidence of the Revolutionary and early national generations made it difficult for them to believe that the Indians would not also see the desirability of an end to savagery and their acceptance of civilization.

The essential unity of the period from the Revolution to the late 1820s, when the government decided on the removal of the eastern tribes, can be seen in both the character of Indian-white relations and in the content of the white man's thinking. The process that began with Independence and the expansion of the nation reached a fitting denouement in removal. Similarly, the ideas around which white men constructed their understanding of the relationship between the two societies persisted throughout the period.

In his *Notes on the State of Virginia*, published in the 1780s, Jefferson made the most perceptive summary statement about the nature of Indian society. His interpretation was not so much original or even profound, but it reflected accurately—it summed up in a way that only Jefferson could—the basic thinking of his age on the subject of Indian-white relations. Furthermore, Jefferson held political power for eight crucial years at the heart of the period. After the 1790s, when the last major conflicts (aside from the War of 1812) took place between the eastern tribes and the white man,[1] he had an opportunity to put into effect the policy of incorporating the Indian into the white man's society. In the years following his retirement from office, those who directed the government's relations with the tribes acted under the aegis of Jeffersonian theory and policy. Although the years from the Revolution to removal produced ample diversity in politics and ideology, on the question of the Indian and his relationship to civilization they were substantially Jeffersonian.

Men so disparate in intellectual commitment, political loyalties, and even in temperament as Timothy Pickering and Thomas Jefferson thought and acted in concert on the question of the Indian. Indeed, the policies of the Washington administration, formulated by Henry Knox, were fully consistent with Jeffersonian principles. Some with Federalist connections like Jedidiah Morse and Elias Boudinot, who maintained a scholarly interest in the Indians and held deep sympathies for their welfare, favored the general lines of Jeffersonian policy. Others who opposed Jefferson strongly on certain issues went along with him on the Indian. Clement C. Moore and Gilbert Imlay criticized Jefferson for his views on the Negro, but were in accord with his approach to the Indian. Though strongly antisecularist in their opinions, such men as Moore, Samuel Stanhope Smith, Samuel Worcester, and Jeremiah Evarts could see the wisdom of Jefferson's philanthropic plans for the tribesmen. In the sense that the Indian represented a completely foreign culture or, perhaps more pertinent, because he stood for savagery, the antithesis of civilization, white men found it easy to bury their own differences in dealing with him. If in little else, on the question of the Indian there was a wide consensus of opinion.

In the years after Jefferson's retirement from public office, Indian affairs continued under the direction of men who sympathized with his point of view. Agents in the field such as Benjamin Hawkins and Return J. Meigs, despite the interruption of the War of 1812, worked for the incorporation of the natives. Within the government, Thomas L. McKenney, first as superintendent of Indian trade and then in the 1820s as the head of the Indian office in the War Department, kept up a constant barrage of exhortation in favor of a humanitarian policy for the Indians. Larger policy for the most

1. Edward H. Spicer, *A Short History of the Indians of the United States* (New York, 1969), 11–12.

part fell to the responsibility of the secretary of war. In that office during Jefferson's administration, Henry Dearborn worked to effect the president's policy. His successors, William Eustis, William H. Crawford, John C. Calhoun, and James Barbour, maintained the Jeffersonian position until, during Calhoun's tenure in the mid-1820s, the government turned to removal.

Missionaries of various persuasions carried on much of the actual work of civilizing the natives. Moravians like David Zeisberger and John Heckewelder spent their lives in devoted work among the Delawares in Pennsylvania and the Northwest. Samuel Kirkland, Gabriel Richard, Gideon Blackburn, and Isaac McCoy were only a few of the many missionaries who went into the wilderness to bring Christianity and civilization to the tribes. Finally, in the second decade of the nineteenth century, the American Board of Commissioners for Foreign Missions, in origin a Congregational organization, united its efforts with the policy of the government for the transformation of the southern Indians. As much as did Jefferson, the missionaries demanded of the Indians an end to savagery and the acceptance of civilized ways.

This basic Jeffersonian commitment bound all these people together in their attitudes toward the Indians. Jefferson led the age, not because his ideas were original, but because they represented a consensus. His prominence as a political leader enhanced the importance of his activities in favor of the Indians. Also, his position of influence in scientific affairs gave his opinions on the Indian's future a special stature. In his *Notes on Virginia,* his presidency of the American Philosophical Society, his extensive correspondence with the important minds of the period, and finally in his determination, while he held political power, to change the character of tribal society, Jefferson held a central position in the late eighteenth and early nineteenth centuries. Judged in the light of a widely held body of opinion on the nature of Indian-white relations, the age can be called Jeffersonian.

To be sure, Jeffersonian attitudes toward the native populations had deep intellectual roots. A distinctive set of postulates, of ways of looking at reality, though not often articulated fully, informed Jeffersonian opinion. At a practical level, such opinion seemed far removed from its intellectual origins. Men favored certain actions with only the most attenuated perception of their intellectual foundations. Practical men took what they believed to be practical actions with little consideration of their ramifications. Some, of a more profound turn of mind—Jefferson himself, Samuel Stanhope

Smith, Benjamin Rush, Jedidiah Morse, Albert Gallatin, DeWitt Clinton—thought out some of the implications of their beliefs. In fact, few literate men in the late eighteenth and early nineteenth centuries went completely untouched by a "style of thought"[2] that impelled them to look favorably on the Indians and to advocate their social incorporation with the white man. The coherence of the ideas, their internal logicality, existed aside from their comprehension in one particular mind. Perhaps Jefferson came closest to being a complete Jeffersonian. But few who dealt with Indian affairs in the period from the Revolution to 1830 did not think within the limits of that intellectual frame.

The Indian became a victim of the white man's proclivity for conceptualization and idealization. Though at any given time ideas only partially coerced events, few areas of public interest were as immediately susceptible to the influence of big ideas as the relations between primitive man and civilization. Typically, Jeffersonian thinking stressed the improving aspects of the human situation. In the manner of the eighteenth-century rationalist mind, Jefferson and his generation viewed the future optimistically. Indeed, nature itself provided the means for its own improvement. Human will became less important than the unfolding development of nature's self-realization. And this process was inclusive: nature produced no sports, no extraneous energies, no incongruous elements. The same cosmic verities, easily discernible, reassuring, and intrinsically progressive, characterized all of creation. An extension of this principle of inclusion brought the human being into close relationship with his physical surroundings and opened him to environmental influence. Tightly bound within the ever-changing and beneficent order of nature, men became in great measure what the world made them. Differences among men, variety in nature, could be explained by environmentalism, as could any changes induced by a reaction to nature or by positive human decision.

Moreover, the ends of human development came within the broad conceptions of paradise and the noble savage. These stereotypes explained the differences between civilization and primitive existence, and they also presented the white man with an ideal his whole society might strive to reach. Most writers employed the

2. I have in mind here the term Karl Mannheim uses to describe a way of thinking distinct from the schools of formal philosophy and closely related to its social background. See Karl Mannheim, *Essays on Sociology and Social Psychology*, ed. Paul Kecskemeti (New York, 1953), 74–77.

concepts for rhetorical convenience or sometimes to relieve the frustrations of civilized life. But paradise and the noble savage also drew on powerful motive forces in Western thought—forces that, together with environmentalism, the Jeffersonian age set to work for the purpose of civilizing the Indian.

A deep-seated benevolence, intending for the Indian the best that civilization could offer, translated this theoretical statement into a design for action. Furthermore, the conviction that the Indian had only a short period in which to complete the work of incorporation added an element of realism. The force of frontier extension pressed heavily against the successful completion of the philanthropic plan. And when the native did not make the progress expected of him, doubts that had been only fleeting before became profound fears that he would be destroyed. Philanthropy, as a consequence, though still reflecting the optimism of the age, became anxious and itself seemingly aggressive. The full import of Jeffersonian theory and the intensity of philanthropic anticipation imposed the necessity of success. When nature did not yield immediate results, when the actualities of acculturation[3] stretched the process beyond the time afforded by the advancing frontier, Jeffersonian optimism turned to compulsion, mostly covert but sometimes frankly espoused, to complete its task.

Still, the aggressiveness of philanthropy arose from deeper sources than the tension between Jeffersonian hope and the historical obstacles to its realization. The philanthropic mind was at base obtrusive and compulsive in its determination to have its way. Though it praised the Indian for his many abilities, it conceded native society nothing in the way of permanence. Philanthropy treated the tribes as objects of commiseration whose sole purpose after the arrival of the white man should have been the speedy adoption of

---

3. I am using "acculturation" as classically defined as "those phenomena which result when groups of individuals having different cultures come into continuous firsthand contact, with subsequent changes in the original cultural patterns of either or both groups." See Robert Redfield, Ralph Linton, and Melville J. Herskovits, "Memorandum for the Study of Acculturation," *American Anthropologist*, N.S., XXXVIII (1936), 149. Also Bronislaw Malinowski, *The Dynamics of Culture Change: An Inquiry into Race Relations in Africa*, ed. Phyllis M. Kaberry (New Haven, 1945), chap. 2; Melville J. Herskovits, *Acculturation: The Study of Culture Contact* (New York, 1938); Ralph Linton, ed., *Acculturation in Seven Indian Tribes* (New York, 1940); Edward H. Spicer, ed., *Perspectives in American Indian Culture Change* (Chicago, 1961), chap. 8; The Social Science Research Council Summer Seminar on Acculturation, 1953, "Acculturation: An Exploratory Formulation," *Am. Anthro.*, N.S., LVI (1954), 973–1002; Evon Vogt, "The Acculturation of American Indians," *The Annals*, CCCXI (1957), 137–146.

civilization. It demanded a total transformation in full confidence that what was to come would in all ways be superior to what had been. If philanthropy seemed supercilious, it betrayed no false voice to the Indian. Self-satisfied, righteous, morally aggressive, and paternal, it tended to infantilize the Indian and to destroy the integrity of his culture. But the strength of its moral drive only reflected the consistency of its principles and the profoundest good-will. Because it believed itself in league with the cosmos, philanthropy imposed a terrible burden on the Jeffersonian conscience, and it asked of the Indian an impossible achievement.

Specifically, the philanthropic plan required that the Indian abandon the hunter-warrior culture, the tribal order, and the communal ownership of land. It commanded him to become civilized by adopting a variety of manners and artifacts and, most important, by choosing to live according to the white man's individualist ideology. Had such a change been possible, it would have meant a total upheaval in the native's social order. But for the white man, the step did not seem so great. Americans had always conceived of their version of civilization as distinct from Europe's, a peculiar growth of the new continent. The Indian should have found no difficulty in adjusting his primitive but distinctly New World manner of life to the similarly distinct middling conception of society familiar to the Jeffersonian age. Envisioning only a minor transition from the wilderness to the garden, philanthropy could afford to be confident.[4]

What the philanthropists intended for the Indian bore little resemblance to the reality. The relations between white and Indian, both the formal efforts at conversion and the informal contacts between the two societies, profoundly affected the tribal order. Civilization introduced new artifacts, redirected the economic and social life of the tribes, and severely damaged substantial portions of tribal culture. Indian life changed as a consequence of meeting the white man; many Indians took significant steps in the direction of becoming civilized. But the tribal order remained intact. Despite

4. See John William Ward, *Andrew Jackson: Symbol for an Age* (New York, 1962), 40–41, 228, n. 28, for the contention that civilizing the Indian meant admitting him to the pastoral garden. Roy Harvey Pearce, *The Savages of America: A Study of the Indian and the Idea of Civilization*, rev. ed. (Baltimore, 1965), 3–4, makes a stricter division between civilization and savagery and notes the desire to master the Indian by civilizing him (pp. 41–42, 73–74). He deals with symbols, however, and not with the actualities of Indian-white relations. See David Bidney, "The Idea of the Savage in North American Ethnohistory," *Journal of the History of Ideas*, XV (1954), 322–327.

much disintegration and malaise, and also a noticeable degree of acculturation among the native peoples, they remained recognizable as Indians. Philanthropic ideology, with scarcely any recognition of the tendency of culture to persist or of the inherent tentativeness in the acculturative process, had asked the Indian to abandon totally his ancient manner of life. The simplicity of Jeffersonian theory, which supposed such cultural obliteration possible, left the philanthropic mind unprepared for the failure of its program.

This hiatus between what the Jeffersonian age expected would occur as a consequence of its plans for the native tribes and what actually did happen raises a problem of interpretation. In effect, the philanthropic mind formulated its conception of Indian society and its proposal for how that society ought to evolve in relation to civilization with little attention to the actualities of the Indian experience. Jeffersonian theory operated with considerable coherence in one sphere and provided those who believed in it with a rationale for profoundly influencing the native way of life, but it offered no explanation for what really happened to the Indian. It could account for none of the negative consequences of Indian-white relations: the breakdown of tribal society, the failure of the civilizing program to lead to the incorporation of the Indians into the white man's world, and the steadfast refusal of many Indians to take the final step into civilization. While the Indians grappled with the disorientation of their societies and the acquisition of new ways of living, philanthropic thinking remained static. No major changes occurred in Jeffersonian theory between the Revolution and 1830. The decision to support removal in the 1820s had as its purpose the preservation of the theoretical structure rather than any fundamental revision. It in no way affected the philanthropic commitment to the eventual incorporation of the natives. As a consequence, the philanthropic mind can best be explained by a logical but static exposition of its internal content. The description of policy and its effects on native society, however, must be seen developing in time as the Indians reacted to the application of the white man's power.

Furthermore, since Jeffersonian theory had so utterly misconstrued the nature of tribal culture and the possibilities for its reform, the historical guilt so often imputed to the white man could scarcely be applied to the philanthropist. True enough, philanthropy played its part in the overall attack on the native society; it intended to destroy the Indian's world. But it made no such frontal assault on the tribes as did the Indian-hating frontier. Its crime, if it committed one, could be ascribed to naïveté, perhaps even an excess of goodwill, but not the intentional inflicting of pain on a less powerful people. More to the point, the Jeffersonian brand of philanthropy could be justly accused of treating the native more like a precious abstraction than a living human being. For the Indian it wanted only the best, but that meant ultimately the elimination of the tribal order, for which the Jeffersonian age must bear its share of responsibility. Its crime was a willful failure of the intellect but not of the will.[5]

5. For a discussion of the historian's tendency to consider the white man guilty for the destruction of Indian society, see the author's "Indian-White Relations in Early America: A Review Essay," *William and Mary Quarterly*, 3d Ser., XXVI (1969), 267–286.

Metaphysics

Chapter I

Environmentalism

I

The Jeffersonian generation had a special affinity for natural history. Travelers, missionaries, traders, members of the American Philosophical Society, all relished the variety and beauty of the natural world. Jefferson himself spent many hours carefully observing his surroundings, collecting specimens, and compiling information. By far the most interesting natural phenomenon was the Indian, worthy of observation certainly and, because he possessed a distinctive style of living, the subject of extensive investigation. The special vision of reality derived from the study of natural history influenced all aspects of Jeffersonian thought. For the question of Indian-white relations and the philanthropic desire to civilize the native, it was crucial.

Yet as a science, natural history lacked the intellectual breadth characteristic of much Enlightenment thought. Based primarily on almost random observation, it was necessarily superficial. The observer accepted things as they appeared; surface manifestation became the salient character of nature. Because it was unidimensional, this surface revealed a basic coherence, an order that pervaded all of nature from the most finite element to the cosmos itself. The very superficiality of the science of natural observation evinced the security with which a scientist such as Jefferson could pick over his world. It held no terror for him, no fear that the facts would not fit into an overall scheme or that his somewhat carefree rummaging would turn up some bit of knowledge beyond the capacities of human comprehension. Jefferson as a scientist possessed the serene confidence of his age.

Seeing the American Indian as part of nature, Jefferson and his contemporaries described and measured him. Though perceptive enough, and revealing of much basic information on Indian life, their science never probed deeply into the anthropology of tribal existence. Because the native population lived a peculiar tribal form of social life and because Indian manners and customs were so different from the forms familiar to the white man, the merely descriptive capacities of natural history were insufficient for explaining the native world. The obvious differences between white and Indian called for a more inclusive philosophical frame. Since relations between the two societies had always been difficult and had reached a level of crisis in the late eighteenth century, the Jeffersonian age urgently required that Indian and white be kept within the same natural order.[1] Just as the primary vision of natural history provided an unquestioned method for observing the environment, the age of Enlightenment offered a cosmology that was more than adequate to encompass all the disparate elements in reality.

For the Jeffersonian period, the most extensive effort to combine natural history and Enlightenment cosmology could be found in the *Histoire naturelle* of the comte de Buffon. In its major conclusions, this work vindicated an ordered universe, but it also illustrated a danger that lay at the heart of natural history. Observation and description tended toward a particularization of nature. Buffon was chary of the Linnaean system, which erected an elaborate order of fixed species. With his attention directed to the great variety of nature rather than to a rigid system of classes, Buffon described individuals. The scarcely perceptible gradation in nature from one creature to the next seemed more revealing to him than the distribution of plants and animals into specific categories. Buffon averted, however, a collapse of all system into atomism. And in his later writings, he followed the main lines of Linnaean science, though he retained his fondness for the similarities in nature rather than for its sharp distinctions.[2]

---

1. Robert A. Nisbet, *Social Change and History: Aspects of the Western Theory of Development* (New York, 1969), chap. 4; Daniel J. Boorstin, *The Lost World of Thomas Jefferson* (New York, 1948), 226, 272, n. 17.

2. See Ernst Cassirer, *The Philosophy of the Enlightenment*, trans. Fritz C. A. Koelln and James P. Pettegrove (Princeton, 1951), 78–79; Arthur O. Lovejoy, *The Great Chain of Being: A Study of the History of an Idea* (Cambridge, Mass., 1936), 229–231, 361n; Arthur O. Lovejoy, "Buffon and the Problem of Species," in Bentley Glass *et al.*, eds., *Forerunners of Darwin* (Baltimore, 1959), 84–113. On p. 91 of the latter article, Lovejoy sums up the significance of Buffon's reliance on what he calls the principle of continuity: "Though itself the product of the extreme of philosophical rationalism [it] tended in a mild way towards a sort of anti-rationalism, towards a distrust of over-sharp distinctions and over-simple conceptions, towards a sense of a certain incommensurability between the richness of reality and the methods of conceptual thought." See also John C. Greene, *The Death of Adam: Evolution and Its Im-*

What Buffon disclosed to the Jeffersonian age, consequently, was a certain tension between his conception of natural order and his love for the disparate elements in nature. As a natural historian, he perceived the uniqueness of individuals, describing and measuring with an eye to the discrete properties of an entity. Considered in its entirety, Buffon's work, prodigious in its scope, was a deliberate effort to impose pattern on the natural world.

Jefferson's writings were more casual, amateurish by comparison; but his conception of nature, based on broad principle, emerged finally on the side of order. He advocated classification and attacked Buffon for the individualist tendencies of his early cosmology, yet he could also sound like the ultimate atomist. In a letter to Dr. John Manners in 1814, he stated that nature's "creation is of individuals." Nothing in nature was precisely like any other thing— "no two particles of nature are of exact resemblance." Efforts to reduce natural phenomena into specific departments could only be fanciful, but the scientific enterprise required just such a reduction. His own system was instrumental. The arrangement of nature into classes made memory easier and facilitated communication. He condemned what he called the "no-system of Buffon" because its consequences were regressive and individualist and made scientific discourse impossible.[3]

In his actual work as a natural historian, Jefferson posed a broadly inclusive interpretation of nature. His search for the skeletal remains of the mammoth and the megalonyx prompted him to insist that the cosmos was designed on a grand scale.[4] He persisted

pact on Western Thought (Ames, Iowa, 1959), 138–155; Loren Eiseley, *Darwin's Century: Evolution and the Men Who Discovered It* (Garden City, N.Y., 1958), 39–45. For evidence that the great Linnaeus himself came to doubt the fixity of species, see *ibid.*, 18–19, 24–25. George Gaylord Simpson, *This View of Life: The World of an Evolutionist* (New York, 1964), 7–8, notes that through his theory of degeneracy Buffon believed that species could change but that he was not an evolutionist in the sense of thinking that one species evolves from another. He notes also Linnaeus' tendency in later life to doubt the rigidity of his categories. For the relation between the Linnaean science and the Chain of Being, see Winthrop D. Jordan, *White Over Black: American Attitudes Toward the Negro, 1550–1812* (Chapel Hill, 1968), 218–228.

3. Jefferson to John Manners, Feb. 22, 1814, Andrew A. Lipscomb and Albert Ellery Bergh, eds., *The Writings of Thomas Jefferson* (Washington, D.C., 1903–1904), XIV, 97–103; Manners to Jefferson, May 20, 1817, Jefferson Papers, Library of Congress (microfilm); Jefferson to John Vaughan, Aug. 15, 1805, *ibid.* Jefferson apparently did not know of Buffon's later change in his theory.

4. Charles Willson Peale to Thomas Jefferson, July 17, 1803, Jefferson Papers; Meriwether Lewis to Jefferson, Oct. 3, 1803, Donald Jackson, ed., *Letters of the Lewis and Clark Expedition, with Related Documents, 1783–1854* (Urbana, 1962), 126–132; Jefferson to Caspar Wistar, Feb. 25, 1807, Lipscomb and Bergh,

in tracing the remains of the mammoth, knowing full well that the evidence of the past existence of the creature demonstrated its continued existence. "Such was the economy of nature," he contended, "that no instance can be produced of her having permitted any one race of her animals to become extinct; of her having formed any link in her great work so weak as to be broken." Although Indian legend offered corroboration that the mammoth still roamed in the far Northwest, Jefferson required no empirical proof for his theory. Testimony of any sort "would be adding the light of a taper to that of the meridian sun."[5] His conclusion concerning the essential order of nature was a priori. No collection of evidence could have adequately supported it, though its expression was certainly occasioned in Jefferson's mind by his study of natural history.

The megalonyx, a giant sloth long since extinct, presented a more difficult scientific problem. The evidence was the same—skeletal remains—but there was much less of it. Yet the mere existence of the bones presented the probability that the class survived: "put into a train of motion," there was every reason to suppose that it would continue in that mode of existence. Indeed, should one of the links in "nature's chain" be lost, the very system itself would be in danger of collapse. But the "local disappearance of one or two species of animals, and opposed by the thousands of instances of the renovating power constantly exercised by nature for the reproduction of all her subjects, animal, vegetable, and mineral," certainly did not warrant such a conclusion. A loss so small, Jefferson seemed to say, would go unnoticed in a universe so diverse and so perfectly designed. Furthermore, in a universe so ingeniously contrived, a creature as dangerous as the megalonyx would be produced sparingly. "If lions and tygers multiplied as rabbits do, or eagles as pigeons, all other animal nature would have been long ago destroyed, and themselves would have ultimately extinguished after

eds., *Writings of Jefferson*, XI, 158–159. See also Thomas Jefferson, "A Memoir on the Discovery of certain Bones of a Quadruped of the Clawed Kind in the Western Parts of Virginia," American Philosophical Society, *Transactions*, IV (1799), 246–260.

5. Thomas Jefferson, *Notes on the State of Virginia*, ed. William Peden (Chapel Hill, 1955), 43–44, 53–54. There is an interesting letter from Ezra Stiles to Jefferson, June 21, 1784, in which the tough-minded New Englander refused to credit the Indian fables concerning the existence of the mammoth. Julian P. Boyd, ed., *The Papers of Thomas Jefferson* (Princeton, 1950–), VIII, 315. The argument was also opposed by Gilbert Imlay, *A Topographical Description of the Western Territory of North America: containing a Succinct Account of its Soil, Climate, Natural History, Population, Agriculture, Manners, and Customs . . .* , 3d ed. (London, 1797), 31–32.

eating out their pasture."[6] In the end, he succeeded in upholding the coherence of nature, though his arguments were more diverse and also more tenuous.

Jefferson's conception of nature differed little from the common opinion of Enlightenment observers. He had read Buffon, faced the same problems of order and diversity, and concluded that the study of natural history affirmed the essential coherence of the world. The versatility of his arguments did not mask the fundamental truth that empirical evidence could do little more than enhance existing conclusions.

This basic commitment to the order of nature had profound implications. Natural history brought into relief the singularity of the Indian, though its superficiality tended to blur the clarity of outline. In addition, the Indian held a fixed and integral place in the broad vision of Jefferson and his age. He was governed by the same rules that ordered the white man's existence, which granted his separateness at the same time that they confirmed the universality of the system. And it was the universality that counted most for the relations between the two societies. Moreover, the orderliness of the natural scheme implied a moral imperative. The rightness of the system grew out of its very consistency; the integrity of any particular arrangement could not be questioned.

This idea rested precisely at the root of the Jeffersonian attitude toward the Indian. His way of life was peculiar. And though nature certainly sanctioned the native's existence, it could never be said to have been responsible for the particulars of his mode of living. The universality of the design placed a high value on similarity within a particular class. The Indian's way of life set him off from the exemplar for humanity—the white man—and, consequently, from the accepted attributes of his type. Jefferson and his contemporaries insisted that the particulars of the Indian's life should be changed so that he would fit more snugly into the natural order.

2

Although the doctrine of human equality stemmed directly from the universalizing tendency of Enlightenment cosmology, Chris-

6. Jefferson, "Memoir on the Discovery of certain Bones," Am. Phil. Soc., *Trans.*, IV (1799), 255–256; DeWitt Clinton, "Introductory Discourse Delivered before the Society on 4th of May, 1814," Literary and Philosophical Society of New-York, *Transactions*, I (1815), 58, 114–116. A position slightly different from Jefferson's was taken by John Filson, *The Discovery, Settlement and present State of Kentucke: and An Essay towards the Topography, and Natural History of that important Country* . . . (Wilmington, 1784), 35–36.

tianity confirmed it. Indeed, for a substantial body of savants in the Jeffersonian period, whose benevolence was largely religious, the secular wisdom was better stated in Genesis. William Robertson, for example, in his *History of America,* a work widely read and quoted in the New World, recorded the basic principle: "We know, with infallible certainty, that all the human race sprung from the same source, and that the descendants of one man, under the protection as well as in obedience to the command of Heaven, multiplied and replenished the earth." James Adair, the trader and historian, writing specifically of the Indian, united both the secular and the religious argument: "The works of a being, infinitely perfect must entirely answer the design of them." Hence, for him there was only one creation: "Had there been a prior, or later formation of any new class of creatures, they must materially differ from those of the six days' work; for it is inconsistent with divine wisdom to make a vain, or unnecessary repetition of the same act." God had organized his universe with the neatly arranged symmetry of nature itself. Indian and white man differed little in their internal construction and their external appearance. "Indians have lineally descended from Adam," he insisted, "the first, and the great parent of all the human species."[7]

From his secular world of observation, Jefferson proposed a similar doctrine. "We shall probably find," he wrote of the Indians, "that they are formed in mind as well as in body, on the same module with the 'Homo sapiens Europaeus.' " Or as Jedidiah Morse put it a generation later: "Without fear of contradiction, then, we assume this point established. Indians are of the same nature and original, and of one blood, with ourselves." Samuel Stanhope Smith had voiced the same argument, though with a greater sense of its refinements. "The doctrine of one race . . . ," he explained, "renders human nature susceptible of system, illustrates the powers of physical causes, and opens a rich and extensive field for moral science."[8] Jefferson had stated the bare fact; Smith carried the principle to a moral imperative. Both white and Indian, consequently, lived in a

7. William Robertson, *The History of America,* 10th ed. (London, 1803), II, 24; James Adair, *The History of the American Indians* . . . (London, 1775), 12.

8. Jefferson, *Notes on Virginia,* ed. Peden, 62; [Jedidiah Morse], *The History of America,* 3d ed. (Philadelphia, 1798), 94; Morse, *A Report to the Secretary of War of the United States, on Indian Affairs, Comprising a Narrative of a Tour Performed in the Summer of 1820* . . . (New Haven, 1822), 82; Samuel Stanhope Smith, *An Essay on the Causes of the Variety of Complexion and Figure in the Human Species* . . . (Philadelphia, 1787), 110.

world in which forces tended to converge. Equality was as much a moral necessity as it was a descriptive fact.

Similarly, Benjamin Rush went beyond the mere reiteration of the basic principle of human unity. Drawing on the popular materialism of the day, he contended that there was nothing in the mind that had not come through a sensory and hence material impression. He pointed out, in accepted Enlightenment terms, the close connection between the mind and the body. If the Indian and the white man possessed the same basic human qualities, then they could be expected to react similarly to the same stimuli. He attributed distinctions among men, not to inherent differences, but to the diversity of external influences.[9] The argument was simple, but the implications were profound. By the common formula, the doctrine of equality within the species sustained the integrity of the human organism, but at the same time, human susceptibility to influence by the environment provided the means for change.

The lines of thought came together in the doctrine of environmentalism. It not only explained how men lived in and adapted to nature but also carried the primary perception of natural history into the realm of action. As natural history tended toward the passivity of disinterested observation, environmentalism dealt with the interaction that took place in the physical setting. The universality of the system and the equality of the human elements within it provided a stable basis for the environmental process. Change in nature occurred within the limits of an ordered cosmos. The very character of the design required that alteration conform to the set pattern of the natural state. As part of that scheme, the Indian was expected to change as his condition dictated, to take on the characteristics that the mechanics of environmentalism selected, and yet to remain securely within the confines of the natural human condition.

Samuel Stanhope Smith, a close ally of the Scottish commonsense philosophers, wrote thoughtfully about environmentalism. He confronted the familiar questions. Did the fixed order of Linnaeus actually reflect reality? What were the verifiable criteria for the definition of a species? He favored order, of course, but he had different notions on the question of membership in the various species. Buffon and his popularizer, the Abbé Raynal, had defined a species by

9. Benjamin Rush, "On the Influence of Physical Causes in Promoting an Increase of the Strength and Activity of the Intellectual Faculties of Man," in *Sixteen Introductory Lectures* . . . (Philadelphia, 1811), 88–89.

the capacity of members to breed fertile descendants. Smith followed the German anatomist J. F. Blumenbach in contending that the unity of a species required only that the "general form and properties" of its members resemble one another.[10] By softening the rigidity of outline and broadening the technique of classification, Smith significantly shifted the focus of nature. Biological function as the criteria for identification within a species was specfic and easily discovered. Smith's method utilized observation primarily. The measured clarity of the Linnaean universe gave way to a vague distribution of properties, more or less similar, in a given group of organisms. Visual perception became the source of his taxonomy of nature. Smith viewed the natural order through its tentative shading of particularity rather than through the fixed arrangements of specific classes.[11]

Yet Smith believed in the viability of species and the equality of mankind. He emphasized the particular because the process of change affected individuals within a species. Varieties of a basic type changed as a consequence of environmental influence, but such alterations did not affect the integrity of the species. For example, Smith disputed Lord Kames's theory of special creation on the ground that the savage state could only be explained by the concept of varieties. Special creation would have established savagery as a separate and fixed category in nature, a species that by definition "must be subject to different laws both in the physical and moral constitution." There could have been no movement from the savage state to civilization. Since the Indian as a savage was a variety of

10. Samuel Stanhope Smith, *An Essay on the Causes of the Variety of Complexion and Figure in the Human Species* . . . , 2d ed. (New Brunswick, N.J., 1810), 13–14. See also Terence Martin, *The Instructed Vision: Scottish Common Sense Philosophy and the Origins of American Fiction* (Bloomington, 1961), 3–14; Pearce, *Savages of America*, 97–100. The best discussion of Smith is Winthrop D. Jordan's introduction to his edition of Smith's *Essay on Variety* (Cambridge, Mass., 1965), vii–liii.

11. See Jefferson to John Manners, Feb. 22, 1814, Lipscomb and Bergh, eds., *Writings of Jefferson*, XIV, 100–101: He objected to the systems of Linnaeus, Blumenbach, and Cuvier because they gave too much to the "province of anatomy." Indeed, he went on, anatomy might be considered part of natural history. He preferred, however, to think that, "as soon as the structure of any natural production is destroyed by art, it ceases to be a subject of natural history, and enters into the domain ascribed to chemistry, to pharmacy, to anatomy, etc. Linnaeus' method was liable to this objection so far as it required the aid of anatomical dissection, as of the heart, for instance, to ascertain the place of any animal, or of a chemical process for that of a mineral substance. It would certainly be better to adopt as much as possible such exterior and visible characteristics as every traveller is competent to observe, to ascertain and to relate."

the human species, it was the integrity of the overall type that made change possible. Also, because the white man represented the quintessence of the kind, he directed the change toward civilization. The process would take place as a consequence of "varying their culture, and, sometimes, by transferring them to a different soil, or climate; but to all these varieties, where there is no radical diversity of *kind,* the same general laws will still apply." An ordered nature, fixed species, and the flexibility of particular varieties, as interpreted by Smith for the Jeffersonian age, constituted the basis for the environmentalist conception of nature.[12]

Conversely, classes in nature tended to break down. The process could be seen in the superficiality and particularization of natural history, and it was evident also in the cosmology of Buffon and Jefferson. The attention paid to varieties because of their potentiality for change further contributed to the signs of wear in the Linnaean fabric. In 1799 Charles White, a London physician and intellectual harbinger of things to come, writing in direct response to Smith, argued against environmentalism and for special creation. White's methodology left nothing to the superficial observation of natural history. His attack was organic: physical composition in all its ramifications, skeletal structure, bulk, texture, color, all possible evidences of individuation. He seemed bent on establishing a new racially static conception of nature. But, paradoxically, he ended by working out the details of Buffon's nuance and Smith's particularization. So determined was he to define every possible separate organism that he markedly increased their number and diminished the intensity of the differences among them. For the human species, White demonstrated the moderate shading from one kind to the next. The breakdown of order seemed designed to prove the close relationship among the varieties of humankind.[13]

Furthermore, the movement away from the strict delineation of species was closely related to the idea of the "Chain of Being." Traditionally, the chain image had served as one of the principal conceptions of order. By arranging nature, or the entire cosmos,

12. Smith, *Essay on Variety,* 2d ed., 11–13, 28. On special creation, see [Henry Home], Lord Kames, *Sketches of the History of Man* (Dublin, 1775) , I, 9; Bernard Romans, *A Concise Natural History of East and West Florida* . . . (New York, 1775) , 38, 54–56; Benjamin Smith Barton, *New Views of the Origin of the Tribes and Nations of America* (Philadelphia, 1797) , cii-civ; Don Cameron Allen, *The Legend of Noah: Renaissance Rationalism in Art, Science and Letters* (Urbana, 1949) , 132–137.

13. Charles White, *An Account of the Regular Gradation in Man* . . . (London, 1799) , 1–2, 10, 13, 133–138.

along a single hierarchical line from the lowest element to the highest, Enlightenment thought possessed an inclusive and coherent scheme from which no natural factor might stray. Although neither Linnaeus nor Blumenbach in establishing their schematic interpretations had used a hierarchical plan, the idea was pervasive in the eighteenth century, particularly in Jeffersonian America. Certainly the rhetorical content of Jefferson's notion of order was distinctively teleological. When his study of the mammoth and the megalonyx raised the question of a gap in the universal design, he dismissed the possibility with a reassuring reference to the "Chain of Being." "Link" and "nature's chain" came easily to him. Similarly, John Filson, who believed it most fortunate for mankind that the mammoth had disappeared, used the same terminology. The eighteenth century had a "ravenous appetite for hierarchical principles."[14] Should the fixed categories that lent order to nature collapse, the chain might well carry on without them.

For the Indian the chain offered a middle position within the human species between the white man and the Negro, and it also provided the means for alteration in that status. Besides lending to nature a static definition, it also presented an analogy of movement. One of the principal happenings in eighteenth-century thought, the "temporalizing" of the chain, saved the Indian from the implications of the disintegration of the natural order. The perfection of any particular form "came to be conceived by some, not as the inventory but as the program of nature, which is being carried out gradually and exceedingly slowly in the cosmic history."[15] In this instance the ultimate form for the human species was the white man. The unfolding gradation meant that the process of nature developed with the white man's character as the necessary end. Since the Indian was already close to the white man, the transition would be swift and certain.

In broader terms, the temporalization of the chain spelled out a scheme of cultural evolution. Nature itself would assure the transformation of human society, and the Indian would be part of that process. "A principle of progressive improvement," wrote Lewis Cass in the 1820s, at a time when the native's place in the melioration of society was seriously questioned, "seems almost inherent in human nature." Early in the period, when the plan for civilizing

14. Filson, *Kentucke*, 35–36; Jordan, *White Over Black*, 220.
15. Lovejoy, *Chain of Being*, 244; Jordan, *White Over Black*, 224.

the Indian had scarcely been formulated, Henry Knox argued for its feasibility in similar terms. He admitted that the task would be fraught with difficulties and would require perseverance, "but to deny that, under a course of favorable circumstances, it could be accomplished, is to suppose the human character under the influence of such stubborn habits as to be incapable of melioration or change—a supposition entirely contradicted by the progress of society, from the barbarous ages to its present degree of perfection." Jefferson inevitably thought of the transition demanded of the Indian as the essential step out of barbarism. He had no fear of new inventions, he asserted to Robert Fulton in 1810, nor was he "bigoted to the practices of our forefathers. It is that bigotry which keeps the Indians in a state of barbarism in the midst of the arts."[16] Within the analogy of the temporalized chain, therefore, the Indian had but one step to go, from barbarism to civilization; yet this one step was possible because of the broad expectations of cultural evolution.

In his most fulsome rhetoric, Jefferson laid out all of the steps in a schematic presentation of human advance on the American continent.

Let a philosophic observer commence a journey from the savages of the Rocky Mountains, eastwardly towards our seacoast. These he would observe in the earliest stage of association living under no law but that of nature, subsisting and covering themselves with the flesh and skins of wild beasts. He would next find those on our frontiers in the pastoral state, raising domestic animals to supply the defects of hunting. Then succeed our own semi-barbarous citizens, the pioneers of the advance of civilization, and so on in his progress he would meet the gradual shades of improving man until he would reach his, as yet, most improved state in our seaport towns. This, in fact, is equivalent to a survey, in time, of the progress of man from the infancy of creation to the present day. I am eighty-one years of age, born where I now live, in the first range of mountains in the interior of our country. And I have observed this march of civilization advancing from the seacoast, passing over us like a cloud of light, increasing our knowledge and improving our condition, insomuch as that we are at this time more advanced in civilization here than the seaports were when I was a boy. And where this progress will stop no one

16. Lewis Cass, "Indian Treaties and Laws and Regulations relating to Indian Affairs . . . ," *North American Review*, XXIV (1827), 391; Henry Knox to Washington, July 7, 1789, *American State Papers. Documents, Legislative and Executive . . .* (Washington, D.C., 1832–1861), *Indian Affairs*, I, 53, hereafter cited as *American State Papers, Indian Affairs*; Jefferson to Robert Fulton, Mar. 17, 1810, Lipscomb and Bergh, eds., *Writings of Jefferson*, XII, 380–381.

can say. Barbarism has, in the meantime, been receding before the steady step of amelioration; and will in time, I trust, disappear from the earth.[17]

By elongating the process of change, stringing out the stages of improvement from nature to the pastoral state, to semi-barbarism, and then to the society of the seaport towns, Jefferson applied the analogy of the chain to the evolutionary history of mankind. He had created a unilinear world, with the end supposedly in doubt but with savagery assuredly in the past. Such in microcosm was the "progress of man," a "cloud of light" drifting forward with the "gradual shades of improving man." The imagery reflected the inexorableness of the process; and the notation that improvement came gradually, in moderate shades of alteration, lent a sense of steady, irresistible advance. With the pattern of improvement so clearly mapped, the Indians' social deficiencies would surely be corrected.

3

At the heart of the Jeffersonian conception of man and his relation to the environment lay the psychological theory of John Locke. Natural history, with its emphasis on observation and with its vision of order perceptible in the external arrangement of things, grew out of this Lockean epistemology. It saw men as particularly susceptible to the influence of their surroundings. And at the same time, because the Lockean theory established the lines of interrelation between men and their world, it tended to set in motion a reciprocal process of change. The major consequence of the ascendancy of Locke was to challenge the integrity of the natural order and to portray nature instead as a constant process of becoming.

According to the Lockean position, the way men saw the world was at least as important as what they saw. The manner of seeing influenced profoundly the nature of the object seen. In consequence, the locus of identity moved from the object to the eye of the subjective viewer. The essences of things were unknowable;

17. Jefferson to William Ludlow, Sept. 6, 1824, Lipscomb and Bergh, eds., *Writings of Jefferson*, XVI, 74–76. Ludlow had organized a utopian community in Pennsylvania; see his proposal to educate the Indians as representative of the Society of Rational Brethren and the Friends of Science, Jan. 15, 1821, Letters Received by the Office of the Secretary of War Relating to Indian Affairs, 1800–1823 (Microcopy 271), Roll 3: 976–982, Records of the Bureau of Indian Affairs (RG 75), National Archives, hereafter cited as Letters Received, Sec. War (M-271), Roll 3. Also, for the stages of human progress, see George W. Corner, ed., *The Autobiography of Benjamin Rush . . .* (Princeton, 1948), 71–73.

men knew the sense impressions in their own minds. Without the stability of the Linnean construction, Locke's interpretation of how mankind perceived its surroundings transferred the center of initiative from the external world to the human mind.[18]

Ultimately, because the content of their minds originated in sense impressions, men depended on the character of the environment. Emptied of innate ideas, men seemed no more than the world had made them. In the Lockean scheme, the sources of knowledge were two: sense impressions and reflection. With the second of these, reflection, the human mind awakened from the inert receptivity of sensory formation and contributed to its own construction. The mind had a capacity for observing itself, for perceiving its own operations. Just as the natural historian observed his environment, he also shaped it. The act of vision was tantamount to an act of formation. From the original stimulus in the environment, which incited and molded the human mind, the Lockean conception gave the human organism the decisive role in affecting creatively that very environment. Although the original stimulus set the limits of possible invention, the environmental world afforded ample room for man's creative genius.[19]

By itself the Lockean world was all flux and becoming; it provided no stable element to contain its tendency toward indiscriminate change. The ordered universe of Linnaeus supplied a solid enough backdrop, and it gave some account of alteration in the concept of varieties. But Lockeanism went beyond the balance between stability and change; it proposed a world of constant fluidity. Most important, in dismissing innate ideas, Locke risked setting men adrift morally. In a world of interminable flux, human behavior possessed no definite direction, nor could the human species make any claim to a distinctive moral stature.

In response to this interpretation, English latitudinarian thought in the late seventeenth century began the process of constructing in the human being a stable organ of moral decision. The earl of Shaftesbury and Francis Hutcheson completed the work in the early eighteenth century with the doctrine of the moral sense. Widely disseminated in the writings of the Scotch commonsense thinkers, especially Lord Kames, the moral sense anchored human activity

18. Ernest Lee Tuveson, *The Imagination as a Means of Grace: Locke and the Aesthetics of Romanticism* (Berkeley, 1960), 25.

19. John Locke, *An Essay Concerning Human Understanding*, 24th ed. (London, 1823), Bk. II, chap. i, pars. 1–5; Jay Wharton Fay, *American Psychology before William James* (New Brunswick, N.J., 1939), 50.

in solid moral ground. And it established for the human psyche, in its relations with the outside world, the kind of coherent focus that the Lockean psychology did not provide. Moreover, the moral sense operated in the realm of feeling and thus satisfied the Lockean requirement for a material moral instrument.[20]

The widespread belief in the moral sense during the Jeffersonian period served an important function for the white man's dealings with the Indian. Because the principle lodged the moral capacity in a mental compartment that was a basic possession of all human beings, it reaffirmed the unity of mankind. And because morality was timeless and organic, the Indian's special circumstances had not affected his moral potentiality. The Indian might be expected to follow the same rules as the white man. The equality so difficult to discern in the character of the two societies could be seen in their identical moral potentiality. The moral sense not only provided the basis on which white and Indian might come together but also, from the white man's point of view, put such relations in a moral context. The unity of mankind became more than a fact, it became a moral imperative.

The principal influence of the commonsense thinkers on Jefferson probably came through Lord Kames, though he also owned copies of the important volumes of Shaftesbury and Hutcheson.[21] A popularizer, Kames had a talent for simplification that was persuasive on the surface but lacked the substance of those who had written earlier on the subject. Jefferson's conception of the moral sense, consequently, was superficial though consistent with his overall vision of reality.

Kames defined the moral sense as an organ of action rather than perception or understanding; he also conceived of it as intimately connected to the order of the universe. Thus Kames defined the law of nature as *"rules of our conduct and behavior, founded on natural principles, approved of by the moral sense, and enforced by natural rewards and punishment."* The equalization of the subjective human being with the objective moral order was

20. Tuveson, *Imagination as a Means of Grace,* chap. 2; Tuveson, "The Importance of Shaftesbury," *ELH,* XX (1953), 267–299; R. S. Crane, "Suggestions Toward a Genealogy of the 'Man of Feeling,'" *ibid.,* I (1934), 205–230; Norman S. Fiering, "Moral Philosophy in America, 1650–1750, and Its British Context" (Ph.D. diss., Columbia University, 1969).

21. Jefferson to Thomas Law, June 13, 1814, Lipscomb and Bergh, eds., *Writings of Jefferson,* XIV, 144; Adrienne Koch, *The Philosophy of Thomas Jefferson* (New York, 1943), 17–18; E. Millicent Sowerby, comp., *Catalogue of the Library of Thomas Jefferson* (Washington, D.C., 1952–1959), II, 12–13.

perfect. Kames created a reality of Newtonian symmetry in the moral realm. Because it directly reflected the natural order, human behavior took on a presumption of necessity. Moral activity became natural activity.[22]

Drawn from the Lockean position in psychology, the moral sense seemed devoid of rational content. It responded instinctively to a situation requiring a moral decision. As with the impulse to self-preservation, the human person did not stop to reflect on the desirability of survival. The object of choice need only be presented for the human organism to select the means to preserve existence. "The authority," wrote Kames, "lyes in this circumstance, that we feel and perceive the action to be our duty, and what we are indispensably bound to perform." Such a direct call to action, similar to a sensate impulse, was akin to the voice of God in man; it commanded the strictest obedience.

Kames was eager, however, to preserve man's free will. The moral faculty presented the choice, but the will freely made it. Though the determinism implicit in reducing the moral capacity to an instinct left no room for the free act, Kames found such a conclusion unacceptable. Nor could he accept the theory that the sole measure of human behavior was the relative intensity of pleasure or pain that might follow from a particular course of action. Both of these notions failed to take into account the possibility of human growth. "People," he wrote, "generally turn wise by experience." Though the moral sense was rooted in nature, though it partook of the directness of an instinct, it also admitted "of great refinements by culture and education." It improved gradually, as did the other human faculties, until it was "productive of the strongest as well as [the] most delicate feelings."[23]

The principle of development in the moral sense led Kames to consider the problem of the Indian and to apply the possibility of growth to his future. He questioned the Hobbesian doctrine that the state of nature was really a state of war. The existence of brutish manners did not imply an innate brutishness, nor did it refute the moral sense theory. The state of nature should be considered only a set of special circumstances that, though tending to limit the acuity of the moral capacity, did not vitiate it. The scarcity of material goods, which forced primitive men to concentrate on the

22. [Henry Home], Lord Kames, *Essays on the Principles of Morality and Natural Religion; with other Essays concerning the proof of a Deity* (Edinburgh, 1751), 53, 122.

23. *Ibid.*, 10–11, 21–33, 63–64, 78, 98–99, 143–144.

basic necessity of survival, presented the major difficulty to life in the natural state. Elemental manners did not destroy the moral sense. "For primitive men," he wrote, "the defect lies in the weakness of their general principles of action, which terminate in objects too complex for savages readily to comprehend." Such a defect could be remedied by "education and reflection," through which the moral sense would acquire its full authority "openly recognized, and cheerfully submitted to."[24]

Finally, then, Kames went beyond the definition of the moral sense as a mere capacity or an inherent tendency. He supplied it also with a list of specific things to do. Both as a natural capacity and as an index of moral activity, the moral sense was subject to improvement by exercise and cultural elevation. Defining the natural capacity as the facility "to consider some actions *fit, right* and *meet* to be done, and to consider others as unfit, unmeet and wrong," Kames declared that there were degrees of morality in different actions. Hostile actions against others were wrong; their opposites, gratitude to benefactors and the meeting of just engagements, were wholly right. On a lesser scale, certain acts that were benevolent and generous came under the heading of neither right nor wrong. They might be both fit and right, but they did not bind as duty. The specific content of the moral sense, the elements Kames listed in the order of importance, were self-preservation, self-love, fidelity, gratitude, and benevolence.[25]

The moral sense, in the writings of Kames, was described with the widest intellectual and social versatility. In affirming human unity, it endowed all men with a faculty for future accomplishment. Moreover, in equating the content of the moral faculty with the major virtues of the white man's culture, Kames prescribed the direction improvement should take. By solving the problem of Lockean subjectivity, bridging the gap between the man and his environment, and giving to humanity a basis from which to act out the human drama in moral terms, the innate moral sense was an important element in the Jeffersonian conception of nature. Jefferson was particularly taken with moral sense theory because it would serve as a basic instrument for introducing human initiative into the development of the American continent.

As Jefferson conceived it, the very order of the universe required a moral sense inherent in the organic makeup of humanity. Though

24. *Ibid.*, 137–142.
25. *Ibid.*, 52, 59–61, 123–129, 143–144.

the individual preceded society, "man was created for social intercourse; but social intercourse cannot be maintained without a sense of justice; then man must have been created with a sense of justice." "The practice of morality being necessary for the well-being of society, he has taken care to impress its precepts so indelibly on our hearts that they shall not be effaced by the subtleties of our brain."[26] Since moral activity was essential to man as a social being, the world itself was infused with moral energy.

Still, the moral sense, in Jefferson's mind, existed prior to the activation of its social function. His materialism brought him, in fact, very close to an instinctual explanation of humanity by interpreting the moral sense as an emotional force. He wrote to Maria Cosway in his dialogue between the head and the heart that morals were too important for man's happiness "to be risked on the incertain combinations of the head." Sentiment, not science, gave morality its foundation. The creator knew his work well when, as with natural rights, morality was not "left to the feeble and sophistical investigations of reason, but is impressed on the sense of every man." Jefferson qualified the principle "that a man owes no duty to which he is not urged by some impulsive feeling" only by insisting that the feeling should have some wide currency and not emanate from a single individual.[27] He believed that the moral sense had deep organic and instinctual sources.

Men could not learn morality. Being similar to an appendage, however, the moral sense could be strengthened by exercise. It might be stronger in the plowman than in the man of education, but either might increase his moral facility by losing no occasion to exercise the disposition "to be grateful, to be generous, to be charitable, to be humane, to be true, just, firm, orderly, courageous etc." In effect, the operation of the sense revealed its content, which was inseparable from the mechanism itself. The standard of virtue was "utility" to man, a simple sense of duty to fellow men "which prompts us irresistibly to feel and to succor their distresses."[28] As an

26. Jefferson to James Fishback, Sept. 27, 1809, Lipscomb and Bergh, eds., *Writings of Jefferson*, XII, 315; Jefferson to Francis Gilmer, June 7, 1816, *ibid.*, XV, 24–25.

27. Jefferson to Maria Cosway, Oct. 12, 1789, Boyd, ed., *Jefferson Papers*, V, 442–445; Jefferson to John Manners, June 12, 1817, Lipscomb and Bergh, eds., *Writings of Jefferson*, XV, 124; Jefferson to Thomas Law, June 13, 1814, *ibid.*, XIV, 139, 144.

28. Jefferson to Peter Carr, Aug. 10, 1787, Boyd, ed., *Jefferson Papers*, XII, 14–15; Jefferson to Thomas Law, June 13, 1814, Lipscomb and Bergh, eds., *Writings of Jefferson*, XIV, 140–141, 143; Jefferson, *Notes on Virginia*, ed. Peden, 93.

intrinsic part of the nature of man, benevolence affected the very order of nature.

An anecdote told by William Bartram in his rambles in the Georgia forest illustrated the depth to which the conception had permeated American thinking. Bartram came upon an Indian one day, and the thought struck him suddenly that the man was intent on murder. But his fear quickly passed when the native assumed a friendly manner and told him to inform the other white men he met that he had been well treated by an Indian. On arriving at the nearby trading post, the whites there told Bartram that the Indian was an outlaw and a notorious murderer who the previous evening at that very post had sworn to kill the first white man he met. Bartram believed that the lesson was clear:

Can it be denied, but that the moral principle, which directs the savages to virtuous and praiseworthy actions, is natural or innate? It is certain they have not the assistance of letters, or those means of education in the schools of philosophy, where the virtuous sentiments and actions of the most illustrious characters are recorded, and carefully laid before the youth of civilized nations: therefore this moral principle must be innate, or they must be under the immediate influence and guidance of a more divine and powerful preceptor, who, on these occasions, instantly inspires them, and as with a ray of divine light, points out to them at once the dignity, propriety, and beauty of virtue.[29]

Bartram found virtue manifested in the simple native character. Living close to nature, without the benefit of civilized manners, the Indian behaved as Jefferson believed the moral sense required.

4

Once Locke had turned the attention of eighteenth-century thinkers to the physical world, the obvious need was for a systematic account of the relationship between man and his environment. Beyond the axiomatic order of nature, the unity of mankind, and the benevolent implications of the moral sense theory, science could portray objectively the reciprocal effects of man and nature in interaction. Man made his mark on nature, just as nature left its imprint on man. Environmentalism not only explained the process but also assumed that it possessed an essential validity. What happened, especially to men, became part of the salutary order of nature. As

29. Francis Harper, ed., *The Travels of William Bartram: Naturalist's Edition* (New Haven, 1958), 16, the whole incident, pp. 14–16; Benjamin Rush, "An Inquiry into the Influence of Physical Causes upon the Moral Faculty," in *Medical Inquiries and Observations*, 2d ed. (Philadelphia, 1805), II, 20; Samuel Williams, *The Natural and Civil History of Vermont* (Walpole, N.H., 1794), 175.

men changed in response to new circumstances, for example the Indian under the influence of the white man, the altered being emerged from the process as part of a new arrangement of nature, possessing all the claims to legitimacy of any previous stage. Natural historians expected such constant flux and tended to consider it wholly desirable.

Conceived most broadly, environmentalism respected no fixed categories in the natural order. All things became subject to the inexorable molding power of the environment. Even Jefferson, for all his insistence on the indestructibility of the chain of nature, admitted the force of environmental influence: "Animals transplanted into unfriendly climates," he wrote, "either change their nature and acquire new fences against the new difficulties in which they are placed, or they multiply poorly and become extinct."[30] Fixed species already allowed for change by varieties within their limits, a point consistent with the environmental theory. But the theory evoked a process of less exact and limiting definition. Its very nature seemed to be flux, a repeated adaptive reconciliation between subject and surroundings. Environmentalism in the Jeffersonian age became the primary method for describing and predicting the manner in which all things would change and eventually be fulfilled.

Even the moral sense could be expected to develop and mature under the prodding of the environment. Benjamin Rush described in fine detail the openness of the moral faculty not only to the effects of climate, diet, and disease but also to such subjective dispositions as idleness, pain, cleanliness, solitude, and eloquence. The anticipated growth would come primarily as a result of the interaction between the physical world and the internal resources of human beings. Jedidiah Morse applied the principle to an evaluation of the American Indians. "Their qualities good and bad (for they certainly possess both), their way of life, the state of society among them, with all the circumstances of their condition, ought to be considered *in connection,* and in regard to their mutual influence."[31] In some respects the environmentalist doctrine could be formulated crudely: man as the unidimensional product of his physical setting. But as used in the Jeffersonian period, it was a subtle instrument for the fusion of such diverse elements as the external world, man's intrinsic potentiality, and the intermingling of the two that had produced the human social character.

30. Jefferson, *Notes on Virginia*, ed. Peden, 169.
31. Rush, "Inquiry into the Influence of Physical Causes upon the Moral Faculty," in *Medical Inquiries*, 2d ed., II, 24–38; Morse, *History of America*, 66.

William Robertson employed the environmentalist conception as the informing principle of his *History of America*. He began by assuming a natural equality among men; as they came from the cradle of nature, they were all of the same capacity. No matter the level of culture that might some day be achieved, "we can discern no quality which marks any distinction or superiority." Hence each human being had an equal capacity for improvement; the "state of society" caused the actual differences. The mind naturally accommodated itself to the external condition from which "it receives discipline and culture." In proportion to human wants and according to the demands of circumstances, the intellectual powers of men were called forth. In Robertson's system, therefore, men were largely responsive, but such would be true of any environmentalist interpretation. At base it required the human entity to emerge as the product of external stimuli. But the organism was never inert, never merely responsive; stimulus from without awakened and formed an internal order that in turn affected the human character.[32]

Samuel Stanhope Smith also used the phrase "state of society," though his definition was more precise. "The state of society," he wrote, "comprehends diet, clothing, lodging, manners, habits, face of the country, objects of science, religion, passions and ideas of all kinds infinite in number and variety." These factors, either alone or in combination with climate, were "adequate to account for all the varieties we find among mankind." Also he contended explicitly that men could influence the world in which they lived. He made the point by listing the shortcomings of savage existence. Primitive men, who had gathered only a small deposit of cultural potential, were far more susceptible to manipulation, thought Smith, than men who had accumulated a substantial cultural fund from which could be drawn the means for altering the world's form. Savages would be more readily shaped to the design of the environment "because the habits and ideas of society among them are few and simple; and to the action of the climate they are exposed naked and defenceless to suffer its full force at once." To be sure, primitive man's condition tended to belie the second-stage environmental reaction that gave the human organism a semblance of initiative. So devoid was the savage of the cultural foundation, upon which future construction could be based, that only the intervention of a foreign influence could be effective. Smith rejected the notion that

32. Robertson, *History of America*, II, 212-213, 226.

civilization was a slow growth from savagery. He could see no way to begin the process, unless God delivered civilization to man already intact. For the Indian, the philanthropist played the divine role. Thus environmentalism and benevolence were neatly combined in the Jeffersonian mind.[33]

Environmentalism, then, supplied the method by which the changing order of existence could be explained. Living things were the product of circumstance; they changed as the world they inhabited changed.[34] Yet the process for humanity was infinitely more complex. After the original impression, the human organism constructed the machinery necessary for shaping reality in new ways. From his environmental origins man became, in effect, a manipulator of the very environment that had formed his original design.

5

Smith began his detailed presentation of the environmental theory with the effects of climate on the human organism. The sun, he maintained, had a tendency to darken the skin, but its impress was regulated by the relative quantity of bile in the body. Either sun or bile alone darkened the skin; together their result was more intensive. In addition, the heat of the sun stimulated a more generous flow of bile, deepening the color tone. In a torrid climate, by the time the bile reached the skin it was less energetic, could not be sweated out, and remained close to the skin producing the sable hue invariably seen in southern regions. Moreover, the vapors from stagnant waters in uncultivated areas, together with fatigue, poverty, and hardship, all tended to increase the bile flow. Moderate cold, conversely, corrected the bile secretions, sent the blood to the surface, and made the complexion clear and florid.[35]

33. Smith, *Essay on Variety*, 25n, 63; *ibid.*, 2d ed., 15–28; Peter S. Du Ponceau, translation of Johann Severin Vater, "An enquiry into the origin of the population of America," 1810, Class 572.97, Nov45d, Library of the American Philosophical Society, Philadelphia.

34. Even when the emphasis was not on the power of the environment to transform the human organism, the 18th century demanded a fundamental congruence between man and his surroundings. See Abbé Raynal, *A Philosophical and Political History of the Settlements and Trade of the Europeans in the East and West Indies*, trans. J. O. Justamond, 2d rev. ed. (London, 1798), VI, 87; Imlay, *Topographical Description*, 130.

35. Smith, *Essay on Variety*, 13–17. See White, *Account of the Regular Gradation in Man*, 99–118, for a critique of Smith. Also John Augustine Smith, "A Discourse, on the Manner in Which Peculiarities in the Anatomical Structure Affect the Moral Character . . . ," in *A Syllabus of the Lectures Delivered to the Senior Students in the College of William and Mary on Government* (Philadelphia, 1817), 79–118; Romans, *Concise Natural History*, 42; Albert Gallatin,

The gradation in complexion, consequently, seemed closely related to latitude. Nearly so, thought Smith, but there were numerous secondary factors of which account should be taken. Countries of great height were usually cool in relation to their latitude; nearness to the ocean had a moderating effect on both cold and heat; large ranges of mountains protected some countries from frigid winds and made them warmer. Soil also had its influence on climate: sand held the heat better than clay, and wooded lands were colder in the North and more temperate in the South. Uncultivated regions also affected the bile. The "putrid exhalations that copiously impregnate the atmosphere" in such places relaxed the nervous system, which, as a result, increased the flow and distribution of the bile through the body. "This liquor tinges the complexion of a yellow colour, which assumes by time a darker hue."[36]

In his *History of Vermont,* Samuel Williams worked out his own version of the environmentalist system and its effect on human color. On the principle that certain colors were suitable for certain climatic conditions, he conceived darkness of shade as fitting for hot regions and lightness for the colder areas. The climate would tend naturally to produce the desirable color, though a transition from white to black was easier than the opposite. Changes of either kind took place very slowly. The Negro, for example, would not in a favorable climatic situation become white any faster than it had taken him to become black. The time lapse for this process had been about four thousand years. To produce the less blatant shade of the Indian, however, had taken probably only six hundred years. Other environmental factors than the weather tended to retard or accelerate color change: wind, dirt, the use of paints and oils.

Williams believed that the Indian's reddish tinge resulted from his exposure to the open air rather than from a specific climatic circumstance. Furthermore, the native had probably been the same color when he arrived on the American continent, since the temperate atmospheric condition of the New World was not conducive to emphatic color changes. In the North the Indians' practices of painting and oiling their skins prevented any noticeable change, though it was also true that the Eskimo's complexion seemed to be lighter than the Indian's. Nevertheless, though the Negro's deep

---

"A Synopsis of the Indian Tribes within the United States East of the Rocky Mountains, and in the British and Russian Possessions in North America," American Antiquarian Society, *Archaeologia Americana (Transactions and Collections,* I–III [Worcester, Mass., 1820–1850]) , II, 130, hereafter cited as Am. Antiq. Soc., *Archaeologia Americana,* II.

36. Smith, *Essay on Variety,* 4–6, 11–12.

skin tone seemed alien to the gentle atmosphere of the New World, the color of the Indians as a whole seemed to fit the temperate character of the continent.[37]

The American continent as a benign haven, impressing its influence with nice discretion on the occupants of its forests, was well within the environmentalist conception, though the theory would have been more decisive had the potentiality of the New World been described in more aggressive and vibrant terms. Without sharp contrast, the land yielded the physical character and temperate virtues of its middling potentiality. In similar language, Hugh Williamson explained the temperateness of the American influence: "There is, and ever will be, in America, a much greater similarity of form and complexion, among the human race, than is to be found upon the other continent. That similarity may produce a more friendly intercourse, and general communication of sentiment. The soil of America, which seems to produce animals of equal strength and firmness, but less ferocity of disposition, than are produced on the other continent, may probably give existence to a race of men, less prone to destroy one another, and more desirous to improve the understanding and cultivate the social virtues." The median color of the Indian, between the blackness of the Negro and the paleness of the white man, reflected this moderate influence of the American land. Also, the accommodating social disposition of the native population proved fitting for the necessary congruence between man and his surroundings.[38]

37. Williams, *History of Vermont*, 387–396. See also Pierre François Xavier de Charlevoix, *Journal of a Voyage to North America*, ed. Louise Phelps Kellogg (Chicago, 1923 [orig. publ. London, 1761]), I, 257; Jeremy Belknap, "On the Colour of the Native Americans and the Recent Population of this Continent," in *A Discourse, Intended to Commemorate the Discovery of America by Christopher Columbus* . . . (Boston, 1792), 125–132; Barton, *New Views*, xvi; Rush, "On the Influence of Physical Causes," in *Sixteen Lectures*, 116–117; Clemens de Baillou, "A Contribution to the Mythology and Conceptual World of the Cherokee Indians," *Ethnohistory*, VIII (1961), 102; Elias Boudinot, *A Star in the West; or, A Humble Attempt to discover the long lost Ten Tribes of Israel* . . . (Trenton, 1816), 137.

38. Though presented widely, the temperate argument was particularly useful in answering the comte de Buffon's criticism of the New World; see chap. 3 below. Hugh Williamson, *Observations on the Climate in Different Parts of America, Compared with the Climate in Corresponding Parts of the Other Continent* . . . (New York, 1811), 179–180. Jefferson to C. F. C. Volney, Feb. 8, 1805, H. A. Washington, ed., *The Writings of Thomas Jefferson* . . . (Washington, D.C., 1853–1854), IV, 569: "I think it a more chearful one [the American climate]. It is our cloudless sky which has eradicated from our constitutions all disposition to hang ourselves, which we might otherwise have inherited from our English ancestors." Adam Ferguson, *An Essay on the History of Civil Society* . . . , 8th ed. (Philadelphia, 1819), 197, 203–204, 214–215.

Although environmental conditioning affected color most obviously, Smith saw it as only part of the entire bodily formation that emerged from the communion of man with his external condition. Witness his description of the effect of cold on the physical structure of the northern native: "Extreme cold likewise tends to form the peculiarities of these races, their high shoulders and their short necks. Severe frost prompts men to raise their shoulders as if to protect the neck, and to cherish the warmth of the blood that flows to the head. And the habits of an eternal winter will fix them in that position."[39] In a similar vein, he described a white girl who had been bound to him as a servant when she was ten years old. Her parents had been very poor, and as a consequence the child was emaciated, sallow in complexion, and well on the way to baldness. "This girl has by a fortunate change in her mode of living, and indeed by living more like my own children than like a servant, become, in the space of four years, fresh and ruddy in her complexion, her hair is long and flowing, and she is not badly made in her person." Smith interpreted a normal return to health by a sickly child, once given proper nourishment and protection from the elements, as similar to the deep-rooted effects of environmental conditioning on the varieties of the human race.[40]

Man's external situation played a correspondingly important role in the formation of his culture. As Robertson put the argument, similar manners among different groups of people, rather than showing a previous connection, proved that they had been nurtured in the same kind of physical surroundings. Using the often-repeated abundance theory that the Indians lived as hunters because the plenty of nature made work unnecessary (hunting was sport, not work), he reasoned that the material circumstances had dictated a certain cultural conformation. More particularly, all societies were formed in their political character by climate:

In the New World, as well as in other parts of the globe, cold or temperate countries appear to be the favorite seat of freedom and independence. There the mind, like the body, is firm and vigorous. There men, conscious of their own dignity, and capable of the greatest efforts in asserting it, aspire to independence, and their stubborn spirits stoop with reluctance to the yoke of servitude. In warmer climates, by whose influence the whole frame is so much enervated, that present pleasure is the supreme felicity, and mere repose is enjoyment, men acquiesce, almost without a struggle, in the dominion of a superior. Accordingly, if we proceed from north to south along the continent of America, we shall

39. Smith, *Essay on Variety*, 39.
40. *Ibid.*, 55n.

find the power of those vested with authority gradually increasing, and the spirit of the people becoming more tame and passive.[41]

The argument could be traced full circle. Originating in the physical condition and concluding with the cultural conformation that grew out of it, the process reflected back on itself. The culture made its mark on the land. What began as a derivative of the simplicity of the Lockean thesis soon went far beyond it and, in the sense that human culture had a significant effect on the physical environment, turned the thesis on itself.

For the native American, specifically, the reflective process of environmentalism was set in motion once the bonds of savagery were broken. The character of human culture began the gradual, imperceptible change of man's physical surroundings. Williamson thought the "established principles of philosophy" sufficient to show that, as the continent was cultivated, the cold of the winters would tend to be mitigated: "When the virtuous industry of posterity shall have cultivated the interior part of this country, we shall seldom be visited by frosts or snows, but may enjoy such a temperature in the midst of winter, as shall hardly destroy the most tender plants." The elimination of the forests would increase the circulation of the air and thus raise the temperature. The general health of the country would be improved by rearranging its unfelicitous surface. "While the face of this country was clad with woods, and every valley afforded a swamp or stagnant marsh, by a copious perspiration through the leaves of trees or plants, and a general exhalation from the surface of ponds and marshes, the air was constantly charged with a gross putrescent fluid. Hence a series of irregular, nervous, bilious, remitting and intermitting fevers, which for many years have maintained a fatal reign through many parts of this country, but are now evidently on the decline." The line of development was clear: from the institution of farming to a change in the landscape that stimulated a rise in the temperature and a general moderation in the atmosphere of the land. As a result of the betterment of the health of the inhabitants, human physiognomy changed, and hence the process returned to its material origins.[42]

Similarly, Benjamin Rush believed in the potentiality of human culture to affect the construction of the continent. He distinguished

41. Robertson, *History of America*, II, 59–60, 132.
42. Hugh Williamson, "An Attempt to account for the Change in Climate, which has been observed in the Middle Colonies in North-America," Am. Phil. Soc., *Trans.*, 2d ed., I (1789), 342–345.

between clearing the land, which might only succeed in reducing its fertility, and cultivation, defined in part as "exhaling the unwholesome or superfluous moisture of the earth, by means of frequent crops of grain, grasses, and vegetables of all kinds," which would increase the salubrity of the country.[43]

If human culture could transmute the face of nature, then man's physical structure could be altered by the same force. Smith maintained that the savage condition increased and the civilized state retarded the effects of climate. More important, social development of a certain level entirely blunted the impact of the environment. By this principle, the Indian's level of achievement made him particularly open to the influence of climate, and, above all, his physical construction became a direct reflection of his mental disposition. The native visage was fixed, stupid, vacant, melancholy, and wild. The first three characteristics stemmed from the supposed absence of ideas in the native brain, melancholy resulted from his solitary life in the forest, and wildness originated in the usual savage state of war. The large and protruded mouth common to the Indian testified to his mental void, which left his face "unexerted," relaxed, and, consequently, with a tendency toward broadness. The protrusion and swelling of the lips arose from the grief that the unhappy condition of his life imposed on the Indian, and the nose was flat and sometimes sunken in the face because of the broadness of his other features.[44]

Furthermore, the changes supposedly wrought in the appearance of whites captured by the Indians and required to adopt the native ways came not merely from the normal effects of climate on the sparsely clothed captive. Infants, so Smith told the story, kidnapped by the Indians before white civilization had made a marked impression on them had been raised in the "solitude and rudeness of savage life" and had taken on the "same apathy of countenance . . . the same swelling of the features and muscles of the face, the same form and attitude of the limbs, and the same characteristic gait, which is a great elevation of the feet when they walk, and the toe

43. Benjamin Rush, "An Inquiry into the Cause of the Increase of Bilious and Intermitting Fevers in Pennsylvania with Hints for Preventing Them," Am. Phil. Soc., Trans., II (1786), 205–212; Rush, "An Account of the Climate of Pennsylvania, and Its Influence upon the Human Body," in Medical Inquiries and Observations (Philadelphia, 1789), 83; Charles William Janson, The Stranger in America: Containing Observations made during a Long Residence in that Country, on the Genius, Manners and Customs of the People of the United States . . . (London, 1807), 63–64.

44. Smith, Essay on Variety, 44, 81–85.

somewhat turned in, after the manner of a duck." These characteristics, together with the darkening of the skin from exposure to the elements, made the white captive hardly distinguishable from the Indian. For Smith this evidence established the principle that the state of society, not climate, created the major physical distinctions between native and white.[45]

Even within white society, variable cultural levels produced groups with distinctive physical attributes. The laboring classes, according to Smith, were usually more "swarthy and squalid" in complexion. Their features were harder, and their limbs more coarse and poorly formed than persons better supplied with the artifacts of the culture. The poor "want the delicate tints of colour, the pleasing regularity of features, and the elegance and fine proportions of person." Of course, exceptions could be found in both the lower and upper strata of society, but the general rule held true.[46]

Smith thought he had found a working example of the effects of culture on the human physical makeup in the case of an Indian student at the College of New Jersey. Unfortunately, the native boy was not a perfect specimen since "he was too far advanced in savage habits to render the observation complete, because, all impressions received in the tender and pliant state of the human constitution before the age of seven years, are more deep and permanent, than in any future, and equal period of life." For this reason, there were some obvious differences between the young Indian and his fellow students: "The largeness of the mouth, the thickness of the lips, in the elevation of the cheek, in the darkness of the complexion, and the contour of the face." But under the influence of American culture, these savage features seemed to change visibly. As the boy lost "that vacancy of eye, and that lugubrious wildness of countenance peculiar to the savage state and acquires the agreeable *expression* of civil life," he more and more took on the appearance of his fellow scholars. "The expression of the eye, and the softening of the features to civilized emotions and ideas, seems to have removed more than half the difference between him and us." Though still a distinctive quality, his color became light enough to reveal a

45. *Ibid.*, 59–60n; also Joseph Doddridge, *Notes, on the Settlement and Indian Wars, of the Western Parts of Virginia & Pennsylvania* . . . (Wellsburgh, Va., 1824), 53.

46. Smith, *Essay on Variety*, 52–53. John Ledyard believed that there was a direct connection between physical features and station in life, as there was between color and civilization. See Stephen D. Watrous, ed., *John Ledyard's Journey through Russia and Siberia, 1787–1788: The Journal and Selected Letters* (Madison, 1966), 178, 180.

blush. The Indian's special characteristics necessarily gave way under the environmental impact of civilization.[47]

6

In his *Notes on Virginia,* under the caption "Productions Mineral, Vegetable and Animal," Jefferson viewed the Indian in a natural and, consequently, in an environmentalist setting. Following the methodology of natural history, he concerned himself with circumstances and style of life. The ease with which he resorted to this relatively open portrayal of manners testified to the strength of the environmentalist proposition. It was at once the most comprehensive and the most incisive way of explaining the native society, for it offered the breadth of the Indian's way of life and the depth of meaning that necessarily attached to his future. Because environmentalism established the conditions of change in nature, Jefferson's interpretation of tribal society opened the way for its future transformation.

The Indian possessed a distinctive complement of manners and mores that set him apart from civilized man. Yet because he had acquired these environmentally, as had the white man his own peculiar way of life, they proved both the natural equality of men and the possibility of change. Delineating carefully the differences between the two cultures, Jefferson defined the basis upon which the Indian could someday become identical with civilized man. Had his description of tribal society been built on static physical characteristics or had he compiled a catalog of inherent and irremediable attributes, such would not have been true. He presented instead a fragmentary but singularly adroit configuration of what he conceived as typical native habits. It was sufficiently plausible to affirm the native integrity but not so permanent as to impede the possibility of improvement.

The Indian, Jefferson thought, was brave—and clever, too, for he used stratagem rather than risk his life foolishly. He met death with deliberation, and he had a special capacity for enduring torture. He showed affection and indulgence toward his children; in adult life he maintained firm friendships. Though his virtues seemed to separate him from the white man, his sensibility was the equal of the European "in the same situation." In a comparison of strength between white and Indian, considering the male and female on either side, the issue rested on the amount of exercise

47. Smith, *Essay on Variety,* 60–62.

common in each society. Pampered white females probably lacked the strength of native women. The lower fertility of the Indians could be explained by "diet and exercise" but also by the practice of Indian women accompanying their husbands on war and hunting expeditions. When married to whites or confined as slaves, they proved as fecund as European women. The drudgery in the lives of the Indian women, a characteristic of barbarism, would be changed by civilization. Finally, Jefferson admitted that all the information had not yet been gathered; but when it was, the Indian would be shown the equal of the white man.[48]

Equality in this sense meant identity. The Indian's highly rated capacities, though treated objectively enough, served as evidence for what he could become rather than as social values that deserved to endure for their own sake. Similarly, the broad theoretical structure, which first established the order of nature and, consequently, the basic equality of human creatures, had also arranged for the process of natural transformation. The Indian's manner of life, therefore, which seemed to separate him from the white man's society, provided the visible justification for his eventual incorporation into civilization. As a variety of humankind, capable but not quite fully accomplished, he could be expected to someday move beyond the limits of the tribal world.

Many who believed that someday the Indian would transcend the limitations of his social order only vaguely understood the theoretical basis for their position, though it could be found with con-

48. Jefferson, *Notes on Virginia*, ed. Peden, 59–63. In striking contrast, Jefferson's treatment of the Negro was static and racial. He was impressed not so much with manners as with physical structure. *Ibid.*, 138–143. For the nearly definitive statement on the subject, see Jordan, *White Over Black*, chap. 12. Conceptually, at least, Jeffersonian environmentalism excluded racism. The Indian's physical character was submerged in his cultural character. Divisions there were between white and Indian, but in the Jeffersonian age, they were not racial. For the opposite point of view on Indian-white relations generally, see Frederick M. Binder, *The Color Problem in Early National America as Viewed by John Adams, Jefferson, and Jackson* (The Hague, 1968) ; Thomas F. Gossett, *Race: The History of an Idea in America* (Dallas, 1963) , 3; William Stanton, *The Leopard's Spots: Scientific Attitudes toward Race in America, 1815–59* (Chicago, 1960) , 2; Dante A. Puzzo, "Racism and the Western Tradition," *Jour. Hist. Ideas,* XXV (1964) , 583; Howard H. Peckham, "Indian Relations in the United States," in John Francis McDermott, ed., *Research Opportunities in American Cultural History* ([Lexington, Ky.], 1961) , 36, 39; and Robert F. Berkhofer, Jr., *Salvation and the Savage: An Analysis of Protestant Missions and American Indian Response, 1787–1862* ([Lexington, Ky.], 1965) , 151. For the contrary view, see Alden T. Vaughan, *New England Frontier: Puritans and Indians, 1620–1675* (Boston, 1965) , 62–63n; Lewis O. Saum, *The Fur Trader and the Indian* (Seattle, 1965) , 28, 32–39; Boorstin, *Lost World of Thomas Jefferson,* 85; and Jordan, *White Over Black,* 22.

siderable clarity in the writings of such men as Jefferson and Smith. But the cogency of the world view that informed Jeffersonian philanthropy was less pertinent than the pervasive sense of becoming that it supplied. Nature seemed to possess a fundamental suppleness, a disposition to respond positively to human desires. Ultimately, the theory supported this perception, but most men, concerned more with action than theorizing, did not go beyond the happy conviction that the world would yield to their purposes. Goodwill toward the Indian tended especially to find justification in the feeling that change for the good was the very marrow of nature.

All the elements in the argument combined to logically justify the incorporation of the Indian. An ordered universe and the doctrine of equality established the basis for it. The Chain of Being contributed teleological development to this natural order. Once nature had been set in motion, stressing, therefore, the process of becoming rather than static identity, the moral sense made it easy to add the connotation of moral necessity to what actually occurred. The transition from the logical justification for the possible alteration of the native culture to the moral need to accomplish that change was even more evident in the science of natural history and the theory of environmentalism.

Although both natural history and environmentalism seemed no more than neutral methods for handling great quantities of information, they were most profoundly entwined in the workings of nature. The natural historian did more than merely observe and describe: environmentalism was more than a description of how things came to be. Both offered a self-contained version of nature, essentially coherent, with its processes operating according to self-validating rules. When environmentalism explained how climate affected color, or culture the lay of the land, or how the Indian changed his character in contact with civilization, it explained how things inevitably came out, not merely how they happened to occur. The environmentalist way of thinking gave to the Jeffersonian age a great confidence in the developing character of nature. It also imposed on the white man the terrible obligation to see that all did indeed come out as the theory seemed to predict. On the Indian, ironically, it imposed the greatest burden of all: to abandon his way of life and become a white man.

Chapter II

Origins

I

Environmentalism associated the Indian with the American land; it tied his future to the future of the continent. But it did so abstractly, with little of the actual material relationships men establish with their physical surroundings. The environmentalist description of change, no doubt, explained how the Indian came to be as he was and how he would probably turn out in the future, but it made no contribution to the history of the Indian. His past, shrouded in mystery, evoked so many exotic possibilities that it had long been a preoccupation of natural historians. But even more important, without some knowledge of the Indian's origin, the description of his potentiality that environmentalism had posited remained incomplete.

Jeffersonian theory had only a tangential relationship to reality, but the dealings between Indian and white society had always been genuine enough. The white man, seeing how the Indian actually lived, inquired how he had lived in the past, how he had come to reside on the American continent. The passion of philanthropy accounted for the persistence with which white men asked the question, and the historical interest common to Enlightenment thought was more than adequate to justify a continuing inquiry.[1] Men with the Jeffersonian cast of mind, who were required to deal with a people of such different social character, raised the most obvious practical question. From whence had these people come?

The study of the native past took on certain didactic connotations. The Jeffersonian generation, eager to civilize the Indian, had an interest in defending him, in making sure that he presented himself for admission into civilization with the best possible antecedents. Could the Indian, strange in his social composition and

---

1. For the place of history in 18th-century thought, see Alfred Cobban, *In Search of Humanity: The Role of the Enlightenment in Modern History* (London, 1960), 105, 107; Peter Gay, *The Enlightenment: An Interpretation. The Rise of Modern Paganism* (New York, 1966), 32.

isolated from the main course of civilized development, now be considered a fit subject for incorporation into the civilized order? By associating the native with the familiar geography of human beginnings and by filling in the story of his supposed wanderings with specific events, the Indian became less a curious anomaly and more an acceptable, if temporarily separated, member of society. Discovering the native's origin humanized him and also added coherence to the story of mankind.

The explanation of the Indian's past for the pursuit of philanthropic ends or for purely scientific ends derived its significance from the universalizing tendency of an age that considered the unity of mankind axiomatic. Thus, despite the vagueness of his origins, the Indian would not have been denied full membership in the human family, especially so because of the tendency in Jeffersonian thought to place a high premium on inclusiveness. "There can be no reasonable ground to doubt," noted the physician and natural philosopher James H. McCulloh as late as 1829, "the one origin of the species." The principle, at root religious, was fundamental to the Christian message. The scripture, declared Caleb Atwater after his examination of the western earthworks for traces of the native past, cast "a strong and steady light on the path of the Antiquarian." In poking about the ancient remains, Atwater found evidence that he thought was at least as reliable for supporting the doctrine of human unity as any of the secular rationalizations of the age.[2]

Jefferson had a deep interest in a solution to the problem of Indian origins. He not only knew the extensive literature on the subject but also owned most of the important writings.[3] Whatever conclusion might be drawn from the investigations then being pursued, he believed that the truth would come from the study of Indian languages. Above all, he opposed reckless speculation and idle theorizing. In a letter to John Adams, Jefferson criticized Joseph François Lafitau, an early eighteenth-century Jesuit historian, for drawing extensive parallels between the American Indians

2. J. H. McCulloh, *Researches, Philosophical and Antiquarian, concerning the Aboriginal History of America* (Baltimore, 1829), 418; Caleb Atwater, *Description of the Antiquities Discovered in the State of Ohio and Other Western States . . .* ([Circleville, Ohio], 1820), 205–206.

3. For a résumé of 16th- and 17th-century literature concerning the origin of the Indian, see: Lee Eldridge Huddleston, *Origins of the American Indians: European Concepts, 1492–1729* (Austin, 1967); Allen, *Legend of Noah,* 120–130. See also John H. Powell, *On the Origin of the American Indians* (Philadelphia, 1946); Marc Maurice Wasserman, "The American Indian as Seen by the Seventeenth Century Chroniclers" (Ph.D. diss., University of Pennsylvania, 1954), chap. 16.

and ancient civilizations. "He selects . . . all the facts," Jefferson observed, "and adopts all the falsehoods which favor this theory, and very gravely retails such absurdities as zeal for a theory could alone swallow." At a later date, after disposing of a host of bizarre interpretations, he wrote Adams that "the question of Indian origin, like many others, pushed to a certain height must receive the same answer, 'Ignoro.' "[4] Language study, of course, would lead to very different conclusions.

Adams shared Jefferson's opinion of the recent speculations. He suggested that he "could make a System too. The seven hundred Thousand Soldiers of Zingis, when the whole or any part of them went to battle, they sett up a howl, which resembled nothing that human Imagination has conceived, unless it be the Supposition that all the Devils in Hell were let loose at once to set up an infernal Scream, which terrified their Ennemies and never failed to obtain them Victory. The Indian Yell resembles this: and therefore America was peopled from Asia."[5] Although his humor may have missed the mark, Adams had not unduly exaggerated the uncritical nature of some investigations.

A more limited approach, and probably the least popular, came from Peter S. Du Ponceau, the linguist and president of the American Philosophical Society, who advocated scientific investigation for its own sake, without the encumbrance of weighty hypotheses. Referring to Benjamin Smith Barton's *New Views of the Origin of the Tribes and Nations of America,* Du Ponceau complained that

4. Jefferson to Adams, June 11, 1812, and May 27, 1813, Lester J. Cappon, ed., *The Adams-Jefferson Letters: The Complete Correspondence Between Thomas Jefferson and Abigail and John Adams* (Chapel Hill, 1959), II, 305–307, 323–324.

5. Adams to Jefferson, June 28, 1812, *ibid.,* 310; Noah Webster's letter to the editor of *The American Museum,* VIII (1790), 11–12, offered a typical speculation on Indian origins: "What will the public say of the following opinions, that the Southern Indians, in Mexico and Peru, are descended from the Carthaginians or other Mediterranean nations, who found their way to the continent at a very early period, and spread themselves over North as well as South America—that these nations had become more civilized, than the present northern Indians, tho' not acquainted with the use of iron—that at a late period of time, perhaps four or five centuries ago, the Siberian Tartars found their way to the North West parts of this country, and pushed their settlements till they met the southern and more ancient settlers—that, accustomed to a colder climate and more active and hardy life, they were the Goths and Vandals of North America, and drove the more ancient settlers from their territory—that in the contest between these different tribes or races of men, were constituted the numerous fortifications discovered on the Ohio, the northern lomes, and in all parts of the western territory. What facts may be found to support this idea, must be left to further investigation."

the author had not kept strictly to the philological task of adding information on American Indian languages to the great work of the German scholar Peter S. Pallas. "Happy would it have been," Du Ponceau wrote, "if he had not suffered his imagination to draw him away from that simple but highly useful design! But he conceived that by comparing the American with the Asiatic languages he could prove the origin of our Indians from the nations which inhabit the opposite coast of Asia; and thus he sacrificed the real advantage of science to the pursuit of a favourite theory." Du Ponceau's reputation as editor of David Zeisberger's Delaware grammar, a formidable scholarly achievement, added weight to his opinion.[6]

Yet the Jeffersonian age produced little in the way of disinterested scholarship. In the same way that Jeffersonian thought mixed the problem of the Indian's origin with the question of his future relation to civilization, it subordinated the study of primitive languages to the value these investigations might have for philanthropic goals.

2

The remnants strewn throughout the Mississippi valley of what appeared to be a pre-Indian culture aroused much curiosity in the Jeffersonian period. Of special interest were the remains of the Mound Builders' era. These structures took various shapes, most frequently a large rectangular earth-walled area pierced by a number of openings. Burial mounds, similar to the one on the Rivanna described by Jefferson in his *Notes on Virginia*, were also a common sight.[7]

The remnants afforded ample opportunity for imaginative the-

6. Peter Stephen Du Ponceau, "Preface" to David Zeisberger, "A Grammar of the Language of the Lenni Lenape or Delaware Indians," Am. Phil. Soc., *Trans.*, N.S., III (1830), 66.

7. Jefferson, *Notes on Virginia*, ed. Peden, 97–100; Thomas Ashe, *Travels in America* . . . (London, 1809), 131–138, describes in detail his careful opening of a number of mounds on the Muskingum; he also condemns (pp. 175–176) the "profane and violating hands" that had destroyed what he believed were "mummies" in a cave near Lexington, Ky. The earthworks in their various manifestations are now attributed to the Hopewell culture (ca. A.D. 900–1300) and its various connections. Paul S. Martin, George I. Quimby, and Donald Collier, *Indians before Columbus: Twenty Thousand Years of North American History Revealed by Archeology* (Chicago, 1947), 267–268. George E. Hyde, *Indians of the Woodlands: From Prehistoric Times to 1725* (Norman, 1962), 33–34, contends that the enclosed areas were neither fortifications nor villages, as had been claimed, but ceremonial enclaves; for a similar opinion in the Jeffersonian period, see *The Western Review*, I (1819), 96–100.

orizing. Jefferson shared the common interest in them, but once again he regretted the tendency to leap to exaggerated and ill-founded conclusions. Charles Thomson forwarded a letter to him in Paris written by John Cleves Symmes, who followed William Robertson's speculation that the western earthworks were the original home of the Aztecs. The writer contended that this highly cultured people had been forced to migrate by the primitive Indians who then lived in the West.[8] In reply, Jefferson cautioned that those who examined the native antiquities should "make very exact descriptions of what they see of that kind, without forming any theories." He reasoned that the moment a person adopted a theory he tended to see only those facts that would enhance it. Thus very little reliable information had been gathered. He proposed that the American Philosophical Society "collect exact descriptions of the several monuments as yet known, and insert them naked in their transactions, and continue their attention to those hereafter to be discovered. Patience and observation may enable us in time to solve the problem." A decade later, in 1798, the society appointed a committee that sent out a letter soliciting information on various facets of Indian life including the ancient fortifications and tumuli. Jefferson, who had been elected president of the society in 1796, was appointed to the committee, whose diverse membership included Caspar Wistar, Charles Willson Peale, and James Wilkinson.[9]

Most observers tended to deny any connection between the Indians and the Mound Builders. As Jeremy Belknap succinctly explained: "The form and materials of these works seem to indicate the existence of a race of men in a stage of improvement superior to those natives of whom we or our fathers have had any knowledge; who had different ideas of convenience and utility; who were more patient of labour, and better acquainted with the art of defence." Jonathan Heart elaborated the argument by contending that the ancient American population "must have been under the subordination of law, a strict and well-governed police, or they could not have been kept together in such numerous bodies, and made to contribute to the carrying on of such stupendous works." The remains yielded evidence, concluded Gilbert Imlay, "of a people far more advanced in civilization than any which have yet

8. Charles Thomson to Jefferson, Apr. 28, 1787, Boyd, ed., *Jefferson Papers*, XI, 323–324; John Cleves Symmes to Charles Thomson, Feb. 4, 1787, New-York Historical Society, *Collections*, XI (New York, 1878), 233–239.

9. Jefferson to Thomson, Sept. 20, 1787, Boyd, ed., *Jefferson Papers*, XII, 159; "Circular Letter," Am. Phil. Soc., *Trans.*, IV (1799), xxxvii–xxxix.

been discovered in this part of the continent." Similarly, DeWitt Clinton thought that enough had been written "to demonstrate the existence of a vast population, settled in towns, defended by forts, cultivating agriculture, and more advanced in civilization than the nations which have inhabited the same countries since the European discovery." One on-the-spot observer, Moses Fiske, writing from Tennessee, noted traces of pottery of various sizes and shapes, some of which, found near the licks, indicated the use of salt. Also, numerous stone utensils of some refinement—axes, spikes, mortars, pounders, plates—pointed toward a society of a relatively high level of proficiency. More cautious, Caleb Atwater placed the builders of the works at a median level, between the primitive Indian and the advanced European. The ancestors of the Indians, he maintained, had lived by hunting, while those of the Mound Builders were shepherds and farmers. After examining various sites, he concluded that the country in which they were found had once been heavily populated, that the people who erected them had used iron—possibly steel, gold, silver, and copper—and knew the art of brickmaking.[10]

A Jefferson correspondent, Yale's president Ezra Stiles, shared these views. He wrote Jefferson in 1786, enclosing a letter on the earth formations from Samuel Holden Parsons, a Connecticut politician and speculator in western lands. Parsons had made a sketch of a formation at the mouth of the Muskingum River. From the existence of pottery and bricks in the earthworks as well as from the great height of the mounds, he concluded that the builders

10. Jeremy Belknap, *A Discourse, Intended to Commemorate the Discovery of America by Christopher Columbus* . . . (Boston, 1792), 45; "A letter from Major Jonathan Heart to Benjamin Smith Barton . . . ," Am. Phil. Soc., *Trans.*, III (1793), 217–218; Imlay, *Topographical Description*, 21, and ed. note, 597; DeWitt Clinton, *A Memoir on the Antiquities of the Western Parts of the State of New-York* (Albany, 1818), 16; Moses Fiske, "Conjectures respecting the Ancient Inhabitants of North America," Am. Antiq. Soc., *Archaeologia Americana*, I, 300–307. Atwater, *Description of Antiquities*, 120, conceded, however, that the builders of the works had no glass and that their pottery was unglazed and of poor quality. For a selection of other spokesmen favorable to the position see: Frances Latham Harriss, ed., *Lawson's History of North Carolina*, 2d ed. (Richmond, 1952), 179–180; "A Letter on the supposed Fortifications of the Western Country, from Bishop Madison of Virginia to Dr. Barton," Am. Phil. Soc., *Trans.*, VI (1809), 132–142; Ashe, *Travels in America*, 184–185, 188; "On the Population and Tumuli of the Aborigines of North America. In a Letter from H. H. Brackenridge, Esq. to Thomas Jefferson," Am. Phil. Soc., *Trans.*, N.S., I (1818), 151–155; "Reflections on the Institutions of the Cherokee Indians . . . ," *The Analectic Magazine*, XII (1818), 37–38.

had been superior to the Indians in their knowledge of the arts. The Indians' ignorance of the remains and the great height of the trees that grew on them led him not only to believe that they had been abandoned long before the coming of the Europeans but also to doubt that there was any connection between the western Indians and the ancient builders. Stiles seemed to agree with Parsons. Probably, he wrote, there had been "European or Asiatic Inhabitants there in antient ages." He noted also that John Smith claimed to have met Indians in Virginia "who descended from those who read in a Book."[11]

But Jefferson remained unimpressed. He wondered whether Parsons had actually seen the bricks as part of the old fortifications. Perhaps these ancient people had the capacity to pile earth in mounds and to dig entrenchments, but making bricks seemed beyond their ability. Certainly those who inhabited the region east of the mountains had been as culturally advanced as the Mound Builders in the West. The white men had been in the East for some time and had found no sign that any previous occupants had used iron. Since the production of iron usually preceded the art of brickmaking, Jefferson thought it unlikely that Parson's observations had been accurate. Besides, he doubted that men in the hunter state would have the industry to make either bricks or iron.[12]

Jefferson had much evidence to back his contention. Tribal culture, for instance, operated at a low technological level, and this technology had improved very little since the white man's arrival. If the earthwork builders in the Mississippi valley had possessed a relatively high degree of culture, then either the Indians had no connection with them or the native society had suffered a very serious decline. Neither proposition solved the problem of the Indians' origin. The current aboriginal inhabitants might well have destroyed a superior civilization, as barbarians had done repeatedly in the past; but then the origins of the earlier people still required explanation. The possibility of decline among the Indians was seriously considered and never totally discarded. Jefferson's proposal that the builders of the earthworks had been primitive ancestors

11. Samuel Holden Parsons to Ezra Stiles, Apr. 27, 1786, enclosed in Stiles to Jefferson, May 8, 1786, Boyd, ed., *Jefferson Papers*, IX, 478, 476.

12. Jefferson to Stiles, Sept. 1, 1786, *ibid.*, X, 316. Ashe, *Travels in America*, 32–33, was particularly critical of Jefferson's position concerning the natives' ancestors. He admonished him to visit the western remains and diligently search among them before passing judgment on the cultural credentials of their builders.

of the Indians accounted for the verifiable facts, but it remained a minority position.[13]

Benjamin Smith Barton, a botanist and professor of medicine, presented the most convincing case for the decline of the Indians. Their own traditions, he wrote, proved that they had long been plagued by divisions and had eventually split into many antagonistic tribes. He viewed the natives of his own time as much less polished than their ancestors of two centuries earlier. Furthermore, since any observer could see that the tribes were then passing into a "melancholy decay," he believed that the decline had begun before the European arrival and had continued since. Indian society showed many signs of a past eminence. Its mythology, for example, seemed Asiatic in origin, and the astronomy practiced by the Indians appeared similar to the Aztec version of that science. Moreover, the sense of reverence and courtesy that characterized the behavior of the northern Indians associated them in Barton's mind with the refinements of the Aztec empire. Finally, the structure of the Indian languages revealed that they had once been of superior quality; the small number of basic language groups argued for some previous degree of unity.[14]

A North Carolina historian, naturalist, and politician, Hugh Williamson, made effective use of the theory of decline. The western earthworks, he noted, demonstrated that the original North American settlers had been "artists and husbandmen" who, for some time after arriving, had cultivated the arts in their new settlements. When they found a shortage of tillable soil, however, they established small outlying colonies with instructions to live by hunting. This step, according to Williamson, constituted an irreversible

13. Leo Deuel, *Conquistadors Without Swords: Archaeologists in the Americas* (New York, 1967), 393–396. Hyde, *Indians of the Woodlands*, 32, says that in fact the Mound Builders were "in their everyday life barbarous. . . ." A writer in *The North American Review*, VI (1817–1818), 137, maintained "that these masses of the earth were formed by a *savage people*. Yet doubtless possessing a greater degree of civilization than the present race of Indians." For agreement with Jefferson on this issue, see Joseph de Acosta, *The Natural & Moral History of the Indies*, ed. Clements R. Markham (London, 1880), I, 69–70; Robertson, *History of America*, II, 32; Williams, *History of Vermont*, 200–201; Jonathan Carver, *Three Years Travels Through the Interior Parts of North-America* . . . (Philadelphia, 1796), 36–37; and Thaddeus Mason Harris, *The Journal of a Tour into the Territory Northwest of the Alleghany Mountains* . . . (Boston, 1805), 153. Ashe, *Travels in America*, 34, in a different mood, had doubts about the level of the Mound Builders' culture.

14. Benjamin Smith Barton, "Observations and Conjectures concerning Articles which were taken out of an ancient Tumulus, or Grave . . . ," Am. Phil. Soc., *Trans.*, IV (1799), 188–197.

move into savagery. From that day the American Indian had steadily receded from his illustrious past.[15]

Benjamin Rush held a similar view of the Indians' past. Their ancestors had indeed constructed the earthworks, but had "become savages in consequence of their having lost the use of letters or written characters and the knowledge and habits of religion . . . without both of which nations seldom or perhaps never become civilized or preserve their civilization." He traced the cause of this loss to the too easy abundance available on the new continent: "The extent of our country, and the facility of subsistence by fishing and hunting and the spontaneous fruits of the earth, would naturally accelerate the progress of the descendants of the first settlers of our country to the savage state."[16]

One widely disseminated theory associated the Indians with the high level of civilization that had existed in Mexico. Barton gave credence to the suggestion that the tumuli and earthworks had been built by the Aztecs. (He maintained also that the Danes were the ancestors of the Mexicans!) Albert Gallatin and Samuel L. Mitchill also speculated about a link between Mexico and the Mississippi valley. But as Jefferson had noted, commenting on a similar contention by William Robertson, the evidence was feeble.[17]

The details of this elaborate investigation of the ancient remains seemed less important than the establishment of some relationship between the Indians and those who had built them. The principle of human homogeneity made such a connection likely, although the theory that attributed the works to a people of much superior attainments than the natives skirted dangerously close to severing all links between the two societies. The theory of Indian decline, though held by only a few observers, provided a convenient explanation for the low level of native accomplishment, while retaining

15. Williamson, *Observations on Climate*, 115–116.

16. Benjamin Rush to David Hosack, Sept. 25, 1812, L. H. Butterfield, ed., *Letters of Benjamin Rush* (Princeton, 1951), II, 1163. Du Ponceau, Am. Phil. Soc., *Trans.*, N.S., III (1830), 85–86, rejected the notion that the intricate structure of the native languages was evidence for the existence on the American continent of an ancient civilization of high quality. In his opinion, the natural logic given to man by God was sufficient for all people to formulate adequate languages.

17. Barton, "Observations concerning Articles," Am. Phil. Soc., *Trans.*, IV (1799), 186*n*; Gallatin, "Synopsis of the Indian Tribes," Am. Antiq. Soc., *Archaeologia Americana*, II, 147–148; Samuel L. Mitchill, "The Original Inhabitants of America consisted of the same Races with the Maylays of Australasia, and the Tartars of the North," *ibid.*, I, 324–325; Atwater, *Description of Antiquities*, 244–251; Harris, *Journal of a Tour*, 162–167; Jefferson to Charles Thomson, Sept. 20, 1787, Boyd, ed., *Jefferson Papers*, XII, 159.

the relationship with the higher order of technology represented by the remains. In refusing to credit the supposed abilities of the Mound Builders, Jefferson obviated even this need. More significant, the investigation, regardless of the answer or the absence of subtlety in reaching it, clarified the Indian's position in the world by bringing him within the greater orbit of civilized achievement. If the Mound Builders had done such things, then the Indians could do them too. If what the Mound Builders had really accomplished proved of little moment, then at least the Indians now had a past, a place in history.

3

Native languages yielded more reliable evidence of the Indian's origin than had the Mississippi valley earthworks. Even without the help of the Old Testament, wrote Barton, the "pure certainty of science" would establish the origins of man in Asia through the study of comparative linguistics. He quoted the French historian Charlevoix to show that similarities in customs and traditions between one people and another were undependable for determining relationships. "New Events, and a new Arrangement of Things give Rise to new Traditions, which efface the former, and are themselves effaced in their Turn. After one or two Centuries have passed, there no longer remain any Marks capable of leading us to find the Traces of the first Traditions." Yet language held an immunity to these ravages of time; it remained stable at its core and gave the scholar the key to the past.[18]

Jefferson did not entirely share this view. He distinguished the mere relationship between two societies from the direction of transmission. Similarity in language might prove that two groups had once been in contact, but it would not identify the parent stock.[19] Still, as a measure of his commitment to the importance of linguistics, he devoted years to the compilation of a comparative In-

18. Barton, "Hints on the Etymology of certain English words . . . ," *Am. Phil. Soc., Trans.,* VI (1809), 155, and "Preliminary Discourse," in *New Views,* viii–ix. It should be noted that some critics had doubts about the usefulness of language study in the determination of origins; see "Heads of that Part of the Introductory Discourse Delivered November 7, 1816, by Dr. [Samuel L.] Mitchill . . . ," *Am. Antiq. Soc., Archaeologia Americana,* I, 340; McCulloh, *Researches, Philosophical and Antiquarian,* 38–39.

19. Jefferson to Benjamin Hawkins, Aug. 4, 1787, Boyd, ed., *Jefferson Papers,* XI, 683; Jefferson to John Sibley, May 27, 1805, Lipscomb and Bergh, eds., *Writings of Jefferson,* XI, 79–81; Jefferson to John Severin Vater, May 11, 1811, *ibid.,* XIII, 60–61. Barton, "Preliminary Discourse," in *New Views,* lxxxviii, made the same point.

dian language list. Although he had broader philological interests, he seldom failed to relate his word collecting to the question of Indian origins.[20]

From years of avid vocabulary hunting, Jefferson brought together a list of approximately 250 words in as many as fifty Indian languages. He arranged these in order to compare the various Indian words for one particular object and to illustrate the wide diversity in the Indian tongues. Also, he juxtaposed to the Indian words a selection of European equivalents with the purpose of discovering a possible relationship between them. He intended his own work as a complement to the extensive comparative vocabulary compiled under the patronage of Catherine the Great by Peter S. Pallas.

An air of misfortune hung over Jefferson's language study from the beginning. As early as 1786 he wrote to Benjamin Hawkins from Paris of his fear for the loss of his work. To the same correspondent in 1800, he spoke of the danger of risking the collection any longer and his determination to put it into print. Yet in 1806 it had not been published, and he wrote that he expected it would not be for "a year or two more." In 1809, before his precious work reached the public, Jefferson described how an "irreparable misfortune" had finally deprived him of thirty years' labor. The tale was certainly a sad one. His intention had been to publish his work before retiring from the presidency, but he had received a large selection of western Indian words gathered by Meriwether Lewis on the famous expedition, and he had not had the time to collate them into his own lists. He put off the task until his return to Monticello. On leaving Washington, he had all the Indian language material packed in a trunk and shipped by water. On the voyage up the James River, a thief broke open the trunk and emptied the papers into the river. A few tattered, mud-stained remnants floated ashore, but most of the material disappeared. Jefferson later sent what could be salvaged to the American Philosophical Society at Philadelphia where, even in their mutilated condition, they testify to the quality of his labor. Although he planned to compile a new list, he could never bring himself to begin it.[21]

20. Jefferson to James Madison, Jan. 12, 1789, Lipscomb and Bergh, eds., *Writings of Jefferson*, VII, 267; Jefferson to William Dunbar, Jan. 12, 1801, *ibid.*, X, 192–193; Jefferson to Peter Wilson, Jan. 20, 1816, *ibid.*, XIV, 402. See also Koch, *Philosophy of Jefferson*, 108–109; Pearce, *Savages of America*, 80.

21. Thomas Jefferson, "A Manuscript Comparative Vocabulary of Several Indian Languages," Class 497, No. J35, Lib., Am. Phil. Soc., Philadelphia. See

Nevertheless, Jefferson drew one major conclusion and a corollary from his long study of the Indian languages: the radical diversity of the native tongues, from which he inferred that the Indians had lived on the American continent long enough to be the parent stock of Asia. Speaking from memory in 1816 of his own word lists, he wrote that he was "certain more than half of them differed as radically, each from every other, as the Greek, the Latin, and Icelandic. And even of those which seemed to be derived from the same radix, the departure was such that the tribes speaking them could not probably understand one another. Single words, or two or three together, might be understood, but not a whole sentence of any extent or construction." These differences, as he made clear, went to the very root of the languages.[22]

If, according to Jefferson in his *Notes on Virginia,* one arranged the Indian languages

under the radical ones to which they may be palpably traced, and doing the same by those of the red men of Asia, there will be found probably twenty in America for one in Asia, of those radical languages, so called because, if they were ever the same, they have lost all resemblance to one another. A separation into dialects may be the work of a few ages only, but for two dialects to recede from one another till they have lost all vestiges of their common origin, must require an immense course of time; perhaps not less than many people give to the age of the earth. A greater number of these radical changes of language having taken place among the red men of America, proves them of greater antiquity than those of Asia.[23]

Apparently, however, Jefferson never became fully convinced that the population of Asia had its source in America, and he proposed an alternative solution. Americans, in dealing with the Indians, had found them reluctant to use a language other than their own, even when they had full knowledge of the other tongue. Also, judging from the Indians' well-known addiction to domestic feuds, would it not be fair to assume that a tribal faction alienated from the original body would refuse to employ a language still in use

also Jefferson to Benjamin Hawkins, Aug. 13, 1786, Boyd, ed., *Jefferson Papers,* X, 240; Jefferson to Hawkins, Mar. 14, 1800, Lipscomb and Bergh, eds., *Writings of Jefferson,* X, 161; Jefferson to Levett Harris, Apr. 18, 1806, *ibid.,* XI, 102–103; Jefferson to Benjamin Smith Barton, Sept. 21, 1809, *ibid.,* XII, 312–313; Jefferson to Peter S. Du Ponceau, Nov. 7, 1817, *ibid.,* XV, 153.

22. Jefferson to Peter Wilson, Jan. 20, 1816, Lipscomb and Bergh, eds., *Writings of Jefferson,* XIV, 402.

23. Jefferson, *Notes on Virginia,* ed. Peden, 102; Jefferson to Ezra Stiles, Sept. 1, 1786, Boyd, ed., *Jefferson Papers,* X, 316; Jefferson to Charles Thomson, Sept. 20, 1787, *ibid.,* XII, 159.

among those with whom it had quarreled? The dissident faction would be likely to form its own language. Since the natives needed but few words, it would take little effort to invent the requisite number. Jefferson upheld the principle of diversity only by engaging in some of the imaginative theorizing he had previously opposed.[24]

His argument for the priority of America over Asia did not pass without criticism. Joseph Doddridge thought it "a gigantic conclusion! A conclusion which an accurate knowledge of one hundred of the languages of America and Asia, would scarcely have warranted." Though willing to grant Jefferson his due as a philosopher, he thought that his zeal for the honor of the aborigine had led him astray. Clement C. Moore advanced a more substantial criticism. He accused Jefferson of rejecting Scripture. The Bible, said Moore, proved that mankind had its origin in Asia. Jefferson had cast doubt on this truth through his speculations on native language diversity in America and, furthermore, he had implied that the world was not as old as biblical scholars believed.[25]

Jefferson's minority view on diversity became more and more tenuous as the study of philology advanced and the interrelations among Indian languages became evident. Barton had long seen the point. While admitting the great variety in Indian languages, certainly since the coming of the European, he attributed these differences to dialect, which did not reach the heart of the language. Also, he criticized Jefferson for reasoning from diversity to the conclusion that America had probably populated Asia. Yet, except over the nature of the admitted diversity, the two had no cause for argument. Jefferson assumed a connection between the languages of Asia and America—at the source there had been language unity. He stressed the deep-seated diversity found in the native languages

24. Jefferson, *Notes on Virginia*, ed. Peden, 282, ed. note; Jefferson's addition has been inserted after p. 162 in the rebound volume that was his copy of the Stockdale edition, Alderman Library, University of Virginia, Charlottesville. Jefferson was not alone in contending for the great diversity of Indian languages; see Wasserman, "American Indian as Seen by Chroniclers," 107–108; Harriss, ed., *Lawson's History of North Carolina*, 26, 239; John Oldmixon, *The British Empire in America* . . . (London, 1708), I, 99–101; Archer Butler Hulbert and William Nathaniel Schwarze, eds., "David Zeisberger's History of the Northern American Indians," Ohio Archaeological and Historical Society, *Publications*, XIX (1910), 141; "A letter from Heart to Barton," Am. Phil. Soc., *Trans.*, III (1793), 220; and Williams, *History of Vermont*, 198–201.

25. Doddridge, *Notes, on Settlement and Indian Wars*, 46–47; Clement C. Moore, *Observations upon Certain Passages in Mr. Jefferson's Notes on Virginia, which Appear to have a Tendency to Subvert Religion, and Establish a False Philosophy* (New York, 1804), 15–19.

as spoken in his own time. The question of how much time had
elapsed between the period of primary language unity and the
dispersion hinged on the nature of the differences. But whether
these were fundamental or superficial, both Jefferson and Barton
agreed that the diversity had been preceded by an original unity.
Both believed that the Indians, at least from the evidence of their
languages, came from the same source. And both made the significant connection with Asia, even if, for a time, Jefferson had the
direction wrong.[26]

4

The mystery of Indian origins, however, invited fewer careful
scientific investigations than it did outlandish explanations. More
than one generation of New Englanders, for example, puzzled over
the ancient inscriptions found on the Dighton Rock at Taunton,
Massachusetts, and attributed them at one time or another to
Siberian Tartars, Canaanites, Phoenicians and their Carthaginian
relatives, followers of a mythic prince of Atlantis, Egyptians,
Hebrews, and a group of Tyrian sailors in the reign of King Solomon. Jeffersonian opinion on the Indian's origin frequently reached
similar misty realms. Such speculations might be condoned only
because they tended to give the American Indian an assured place
within the natural and historical order.[27]

26. Pearce, *Savages of America*, 80, n. 8, cites William Dunbar, "On the Language of Signs among certain North American Indians," Am. Phil. Soc., *Trans.*,
VI (1809), 1–8, as evidence that opinion in the late 18th century had turned in
favor of language unity among the Indians. But Dunbar, in fact, said just the
opposite. He contended that the use of common signs could be found among
the American Indians and also in Asia, "although their respective oral tongues
are frequently unknown to each other. . . ." Barton, "Observations concerning
Articles," Am. Phil. Soc., *Trans.*, IV (1799), 192n, 194, and "Preliminary Discourse," in *New Views*, lvi–lvii, lxxii, lxxix. See also Gallatin, "Synopsis of the
Indian Tribes," Am. Antiq. Soc., *Archaeologia Americana*, II, 142–144; Du
Ponceau to John Heckewelder, Aug. 30, 1816, "A Correspondence . . . respecting the Languages of the American Indians," Am. Phil. Soc., *Transactions of
the Historical and Literary Committee*, I (1819), 430–431; and Reuben Gold
Thwaites, ed., *Original Journals of the Lewis and Clark Expedition, 1804–1806*
(New York, 1904–1905), I, 132.

27. Edmund B. Delabarre, "Early Interest in Dighton Rock," Colonial Society
of Massachusetts, *Publications*, XVIII (1915–1916), 291; Samuel Eliot Morison,
The European Discovery of America: The Northern Voyages, A.D. 500–1600
(New York, 1971), 244–247; Brooke Hindle, *The Pursuit of Science in Revolutionary America, 1735–1789* (Chapel Hill, 1956), 323–324. For evidence that
bizarre speculations concerning Indian origins may be found in the post-
Enlightenment age, see Robert Wauchope, *Lost Tribes & Sunken Continents:
Myth and Method in the Study of American Indians* (Chicago, 1962); Harold
Sterling Gladwin, *Men Out of Asia* (New York, 1947); and Kenneth Macgowan
and Joseph A. Hester, Jr., *Early Man in the New World*, rev. ed. (New York,
1962), 248–259.

The most prominent rival to the Asian theory of Indian origins traced the native American population to the lost tribes of Israel. Since these missing Semites might have crossed Asia before reaching the American continent, the two theories were not contradictory. They did, however, remain separate interpretations of the native past. Coupling the Indians with the Jews yielded obvious theoretical advantages. Since the European man had his spiritual origin in Israel, it would certainly improve the anomalistic situation of the Indian to find his historical beginnings there. Significantly, much of the effort to associate the Jews and the Indians occurred after 1815 and grew out of the realization of Protestant America that its plans to proselytize the tribes had failed. In the face of this rejection by the Indians, the white man consoled himself with the thought that God had always needed patience in dealing with the Israelites.[28]

Amerigo Vespucci, reputedly, originated the theory that the Indians were Semitic in origin. In the seventeenth century, Thomas Thorowgood, quoting Roger Williams for support, promoted a Jewish origin for the Indian. Writing in 1708, John Oldmixon noted that William Penn held a similar opinion. Later in the century, the Indian trader James Adair swept all rivals aside as the undisputed champion of the idea. His monumental *History of the American Indians* (1775) employed every tool and an unbearable prolixity to prove that the Indians had indeed descended from the wandering tribes of Israel. He listed every possible similarity between the Indians and the Jews. Both people divided themselves into tribes and believed in a monotheistic religion. Both employed a theocratic form of government and looked with respect upon the prophets and priests who guarded their religious shrines. Moreover, Adair found the languages spoken by the American natives similar to the ancient Hebrew in construction and vocabulary. Besides these major points, he gathered a formidable list of parallel Indian and Jewish customs that added weight to his argument in favor of their past connection.[29]

In 1816 Elias Boudinot, who had a long-standing philanthropic interest in the Indian, published his last volume, *A Star in the West*. He adduced once again all the available evidence to prove the Semitic ancestry of the Indians. He ran through the usual categories—language, traditions received by the Indians from the

28. Powell, *Origin of Indians*, 8–9; Pearce, *Savages of America*, 61–62.

29. Robert F. Spencer, Jesse D. Jennings *et al.*, *The Native Americans: Prehistory and Ethnology of the American Indians* (New York, 1965), 14; Allen, *Legend of Noah*, 126; Wasserman, "American Indian as Seen by Chroniclers," 464–468; Oldmixon, *British Empire*, I, 164; Adair, *History of American Indians*, 15–194 *passim*.

Jews, customs then practiced by the Indians, religious opinions and ceremonies, all of which, he thought, pointed to a cultural tie between the two peoples. Though he would not say "past all doubt" that the Indians had descended from the Jews, he thought the evidence could hardly have been more conclusive.[30]

Of the older authorities on the problem of Indian origins, Grotius, Acosta, and Charlevoix had rejected the notion of descent from the Jews. In a later period, some authorities, such as Hugh Jones and Joseph Doddridge, though doubtful about a Hebrew connection, treated the idea with some respect. Others, such as Jonathan Heart, believed it positively false. He argued that proofs based on a purported similarity in customs failed to note that the children of Israel had themselves lived at a very simple level. Similarities between the Indian and Jewish ways resulted from a similar stage of development, not an ancestral relation. James H. McCulloh, completely out of patience with the farfetched evidence, dismissed the Hebrew theory as a "ridiculous conceit."[31]

Somewhat less persistent than the imputed Semitic origin, but a bit more romantic, was the attempt to link the Indians with the Greeks through a lost Alexandrian fleet of the fourth century B.C. One traveler saw proof in the hieroglyphic symbols found in a cave on the Ohio River. Others found it in the noble native visage and in the Indians' universally applauded eloquence.

The effort to associate the Indians with a group of lost Welshmen who followed Madoc across the ocean in the twelfth century proved as durable as the theory of the lost tribes of Israel, though it was

30. Boudinot, *Star in the West*, 88, 281; George Adams Boyd, *Elias Boudinot: Patriot and Statesman, 1740–1821* (Princeton, 1952), 254–255. The pervasive, uncritical character of the Hebrew theory is illustrated by Erminie Wheeler-Voegelin, ed., "John Heckewelder to Peter S. Du Ponceau, Bethlehem 12th Aug 1818," *Ethnohistory*, VI (1959), 72–73: "What regards the *Origin* of the Indians, I chose from the beginning to be silent. True, we all *believe* (and Pyrlaeus did believe the same) that the Indians were the Offspring of the 10 Tribes whoom the King of Assyria led away Captive—etc.—but this is only an *Opinion* of ours —No one of us will undertake to *prove* the fact, and opinions without facts— without reasons for so believing, are worth nothing."

31. Hugo Grotius, *On the Origin of the Native Races of America* . . . , ed. Edmund Goldsmid (Edinburgh, 1884), 14–17; Acosta, *Natural & Moral History*, ed. Markham, I, 64–69; Charlevoix, *Journal of a Voyage*, ed. Kellogg, II, 139; Hugh Jones, *The Present State of Virginia* . . . , ed. Richard L. Morton (Chapel Hill, 1956), 50; Doddridge, *Notes, on Settlement and Indian Wars*, 53–54; "A letter from Heart to Barton," Am. Phil. Soc., *Trans.*, III (1793), 221; McCulloh, *Researches, Philosophical and Antiquarian*, 89, 99, 102–103; Thomas S. Woodward, *Woodward's Reminiscences of the Creek, or Muscogee Indians* . . . (Tuscaloosa, Ala., 1939 [orig. publ. Montgomery, Ala., 1859]), 11–12, 33–34.

never presented with as much erudition. Isaac Stewart, one of the many captives of the Indian wars, described his wilderness wandering after being released by the Indians on the Wabash River. He accompanied a Spaniard and a Welshman across the Mississippi River and seven hundred miles up the Red River, where they came upon a tribe speaking the Welshman's language. The native chiefs claimed that they had come from a foreign land to West Florida and had moved to their present location when the Spaniards captured Mexico. They possessed parchment scrolls written in blue ink. The Welshman, being illiterate, could not read these ancient documents, but he partook of the oral sociability available and remained with the tribe. The story was typical. Accounts of blond, light-skinned, Welsh-speaking natives cropped up repeatedly well into the nineteenth century. As with the Jewish and Greek explanations, the Welsh interpretation received serious attention by men of respectable opinion.[32]

But all other opinions paled before the general consensus that the Indian had in some way crossed to the American continent from Asia. The Spaniard Joseph de Acosta had early discussed the feasibility of such a migration. He found it impossible to believe that the natives had reached their destination by sea. They possessed nothing like the requisite navigational equipment, nor had the ancients from whom they were reported to be descended. Perhaps a ship had been blown off course and reached the New World by accident, but how then would this account for the presence of animals in America. Some useful and desirable animals might have been brought, but certainly no other kind. The riddle would be solved, thought Acosta, only by the discovery of a land passage between the two continents.[33]

32. For Isaac Stewart's story, see *Affecting History of the Dreadful Distresses of Frederick Manheim's Family* . . . (Exeter, N.H., 1793), 16–19. Amos Stoddard, *Sketches, Historical and Descriptive, of Louisiana* (Philadelphia, 1812), chap. 17; Ashe, *Travels in America*, 231–237; Josiah Priest, *American Antiquities, and Discoveries in the West* . . . , 2d ed., rev. (Albany, 1833), 44–47; Antonello Gerbi, *La disputa del nuevo mundo: historia de una polémica, 1750–1900* (Mexico, 1960), 239n. See also David Williams, "John Evans' Strange Journey," *The American Historical Review*, LIV (1948–1949), 277–295, 508–529; Aubrey Diller, "James Mackay's Journey in Nebraska in 1796," *Nebraska History*, XXXVI (1955), 123–128; "A letter from Heart to Barton," Am. Phil. Soc., *Trans.*, III (1793), 222; Morse, *Report on Indian Affairs*, 31; "On the Existence of a Welsh Colony in America," *Analectic Mag.*, II (1813), 410–413; "The Nicholas Biddle Notes" in Jackson, ed., *Letters of Lewis and Clark Expedition*, 515–516; Filson, *Kentucke*, 95–97; Janson, *Stranger in America*, 271–277.

33. Acosta, *Natural & Moral History*, ed. Markham, I, 45–46, 63–64.

On this crucial point, Jefferson summed up the opinion of the late eighteenth century. A voyage by sea to America had always been a possibility, even with the inferior navigational facilities of early times. From the east the transit from Norway by way of Iceland, Greenland, and Labrador seemed without difficulty. Probably the Eskimos had used this route from northern Europe. The recent voyages of Captain Cook in the far Northwest revealed only a narrow expanse of water between Asia and America.[34]

The Jeffersonian generation used a wide miscellany of information to support the conclusion that the American Indians had originated in Asia. The Indians themselves helped. Their own traditions, almost universal if the white man's sources could be credited, told of their migration from the West. For the natural historian, such original information added considerable weight to the argument in favor of Asia. Some, both Indians and whites, doubted the proposition. The Mandan tradition, for instance, told of how the forefathers of the tribe had come to their country through a hole in the earth; the Shawnee talked of having once lived in Cuba until expelled by the Spaniards. Yet only a minority disagreed with the common interpretation. The Indians said that they had come from the direction of the setting sun. White men believed that they had good reason to trust the native memory.[35]

34. Jefferson, *Notes on Virginia*, ed. Peden, 100–101. Jedidiah Morse, *The American Universal Geography* . . . (Boston, 1796), I, 84, agrees with Clavigero and Buffon that at one time Asia and the northwestern part of America were connected as also were South America and Africa. John Ledyard, *A Journal of Captain Cook's Last Voyage* . . . (Hartford, 1783), 88, 175; McCulloh, *Researches, Philosophical and Antiquarian*, 428. See also Macgowan and Hester, *Early Man in New World*, 17–20.

35. For a selection of opinion favoring the Indian tradition see Robert Rogers, *A Concise Account of North America* . . . (London, 1765), 252–253; Adair, *History of American Indians*, 194; William Bartram, *Travels through North and South Carolina, Georgia, East and West Florida, the Cherokee Country, the Extensive Territories of the Muscogulges or Creek Confederacy, and the Country of the Chactaws* . . . (London, 1792), 365–366; Barton, "Preliminary Discourse," in *New Views*, xci–xcii; Robertson, *History of America*, II, 46–47; and John Heckewelder, "An Account of the History, Manners, and Customs, of the Indian Nations who Once Inhabited Pennsylvania and the Neighboring States," Am. Phil. Soc., *Trans. of Hist. and Lit. Comm.*, I (1819), 29. Among those who doubted the validity of the tradition, the most important were Zeisberger and Clinton, in Hulbert and Schwarze, eds., "Zeisberger's History," Ohio Archaeol. and Hist. Soc., *Pubs.*, XIX (1910), 31, 132, and Clinton, *Memoir on Antiquities*, 3–4. For the Mandan story, see Gallatin, "Synopsis of the Indian Tribes," Am. Antiq. Soc., *Archaeologia Americana*, II, 125, and for the Shawnee, see Randolph C. Downes, *Council Fires on the Upper Ohio: A Narrative of Indian Affairs in the Upper Ohio Valley until 1795* (Pittsburgh, 1940), 9.

The travelers' accounts of the eighteenth and early nineteenth centuries contributed bits of corroborative evidence. Some of the information came at secondhand or more, but it tended invariably to trace the Indian to Asia. Josiah Meigs, for example, quoting Ezra Stiles, related to Samuel L. Mitchill an incident concerning the artist John Smibert. When Smibert arrived in America with Bishop Berkeley, the story went, he identified a group of Narragansett Indians in Newport with the Tartars he had been employed to paint at the court of the grand duke of Tuscany. In a similar vein, the traveler John Ledyard, in a letter to Jefferson from Siberia in 1787, explained that the appearance and circumstances of the inhabitants of northern Asia convinced him of their close relation to the Indians. After viewing some Russian figures on the population of the Siberian Tartars and then much later hearing the account of Captain Peter Pond of Melford, who had explored the Indian lands beyond the Great Lakes, Ezra Stiles said he believed that the sparse distribution of people found in both places constituted substantial evidence of a connection.[36]

The clinching arguments in the Jeffersonian period for the Asian origin of the Indians were no more critical than these rumors and stray tales. Imlay presented a convenient summation of the most commonly heard evidence. Native America, he began, had always been more heavily populated on the side towards Asia. The Indian way of life resembled the Tartar manner; neither showed much artistic talent. Both had similar skin coloring. Climate and "those mixtures with which the Americans rub themselves" accounted for any differences. The wild animals on the northern continent could only have come from Asia, and they could not have been transported by sea. And finally, the American bison and the Scythian buffalo held membership in the same species. He might have added the possible kinship in language, beside the wide assortment of customs that one observer after another saw paralleled in Asia and America. But the conviction, accurate as it may have been, had little solid, empirical evidence behind it.[37]

36. Delabarre, "Early Interest in Dighton Rock," Col. Soc. Mass., *Pubs.*, XVIII (1915–1916), 274–275; John Ledyard to Jefferson, July 29, 1787, Boyd, ed., *Jefferson Papers*, XI, 638; Watrous, ed., *Ledyard's Journey through Russia*, 164, 165, 175, 177, 195, 198, 226–227; Franklin Bowditch Dexter, ed., *The Literary Diary of Ezra Stiles . . .* (New York, 1901), I, 356, III, 386.

37. The arguments in the late 18th century for the Asian origin of the Indian were not unlike those offered by Edward Brerewood, *Enquiries touching the diversity of Languages, and Religions, through the chiefe parts of the World* (London, 1614); Allen, *Legend of Noah*, 122–123; and Powell, *Origin of Indians*, 20. For a survey of the common opinion see Imlay, *Topographical De-*

Ultimately, the quest for Indian origins served the purposes of Jeffersonian philanthropy. The age could not be held responsible for the superficiality of the evidence. If some observers seemed less precise and more gullible than need be, even in that age of rudimentary science, the answer to the question of origins obviated any defects in methodology. And even the process itself of searching for the tribal past awakened a deep interest in the Indian's welfare. All the ramifications of the study of native origins—archaeological, philological, and historical—conspired to rivet the white man's attention on the Indian and to demand that tribal society be interpreted through the same methods used by the white man to understand his own society. Philanthropy had asked no more, after all, than that the Indian should be seen through the same lens used by civilization to see itself.

Undoubtedly, the superficiality of the enterprise revealed another equally important aspect of the search for origins. Finding the Indian's beginnings in Asia corroborated conclusions long since reached by another means. The unity of mankind could not have been seriously threatened by any collection of archaeological or historical evidence. Its justification had always been more axiomatic than empirical. The stature of tribal society, its capacity to nurture a facile and adaptable people, already established in environmentalist theory, needed no further support. The thin layer of substance behind the argument for the Asian origin of the Indians merely acknowledged the truth that the decision had already been made.

Yet the Jeffersonian age could not have chosen to avoid one line of investigation because it promised only a limited return. The philanthropic drive employed every means to insure its success. Its appetite for knowledge of the Indian and for substantiation of its interpretation of the native character was promiscuous. No question could be left unanswered. Environmentalism had introduced the element of necessity into the Indian's future. The process of change

scription, 2–3; Samuel L. Mitchill, "The Original Inhabitants of America shown to be of the same family and lineage with those of Asia . . . ," Am. Antiq. Soc., Archaeologia Americana, I, 326–328; Mark Catesby, The Natural History of Carolina, Florida, and the Bahama Islands . . . (London, 1771), vii; Jefferson, Notes on Virginia, ed. Peden, 101; Filson, Kentucke, 92–93; Smith, Essay on Variety, 67; Williams, History of Vermont, 188–193; Carver, Three Years Travels, 133–134; Barton, New Views, 8–81; [Morse], History of America, 110–111; Robertson, History of America, II, 35–45; Dunbar, "On the Language of Signs," Am. Phil. Soc., Trans., VI (1809), 1–3; Williamson, Observations on Climate, 3, 95, 104; and Gallatin, "Synopsis of the Indian Tribes," Am. Antiq. Soc., Archaeologia Americana, II, 142.

in nature admitted no possibility for failure or even for doubt. The moral component of the philanthropic plan for the Indian required the use of every possible means, the acquisition of all possible knowledge.

Moreover, much can be said for the plain good sense of the Jeffersonian era. Extravagant speculations and feeble evidence aside, the consensus described accurately the origins of the native tribes. It relied on an ancient deposit of knowledge in Western civilization that located the origins of all mankind in Asia. Even Jefferson and some of the more scientific investigators made use of this long-accepted body of knowledge. If it could be shown that the Indians had descended from lost Hebrews or Welshmen or had migrated from Asia, the accepted source of civilized population, they would, at least in theory, be incorporated within the limits of civilized identity. The process doubtless worked both ways. The traditional interpretation tended to insure that the Indian would be assigned the proper past; having been so assigned, he came that much closer in his relationship to the white man. Far from arranging a new and exotic past for the native tribes, the Jeffersonian generation made an earnest effort to include him within the ordinary development of mankind.

Chapter III
Deficiency

The immediate occasion for the Jeffersonian evaluation of Indian society was the comte de Buffon's attack on the potentiality of the New World and the deeper implications of this theory for all the inhabitants of the continent. Jefferson, of course, and many other serious-minded Europeans and Americans had shown interest in the native population before Buffon and his contemporaries, the Abbé Raynal, Cornelius de Pauw, and William Robertson, made their views known. But the Buffon theory came at a particularly sensitive moment for the development of the Jeffersonian conception of the Indian. With the wide acceptance of the environmentalist economy, the Jeffersonians could scarcely abide a direct contradiction of their understanding and their hopes. The Buffon conception cut directly to the heart of Jeffersonian optimism. By defining the American land as naturally deficient,[1] it accepted the validity of environmentalism and then went on to predict the most doleful results for those who came under the influence of the new land. From the idea of the continent's hopeful youth, Buffon reasoned to its hopeless inferiority. Conceived of as a howling wilderness, the continent, at least, possessed some definite stature, some decisive quality, though it may have been negative. The deficiency theory left the New World shorn of the basic gift of self-fulfilling energy that the Jeffersonian age tended to see as fundamental to the natural order. Jefferson replied, no doubt, because

---

1. Buffon's theory is often described as proving the degeneration of the continent. This is true, in so far as de Pauw and Raynal described the decline of the animals and men who came from Europe. But more crucial for the Jeffersonian position was the accusation of basic deficiency. See Durand Echeverria, "Roubaud and the Theory of American Degeneration," *The French American Review*, III (1950), 27–28.

Buffon had attacked the American character and the basis for its customary optimism, but the theory had even deeper implications for the vitality of nature itself.

Paradoxically, Jeffersonian theory provided ample support for the deficiency hypothesis. By building nature on an environmentalist base and assuming that the lay of the land, temperature, and humidity profoundly influenced man's physical and mental constitution and in part his moral capacity, Jeffersonian cosmology was deeply implicated in the Buffon interpretation. The natural processes by which the human organism responded to its surroundings remained intact. While the land and the climate retained their vigor and healthfulness, environmentalism yielded salutary results. But when the land turned hot and let off debilitating vapors that lulled its animal and human inhabitants into enfeeblement, the theory became a source of enervation.

The newness of the land, an idea so important for Jeffersonian optimism, became in France an explanation for the inadequacy of the continent. By a curious transposition of meaning, the symbolic youth of the new continent that had enabled the romantic imagination to picture it as an alternative to corrupt civilization took on the definition of literally new—new as a geological fact. Youth in this interpretation stood for unaccomplished potential, for matter without the mature evidence of long-established productive capacity. The theory did not deny the future, but it did impose an unhappy evaluation on the past accomplishments of the American continent.

Buffon's thesis and the popular extension of it by Raynal and de Pauw struck a blow for Europe and civilization against America and progress. It cleverly left the machinery of progress untouched, however, and attempted to destroy only the material from which, supposedly, progress arose. Buffon and his followers, by implication, affirmed their satisfaction with the way things had come to be in Europe without the assistance of America. By denying the potentiality of the New World, they had devised an ingenious instrument for deflating the overblown pretensions of America.

Furthermore, the colonial experience led many Frenchmen to see the new continent as a menace. Only failures and undesirables settled in these distant regions. Though colonies might have proved the capacity of the Old World to spread its way of life to new lands, the French believed that the settlements drained the motherland of support. Wild speculation in colonial enterprise had produced John Law's inflationary bubble; new diseases had been brought from exotic places; and France had suffered defeat and humiliation in wars to protect its far-flung and shaky empire. As a consequence, men like Montesquieu considered colonies liabilities that would eventually strip the homeland of its substance. Buffonian theory supplied the justification for the negative connotations the French already associated with the possession of colonies.[2]

Buffon presented the nucleus of his theory in the first edition of his *Histoire naturelle* in 1761. Because of his stature as a natural historian and the collector of a tremendous storehouse of information about the physical world, Buffon endowed his idea with a prestige far beyond its intrinsic merits. Although he proposed his theory originally with limitations and cautionary words, Jefferson and those who thought as he did took it as an interpretation of the fundamental incapacity of their continent.

Buffon began by comparing the size of the animals of the southern continent of the New World with those of the warmer regions of the old. He found the quadrupeds of Africa "four, six, eight, and ten times larger than" those of South America. In addition, he argued that European animals taken to the American continent had become smaller, as had those common to both continents at the time of the discovery. From these facts, he concluded that the New World possessed "some combination of elements and other physical causes" that militated against the vigorous development of "animated Nature." Whatever the nature of this mysterious flaw, it constituted an insurmountable obstacle to any impressive germinal growth. Even living organisms that had flourished in a more favorable atmosphere would be stunted if transported to America.

Evidence of the continent's deficiency could be found in an examination of its native inhabitants as well. Buffon portrayed the Indian as no more than the first among animals, a weak automaton who had proved incapable of mastering his environment. In return the New World had denied him the basic life-giving spirit of love, so that he exhibited no desire to perpetuate himself. Though the savage equaled the European in size, his "organs of generation are

---

2. This discussion of the background of the degeneracy thesis is taken from: Durand Echeverria, *Mirage in the West: A History of the French Image of American Society to 1815* (Princeton, 1957), 4–7. For the transference of the characteristics of the new land and Indian to the white colonist, see Michael Kraus, "America and the Utopian Ideal in the Eighteenth Century," *The Mississippi Valley Historical Review*, XXII (1936), 490–491.

small and feeble." He had no hair and little sexual inclination toward his female. More nimble than the European, his sensations were dull and his body weak. The Indian was more timid than the European. He seemed lacking in verve because the fundamental needs of food and drink determined his physical reactions. Without these basic stimulants, he could not be aroused. The Indian's feeble sexual drive and the faint spark of affection between parents and children resulted in weak family ties and no political order. Cold-hearted and naturally cruel, the Indian reduced his women to servants and beasts of burden. And finally, he manifested no broad love of mankind.[3]

A more dismal picture of life on the American continent could scarcely be drawn, though Buffon excepted the European colonists from the consequences of his theory. In an effort to spell out the physical laws from which he derived his grim conclusions, he went into considerable detail about the various environmental factors that proved the continent's lack of fecundity. He spoke of the newness of America, the relative degrees of heat and moisture in the different parts of the continent, the location and height of the mountains, the quantity of the running and stagnant waters, and the extent of forested areas, all of which, he believed, played an important part in releasing a very low level of primal energy. Although he based many of the particulars of his argument on doubtful authority and made only vague connections between the land and the men formed by its influence, his approach remained well within the accepted confines of natural history. Not only did Buffon's work uphold the environmentalist supposition, but his methodology, the detailed descriptive elaboration, placed it within the best tradition of Enlightenment science. And this made the indictment all the more disturbing.[4]

The Dutch naturalist Cornelius de Pauw, a typical philosophe with a taste for the exotic but no sympathy for the primitive, first applied Buffon's theory to the European settlers. Exaggerating slightly, he followed the main lines of Buffon's discussion. He depicted American animals as a thousand times less dangerous than

3. [George Louis Leclerc], Count de Buffon, *Natural History, General and Particular* . . . , trans. William Smellie, new ed. (London, 1812), VI, 25–253; Gerbi, *La disputa del nuevo mundo,* chap. 1; Gilbert Chinard, "Eighteenth Century Theories on America as a Human Habitat," American Philosophical Society, *Proceedings,* XCI (1947), 31.

4. Echeverria, "Roubaud and the Theory of American Degeneration," *French Am. Rev.,* III (1950), 25; Chinard, "Eighteenth Century Theories on America," Am. Phil. Soc., *Procs.,* XCI (1947), 31.

those of Asia and Africa. Creatures brought to the New World from elsewhere invariably became weaker under American conditions and in succeeding generations grew more debilitated. The native populations could not be compared in energy or accomplishment with those of the civilized world. But most serious, de Pauw maintained that the general deficiency of America had its effect also on the white colonist. The New World, in his opinion, had produced neither a scholar of high repute nor one who could be compared with the great minds of Europe.[5]

The Abbé Raynal, a philosophe and historian of sorts with a talent for making good use of other people's ideas, popularized the opinions of Buffon and de Pauw. Following the familiar course of argument, he asserted that the indigenous inhabitants of the New World showed less strength and courage than the people of the old continent, seemed less lively and affectionate, and, because of the indolence of the men, subjected their women to unnecessary toil. With direct reference to Buffon, he believed that their ineffectual sexual impulse implied an organic imperfection that subjected the people of America to a perpetual childhood. Furthermore, he agreed with de Pauw's contention that the climatic deficiency of the continent would necessarily affect the level of culture attained by the European settler. In mock astonishment, he noted that America had reared neither a good poet nor an able mathematician nor, for that matter, a man of genius in any of the arts or sciences.[6]

When Buffon perceived that his theory had assumed the proportions of an irresponsible slander against the New World—Peter Kalm used it in his *Travels,* as did William Robertson in his widely read *History*[7]—he reevaluated its basis. Because of an important gap in its original formulation, he had never made it clear whether America suffered from an organic and incurable deficiency or some less basic defect. At times Buffon seemed to say merely that the

5. [Cornelius] de P[auw], *Recherches philosophiques sur les Américains . . .* (London, 1770), I, 8–9, 125–126, II, 164–165, 167–168; Gerbi, *La disputa del nuevo mundo,* 49–55; Echeverria, *Mirage in the West,* 9–11; Henry Ward Church, "Corneille de Pauw, and the Controversy Over His *Recherches philosophiques sur les Américains,*" *PMLA,* LI (1936), 178–189.

6. Guillaume Thomas François Raynal, *Histoire Philosophique et Politique, Des Établissemens & du Commerce des Européens dans les deux Indes* (Amsterdam, 1770), VI, 193–194, 376; Gerbi, *La disputa del nuevo mundo,* 42–47; Echeverria, *Mirage in the West,* 13–14.

7. Adolph B. Benson, ed., *The America of 1750: Peter Kalm's Travels in North America* (New York, 1937), I, 55–56. For a defense of Kalm against the charge of credulity, see Martti Kerkkonen, *Peter Kalm's North American Journey: Its Ideological Background and Results* (Helsinki, 1959). Robertson, *History of America,* II, 16–24.

continent's youth accounted for its inadequacies. In his *Époques de la nature* of 1778, he finally returned to this neat compromise, which dissociated him from the rash conclusions of his followers and made it easier to maintain the validity of natural history and the environmentalist conception. And, significantly, this delicate adjustment brought Buffon's theory into closer conformity with Jeffersonian optimism. If the American problem stemmed only from the continent's recent emergence from primeval quiescence, then the possibilities for growth seemed clear enough. And with its youth unsullied by the decadence of age, it could expect an even brighter future. Buffon remained antiprimitivist and a staunch defender of civilization, but his argument skirted very close to primitivism.[8]

The greater purport of Buffon's thesis, however, concerned the problem of natural order. As first presented, his notion proposed a hiatus in the order of nature that grievously impaired its ability to produce normal development in America; in effect, a portion of nature had turned up without its proper potentiality. The contention seemed fully consistent with Buffon's early atomism—a conception that denied nature the clarity and order established by the Linnean system. As Samuel Miller said in his review of eighteenth-century scientific thought, despite Buffon's "splendid publications" and "captivating style," his hypotheses were frequently "whimsical, extravagant, and delusive." But more pointedly: "His neglect of regular systematic arrangement is a great defect, and must ever lessen the value of his works." The Jeffersonian reaction to the deficiency theory, consequently, came from a source deeper than the wounded ego of self-confident, progressive America. Beyond being optimistic about America's destiny, Jeffersonians also required a pattern of order and predictability in nature. Buffon disappointed them on both counts.[9]

2

Understanding the potential consequences of the Buffon theory, Jefferson and his generation reacted sharply. Benjamin Franklin, though doubtless appalled by the European position, answered the charge with delicate mockery. The dinner party at which he invited his American companions to compare their impressive heights with the diminutive sizes of his French guests and his amusement when

8. Gerbi, *La disputa del nuevo mundo,* 139–141; see the review of the Gerbi volume by George Boas, *Jour. Hist. Ideas,* XVII (1956), 425.

9. Samuel Miller, *A Brief Retrospect of the Eighteenth Century . . .* (New York, 1803), 115–116; Gerbi, *La disputa del nuevo mundo,* x, 30–31.

the Abbé Raynal believed the Polly Baker ruse revealed his attitude toward such ponderous theories.[10] John Adams, according to his own account, spent much energy in counteracting the "shameless falsehoods" of the Europeans concerning America, though finally he gave up the task as hopeless. But Jefferson occupied the role of principal defender of the integrity of the New World. He found little humor in the European slanders, and he never had any thought of surrendering the field of propaganda to them. By the sheer dint of his own energy and scholarly enterprise, he intended to vindicate America's honor.[11]

Jefferson made his formal reply to Buffon and his followers in his *Notes on Virginia.* He directed his refutation mainly at Buffon and Raynal, the latter for his application of the original theory to white Americans. Impelled by both American patriotism and his commitment to a particular brand of eighteenth-century cosmology, Jefferson also reacted because of his characteristic distaste for disembodied theories. Buffon, he believed, had violated one of the primary canons of the comparative method by treating the Indian and the European as though they had reached the same state of development, when they obviously had not. De Pauw and Robertson he considered mere compilers, unworthy of serious refutation.[12]

Following the line of argument pursued by Buffon and his allies, Jefferson first dealt with the land: "As if both sides were not warmed by the same genial sun; as if a soil of the same chemical composition, was less capable of elaboration into animal nutriment; as if the fruits and grains from that soil and sun, yielded a less rich chyle, gave less extension to the solids and fluids of the body, or produced sooner in the cartilages, membranes, and fibres, that rigidity which restrains all further extension, and terminates animal growth." His argument carefully avoided any criticism of the mechanism by which Buffonian nature influenced the creatures within its grasp—it was sufficient, rather, to show the basic similarities between the two continents.[13]

10. Leonard W. Labaree *et al.,* eds., *The Papers of Benjamin Franklin* (New Haven, 1959–), III, 120–125; Raynal, *Philosophical and Political History,* trans. Justamond, V, 365; "Biographical Sketches," Lipscomb and Bergh, eds., *Writings of Jefferson,* XVIII, 170–172; Max Hall, *Benjamin Franklin and Polly Baker: The History of a Literary Deception* (Chapel Hill, 1960), 58–66, 79–81.

11. John Adams to Philip Mazzei, Dec. 15, 1785, Boyd, ed., *Jefferson Papers,* VIII, 678–679.

12. Jefferson to Chastellux, June 7, 1785, *ibid.,* VIII, 184–186.

13. Jefferson, *Notes on Virginia,* ed. Peden, 47; Jefferson to Benjamin Vaughan, Dec. 29, 1786, Boyd, ed., *Jefferson Papers,* X, 646; Vaughan to Jefferson, Jan. 26, 1787, *ibid.,* XI, 72.

Summarizing the Buffon position in four points, Jefferson disputed each. By the Frenchman's reckoning, American animals, common also in Europe, grew to a smaller size; indigenous species were constructed on a diminutive scale; animals brought from the Old World and domesticated in the New degenerated; and finally, America supported fewer species. Buffon based these conclusions, said Jefferson, on the supposition that a hot, dry climate stimulated growth while a cold, moist atmosphere retarded it. He assumed that America was cold and moist. Jefferson declined to speak authoritatively about the relative climatic conditions of Europe and America, but even assuming the validity of Buffon's proposal, he thought that an examination of the quadrupeds under the first two categories would prove the American animals of a larger size. On the third point, Jefferson conceded that some domestic animals imported from Europe appeared to degenerate from the original stock. "In a thinly peopled country," reasoned Jefferson, "the spontaneous productions of the forests and waste fields are sufficient to support indifferently the domestic animals of the farmer, with a very little aid from him in the severest and scarcest season. He therefore finds it more convenient to receive them from the hand of nature in that indifferent state, than to keep up their size by a care and nourishment which would cost him much labour." The last item in Buffon's indictment, that America had fewer distinct species, would not stand in light of the extensive list Jefferson had compiled in disproving the previous points.[14]

Furthermore, even conceding Buffon his basic inference that heat and dryness aided physical growth and cold and moisture checked it, Jefferson believed that the actual conditions of the two continents failed to support his conclusions. Considering the whole of the American continent, from the hottest to the coldest region, the New World enjoyed a warmer climate. Yet he reasoned from this proposition that America and Europe should have been equally congenial to growth since each possessed at least one of the requisite attributes: America may have been warmer than Europe, but Europe was drier.[15]

The remains of the mammoth and the megalonyx, of course, supplied the primary evidence in support of Jefferson's claim for America's potentiality. Objective science aside, these enormous beasts served ulterior purposes in the argument with Buffon. In

14. Jefferson, *Notes on Virginia*, ed. Peden, 47–58; Gerbi, *La disputa del nuevo mundo*, 231–244.
15. Jefferson, *Notes on Virginia*, ed. Peden, 48.

Jefferson's view, investigation proved the mammoth unique to the American continent and not, as claimed by some Europeans, identical with the elephant. Five or six times the size of the elephant, the mammoth probably possessed larger, more distinctly formed teeth. No one had ever discovered a sign of the elephant in America, and undoubtedly none would ever be found, since it seemed native only to tropical regions. Nor, for that matter, had any mammoth bones been unearthed in the warmer sections of the New World.[16] While Jefferson served as its president, the American Philosophical Society sought information about the mammoth. Both Lewis and Clark, at his request, sent specimens from the West. And Charles Willson Peale, a scientist with a flair, ensconced these remains in his Philadelphia museum to advertise the capacity of the continent for the nurturing of spectacular creatures.[17] When first brought to his attention, Jefferson believed the megalonyx an even more impressive beast. Smaller than the mammoth or the elephant, but a carnivore of larger size than either the lion or the tiger, this creature seemed ideal for his purposes. Jefferson's enthusiasm faded when he discovered that his prized specimen resembled the megatherium, a herbivorous South American sloth named by Cuvier. Yet the animal's size, if not its carnivorous ferocity, still credited the American land with the capacity for supporting formidable creatures.[18]

In his determination to overwhelm Buffon and his followers with a body of irrefutable evidence, Jefferson asked General John Sullivan to send a variety of specimens to Paris from the wilderness of northern New England. Sullivan outdid himself with an elaborate and expensive selection of skins, skeletons, and antlers to support Jefferson's argument. Somewhat overwhelmed himself, Jefferson shipped the lot to Buffon with apologies that the moose skin had

16. *Ibid.*, 43–47, 53–54. In proving the greater size of the American animals, Jefferson refuted Buffon at a particularly sensitive point. One of the Frenchman's underlying assumptions was precisely the superiority of larger over smaller animals; see Gerbi, *La disputa del nuevo mundo*, 14–19.

17. "Circular Letter," Am. Phil. Soc., *Trans.*, IV (1799), xxxvii–xxxix; Meriwether Lewis to Jefferson, Oct. 3, 1803, Jackson, ed., *Letters of the Lewis and Clark Expedition*, 126–130; Jefferson to Caspar Wistar, Feb. 25, 1807, Lipscomb and Bergh, eds., *Writings of Jefferson*, XI, 158–159; Jefferson to Monsieur de la Cepede, July 14, 1808, *ibid.*, XII, 83–88.

18. Jefferson, "A Memoir on the Discovery of certain Bones of a Quadruped of the Clawed Kind in the Western Parts of Virginia," Am. Phil. Soc., *Trans.*, IV (1799), 246–260; Julian P. Boyd, "The Megalonyx, the Megatherium, and Thomas Jefferson's Lapse of Memory," Am. Phil. Soc., *Procs.*, CII (1958), 420–435.

shed some hair and assurances that these were diminutive examples indeed of what America might yield. From Sullivan he begged no more favors. But as comical as it appeared, Jefferson showed to what lengths he would go to prove his case against the Buffon theory.[19]

Ultimately, the dispute turned to the capacity of the American Indian, not because Buffon had rested his case on the native, but because symbolically nothing could better represent the youth and vitality of the new continent. Europeans had long conceived of America in such terms, and the Americans themselves, though less taken with mythic thinking, saw the aptness of the relationship between the Indian and the New World. Without hesitation Jefferson put forward a defense of the tribesmen at the same time that he spelled out the virtues of the virgin continent.

3

Though limited to a few paragraphs, Buffon's attack left little of the Indian's reputation unscathed. Jefferson replied point by point in his *Notes on Virginia* with the general intention of upholding the essential vigor of the native's physical makeup and of ascribing the deficiencies to the state of his society. Sexuality, and the human qualities that flowed from it, held a central place in Buffon's interpretation, as it did also in Jefferson's response. He had no doubt that the Indian possessed a powerful sexual drive. In reaction to the common association of sexuality with hairiness, Jefferson assured his readers that the Indian had been plentifully endowed with hair but found it vulgar and plucked it out. Indian women exhibited considerable strength and seemed sufficiently fertile. In war the men viewed bravery as a virtue, endured pain in silence, and met death stoically. The Indian owned a lively, indulgent, and affectionate temperament, and, above all, his enthusiasm for hunting and games of chance proved the acuteness of his mind.[20]

Jefferson exploited one of the more obvious openings in Buffon's position. The Frenchman had admitted that both European and Indian possessed a similar physical construction. But he had also detected certain shortcomings in the native's moral capacity. Buffon should have seen, Jefferson claimed, that materialism and environmentalism required a close relationship between the human body

19. John Sullivan to Jefferson, Mar. 12, 1784, and June 22, 1784, Boyd, ed., *Jefferson Papers*, VII, 21–24, 317–320; Jefferson to Buffon, Oct. 1, 1787, *ibid.*, XII, 194–195; Jefferson to Sullivan, Oct. 5, 1787, *ibid.*, 208–209; Anna C. Jones, "Antlers for Jefferson," *The New England Quarterly*, XII (1939), 333–348.

20. Jefferson, *Notes on Virginia*, ed. Peden, 59–61.

and the workings of the mind. If he granted the Indian physical equality with the white man, surely moral equality would follow. Jefferson merely insisted that Buffon trace out the full implications of environmentalism. An Indian built on the same physical model as the European would enjoy similar mental and moral abilities.[21]

Evidence for the Indian's mental abilities could be seen in the character of his society. With neither a conception of the principle of compulsion nor any visible political constraints, the bond of cohesion in native society rested on personal influence and persuasion. The Indians put great emphasis on "eloquence in council, bravery and address in war." The white man's experience supplied many examples of the native talent in diplomacy. Jefferson particularly liked the speech of the Mingo chief Logan as a sample of the Indian's ability to appraise his own situation realistically and express his feelings with deep pathos. "I may challenge the whole orations of Demosthenes and Cicero, and of any more eminent orator, if Europe has furnished more eminent, to produce a single passage, superior to the speech of Logan." Yet such notable talents did not permit a comparison of Indian society with Europe before Rome's expansion to the north. The Indians lacked numbers and hence did not have the advantage of "emulation" that Europeans possessed. Even so, he concluded, how long did it take European society to produce a Newton?[22]

Jefferson countered the Abbé Raynal's comments on the American settlers with a brief recitation of the American litany of genius: Washington, Franklin, Rittenhouse. In proportion to her numbers and age, America compared well with the older nations. Especially so with Great Britain, whose sun could be seen "descending to the horizon. Her philosophy has crossed the Channel, her freedom the Atlantic, and herself seems passing to that awful dissolution, whose issue is not given human foresight to scan."[23] Jefferson might temporize when describing the Indian's accomplishments, but he saw no reason to do so when speaking of the whites.

In his desire to enlist all the aid possible, Jefferson submitted the manuscript of his *Notes on Virginia* to more than one philosophical acquaintance for comment. One of these, Charles Thomson, the secretary of the Continental Congress, returned an extensive discussion which so pleased Jefferson that he appended it to the privately printed version of the *Notes* in 1785 and to the Stockdale

21. *Ibid.*, 61–62.
22. *Ibid.*, 62–63.
23. *Ibid.*, 64–65.

edition of 1787. Thomson had played an active role in Pennsylvania Indian affairs and had some familiarity with the Delaware tribe. He followed Jefferson's line of argument in refuting Buffon, though he usually took higher ground. Even Buffon's concession of equality in size proved unacceptable, since, according to Thomson, the Delaware attained a greater height and the Iroquois a larger size than the white man. He knew of no evidence to show that the Indians had smaller penises than Europeans. The vanity of the Indian dexterously plucking the hair from his face in order to increase his prowess among the ladies furnished at least some indication of his virility. The tribesmen might have been less inclined to sexual indulgence than the Europeans, but the reason lay not in a natural defect but in manners. From earliest youth, the natives devoted themselves to war and the chase. The survival of their people depended on proficiency in these arts. Sexual dalliance could come only after the fundamental necessities of fighting and hunting had been mastered. "If a young man were to discover a fondness for women before he has been to war, he would become the contempt of the men, and the scorn and ridicule of the women. Or were he to indulge himself with a captive taken in war, and much more were he to offer violence in order to gratify his lust, he would incur indelible disgrace." True enough, Indian women often assumed the initiative in sexual matters, though elderly warriors often took young wives. "Does this savour of frigidity, or want of ardour for the female?"

Thomson found little substance in the rest of Buffon's indictment. Though often undemonstrative, the Indians showed sufficient natural affection. Their bravery and fortitude in the face of torture reminded Thomson of "the old Romans in the time of the Gauls." Their exhausting dances and their ability to carry out extended marches in time of war proved that their bodies responded to more than the simple demands of hunger and thirst. Custom accounted for the work load demanded of native women. And the strength of the tribal bond should have been clear enough from the sensitivity with which an entire tribe reacted to an insult offered to one of its members.[24]

The idea of American deficiency seemed so extraordinary to Hugh Williamson that he searched for hidden motives among its proponents. With so little evidence to support the thesis, he supposed that pride or a provincial love of their own native surround-

24. *Ibid.*, 199–202, 296, ed. note.

ings had led the Europeans to formulate it. Perhaps some merely absorbed a fashionable notion, but the most insidious adopted the concept of American inferiority because they wished to subvert the unity of man based on the Mosaic law.[25] Surely, Jefferson's article on the megalonyx furnished evidence that the new continent had once nurtured beasts of great size, larger than the elephants and lions of the Old World. Williamson attributed the inferiority of American domestic animals to the easy ways that accompanied American abundance, not to a natural incapacity. "Nothing less than necessity," wrote Williamson, "has ever produced diligence in any kingdom or state."[26]

Though he considered much of the European information on the American tribes erroneous, Williamson agreed that they had not yet risen to the standards of civilization. But he found the reasons for the Indian's laggard performance in his hunting culture. As brave as any other man, the Indian relied on stratagem because it was the prudent thing to do. He occasionally mistreated his wife, but so did Russians and Arabians, and no one impugned their natural powers. Besides, how could an Indian whose strength had been so fundamentally undermined be capable of treating anyone with severity? The parity in size between Europeans and Indians substantiated their equality in strength. New England Indians who had adopted the white man's ways and especially his diet had proved able workmen in the Nantucket fishery. The relative inferiority of native culture, therefore, should not be attributed to an irreversible impediment any more than should similar conditions elsewhere: "No man will say that Greece is a country in which the human race naturally degenerate. The birth place of Homer, Pindar, Demosthenes, Hypocrates, Zeuxes, and Apelles, cannot be mentioned as the grave of genius; but the inhabitants of that region have no pretensions, at present, to any superiority over the American Indians."[27]

Some Americans obtained their information about the Indians from firsthand observation, but like Jefferson most depended on the word of travelers, Indian traders, and frontier fighters, many of whom put their knowledge into print. One European observer at least went to the sources. William Robertson wrote to the Pennsylvania trader George Croghan in search of an authentic account of aboriginal life. Croghan answered a list of questions, some

25. Williamson, *Observations on Climate*, 140–141.
26. *Ibid.*, 78–82.
27. *Ibid.*, 87–94, 122–123.

in great detail. He offered the usual environmentalist description of native society, and to two questions, obviously based on the Buffon thesis, he returned explicit answers. He found it difficult to judge the relative vigor of the Indians and the inhabitants of the ancient continent "butt its Gineraly alowd. they Can Carry Greater burdens on thire backs, then the Europians, and bear more hard-shipes in traveling and hunger." On the crucial issue of the Indian's passion, Croghan went to the heart of the Buffon contention: "The Indians are No way Deffective in the Animal Passions for thire feamales, and have as Great Desiers and abilitys I blive as any Nations can have, butt they have a Natural Modiesty in thire be-haver which prevents thire Desier being Easly Discoverd and phaps they have more affection for thire Children and Relations then any other Nations on Earth."[28]

Possibly Croghan's replies never reached Scotland, though in the *History* Robertson referred to his *Journal* when reporting on the mammoth bones from the Kentucky salt licks. In any case he made no obvious use of Croghan's views. Robertson interpreted the New World through a neat combination of the Buffon thesis and environmentalism. The principle of life on the American continent seemed weaker than in Europe, the animals smaller and fewer in number. The Indians, weak and indolent, lacked social affection and made their women "neither the objects of that tender attach-ment which takes place in civilized society, nor of that ardent de-sire, conspicuous among such nations." This absence of vibrant energy, however, arose from the primitive condition of the land and not from an intrinsic flaw as in the Buffon-Raynal-de Pauw theory. Robertson had great faith in the efficacy of cultivation, and he believed that both the land and the Indian would be changed as soon as they became the subject of civilized exploitation.[29]

Croghan's futile effort to keep the record straight revealed a pro-found truth about the Jeffersonian-Buffon dispute. Both sides, no doubt, cared for an accurate natural history of the American conti-nent. Yet the facts, no matter how high the Americans heaped them, would not really supply the needed answer. Buffon had posited an organic defect in the American continent that no list of particular attributes could quite counter. The frustration arising

28. Nicholas B. Wainwright, "The Opinions of George Croghan on the American Indian," *The Pennsylvania Magazine of History and Biography*, LXXI (1947), 152–159; Wainwright, *George Croghan: Wilderness Diplomat* (Chapel Hill, 1959), 283.

29. Robertson, *History of America*, II, 61–65, 349–350.

from this knowledge led to the American touchiness on the subject, to an unwillingness to let any European criticism pass, and to a determination to correct every error. Also, the Americans seemed to realize that they would have to answer Buffon on the most important issue of all, the Indian's sexual powers.

The basic problem, according to Buffon, rested with the Indian's "small organs of generation." From this woeful defect flowed all the list of calamitous deficiencies that plagued native society; the debility of the primary human resource limited population growth and permitted only a loose ordering of native society. Colonial opinion scoffed at this theory. From the eighteenth-century literary treatment of the Indians, the Jeffersonian generation had learned with certainty of the vigor of the native sexual impulse. In keeping with his generally lively views on relations between the sexes, William Byrd believed that the whole issue of Indian-white relations could be settled by intermarriage. "A sprightly Lover," he wrote, "is the most prevailing Missionary." He never doubted that the natives would be easily enticed to the pleasures of Venus.[30] Byrd merely burlesqued the characteristic view of the Indians' sexual capacity.

Robert Beverley found no shortage of sexual energy among the Indians, though he reported no evidence of prostitution. As he described it, tribal hospitality became a libidinous fantasy. The Indians treated "Strangers of Condition" to a grand entertainment, at the completion of which "a Brace of young Beautiful Virgins are chosen, to wait upon him that night, for his particular refreshment. These Damsels are to Undress this happy Gentleman, and as soon as he is in Bed, they gently lay themselves down by him, one on one side of him, and the other on the other. They esteem it a breach of Hospitality, not to submit to every thing he desires of them." These young ladies did not suffer in reputation because of their behavior. "The excess of Life and Fire, which they never fail to have, makes them frolicksom, but without any real imputation to their Innocence." The trouble came with the English who seemed unable to make the nice distinction between guilt and "harmless freedom" and who insisted on believing the native women incontinent.[31] Either way the Indians possessed a goodly supply of sexual initiative.

30. William K. Boyd, ed., *William Byrd's Histories of the Dividing Line Betwixt Virginia and North Carolina* (Raleigh, 1929), 3–4, 120–122.

31. Robert Beverley, *The History and Present State of Virginia*, ed. Louis B. Wright (Chapel Hill, 1947), 170–171, 188–189. Wright notes that in the 1722 edition Beverley changed his opinion on the sexual freedom of the native girls. See p. xxv.

John Lawson sprinkled his account of the Indians of North Carolina with diverting glimpses of the natives' supposed sexual proclivities, though his view also contained intimations of Buffon. "The Indian Men," he maintained, "are not so vigorous and impatient in their Love as we are." During the period of betrothal, before the brave had paid the full price for his bride, the couple lived together intimately but without consummation. Lawson doubted the capacity of Europeans to bear up under such trying customs. And yet, his overall description of tribal sexuality offered much evidence of venereal ferment. Prostitutes in the tribes, called "trading girls," did a brisk business among the traders. White men knew "how much Frailty possesses the Indian Women, betwixt the Garters and the Girdle." The Indian king held the title of "chief Bawd" with a "Prerogative over all the Stews of his Nation, and his own Cabin (very often) being the chiefest Brothel-House." Open sexuality began at an early age. "The Girls, at twelve or thirteen Years of Age, as soon as Nature prompts them, freely bestow their Maidenheads on some Youth about the same Age, continuing her Favors on whom she most affects, changing her Mate very often, few or none of them being constant to one, till a greater number of Years has made her capable of managing domestic Affairs." Nor, in Lawson's version, did such promiscuity cause scandal in the tribe: "the more Whorrish, the more Honorable." "The Flos Virginis, so much coveted by the Europeans, is never valued by these Savages." Women captured in war from other tribes served the purposes, frequently three or four at a time, of the great men of the village.[32] Doubtless, Lawson's preoccupation with the sexual propensities of the American Indians revealed more about the mind of early eighteenth-century England than about the native society, but it also strengthened the colonial tradition that the Indians enjoyed a strong sexual drive.

In his *History of Virginia,* William Stith noted offhandedly that Powhatan kept twenty concubines. John Oldmixon informed his readers with assurance that "no People in the World make themselves so easie in Wedlock" as the Indians; husbands may be cuckolded without "Crime or Scandal." Indians considered it both "lawful and reputable enough for their Virgins to be as generous to Mankind as they please, before Marriage." In his potboiler on the Indians of the Northwest, Jonathan Carver dismissed the natives' supposed frigidity; they were "the zealous votaries of Venus."[33]

---

32. Harriss, ed., *Lawson's History of North Carolina,* 31, 32, 49, 196–197.

33. William Stith, *The History of the First Discovery and Settlement of Virginia* . . . (Williamsburg, 1747), 58; Oldmixon, *British Empire,* I, 124

The multiplication of opinions added little to the basic theme already well impacted in discussions of native society.

Yet some close observers of the American scene saw merit in the Buffon theory. The Indian did seem to manifest a certain lassitude, a diffident rejection of the humane affinities so dear, to the white man. From one perspective, such detachment could be viewed as a characteristic of the noble savage, though it could also be explained as a major deficiency in the native constitution. The most common theory, the one that answered Buffon at the same time that it preserved the sacred doctrine of environmentalism, attributed the apparent absence of native energy to custom and the lack of stimulus in a primitive existence. Wrote James Adair, "The unconcern, doubtless proceeded originally from a virtuous principle; but now it may be the mere effect of habit: for jealousy and revenge excepted, they seem to be diverted of every mental passion, and entirely incapable of any lasting affections." Samuel Stanhope Smith explained the Indians' "appearance of indifference" by their simplicity of manners "where no studied excitements are used to awaken the passions." Admitting that the Indians showed no ardor for their women, Jedidiah Morse noted that custom helped them avoid the excesses common in Europe. Surely, the native tribes carried on sufficient activity (war and dancing) to insure a basic vitality.[34]

A substantial body of opinion, with a broad conception of the problem, portrayed the Indian as a vigorous character indeed. Stith described Powhatan as "a great Master of all the Savage Arts of Government and Policy . . . , penetrating, crafty, insidious, and cruel." Adair asserted that nothing would terrify the natives to submit to anything contrary to "their general idea of liberty." In a hodgepodge of current opinion of the Indian's virtues and vices, as much accurate as not, Bernard Romans included one passage that summed up the positive side: "They are strong and active, patient in hunger and the fatigue of hunting and journeying, but impatient and incapable of bearing labour, they are incredibly swift of foot; their discourse is generally of war, hunting, or indecency; their women are handsome, well made, only wanting the colour and

(Oldmixon offered a different version on p. 285) ; Carver, *Three Years Travels,* 245, 247.

34. Adair, *History of American Indians,* 99; Smith, *Essay on Variety,* 91n; [Morse], *History of America,* 90–92, 94. Support for Buffon came from Benjamin Rush, *Three Lectures upon Animal Life . . .* (Philadelphia, 1799), 56; [John Mitchell], *The Present State of Great Britain and North America . . .* (London, 1767), 257–260; Kames, *Sketches of History of Man,* III, 72.

cleanliness of our ladies, to make them appear lovely in every eye; their strength is great, and they labour hard, carrying very heavy burdens, a great distance; they are lascivious, and have no idea of chastity in a girl. . . ." And with more pretension to scientific exactitude, as distinguished from the conventional literary inter- pretation, Rush announced his conclusions as a man of medicine: "After much inquiry, I have not been able to find a single instance of FATUITY among the Indians, and but few instances of MELAN- CHOLY and MADNESS."[35] All in all, American opinion before the Buffon attack, and during the Jeffersonian period in direct response to it, saw the Indian as a creature of formidable parts. Jefferson and his generation had no need to invent new arguments to defend the native. They could draw upon the literary evidence that had been accumulating for generations and add to it the results of their own investigations.

Beginning with a positive opinion of the native's sexuality and a defense of the general strength of his character, the Jeffersonians ended with a self-confident hymn to all things American. The land particularly had to be guarded against Buffonian criticisms. Ben- jamin Smith Barton dismissed even the supposed physical infancy of the continent as "one of the many dreams of the slumbering phi- losophers of our times." William Barton praised America's invigo- rating climate, noting also that the congenial warmth of the summers could only increase "the generative principle of animal nature." The variety of the landscape, "with hills and vallies, moun- tains and plains" added to the healthfulness of the climate, justified America's singular position among the continents of the globe. Toward the end of the Jeffersonian age, in an expansive rhetoric, John Bristed spoke of the continent's "prodigious *physical* capabili- ties. . . . Indeed, the whole aspect of *Nature* here, in America, has a direct tendency to enlarge and elevate the mind of the sensible and refined spectator. Little are the feelings of that being to be envied, whose heart does not swell with sublime emotions, when he sees with what a bold and magnificent profusion the living God has scattered the great works of his creation in this quarter of the globe; on how vast and awful a scale of grandeur *He* has piled up the

35. Stith, *History of First Discovery of Virginia*, 154–155; Adair, *History of American Indians*, 371; Romans, *Concise Natural History*, 43–44; Benjamin Rush, "An Inquiry into the Natural History of the Medicine among the In- dians of North America, and a Comparative View of Their Diseases and Reme- dies with Those of Civilized Nations," in *Medical Inquiries and Observations*, 3d ed. (Philadelphia, 1809) , I, 119.

mountains, spread out the valleys, planted the forests, and poured forth the floods."[36]

In order to emphasize the significance of native customs in upholding environmentalism, the Americans sought eagerly for any incidental but perhaps revealing mistakes made by the other side. Because of the diversity of native manners, the distant European knew little of the actuality and often hit upon the stereotype. For example, he associated hair with racial vigor. Supposing the native constitutionally weak and then noting his lack of hair, he easily concluded that smooth skin demonstrated the tribesmen's natural deficiency. Delighting in every opportunity to correct the misinformed European, the Jeffersonian literature dwelled with almost obscene pleasure on the Indians' practice of picking the hair from their bodies. Once again, the supposed basic defect turned out to be only a question of manners and proved nothing of overriding importance about the aboriginal constitution except perhaps an eccentric notion of beauty.[37]

Of somewhat greater import, the reputed native capacity for the endurance of hardship and pain also supported the argument from manners and the environmentalist assumptions of both sides. Buffon and his followers took what some Americans saw as stoical virtue as evidence of an essential lassitude in the Indian physique. Smith sought an explanation in the relative simplicity of the native mental processes that made Indians less sensitive to discomfort. Both sides drew on the same cultural material, the endurance of pain, and both operated from a basic environmentalist principle, but they offered different explanations.[38]

In making his contribution to Buffon's education, Morse reached beyond the American literary experience to the accounts of native societies on the southern continent by José de Acosta and Francisco Xavier Clavigero, which described the construction of advanced

36. Barton, "Preliminary Discourse," in *New Views*, cvii–cviii; William Barton, "Observations on the probabilities of the Duration of Human Life, and the progress of Population, in the United States . . . ," Am. Phil. Soc., *Trans.*, III (1793), 53; John Bristed, *The Resources of the United States of America . . .* (New York, 1818), 12.

37. For a few of the many references, see Adair, *History of American Indians*, 6; Williams, *History of Vermont*, 157–158; Morse, *History of America*, 70–71; and Heckewelder, "Account of the Indian Nations," Am. Phil. Soc., *Trans. of Hist. and Lit. Comm.*, I (1819), 197–198.

38. [William Stork], *A Description of East-Florida, with a Journal, Kept by John Bartram of Philadelphia . . .* , 3d ed. (London, 1769), 2; Smith, *Essay on Variety*, 2d ed., 404–411; [Morse], *History of America*, 73–77; William Barton, "Observations on the probabilities of the Duration of Human Life," Am. Phil. Soc., *Trans.*, III (1793), 50; Williams, *History of Vermont*, 165.

civilizations in America. Directing the discussions to de Pauw in particular, he described the native accomplishments in government, law, history, painting, and calendar making. An indigenous American civilization in Mexico used the arch in building, installed vapor baths in its palaces, used a form of money in its commerce, and amused itself with the science of astronomy. Moreover, he quoted Acosta's defense of the Aztecs against the charge of cowardice in their war with Cortés. The Spaniards, he maintained, had many more men than had been reported, and they made use of Indian allies. Besides, when the conquistadores arrived, the Aztec monarchy was already in danger of collapse. Morse concluded his survey of Latin American history with a broad environmentalist statement that gave the northern tribes the full benefit of the virtues he had discovered in the South. "After such long experience and study of them, from which we imagine ourselves enabled to decide without danger of erring, we declare to M. de Pauw, and to all Europe, that the mental qualities of the Americans are not in the least inferior to those of the Europeans; that they are capable of all, even the most abstract, sciences; and if equal care was taken of their education, if they were brought up from childhood in seminaries, under good masters, were protected and stimulated by rewards, we should see rise among the Americans, philosophers, mathematicians, and divines, who would rival the first of Europe."[39]

4

In affirming the environmentalist thesis and then denying the Indian the meliorist results that flowed from it, Buffon presented the Jeffersonians with an extraordinarily difficult polemical situation. Few Americans perceived, as did Jefferson, the environmentalist basis of the European theory. Most American replies assumed that the Buffon-Raynal-de Pauw interpretation rejected this indispensable dogma of eighteenth-century progress.

By isolating the American defect in some mysterious natural impotence, European theorists imposed a static inequality on the new continent and on its native race. Buffon unquestionably referred to the basically material origins of the problem, and he certainly intended to deny to the Indian the possibility of an improved condition. He made use of environmentalism, but for the wrong purpose: not to point the way to a better future, but to make that future organically impossible. Although he never took the further step of applying the thesis to the white man, Raynal and

39. [Morse], *History of America*, 67, 77–86.

de Pauw filled that gap in logic. Had they not taken this step, the American argument might have been less frenetic, though it would have been no less earnest. Environmentalism established a profound relationship between Americans and the land. Buffon opened the discussion at this most basic of all levels, and the Jeffersonian generation replied in kind.

In its extensive treatment of native customs, the Jeffersonian argument had the effect of sustaining environmentalism. The Indian could be easily defended on such questions as his sexual potency and his eloquence, but Buffon and his followers had broached many other issues on which the Americans came to the natives' defense only reluctantly. Frequently, Jeffersonian observers of Indian life seemed just as inclined as Buffon to criticize tribal society. Indeed, philanthropists called for fundamental changes in native society precisely because they found it wanting by the standards of civilization. Answering Buffon by attributing Indian deficiencies to custom provided the basis for this coming alteration. In this sense the Jeffersonian mind showed no more respect for the integrity of Indian culture than did Buffon. The Jeffersonians proposed to do something about it, and they resented the implication that because of a natural flaw this might be a futile enterprise.

In summary, Buffon defined a threefold cause for the varieties among men: first, the effects of climate; second, food that in turn depended on climate; and third, manners, on which climate had an even greater influence. Applied to the New World, his theory offered the Indians no improvement. He intended, as Gilbert Chinard has pointed out, only to defend civilization against the primitive, not to condemn humanity itself to an empty future. Nature, he wished it understood, could be a ruthless adversary when untamed by human hands. In America the white settler employed a wide variety of means to improve his condition, in contrast to the Indian, who reacted passively to his environment. Buffon seemed to be saying that the irrevocable defect in the character of the continent might be surmounted, though not by the tribesman, since he had shown no inclination to rise from his primitive condition. The white man, having been nurtured in Europe, would contribute the necessary energy for the transformation of the New World.[40]

Thus Buffon asserted the power of men over their environment. Human society could be so formed as to create men capable of directing the aimless wanderings of nature. Jefferson voiced as

40. Buffon, *Natural History*, trans. Smellie, III, 372–374; Chinard, "Eighteenth Century Theories on America," Am. Phil. Soc., *Procs.*, XCI (1947), 31–32.

strong a conviction but with a slightly different twist. In 1797, at the time of his enthusiasm over the discovery of the megalonyx, he told his friend James Madison that in nature men held the first position as destroyers: "The Lions and tygers are mere lambs compared with man as a destroyer, we must conclude that it is in man alone that Nature had been able to find a sufficient barrier against the too great multiplication of other animals and of man himself, an equilibrating power against the fecundity of nature."[41] Although in disputing Buffon's interpretation of American potentiality, Jefferson and his followers showed signs of granting the American land a limitless future, they could also offer a more balanced view of the natural condition. Jefferson believed that civilization, though capable of great accomplishments, also taught men to disdain their environment, to treat it selfishly, and eventually to destroy it.

5

Buffon and his followers struck America's open nerve. If Jefferson responded to them with restraint, the rhetorical hotheads who followed him did not. The argument, begun in the sedate phrasing of Jefferson's pen, became increasingly shrill and grandiloquent. Witness Bristed referring to the American land and its civilized inhabitants: "These vast territorial domains are held by a population, free as the air they breathe—a population, powerful in physical activity and strength; patient of toil, and prodigal of life; brave, enterprising, intelligent, and persevering; presenting both in body and mind, the noblest materials for the formation of national greatness, prosperity and influence." With an eye to certain French savants who had dared impugn the American character, he went on to make the New World's claim explicit. "The truth is, that the great mass of the American people *surpasses* that of all other countries in shrewdness of intellect, in general intelligence, and in that vast versatile capacity which enables men to enter upon and prosecute successfully, new situations and untried employments."[42] American self-confidence and anticipation of a great future needed no artificial stimulus.

For the Jeffersonians, the Buffon theory served as an important

41. Jefferson to Madison, Jan. 1, 1797, Lipscomb and Bergh, eds., *Writings of Jefferson*, IX, 359–360.

42. Bristed, *Resources of America*, 2–3, 307, 309. The Americans remained sensitive on the subject; see Henry Nash Smith, *Virgin Land: The American West as Symbol and Myth* (Cambridge, Mass., 1950), 27–28; Clinton, "Introductory Discourse," Lit. and Phil. Soc. of N.-Y., *Trans.*, I (1815), 21–23, 79–80, note A.

basis for the articulation of American self-consciousness. Yet the number of European intellectuals who held the position was small, and they made efforts in the 1770s and 1780s to soften its consequences. Eventually it proved no more than an aberration in the general development of Western thinking.[43] But it challenged the Americans to respond; it galvanized a counter theory. In self-defense the Jeffersonian generation applied itself to self-examination and also to theoretical explanation. America defined its greatness in the vindication of nature against Buffon's churlish dissent—a greatness short of accomplishment but wholly within the scheme of environmental development. Buffon may have been no more than a convenient foil for America's already substantial confidence in its own future—though no less important for that. He skewered precisely the right elements in American progressivism and thus more securely united the land and the Indian in both the European criticism and the Jeffersonian defense.

43. Echeverria, *Mirage in the West*, 29–31, 64–66.

Chapter IV

The Noble Savage

I

Environmentalist theory offered a mechanical definition of human development. Although satisfactory for describing the Indian's society and vital for plotting his future, it was little commensurate with the grandeur of the meliorist enterprise. The Jeffersonian generation saw the transformation of the continent and the Indian in epic dimensions. It would not be entirely satisfied with the slow, unfolding progress of environmentalism. The desert must blossom, and the Indian must prove himself ready for prompt incorporation into the unique design of American civilization. Jeffersonian optimism required a broad formulation, sufficiently supple to accommodate the environmentalist contrivance, yet compelling enough to transport the American Indian into the realm of perfection.

The New World as paradise, inhabited by noble savages, supplied the needed formula. Though superficially a conception of static perfection, it served more often as a utopian goal. From the simplest improvements in the human condition to the grandest flights of achievement, the vision of a perfect order on earth operated as a basic force in the development of civilization.[1] The discovery of the

1. For a survey of the utopian spirit in Western thought, see Ernest Lee Tuveson, *Millennium and Utopia: A Study in the Background of the Idea of Progress* (Berkeley, 1949); Henri Baudet, *Paradise on Earth: Some Thoughts on European Images of Non-European Man* (New Haven, 1965); Lois Whitney, *Primitivism and the Idea of Progress in English Popular Literature of the Eighteenth Century* (Baltimore, 1934), chap. 1; Charles L. Sanford, *The Quest for Paradise: Europe and the American Moral Imagination* (Urbana, 1961), chaps. 1–7; Eric Voegelin, *The New Science of Politics* (Chicago, 1952), chap. 4; George Boas, *Essays on Primitivism and Related Ideas in the Middle Ages* (New York, 1966 [orig. publ. Baltimore, 1948]); Norman Cohn, *The Pursuit of the Millennium: Revolutionary Messianism in Medieval and Reformation Europe and Its Bearing on Modern Totalitarian Movements*, 2d ed. (New York, 1961); Gilbert Chinard, *L'Amérique et le rêve exotique dans la littérature française ou XVIIᵉ et ou XVIIIᵉ siècle* (Paris, 1934).

New World and the interpretation of its future through the paradisaic conception added an element of reality to an already old system of ideas. By the Jeffersonian age, the noble savage had become
the most important conventionalized term for the Indian.

Untouched by the hands of man, the environment defined the
qualities of the noble savage—impulsive, unrestrained, unburdened
by social conventions, sometimes toughened by a puritan simplicity,
limited in his requirements, and content in a world that demanded
nothing of him.[2] More significant, as part of the landscape of paradise, the noble savage reflected a unidimensional image. Rather
than standing aside from his surroundings, as did civilized man, the
noble savage blended into the surface of paradise. In effect, he could
not be differentiated from a natural resource, and the white man
tended to treat him as such.

Together with the paradisaic conception of the New World, the
Jeffersonian age frequently used two other mythic formulations.
One interpreted the new continent as a most unpleasant place, a
howling wilderness peopled by vicious savages,[3] and the other defined a judicious middle position, a place neither so menacingly in-
hospitable nor so invitingly benign. This middling alternative, the
pastoral garden, idealized the New World, but it also left room for
the existence of society.[4] But at base, both the anti-image and the
pastoral garden offered a timeless conception of the world, which
saved it from the complexities of historical development. Defining
nature univocally, they bound man and environment together in an
inseparable union. As an ideal, the pastoral garden was a progressivist conception, and although the noble savage had been designed
specifically for paradise, he also found it congenial.

By the last decades of the eighteenth century, it became clear that
the American Indian had failed to fulfill the promise of his idealization. He had not become civilized, at least not in the way that the
white man expected he would. The continent had yielded to civilization's molding influence. Through the same process, the native as
noble savage, indistinguishable from the land, should have gradually taken on the virtues, though not the vices, of the civilized

2. Arthur O. Lovejoy and George Boas, *Primitivism and Related Ideas in
Antiquity* (Baltimore, 1935), chap. 1; Baudet, *Paradise on Earth*, 34–35.

3. Howard Mumford Jones, *O Strange New World. American Culture: The
Formative Years* (New York, 1964), chap. 2; Roderick Nash, *Wilderness and
the American Mind* (New Haven, 1967).

4. Leo Marx, *The Machine in the Garden: Technology and the Pastoral
Ideal in America* (New York, 1964), chap. 3.

world. The ideal that defined the ultimate possibility in pushing back the wilderness supplied a basis for the eventual incorporation of the Indian within the white man's culture. But this transference of the idealized economy of paradise and the noble savage into the actual interworkings of the conflict of culture imposed on the Indian an impossible demand. He could no more be the noble savage in reality than he could consciously slough off the cultural accretions of a millennium. Still, the Jeffersonian generation persisted in its idealistic expectation that the Indian would some day meld into the white man's society.[5]

2

Americans in the Jeffersonian period showed a strong tendency to view their position on the new continent in paradisaic images. In European thought, the infusion of the land itself with the ultimate in human promise took place in the seventeenth century. The great achievement of that age was to instill the wish for paradise into the very tissue of reality. The earth took on a new and flagrantly hopeful meaning. In the expected edenic transformation, E. L. Tuveson has noted, "Our planet assumed the burden of eschatological interest: so that the very rocks, the seas, the caverns about men took on a sublimity and dramatic power." The New World had already been established as the repository of paradisaic expectation, hence its physical properties, both material and human, could only be described in a rhetoric fitting to its potentiality.[6]

Though his prose usually inclined to an elegant discipline, Jefferson entertained a profound respect for the American land and was not above depicting it in sweeping panoramic rhetoric. In his *Notes on the State of Virginia,* he painted two celebrated portraits of his favorite Virginia scenes. Of the Natural Bridge in Rockbridge County, he wrote that it was "impossible for the emotions, arising from the sublime, to be felt beyond what they are here: so beautiful an arch, so elevated, so light, and springing, as it were, up to heaven, the rapture of the Spectator is really indiscribable!" Also his prose sketch of the confluence of the Potomac and the Shenandoah, less scenic, conveyed the impression of overwhelming primeval force,

5. Pearce, *Savages of America,* 48, detects the prevalence of the natural-man theme, but contends that the prospect of civilizing the Indian was no more than a forlorn hope after the middle of the 18th century. Hoxie Neale Fairchild, *The Noble Savage: A Study in Romantic Naturalism* (New York, 1928), 299, believes that the noble savage convention was in use until the second decade of the 19th century.

6. Tuveson, *Millennium and Utopia,* 106; Smith, *Virgin Land,* 3–13.

the rivers surging together and bursting apart the mountains to make their way to the sea.[7] Jefferson had caught in his portrayals the duality of the utopian-progressive spirit, the combination of sublime rapture and thrusting energy that summed up the paradisaic destiny of the new continent.

Among the many travelers who invaded the American wilderness, one could hardly find a more enthusiastic wanderer than the New England minister and librarian, Thaddeus Mason Harris. Cavorting amid shady groves, verdant pastures, and ripening grain might have its pleasures, he thought,

but the majestic features of the uncultivated wilderness, and the extensive views of nature gained from the brows of a lofty mountain, produce an expansion of fancy and an elevation of thought more dignified and noble. When these great scenes of creation open upon the view, they rouse an admiration exalting as it is delightful: and while the eye surveys at a glance the immensity of heaven and earth, the mind is rendered conscious of its innate dignity, and recognises those great and comprehensive powers with which it is indowed. THE SUBLIME IN NATURE, which, in its effect is equally solemn and pleasing, captivates while it awes, and charms while it elevates and expands the soul.[8]

Enraptured by the sublime scenery, he also contemplated its power. The impression of natural beneficence and dignity created the basis for human well being.

Edenic enthusiasm appeared even among naturalists devoted to the sober examination of the American landscape. One of the very best of the type, William Bartram, resorted to the sublime in his otherwise careful description of the southern wilderness. In virtually his first step beyond the settled regions, he fell into an evening reverie: "The skies serene and calm, the air temperately cool, and gentle zephyrs breathing through the fragrant pines; the prospect

7. Jefferson, *Notes on Virginia*, ed. Peden, 19, 24–25; Jones, *O Strange New World*, 358–359. For a description similar to Jefferson's of the Potomac and the Shenandoah, see the tory traveler J. F. D. Smyth, *A Tour in the United States of America* . . . (London, 1784), I, 37.

8. Harris, *Journal of a Tour*, 71–72. See also Smyth, *Tour in the United States*, I, 308, on the view from Wart Mountain in southwest Virginia: "Throughout the whole of this amazing and most extensive perspective, there is not the least feature or trace of art or improvement to be discovered.

"All are genuine effects of nature alone, and laid down on her most extended and grandest scale.

"Contemplating thereon fills the eye, engrosses the mind, and enlarges the soul.

"It totally absorbs the senses, overwhelms all the faculties, expands even the grandest ideas beyond all conceptions, and occasions you almost to forget that you are a human creature."

around enchantingly varied and beautiful; endless green savannas, checquered with coppices of fragrant shrubs, filled the air with the richest perfume. The gaily attired plants which enamelled the green had begun to imbibe the pearly dew of evening; nature seemed silent, and nothing appeared to ruffle the happy moments of evening contemplation."[9] On one of his earlier expeditions, Bartram had paused to consider the harmony of the natural order. He recorded that being awakened on

a pleasant morning attended by the feather'd inhabitants of these shady retreats with joyfull song invites us forth, the elivated face of this Hilly country breathes an elastic pure air, inspireing health and activity, I arose and joyfully contributed My aid in the contemplation of the wonderful Harmony and perfection in the lovely simplicity of Nature tho naked yet unviolated by the rude touch of the human hand. tho admiting that, human inventions[,] Arts and sciences to be a part in the progress of Nature[,] yet are perpetually productive of inovations, and events, that shew the defects of human Policy; What a beautifull scenery is Vegitable Nature![10]

But the archetypal interpretation of the American land came from Daniel Boone. From his explorations of Kentucky, he became a crucial figure in the understanding of civilized man's relation to the new continent. He described his impressions of nature through the imagination and pen of his popularizer, John Filson. When not warding off dangerous Indians, Boone thought of his excursion as a ramble in elysium. "Nature was here a series of wonders, and a fund of delight. Here she displayed her ingenuity and industry in a variety of flowers and fruits, beautifully coloured, elegantly shaped, and charmingly flavoured." The wilderness provided peace for a troubled spirit, scenic delights for a poetic temper, and food for a hungry body:

One day I undertook a tour through the country, and the diversity and beauties of nature I met with in this charming season, expelled every gloomy and vexatious thought. Just at the close of day the gentle gales retired, and left the place to the disposal of a profound calm. Not a breeze shook the most tremulous leaf. I had gained the summit of a commanding ridge, and, looking round with astonishing delight, beheld the ample plains, the beauteous tracts below. On the other hand, I surveyed the famous river Ohio that rolled in silent dignity, marking the western boundary of Kentucke with inconceivable grandeur. At a vast distance I

9. Harper, ed., *Bartram's Travels*, 14–15.

10. William Bartram, "Travels in Georgia and Florida, 1773–1774: A Report to Dr. John Fothergill," ed. Francis Harper, Am. Phil. Soc., *Trans.*, N.S., XXXIII (1943), 140. For a treatment of Bartram's understanding of nature, see N. Bryllion Fagin, *William Bartram: Interpreter of the American Landscape* (Baltimore, 1933), Pt. I, chap. 2.

beheld the mountains lift their venerable brows, and penetrate the clouds. All things were still. I kindled a fire near a fountain of sweet water, and feasted on the loin of a buck, which a few hours before I had killed.[11]

Boone was more pleased by Filson's account of his career than by the epic treatment he received from his wife's relative, Daniel Bryan. In *The Mountain Muse,* Bryan portrayed a fictional Boone in a series of preposterous exploits, involving a displaced Balkan nobleman, a brigand band, a captive maiden, and an assortment of febrile lovers. He also used paradise for the setting of his story. Overawed by "the *bold* sublimity of the *new world*," he contended that no city with all its "pomp" and "polish'd Art," its "flapping sails of richest Commerce" and "Luxury's costly Magazines,"

> Could half so much delight have given his mind,
> As the unfolding WORLD OF WONDROUS CHARMS,
> Sublime, majestic, beauteous, splendid, fair,
> Which oped its wild luxuriance on his eye
> Wheree'er he trod—Ohio's limpid flood
> Innumerous Beauties in itself contain'd,
> And Majesty and glorious Grandeur too![12]

Bryan also bounded the path of his travelers with lighter, more carefree images:

> The Queen of Spring, mellifluous-breathing May,
> Walk'd with them o'er the wood-land wilds, and steep'd
> In honey-dews the young expanding leaves;
> And through the fleckered forest flung perfumes;
> While flowerets, blooms, and fragrant foliage fill'd
> The extended boundaries of her balmy reign.
> Along the wilds, and feather-winnow'd air,
> In animating undulations flow'd
> The sweetly modulated songs of Spring.

After crossing the "Alleganean Battlements" and entering Kentucky there appeared: "Before their fascinated eyes, / In careless pomp, great NATURE'S GARDEN, deck'd / With all the flecker'd pride of Paradise."[13]

---

11. Filson, *Kentucke,* 51–52, 54–55.
12. Daniel Bryan, *The Mountain Muse: Comprising the Adventures of Daniel Boone; and the Power of Virtuous and Refined Beauty* (Harrisonburg, Va., 1813), 112, 133–134.
13. *Ibid.,* 61, 112–113. Testifying to the intensity with which the age was affected by the paradisaic convention, Timothy Flint, while recognizing that Kentucky was not the paradise Bryan had claimed, went on to describe the

To be sure, nature had its pitfalls: Bartram eluded crocodiles, Boone outwitted the Indians, and Bryan foiled the plans of kidnappers. Yet, in the Jeffersonian period the language of paradise pervaded most interpretations of the American land. Furthermore, the common view of nature was frankly progressive. As pleasant as the pristine condition might be, as exuberantly as its praises might be sung, civilization as a desirable goal always loomed on the horizon.[14]

Even though he wrote in paradisaic terms, Jefferson cannot be accused of idle theorizing; his ideology called for "a conscious program of action." Even with his liking for agriculture, he looked forward to a developing, civilized continent.[15] Bartram, viewing with delight the spacious plains of the Seminoles, envisioned their future development under the direction of "industrious planters and mechanicks."[16] Filson's Boone, despite his need for elbowroom, predicted that the forest would one day resound to the praises of Christianity and that cities would rise in Kentucky to "rival the glory of the greatest upon earth."[17] But Bryan, the most effusive painter of edenic scenes, promoted the transformation of the wilderness most enthusiastically. He welcomed Boone and his followers into Kentucky: "Swift on, o'er the rude-featured Wilderness / The sinewy sons of Enterprise proceed." Crossing the untouched land, Boone applied his own enterprising imagination to its future, and

> Here, like the primary lord of Paradise,
> The Nomenclature of an opening world
> He form'd! bestowing *names* on streams and founts,

vision of the first settlers: "In its surface so gently waving, with such easy undulations, so many clear limestone springs and branches, so thickly covered with cane, with pawpaw, and a hundred species of flowering trees and shrubs, among which fed innumerable herds of deer and buffaloes, and other game, as well as wild turkeys and other wild fowl. . . ." Boone, he went on, "this Achilles of the West wants a Homer, worthily to celebrate his exploits." Timothy Flint, *Recollections of the Last Ten Years* . . . (New York, 1968 [orig. publ., Boston, 1826]), 66–67, and Flint, *Indian Wars of the West* . . . (Cincinnati, 1833), 223–224.

14. Perry Miller, "The Romantic Dilemma in American Nationalism and the Concept of Nature," *Harvard Theological Review*, XLVIII (1955), 241; Tuveson, *Millennium and Utopia*, 99, 142–143.

15. Koch, *Philosophy of Jefferson*, 190; Roland Van Zandt, *The Metaphysical Foundations of American History* (The Hague, 1959), 103; Boorstin, *Lost World of Thomas Jefferson*, 241–242.

16. Harper, ed., *Bartram's Travels*, 148; Fagin, *Bartram*, 55.

17. Filson, *Kentucke*, 49–50. For Boone's celebrated affinity for space, see "James's Account of S. H. Long's Expedition, 1819–1820," in Reuben Gold Thwaites, ed., *Early Western Travels, 1748–1846* (Cleveland, 1905), XIV, 169.

> On plants and places yet anonymous,
> And yet unvisited by other eye
> Emiting Civilizement's softened beams,
> Than the Adventurer's own.

Bryan derived his optimism for the future of the western wilderness from the very beauty and serenity of the land.

> To introduce within a land so fair,
> Luxuriant, healthful, picturesque and gay,
> The social graces and sublime delights
> Of Civilizement, was a task so grand,
> Heroic and humane; that Boone beheld
> No hindrance, difficulty, danger, pain,
> Nor toil, that could a moment cool the zeal
> And ardent eagerness, with which his soul,
> The achievement of his glorious purpose sought.[18]

The anticipation that the Indian would adopt civilization rested precisely on his identification with the land. The untrammeled beauty and simplicity of the landscape reflected corresponding qualities in the human heart. "There is something in the character and habits of the North American savage," said Washington Irving, "taken in connection with the scenery over which he is accustomed to range, its vast lakes, boundless forests, majestic rivers, and trackless plains, that is, to my mind, wonderfully striking and sublime. He is formed for the wilderness, as the Arab is for the desert."[19] This very simplicity of relationship offered the profoundest hope of improvement. Jefferson never ceased promoting the Indian's transformation. Bartram committed himself explicitly in the first pages of his *Travels*. He believed the Indians both willing and capable of absorbing civilized ways, and he recommended that the government propose a specific program to that end. Bryan concluded his epic with the hope that the "delicate" and "glorious" task would soon be accomplished.[20]

18. Bryan, *Mountain Muse*, 112, 144, 189; Smith, *Virgin Land*, 56–57; Arthur K. Moore, *The Frontier Mind: A Cultural Analysis of the Kentucky Frontiersman* ([Lexington, Ky.], 1957), 146–147. Flint, *Indian Wars*, 55, maintained, however, that "Boone saw the country [Kentucky] only with the eye of a hunter, with very little forecast of its future value and destiny."

19. Washington Irving, "Traits of Indian Character," in *The Sketch Book* (New York, 1929 [orig. publ. New York, 1819]), 284; Sanford, *Quest for Paradise*, 116; Fairchild, *Noble Savage*, 8–9, 215, 288, 376.

20. Harper, ed., *Bartram's Travels*, lx–lxl; Fagin, *Bartram*, 53–54; Bryan, *Mountain Muse*, 30–32.

The seeming incongruity of the continent's development and the extension of this process to the acculturation of the Indian, all described against a backdrop more fantasy than reality, illustrated the tendency in Western thought to push the simplest desires to the limit. Paradise would be embellished, and the noble savage could only gain thereby. Less fantastic but still an idealization, the Indian and the pastoral garden supplied a similarly optimistic design.

3

The rhetoric of paradise and the noble savage conveyed a certain ingenuous clarity. As with all idealizations, it swept aside the ambiguities of human existence. The themes of simplicity and the submergence of man in his idealized environment presented an artless, elemental definition of the human condition. The pastoral garden theme added some of the characteristics of a complex reality absent from the paradisaic formula, yet it also retained a basic element of primitivism: it bound man intimately to his environment. The Indian in paradise drew his virtues from nature, so also did the Indian in the middling landscape.

Accounts of the noble savage in his unformed purity abounded in the Jeffersonian period. In his popular treatment of the new continent, the Abbé Raynal, though generally unsympathetic to primitivism, offered a convenient description. The man of nature, he contended, lived in a timeless world, with the means of subsistence always at hand—obtained by a minimal expenditure of energy because of the perfect congruence between his instincts and physical needs and the potentialities of his environment. He suffered no accretion of artificial desires, and therefore he found no difficulty in satisfying his wants. The limitations of his natural existence required only the simplest form of social organization; without a social hierarchy, no invidious distinctions grew up among men. Enjoying both independence and a secure subsistence, the savage led a happier life than civilized man, who was forced to think of his future and to guard his liberty.[21]

Although on most issues a cultural relativist, William Robertson stressed the "primaeval simplicity" of aborginial life. The natives lived without the necessity of labor or property and enjoyed "almost without restriction or control the blessings which flowed spontaneously from the bounty of nature." Another Scotsman of the commonsense, antiprimitivist school, Adam Ferguson, spoke of the

21. Raynal, *Philosophical and Political History*, trans. Justamond, V, 297–302.

"simple passions, friendship, resentment, and love" characteristic of the uncultivated mind. The savage, he said, "enjoys a delicious freedom from care, and a seducing society, where no rules of behaviour are prescribed, but the simple dictates of the heart."[22]

Despite his extensive trading experience among the Indians, the historian James Adair spoke of tribal life as "derived from the plain law of nature," which excluded "all quibbles of art" and enacted the most basic of all human regulations, the "golden rule."[23] Bartram praised the hospitality of the natives: "O divine simplicity and truth, friendship without fallacy or guile, hospitality disinterested, native, undefiled, unmodified by artificial refinements."[24] At another point in his travels, after stopping for the night in the wilderness with a companion, he became euphoric over natural existence: "How supremely blessed were our hours at this time! plenty of delicious and healthful food, our stomachs keen, with contented minds; under no control, but what reason and ordinate passions dictated, far removed from the seats of strife. Our situation was like that of the primitive state of man, peaceable, contented, and sociable. The simple and necessary calls of nature, being satisfied. We were altogether as brethren of one family, strangers to envy, malice and rapine."[25]

This consonance between the environment and the native formed a consistent motif in the literature of the Jeffersonian era. As Robert Rogers, the Indian fighter, put it in his practical way: "The goodness of the country . . . must render life agreeable and easy to persons who . . . are content with having the demands of nature answered."[26] Even those writers who called attention to the hardships of primitive life retained the basic element of noble savagism. The Vermont historian, Samuel Williams, noted that in times of plenty the Indian gorged himself on the abundance of the country but in the lean season he endured his misfortune with "patience and firmness." The Indian accepted these difficult times because of the natural symmetry between his physical constitution and his surroundings. Without intense desire, he enjoyed the simple rewards offered by nature.[27]

Only a slight mutation changed nature from an unformed para-

22. Robertson, *History of America*, II, 49; Ferguson, *Essay on Civil Society*, 174, 313–314.
23. Adair, *History of American Indians*, 429.
24. Harper, ed., *Bartram's Travels*, 222.
25. *Ibid.*, 71.
26. Rogers, *Concise Account of North America*, 195.
27. Williams, *History of Vermont*, 136–137, 171.

dise into a pastoral garden. This middling landscape, for all its idealized similarity to paradise, represented a far more subtle effort to explain the meaning of the new continent and man's relation to the land. In the sense that the configuration of the garden contained some limited human contribution, it rejected the purity of the paradisaic order. Yet with a relatively uncomplicated design, the garden played a vital role in forming those who lived under its influence. Moreover, as it came from the anguished deliberations of St. John de Crèvecoeur, it provided an escape from the difficulties of the civilized world.[28] Both as an ideal state yet to be achieved and as the repository of at least certain human accomplishments, the pastoral garden held out hope for the Indian.

The primitive virtues of the land impressed Crèvecoeur less than its fertility. Its beauty did not mean that the landscape would supply the means for the good life gratuitously. It required some cultivation. Strangely, he also saw the uncultivated forest as the scene of violence, caused not by Indians but most often by white men who had deserted civilization. Finding the wilderness a rich source of comforts, they gave up farming, took to hunting, and soon became idle and licentious. Yet the Indian, who also lived in the woods, escaped such degradation. "The manners of the Indian natives," wrote Crèvecoeur, "are respectable, compared with this European medley." "They most certainly are much more closely connected with nature . . . ; they are her immediate children."[29]

The war of the Revolution interrupted the rural contentment of Crèvecoeur's Farmer. Against their interests and inclinations, the Indians had been forced into the conflict. Unlike the whites, who would shed anyone's blood for sixpence, Crèvecoeur represented the red men as going to war only to avenge the deepest wrongs. But soon most became pawns in the white man's hands. In the midst of this turmoil, the Farmer resolved to join those few Indians who had maintained their independence and who continued in the pastoral life.[30]

By this method Crèvecoeur rescued the Farmer, though dangers still lurked in the wilderness. The high opinion he entertained of the strength of Indian society gave him pause in approaching it. He expected the Farmer to acquire land and to assume a position of

28. Marx, *Machine in the Garden,* 107–116; Echeverria, *Mirage in the West,* 148.

29. J. Hector St. John Crèvecoeur, *Letters from an American Farmer* (New York, 1904 [orig. publ. London, 1782]) , 66–70, 307–308.

30. *Ibid.,* 312.

appropriate rank among the Indians, but caution dictated that his children should remember the customs of their parents; especially, they must not fall to the level of the whites who had succumbed to the untamed wilderness—"those hogs which range the woods." As attractive as the native's way of life appeared to Crèvecoeur, its inherent vigor and the white man's impressibility made him doubt that it should be accepted totally. Seeking to keep the children within the bounds of civilization, Crèvecoeur expected them to work regularly in the fields; for the same reason, he hoped that the Farmer's wife and daughters would not paint themselves like savages. "We can live in great peace and harmony with them," he said, "without descending to every article." Furthermore, he hoped that the Farmer would increase the security of his position by aiding the Indians through his wife's skill in inoculation, in this way repaying the natives for their hospitality.[31]

Crèvecoeur proposed a neatly equivocal design. The Farmer escaped the corruption of civilization, represented by the brutality of war, by moving deeper into the wilderness, but he never fully embraced primitivism. He accepted the Indian's world only because it approximated the pastoral ideal.

> I will revert [he said] into a state approaching nearer to that of nature, unincumbered either with voluminous laws, or contradictory codes, often galling the very necks, of those whom they protect; and at the same time sufficiently remote from the brutality of unconnected savage nature. . . . where, far removed from the accursed neighbourhood of Europeans, its inhabitants live with more ease, decency, and peace . . . : where, though governed by no laws, yet find, in uncontaminated simple manners all that laws can afford. Their system is sufficiently compleat to answer all the primary wants of man, and to constitute him a social being, such as he ought to be in the great forest of nature.[32]

As with primitivism, the nuclear idea remained nature, but nature without the timelessness of idealism. The middling landscape contained some elements of social development.

Still, Crèvecoeur wrote under the influence of primitivism. He could not be content with the merely practical struggle of getting a living from the world. He needed an abstract vision, a mythic ordering of reality. Although the particulars of his conceptualization showed similarities to both the agricultural life of the American colo-

---

31. *Ibid.,* 315–328; Crèvecoeur, *Sketches of Eighteenth Century America: More "Letters from an American Farmer,"* eds. Henri L. Bourdin, Ralph H. Gabriel, and Stanley T. Williams (New Haven, 1925), 194–195.

32. Crèvecoeur, *Letters from an American Farmer,* 300–301.

nies and to the Indian's tribal existence, his major intentions were far from anthropological. He proposed an unreal idealization that could be achieved only by withdrawing from the existing world, not by accepting it in all of its timeliness and imperfection. He portrayed the Farmer and the Indian in perfect synchronization with nature, by definition an ahistorical state. They had acquired so few artificial desires precisely because of their close relationship with nature, because of the appealing simplicity of their existence. Just as the paradisaic ideal promised an end to human striving, the pastoral conception offered a consummation for the deepest yearnings of the human spirit. The Farmer fled from the world to find this end; so also did the utopian urge impel men to leave the imperfections of civilization in search of paradise. Primitivistic optimism, so easily transposed into a utopian future, made the middling landscape a perfectionist conception.

Yet more so than primitivism, the pastoral ideal bore the stamp of commonsense meliorism. Jefferson, after all, and many of his generation, identified the yeoman farmer, living in a setting very close to the pastoral garden, as the very best of men. And, above all, they hoped that the new nation would preserve these middling social arrangements. The Indian already possessed many of the virtues needed to spend the rest of his days in the tranquility of the American garden. Although skeptical of the possibility of educating the tribesman outside of his native element and conscious always of the important differences between white and native, Crèvecoeur did think that the two races would inevitably mix. Moreover, he encouraged the tribes to increase their agricultural skills.[33] He never doubted that progress included the Indian and that his pastoral ways gave him unique qualifications to take his part in it.

4

By defining the Indian as a noble savage, the white man inevitably failed to treat the tribal order on its own terms. The Indian, in effect, became merely a foil in civilized man's constant efforts at self-examination. As a moral exemplar, drawing his virtues from the timeless realm of paradise, the native served only the white man's special needs. Other slightly exotic peoples—Scythians, various Orientals, Arabs, Negroes—had in the past assumed a similar burden for European civilization. But with the discovery of the new con-

33. *Ibid.*, 307, 320; Crèvecoeur, *Sketches of Eighteenth Century America*, 193–194; and Crèvecoeur, *Journey into Northern Pennsylvania and the State of New York*, trans. Clarissa Spencer Bostelmann (Ann Arbor, 1964), 60–65.

tinent, the Indian gradually took exclusive possession of noble savagism.

Shorn of his historic personality, the Indian presented the white man with an extraordinarily difficult problem. Perhaps in Europe, where the intellectual turmoil of the Enlightenment required a moral counterweight to balance civilization's declining confidence, the noble savage could remain a literary phenomenon or an occasional visitor from a distant land. The European never met the tribesman on his own ground. Americans mythologized the native, but they also dealt with real Indians in a real wilderness. Most important, the Indian persisted as a public phenomenon, an enduring issue in American politics. In this role, despite the paradisaic formula, Indians manifested all the characteristics of a living society, of a cultural reality. Indians reacted to civilized influence, not as evanescent images whose virtues matched their paradisaic environment, but as members of a culture under attack. The white man obtained no aid from noble savagism in understanding this reaction.

The subtle infiltration of noble savagism into the actual relationship between the white man and the native proved fatal to the survival of the Indian and seriously hampered the white man's perception of the consequences of his acts. Even those in most intimate contact with native life, particularly the traders, employed the language of paradise.[34] This paradox of realistic experience set in the mold of mythic expression defined the crucial ambiguity in Indian-white relations. Although noble savagism concerned primarily the problems of civilization, it did present a coherent description of the native, a description so impressive that he could never fill its dimensions. The Indian could not hope to equal the level of virtue attributed to him, because the primitivist formulations drew on a set of presuppositions wholly different from those within the reach of real men. Limited by the inertia of a time-bound culture and threatened by cultural disintegration, the Indian could not but be pitied for his fate.[35]

The primitivistic indictment of civilization and the accompanying acclaim for the Indian relied exclusively on the themes of para-

---

34. Saum, *Fur Trader and the Indian*, 113, notes that "firsthand experience in the crude realities of wilderness existence provided no absolute immunity from the intriguing and perennial passion, the ennobling of the savage." Of course, the frontiersman at war with the native engaged in little speculation and was content with the aphorism concerning good Indians and dead Indians.

35. Pearce, *Savages of America*, 53.

disaic nature and savage simplicity.[36] In the New World, Philip Freneau made one of the more comprehensive of such interpretations. Without any immediate or penetrating knowledge of tribal culture, he had imbibed a large dose of primitivism. Using an historic Creek chief who had visited London with James Oglethorpe in 1734, Freneau created an Indian hero in Tomo Cheeki, a man of independence who had successfully resisted the blandishments of civilization.[37] "The gravity of his deportment, his melancholy aspect, his pithy sayings, and a certain exotic peculiarity of character," established him as a discerning critic of the white man's foibles.[38]

Following his dictum that the world had not been created for the sole benefit of man, Tomo Cheeki viewed nature as a simple and revered entity. He wanted the trees to remain "straight and lofty," the streams "winding and irregular, and not odiously drawn into a right line," the soil unplowed, and the air to retain "that balmy fragrance which was breathed into the lungs of the long lived race of men, that flourished in the first ages of the world." In their efforts to improve the world, men had too much "strayed from the grand simplicity of Nature." The time would soon come when the "ancient chaos of woods . . . , the wild genius of the forest will reassume his empire, and expelling from his domains the tawdry productions of art, will once more uprear his gigantic children of oak in the room of these little foppish trees, these shrubs, and bearers of fruit, that have been transferred from another country."[39]

The more Tomo Cheeki examined civilization, the more he became convinced that men had lost much in forsaking the simple ways of nature. Happiness lay in diminishing man's excessive de-

---

36. Whitney, *Primitivism and Progress*, chap. 2.

37. Lewis Leary, *That Rascal Freneau: A Study in Literary Failure* (New Brunswick, N.J., 1941) , 261.

38. Philip M. Marsh, ed., *The Prose of Philip Freneau* (New Brunswick, N.J., 1955) , 331; Benjamin Franklin, "Remarks concerning the Savages of North America," in Albert Henry Smyth, ed., *The Writings of Benjamin Franklin* (New York, 1905–1907) , X, 97–105, is another attempt to explode the pretensions of civilization by praising the simplicity of the Indians. One of the more interesting aspects of the attack on civilization was the effort to identify the savage state with an over-refined stage of modern civilization. The moral was clearly that the most desirable situation lay at some point before human progress came full circle to sophisticated primitivism. See Raynal, *Philosophical and Political History,* trans. Justamond, III, 64–68; Corner, ed., *Autobiography of Rush,* 71–73; and Alfred Owen Aldridge, "Franklin's Deistical Indians," Am. Phil. Soc., *Procs.,* XCIV (1950) , 398–410. See also Peter S. Du Ponceau to John Vaughan, Apr. 30, 1818, Miscellaneous Manuscript Collection, 1816–1818, Am. Phil. Soc., Philadelphia.

39. Marsh, ed., *Prose of Freneau,* 124–125, 338.

sires. "Endless wants," after all, "are the natural cause of endless cares." In a less hectic world, human desires would be reduced to three or four enjoyments, easily satisfied. According to Tomo Cheeki, natural man resided "amidst the luxuriant vegetation of Nature, the delectable regale of flowers and blossoms, and beneath trees bending with plump and joyous fruits." Quaffing goat's milk and water (the drink of "NATURE"), his every desire became a blessing. Young unmarried women accepted freely "that amiable passion" and lived without jealousy under the "golden star of Love." "Carried along upon the great wheel of things," Tomo Cheeki suffered no social derailments, no uncertainties, no tax gatherers, no oppression of the poor, and no concern for the future. The security of the forest afforded primitive man protection against hostile forces, real and figurative.[40]

Freneau's use of the paradisaic conception cannot be ignored, though his overwrought interpretation may be dismissed as either naïveté or merely as a factitious libel against civilization. Having clothed his savage in the glorious benignity of nature, little reason could be found for separating him from so satisfying an environment. It possessed all the perfection and timeless simplicity of paradise. And yet Freneau directed his argument at civilization, not at the Indian. Though apparently sympathetic to the native, the theory allowed him only a secondary part in its moral economy. Freneau had in mind the progressive transformation of civilization; the importance of the Indian lay in his role as a model. He heaped strictures on the head of civilized man and then showed him an ideal worthy of emulation. If only white men could shake their feet loose from the shackles of the past, they might achieve the kind of perfect state enjoyed by the noble savage. In time the Indian too could expect to be taken up in this meliorist process. His social order would also be changed. Indeed, the overwhelmingly positive image of the Indian that stemmed from the paradisaic formulation made that transformation inevitable.

40. *Ibid.*, 341–343. See also Philip Freneau, "The Arrival at Indian Sam's (Or, Wee-Quali's) Wigwam," Lewis Leary, ed., *The Last Poems of Philip Freneau* (New Brunswick, N.J., 1945), 91–95. See also Marsh, ed., *Freneau's Prose*, 125–126, 256; "The Indian Student," Pattee, ed., *Poems of Freneau*, II, 371–374. But it must also be noted that Freneau was not always so blatantly primitivistic. In his early poem, "The Rising Glory of America," written in 1771 with H. H. Brackenridge and revised in 1809, he praised the white man's expected conquest of the continent. The untamed wilderness and the noble red man were given an easy dismissal: Fred Lewis Pattee, ed., *The Poems of Philip Freneau: Poet of the American Revolution* (Princeton, 1902–1907), I, 49–84; Pearce, *Savages of America*, 180–184.

When faced with the question specifically, Freneau could think of no reasons for civilizing the tribesman. Sufficient that he should carry his condemnation of the white man's world to the limit. The Indian already had what he needed for the good life. Yet in his early poem, "The Rising Glory of America," after first referring approvingly to Arcadia, he rejected it for commercial civilization, not for primitivism. In a poem printed in 1822, he grudgingly conceded that the Indians should be taught "what Reason dictates," so long as the teachers learned from the native that "the child of Nature is the better man."[41] Even Freneau, so deeply estranged from civilization, found it difficult to avoid progressive implications of the paradisaic convention.

5

Together with the propagandistic sociology of a Crèvecoeur or a Freneau, the Jeffersonian age also produced an extensive and realistic literature describing the Indian. One of the bases for the later science of ethnohistory can be found in the innumerable treatments of native society produced by civilized observers from the first association of white and Indian. This rich and valuable literature dealt with virtually every aspect of the native culture. Still, no observer of Indian life, especially in the Jeffersonian era, wrote in an ideological void. Though basically accurate, the writings of this age drew on the familiar conceptualizations of the natural state and the noble savage. Invariably, observers defined native attributes against the generalizations of natural simplicity and the close relationship of man and environment.

Most testimony had high praise for the Indian's physical form, while at the same time doubting that his strength could be compared to the white man's. Samuel Williams attributed the native's "vigour, activity, and health of the body" directly to his primitive condition. Jedidiah Morse recommended the Indian as a perfect model for the sculptor, and Bartram rested with the observation that the natives were shaped "so as generally to form a perfect human figure." Contributing a note of sensuousness, Crèvecoeur described an Iroquois council absorbed in the gravity of its proceedings: "Their blankets of beaverskin fell off their shoulders, revealing their mighty chests and muscular arms on which in their youth various animal and insect figures had been tattooed. At such a scene a painter could have drawn bodies that were perfect in pro-

41. Pattee, ed., *Poems of Freneau,* I, 68–71; "On the Civilization of the Western Aboriginal Country," Leary, ed., *Last Poems of Freneau,* 69–71.

portion, limbs controlled by muscles lightly covered with a kind of swelling that was unknown to the whites, and which among the Indians attests to their vigor, strength, and health: heads and faces of a special type, the like of which one sees only in the depths of the New World's forests."[42] Moreover, from the earliest times Europeans had noted the absence of deformity among the Indians. They often attributed it to infanticide and abortion, but produced no evidence in support of such contentions. Sufficient to say that most observers did not expect to find deformity in the state of nature.[43]

Evidence of the Indian's physical prowess stemmed from his matchless integration with his wilderness environment. Morse thought the native's skill in hunting and forest warfare incomparable:

The great qualities of an Indian warrior are vigilance and attention, to give and avoid a surprise; and, indeed, in these they are superior to all nations, in the world. Accustomed to continued wandering in the forests; having their perceptions sharpened by keen necessity, and living, in every respect according to nature, their external senses have a degree of acuteness which, at first view, appears incredible. They can trace out their enemies, at an immense distance by the smoke of their fires, which they smell, and by the tracks of their feet upon the ground, imperceptible to an European eye, but which they can count and distinguish, with the utmost facility.[44]

Williams also spoke convincingly of the Indian's resourcefulness in the woods. Despite the poor quality of his weapons, he showed himself to great advantage: "Fertile in invention, sagacious in distinguishing and observing, nice and accurate in tracing the animal; indefatigable, and persevering in the pursuit." "An impartial mind," said John Long, the fur trader and Indian interpreter, "will require but little to be persuaded that the Indians are superior to us in the woods: it is their natural element."[45]

42. Williams, *History of Vermont*, 163–164; [Morse], *History of America*, 69–70; Harper, ed., *Bartram's Travels*, 306; Crèvecoeur, *Journey into Pennsylvania and New York*, 53; Catesby, *Natural History*, I, viii.

43. Wasserman, "American Indian as Seen by Chroniclers," 41–51; Beverley, *History and Present State of Virginia*, ed. Wright, 159; [Morse], *History of America*, 69; Robertson, *History of America*, 69–70; Williams, *History of Vermont*, 134; Romans, *Concise Natural History*, 42. Rush, "Inquiry into Natural History of Medicine among the Indians," in *Medical Inquiries*, 3d ed., I, 115, agreed that the Indians exhibited a fine physique, but he believed that this only disguised a basic deficiency in their health.

44. [Morse], *History of America*, 38–39.

45. Williams, *History of Vermont*, 136; J[ohn] Long, *Voyages and Travels of an Indian Interpreter and Trader* . . . (London, 1791), 27. Charles Johnston, *A Narrative of the Incidents Attending the Capture, Detention, and Ransom of Charles Johnston, of Botetourt County, Virginia* . . . (New York, 1827), 152, dissented from the usually high opinion of Indian skill in the forest.

Bartram told of an incident that illustrated the Indian's skill on his own ground in contrast to the ineptitude of the white intruder. He and his companions, along with a group of Indians, set out to survey land that the natives had been forced to surrender as compensation for debts owed to the traders. The party planned to strike the Savannah River at a distant point. The surveyor among the colonials consulted his compass and designated the proper route, at which one of the Indian chiefs stepped forward and protested that they would not reach their object in that direction. The surveyor pointed to his compass, insisting that it could not err. Unpacified, the chief contended that the "little wicked instrument was a liar" and would cheat the Indians out of their lands. To be sure, the compass had been wrong and the native right. The white man discarded his instrument and took directions from the Indian for the rest of the tour. In the forest, the tribesman had no peer.[46]

Across the council fire, also, the white man met the Indians on native ground. He knew well that they liked to talk. Prolix to the point of exhaustion and painstaking in the care with which they unfolded an argument of seemingly immense complexity, the natives larded their speech with repetition and couched it in stereotyped metaphors. Among white men, opinions on the quality of Indian eloquence shaded from John Lawson's, that the red men could barely make themselves understood, to that of Jefferson and Elias Boudinot, both of whom, referring to the Logan speech, thought it equal to Demosthenes, Cicero, and other forensic worthies. Most considered Indian eloquence of a fairly high order. Almost all noted in it a quality important for an understanding of the natural man theme: Indians always spoke in allusions; apparently, they could not express abstractions or even general ideas without some reference to the particular. Hence they bombarded their listeners with allusions to the road that would be swept clean, the fire to be kept lit, and the chain that should be strengthened, all having reference to an anticipated diplomatic alliance. To many who attended Indian conferences, this pictorial language sounded like profound eloquence.[47]

He thought the first settlers had formed extravagant opinions on the subject and that the white man was at least the equal of the Indian.

46. Harper, ed., *Bartram's Travels*, 26; Imlay, *Topographical Description*, 102–103; Isaac Weld, *Travels through the States of North America . . .* (London, 1799), 391.

47. Harriss, ed., *Lawson's History of North Carolina*, 251; Jefferson, *Notes on Virginia*, ed. Peden, 62–63; Boudinot, *Star in the West*, 95. The best collection of Indian eloquence is Julian P. Boyd, ed., *Indian Treaties Printed by Benjamin Franklin, 1736–1762* (Philadelphia, 1938).

Raynal noted the absence of abstractions in the Indian languages, but he ascribed it to the inability of the "infant mind" of the savage to extend its view beyond the immediate object. With only a small number of ideas squeezed into a few verbal compartments, the Indian found few usable phrases. But most observers interpreted this simplicity as one of the primary virtues of natural man. The simple figurative style made Morse hark back to the bold eloquence of the Homeric period. Perhaps the most knowledgeable opinion of native elocution came from Peter S. Du Ponceau: "These elegant shades of expression shew in a very forcible manner the beauty and copiousness of the Indian languages, and the extent and the force of that natural logic, of those powers of feeling and discrimination, and of that innate sense of order, regularity and method which is possessed even by savage nations."[48]

The repetitive rhythm of native eloquence gave its hearers an impression of stately dignity. (The feeling is conveyed even to the modern reader.) One can easily see how the repeated use of a limited number of simple metaphors would convey the sense of a natural, primordial vigor, uncorrupted by the nuances of civilization. "The language of Metaphor," wrote Thomas L. McKenney, "is the language of man in his uncultivated state; and his mountains, and rivers, and forests, and to his eyes, the earth, and the sky, with their quakes, and their lightenings are all full of mystery, which create a darkness well fitted for the workings of the imagination, and fertile in wonders." This "eloquent figurative language," said another critic, made the Indian speeches "partake of the strength and dignity of the language of Nature." Amos Stoddard, who had accompanied a delegation of western Indians to Washington in 1805, stated cogently the theoretical relation between pristine nature and Indian language:

They speak from nature, and not from education. They utter what their subject inspires and never advert to approved models as their standard. Their language is barren; and hence they are obliged to resort to metaphor, or to use much circumlocution in the expression of their sentiments. This is doubtless the practice of all illiterate nations. All languages are figurative in proportion to their barrenness; and this is more pleasing and powerful than the smooth harmony of studied periods. Art will do much but nature much more. Perhaps a profound knowledge of Roman and Grecian literature would have obscured the genius of

48. Raynal, *Philosophical and Political History*, trans. Justamond, V, 126; [Morse], *History of America*, 33; Du Ponceau to John Heckewelder, Aug. 21, 1816, "Correspondence respecting Languages of the Indians," Am. Phil. Soc., *Trans. of Hist. and Lit. Comm.*, I (1819), 421.

Shakespeare. Who at this day, except the untutored sons of nature, can utter the language of Ossian and Homer? What man, trammeled with the forms of modern art, can speak like Logan, mentioned in the notes on Virginia? The language of nature can alone arrest attention, persuade, convince, and terrify; and such is the language of the Indians.[49]

Within its sphere, native discourse showed basic consistency and a remarkable self-assurance, primary qualities of natural man.[50]

49. Thomas L. McKenney to Caleb Atwater, Feb. 16, 1826, Letters Sent by the Office of Indian Affairs, 1824–1881 (M-21), Roll 2: 433, Records of the Bureau of Indian Affairs (RG 75), National Archives, hereafter cited as Letters Sent, Off. Indian Affairs (M-21), Roll 2; *The Miscellaneous Magazine*, I (1824), 275. See also Stoddard, *Sketches, Historical and Descriptive*, 431–432. Stoddard favored the plan for making farmers of the Indians: "This change of life has a tendency to wipe away their savage manners, to restore them to the dignity of human nature, and to make them useful to themselves, and to the world." *Ibid.*, 447–450.

50. The Indians' dependence on stereotyped formulas was evident in their use of wampum. This had a ceremonial function, but it also served as a handy reminder for the Indian of the scheme of metaphor. At one of the Carlisle treaties, the Indian spokesman, Scaroyady, rose and informed the expectant audience: "The *Twightwees* intended to say something to you; but they have mislaid some Strings, which has put their Speeches into Disorder; these they will rectify, and speak to you in the Afternoon." Boyd, ed., *Indian Treaties*, 131. The question of Indian metaphor bears upon the authenticity of the Logan speech. Fairchild, *Noble Savage*, 492, has noted that "the Indian, having a very limited abstract vocabulary, is forced to convey most of his scanty abstract ideas in concrete terms. Hence he frequently appears to be consciously imaginative when he is merely groping for expression." Logan was imaginative enough in his little discourse, and he does not appear to be groping, but, significantly, there is only one mildly allusive phrase ("beams of peace") in the entire piece. Though Logan's speech may be eloquent, it is an eloquence of the biblical rather than Indian sort. It should be used, not to illustrate the peculiar talents of the noble savage, as it was by Jefferson, but to point up the Indian's extraordinary facility in absorbing the white man's culture. Logan's life adds weight to the argument. He was a Mingo and probably a mixed blood, one of those Iroquois who had broken off from the main body of the nation and taken residence on the Ohio frontier, an area of intense conflict between white and Indian. By all accounts he was closely connected with the whites, drank heavily, and died mysteriously. Logan will not do as a noble savage; he represents, rather, the unfortunate, culturally disintegrated Indian. See Jefferson, *Notes on Virginia*, ed. Peden, 62–63, app. 4; Edward D. Seeber, "Critical Views on Logan's Speech," *Journal of American Folklore*, IX (1947), 130–146; Laurence C. Wroth in *DAB* s.v. "Logan, James." Wilcomb E. Washburn, ed., "Logan's Speech, 1774," in Daniel J. Boorstin, ed., *An American Primer* (Chicago, 1966), I, 60–64, believes that the civilized character of the language may be explained by the process of translation. But most other Indian speeches were also translated and they invariably fall within the usual rhythmic formulation. Washburn also sees the speech as "in microcosm, the history of the Indian-white relationship." In this conception, the hospitable native befriends the white, is repaid by some outrage, seeks revenge because "other avenues" are closed, is defeated in the ensuing war, and loses both his land and his spirit. Such, no doubt, was the myth that grew up in humanitarian circles in the 19th century; it illustrates the persistence of noble savagism. The Indian as nonviolent, innocent victim,

Native eloquence seemed to supply a cohesive element in Indian life. The white man never ceased to be fascinated by the contrast between his own society, heavily laden with rules of organization, and the seemingly unfettered operation of the native social system. In his *Notes on Virginia,* Jefferson wrote that the Indians had

never submitted themselves to any laws, any coercive power, any shadow of government. There only controuls are their manners, and that moral sense of right and wrong. . . . An offence against these is punished by contempt, by exclusion from society, or, where the case is serious, as that of murder, by the individuals whom it concerns. Imperfect as this species of coercion may seem, crimes are very rare among them: insomuch that were it made a question, whether no law, as among the savage Americans, or too much law, as among the civilized Europeans, submit man to the greatest evil, one who has seen both conditions of existence would pronounce it to be the last: and that the sheep are happier of themselves, than under care of wolves.[51]

Jeffersonians did not believe that the Indians lived in a state of anarchy without the benefit of social order. At issue was the kind and source of regulation. In keeping with the paradisaic understanding, the organs of control had to be built into, or identified with, the natural condition. In Bartram's terms, the moral duties, so difficult to maintain in the white man's social system "without compulsion or visible restraint," operated in native society "like instinct, with a surprising harmony and natural ease." The tribesmen seemed to be guided by "nothing more than the simple dictates of natural reason." As the Moravian missionary John Heckewelder put it, the Indian had "a government in which there are no positive laws, but only long established habits and customs, no code of jurisprudence, but the experience of former times, no magistrates, but advisors, to whom the people, nevertheless, pay a willing and im-

openly hospitable and sensibly rational, was the Indian as natural man. And the popularity of Logan's speech was doubtless due to its accurate reflection of this attitude. But a more discerning view would take into account the significance of the civilized quality of the language and what it reveals of the gradual infiltration of the native culture, of the slow disintegration of Indian society, rather than its betrayal and defeat by the conscienceless whites.

51. Jefferson, *Notes on Virginia,* ed. Peden, 93; Jefferson to James Madison, Jan. 30, 1787, Boyd, ed., *Jefferson Papers,* XI, 92. Although he was not strongly inclined to the noble savage convention, Jefferson occasionally found it a convenient instrument with which to chastise the faults of civilization. He wrote to John Adams, Jan. 21, 1812, in high dudgeon: "As for France and England, with all their pre-eminence in science, the one is a den of robbers, and the other of pirates. As if science produces no better fruits than tyranny, murder, rapine and destitution of national morality, I would rather wish our country to be ignorant, honest and estimable as our neighboring savages are." See Cappon, ed., *Adams-Jefferson Letters,* II, 291.

plicit obedience, in which age confers rank, wisdom gives power, and moral goodness secures a title to universal respect."[52]

Furthermore, native society exhibited no artificial class distinctions; no division, as Jefferson remarked, between the "wolves and sheep." "They are all equal," wrote Adair, "the only precedence any gain is by superior virtue, oratory, or prowess." They rewarded only merit, and love of country supplied the surest path to social prominence. "The Indians are perfect republicans," wrote Boudinot, "they will admit of no inequality among them but what arises from age, or great qualifications for either council or war." Equality created a free and independent people. To quote Jefferson: "Every man with them, is perfectly free to follow his own inclinations." For Robert Rogers this "great and fundamental" principle of the native's society meant "that no one or more on earth has any right to deprive him of his freedom and independency, and that nothing can be a compensation for the loss of it."[53]

The Indian's conviction of his own superiority, which no doubt contributed to his self-possession, impressed the Jeffersonians as further evidence of his nobility. Again primitive eloquence played an important part in the white man's view. "All their proceedings were conducted with great deliberation," wrote DeWitt Clinton of the Iroquois, "and were distinguished for order, decorum, and solemnity. In eloquence, in dignity, and in all the characteristics of profound policy, they surpassed an assembly of feudal barons, and were perhaps not far inferior to the great Amphyctionic Council of Greece." Repeatedly, the literature of the Jeffersonian era used such phrases as "gravity of appearance," "dignified and circumspect," "reserved," "deliberate," and "composed" to describe the behavior of the Indians, who seemed to lack the insecurity and self-doubt that civilization had saddled upon the white man. The integration of the native with his surroundings gave him the appearance, from the white man's point of vantage, of a natural aristocrat.[54]

Civilization's sense of the native's stature need not have been

52. Harper, ed., *Bartram's Travels*, 134, 312; Heckewelder, "Account of the Indian Nations," Am. Phil. Soc., *Trans. of Hist. and Lit. Comm.*, I (1819), 103.

53. Jefferson to Edward Carrington, Jan. 16, 1787, Boyd, ed., *Jefferson Papers*, XI, 49; Adair, *History of American Indians*, 378–379; Boudinot, *Star in the West*, 160; Jefferson to Francis W. Gilmer, June 7, 1916, Lipscomb and Bergh, eds., *Writings of Jefferson*, XV, 25; Rogers, *Concise Account of North America*, 233.

54. DeWitt Clinton, "A Discourse Delivered before the New-York Historical Society . . . ," N.-Y. Hist. Soc., *Colls.*, II (1814), 50; Williams, *History of Vermont*, 150; Carver, *Three Years Travels*, 81; Harper, ed., *Bartram's Travels*, 307.

drawn from intimate contact, though many whites did have occasion to associate with Indians personally. Traders and missionaries went deep into the wilderness, established their households among the tribesmen, intermarried, and lived in close contact with them. Sir William Johnson, who resided for decades on the fringe of the Indian country, had immediate and confident relations with the Iroquois. He lived openly with the sister of the Mohawk chief Joseph Brant and fathered a numerous brood of children by more than one native companion. Many others, such as John Stuart, Benjamin Hawkins, George Croghan, Conrad Weiser, and John Heckewelder, had long and close associations with the Indians, as did the many anonymous traders and missionaries who wandered the American forest. In 1790 Ezra Stiles copied an epitaph from a gravestone near Norwich, Connecticut, commemorating the union of the two societies:

SAMUEL UNCAS

For Beauty Wit for Sterling Sence
For Temper mild for Eliquence
For Courag Bold For things waureegun
He was the Glory of Mohegan
Whose Death has caused great lematation
Both in the English and the Indian Nation.[55]

Yet for the white man, noble savagism referred usually to the class rather than the individual. The formula, of course, fitted more easily the type than the flesh-and-blood person. Confronted by a particular reality, it tended to dissolve.

More commonly, the literature applied the noble savage thesis to those somewhat mysterious, almost legendary Indian leaders who periodically appeared as the foremost of their people. Powhatan, Opechancanough, Philip, Pontiac, and Tecumseh served as symbols of American nature. In an address delivered in 1829 to demonstrate the native's receptivity to civilization, McKenney wrote of the Indian's long and noble struggle to maintain his independence. From Pontiac to Tecumseh, though often reduced in numbers and power, the tribesman fought proudly for his lands and way of life. "Pontiac! What a noble speciman of man existed in the person, and displayed itself in the acts of this warrior-chief!" And he went on to note that "a like spirit, and under like circumstances, animated

55. Franklin Bowditch Dexter, ed., *Extracts from the Itineraries and Other Miscellanies of Ezra Stiles* . . . (New Haven, 1916), 410.

Tecumthé."[56] But of all the Indian heroes, Opechancanough offered a most revealing legend. Proverbially the most cunning, treacherous, and bloodthirsty of Indians, he succeeded to the leadership of Powhatan's confederation at a time when the white man's encroachments had pushed the Indians to the limit. He launched two desperate attacks on the settlements. The first, in 1622, remains as proportionally the most destructive Indian effort to drive the white man into the sea. Despite Opechancanough's qualifications for a major position in the anti-image, his reputation maintained a high level of nobility and primitive self-assurance.

An anecdote of his captivity at Jamestown in 1644, after the second of his encounters with the colonists, makes the point. Although old and infirm, he resented the humiliation of being put on exhibition for the curiosity of the inhabitants. He called for Richard Kemp, who conducted the affairs of the colony in Governor Berkeley's absence, and informed him haughtily that he would certainly not have been accorded such treatment had Sir William been present. Kemp understood, as have those who have recounted the story since: Opechancanough made claim to aristocracy, doubtless of the wilderness sort, but yet such as to command more discriminating treatment. Kemp halted the public exhibition immediately.[57]

The sense of superiority conveyed by the Indian further convinced the white man that he had found the noble savage. Many Indians persisted in believing their own way of life more attractive than the European, and many whites, who in captivity had learned to live as Indians, refused to return to civilization. Adair thought that most Indians had an "inexpressible contempt" for white men, except those who had adopted Indian ways. The natives called the others *"Nothings"* or the "accursed people." They flattered themselves with the name "beloved people." According to David Zeisberger, the Delaware granted the white man industry and even a certain ingeniousness, but they persisted in regarding his way of life "wearisome and slavish as compared with their own." One of the most striking and often-noted examples of this sense of superior-

---

56. Thomas L. McKenney, *Memoirs, Official and Personal; with Sketches of Travels among the Northern and Southern Indians* (New York, 1846), 235–236. For Pontiac as emperor, see [Morse], *History of America*, 54; Robert Rogers, *Ponteach: or The Savages of America. A Tragedy* (Chicago, 1914 [orig. publ., London, 1766]), 198–205.

57. Beverley, *History and Present State of Virginia*, ed. Wright, 60–62; Oldmixon, *British Empire*, I, 241; William Keith, *The History of the British Plantations in America . . .* (London, 1738), 146. In keeping with Opechancanough's place in the anti-image, he was later shot in the back by one of the common soldiers.

ity occurred at the Lancaster negotiations in 1744. Seeking to woo the Iroquois to a friendlier disposition, the Virginia delegates suggested that they might like to send some of their young braves to be educated at William and Mary. Canasatego, the Onondaga chief, replied with great dignity and some superciliousness, thanking the Virginians for their gesture. He knew that the maintenance of the Indian boys at the school would be a great expense.

> But you, who are wise, must know that different Nations have different Conceptions of things; and you will therefore not take it amiss, if our Ideas of this kind of Education happen not to be the same with yours. We have had some Experience of it; Several of our young People were formerly brought up at the College of the Northern Provinces; they were instructed in all your Sciences; but, when they came back to us, they were bad Runners, ignorant of every means of living in the Woods, unable to bear either Cold or Hunger, knew neither how to build a Cabin, take a Dear, or kill an enemy, spoke our Language imperfectly, were therefore neither fit for Hunters, Warriors, nor Counsellors; they were totally good for nothing. We are however not the less oblig'd by your kind Offer, tho' we decline accepting it; and, to show our grateful Sense of it, if the Gentlemen of Virginia will send us a Dozen of their Sons, we will take Care of their Education, instruct them in all we know, and make *Men* of them.[58]

6

For all his exalted stature (rather, because of it), the white man intended to change the Indian by civilizing him. The utopian idiom invested even the simplest activities in the New World with progressivist implications and led directly to the transformation of

---

58. Adair, *History of American Indians*, 32–33; Hulbert and Schwarze, eds., "Zeisberger's History," Ohio Archaeol. and Hist. Soc., *Pubs.*, XIX (1910), 121–122. See also Franklin, "Remarks concerning the Savages of North America," in Smyth, ed., *Writings of Franklin*, 98–99; Boyd, ed., *Indian Treaties*, 72–73, 76. Heckewelder, "Account of the Indian Nations," Am. Phil. Soc., *Trans. of Hist. and Lit. Comm.*, I (1819), 151–152, recorded a rather comic example of the natives' confidence in their own way of doing things: "For, (said he in his broken English), White man court,—court,—may be one whole year!—may be two year before he marry!—well!—may be then got *very good* wife—but may be *not!*—may be *very* cross!—Well now, suppose cross! scold so soon as get awake in the morning! scold all day! scold until sleep!—all one, he must keep *him!* [Indian languages had only the masculine pronoun.] White people have law forbidding throwing away wife, be he ever so cross! must keep *him* always! Well! how does Indian do?—Indian when he see industrious Squaw, which he like, he go to *him*, place his two forefingers close aside each other, make two look like one—look Squaw in the face—see *him* smile—which is all one *he* say, Yes! so he take *him* home—no danger *he* be cross! no! no! Squaw know too well what Indian do if *he* cross! throw *him* away and take another! Squaw love to eat meat! no husband! no meat! Squaw do every thing to please husband! he do the same to please Squaw! live happy!"

both the land and the native culture. Indian and land became enmeshed in an elaborate ideology that established change as the basic function of nature and perfection as its end. Whatever the reasons advanced for civilizing the Indian, they could not be articulated without the paradisaic formula.

The evidence emerges clearly in the literature of the Jeffersonian period. Through the descriptive mechanism of paradise and noble savagism, land and Indian became inseparable. Commonplace accounts of aboriginal life and apocalyptic paeans to the virgin wilderness all gave the consistent impression of the high potentiality of the continent and its native inhabitants. The subordinate conceptualizations of the pastoral garden and the primitivistic indictment of civilization contributed further to the Indian's stature. The Jeffersonian age thought highly of the Indian and the place in which he lived, and it had at hand a plan for building paradise on earth.

In a particularly vivid way, noble savagism vindicated the environmentalist economy. A unique variety, the noble savage became indistinguishable from his paradisaic surroundings. In this realm of perfection, the processes of environmentalist change became final. Environmentalism lacked the decisive moral clarity that the mythic vision of paradise and the noble savage supplied. Both conceptualizations moved the Indian toward a civilized world, but the paradisaic mode shifted the transit of tribal society onto a rigidly defined ideological track. Noble savagism was all scheme and no life; its purest formulation left no trace of the real Indian.

In the deepest sense, any scheme for social improvement based on the paradisaic conception had to be visionary, not merely because experience should have supplied ample information about the futility of past utopias, but because it drew upon a very basic denial of reality. The paradisaic economy partook of the gnostic delusion, the notion that perfection could be produced on this earth. The world would not only get better day by day, but it would finally transcend the very process of its improvement. It would not reach a final stage in its teleology, but would burst through into the elysium. Progress and change required a teleology, but paradise was timeless, total, and inhuman in its definition. Still, it could not be even described without the assumption of development, of amelioration. But whether it came out of the blue in all its splendid irrelevance or whether humankind built it from the materials of an imperfect world, the terrestrial paradise was no less a delusion, a flight from reality.

This is not to say that the Jeffersonian generation had more than its share of mystic levelers and closeted utopians. It doted on practicality, and it enjoyed ample success. But it did fail with the Indian (it was not the first to do so, nor the last), and in part the reason must be set down to the paradisaic conception. In reality, the meeting of Indian and European began the process of acculturation. The Indian had either to be left alone or to undergo the extraordinarily difficult ordeal of cultural change. If he adopted civilization, then by slow and sometimes excruciatingly painful stages, one culture would replace another. The image of the noble savage provided no conceptual basis for such a process. As culture was a peculiar configuration of manners and mores, noble savagism was a universal statement of perfection; as the notion of culture made extensive change hazardous and tentative, the idiom of paradise predicted instant apocalypse. The Indian was no more a noble savage than the continent was a paradise. Even a practical program for civilizing the Indian, if it took no cognizance of the complexities of cultural change, could only dissolve what it was attempting to mold.

Civilization paid a price for its adherence to the paradisaic conception. As the Indian, noble savage or not, declined, a sense of guilt for his destruction settled upon the white man's conscience. No doubt the Indian had suffered principally because civilized man had invaded his paradise. The myth, in demanding more than reality could offer, returned to haunt those who had attempted to live it. Mythologized as a noble savage, the Indian required the best that civilization could give him. Or to put it another way, the native, submerged in nature, should have enjoyed all the riches that nature itself would bear. Yet the reality yielded only disappointment. Paradise never materialized, and rather than becoming civilized, the Indian seemed to disintegrate. The white man not only killed the Indian, he killed the noble savage—in a sense nature itself—and this was a crime for which there could be no expiation.

Program

Chapter V

Incorporation

1

The noble savage provided the impulse, and environmentalism contributed the mechanism, for the incorporation of the Indian into the white man's society. With this object in view, missionary agencies, supported and guided by the federal government, established schools to teach the tribes the white man's written lore, his efficient methods for obtaining a livelihood from the land, home manufactures, individualism, and the basic work discipline required of a progressive society. Philanthropists intended by this program to effect far-reaching changes in the native culture and in time to alter it so drastically as to accomplish the work of incorporation. Fittingly, the Christian missionary who came into the wilderness bearing a message of total and immediate transformation served as the principal agent for this achievement.[1] Because he sought salvation for the Indians, he lent to the civilizing process a moral component that could not be contributed by any merely secular policy. But the missionaries shared the immediate humanitarian desire to see the Indian change his ways, take on the character of civilization, and become, finally, indistinguishable from the white man.

The missionary impulse had always been important in Protestant civilization's settlement of the American continent. The New England Puritans, supposedly social introverts determined to cut themselves off from an unregenerate world, looked on the proselytization of the tribes as a positive obligation. And the Virginians, secular and practical in their search for a better life, considered the conversion of the natives an important part of the settlement process.

1. Berkhofer, *Salvation and the Savage*, 68–69, 105–106; Clifton Jackson Phillips, *Protestant America and the Pagan World: The First Half Century of the American Board of Commissioners for Foreign Missions, 1810–1860* (Cambridge, Mass., 1969) , 7–12; Pearce, *Savages of America*, 33.

No doubt, English Protestants performed at a disadvantage because of their heavy reliance on the word and on intellectual commitment; nonetheless, they intended to carry the European mode of life to the Indian.[2]

This missionary-civilizing commitment persisted into the Jeffersonian period. The major Christian sects, now including the Catholics, became more determined to carry on the work of civilization. Furthermore, the Quakers, who in the early years of settlement had been reluctant proselytizers, took up the cause after the Revolution with much dedication and organizing skill.[3] Thus at the height of the Enlightenment, religion and secular civilization dealt with the Indian tribes as a united front, and the religious organizations became important instruments for the expansion of the white man's world into the tribal preserve.

The formal relations between Indian and white had always been carried on according to the rules of international politics. Government necessarily served as the primary agent of contact, and in the Jeffersonian era philanthropy fell within its responsibilities. The federal authorities either directed benevolent activities or they made the rules under which private agencies engaged in them. The transformation of the Indian became a public function of the white man's society. Hence from the first acquisition of sovereignty during the Revolution to the removal policy of the 1820s, through all the complexities of war, commercial competition, frontier advance, and native decline, cutting across deep political differences, the incorporation of the Indian occupied the attentions of the new government. In a memorandum to Washington in 1789, Henry Knox stated the philanthropic position as well as it was ever formulated in later years. It pained him, he wrote, that the Indians had disappeared from the states now heavily populated by the whites. Shortly all of the tribes east of the Mississippi would be extinct. How different the situation would be if we "had imparted our knowledge of cultivation and the arts to the aboriginals of the country, by which the

2. Vaughan, *New England Frontier*, chaps. 9, 10, 11; Roy Harvey Pearce, "The 'Ruines of Mankind': The Indian and the Puritan Mind," *Jour. Hist. Ideas*, XIII (1952), 203, 209–210; Wesley Frank Craven, "Indian Policy in Early Virginia," *William and Mary Quarterly*, 3d Ser., I (1944), 71–72; R. Pierce Beaver, *Church, State, and the American Indians: Two and a Half Centuries of Partnership Between Protestant Churches and Government* (St. Louis, 1966), chap. 1; Walter Stitt Robinson, "Indian Policy of Colonial Virginia" (Ph.D. diss., University of Virginia, 1950), 257.

3. Sydney V. James, *A People among Peoples: Quaker Benevolence in Eighteenth-Century America* (Cambridge, Mass., 1963), 298–315.

source of future life and happiness had been preserved and extended." The task would doubtless have been very difficult, requiring the "highest knowledge of the human character, and a steady perseverance in a wise system for a series of years." But it could certainly be accomplished. Otherwise, one would have to concede that human habits lacked the capacity to change—a contention belied by the progress of civilization to its current level. Practically, Knox recommended the distribution of farm implements and domestic animals and the appointment of missionaries to reside among the tribes.[4]

Despite the many factors that militated against the amelioration of the native condition, government policy persisted in trying to civilize the tribes. Tension on the frontier with British forces and the open warfare of 1812 to 1814 worked against the civilizing movement. The inroads of settlers into the Indian territory, the conflict that ensued, and the government's tendency to favor the interests of its own people over even the acknowledged rights of the Indians inhibited success. Though confident of the capacity of goodwill to halt the Indians' social decline, philanthropists feared the possible extinction of the tribes. But this recognition only stimulated them to move toward their goal more quickly. The government attempted to undermine British influence among the tribes. Likewise, the federal authorities made at least sporadic efforts to keep the frontiersmen off Indian lands. Most treaties with the tribes contained provisions designed to accomplish philanthropic ends. Finally, the Congress provided for the regulation of the Indian trade in part to aid in the civilizing program.[5]

Presidents Washington and Jefferson, secretaries of war Knox, Dearborn, Crawford, and Calhoun, and lesser governmental agents such as Thomas L. McKenney promoted the policy at every turn. They encouraged Indian delegations to change their tribal ways; they instructed government agents in the field to do their utmost to further philanthropic ends; and they rendered encouragement and

4. Henry Knox to George Washington, July 7, 1789, *American State Papers, Indian Affairs,* I, 53–54.

5. See for example Art. 14 of the Holston treaty with the Cherokee, July 2, 1791, *ibid.,* 125; Washington's Third Annual Address, Oct. 25, 1791, James D. Richardson, ed., *A Compilation of the Messages and Papers of the Presidents, 1789–1902* (Washington, D.C., 1913) , I, 96–97; Henry Dearborn to W. C. C. Claiborne, William Henry Harrison, and Arthur St. Clair, Feb. 23, 1802, Letters Sent by the Secretary of War Relating to Indian Affairs, 1800–1824 (M-15) , Roll 1: 166–168, Records of the Bureau of Indian Affairs (RG 75) , National Archives, hereafter cited as Letters Sent, Sec. War (M-15) , Roll 1.

assistance to independent missionary efforts. Beginning in 1802, Congress authorized some fifteen thousand dollars annually for Indian affairs.[6] Unfortunately, the elaborate system of Indian negotiations and present giving absorbed these funds. The War Department applied some of the money to a number of desultory projects for which it made no accounting, and a portion went to Benjamin Hawkins for his program among the Creeks. No specific plan was brought forth on which the appropriation might have been expended. With similar lack of planning, the annuities granted to the tribes in exchange for land, though often spent on education, had little direct impact on the Indians' condition. Missionaries, such as Gideon Blackburn and Gabriel Richard, received aid for their separate efforts to educate the Indians. The government did much but never with the method or decision necessary to fulfill philanthropic aims.

The decision of utmost importance came in 1819. According to McKenney, his own initiative in soliciting memorials to be sent to Congress from various humanitarian societies led to the creation of an annual fund of ten thousand dollars for a civilizing program. Though little enough, the appropriation constituted a specific authorization that in the hands of Calhoun and his successor in the War Department, James Barbour, would be spent on a definite plan for the Indians' betterment. More important, the government made formal alliance with the missionary agencies for dispensing this fund. It dispatched a circular soliciting proposals for the establishment of schools in the Indian country and proposing that the government contribute toward the erection of buildings and the support of educational programs.[7]

The severe limitations in application hardly seemed commensurate with the strength of the humanitarian commitment. Determined to do something about the Indians' condition, the government never proved able to translate its principles into a successful program. Indeed, the very size and complexity of the problem—the conversion of an entire culture—more than accounted for the failure or the inadequacy of any plan devised. Yet the main reason for the programmatic deficiencies of Jeffersonian philanthropy could be found in its basic optimism. The philanthropists had no more

6. George Dewey Harmon, *Sixty Years of Indian Affairs: Political, Economic, and Diplomatic, 1789–1850* (Chapel Hill, 1941), 158–159.

7. John C. Calhoun, Circular, Sept. 3, 1819, Letters Sent, Sec. War (M-15), Roll 4: 319; Thomas L. McKenney to John Cocke, Feb. 2, 1827, Letters Sent by the Office of Indian Affairs, 1824–1881 (M-21), Roll 3: 355.

than an inkling of the obduracy of the task before them. Until removal, the desperation derived from recognizing that time worked against success never became sufficiently acute to drive the government to decisive action. Even had the new nation possessed the centralized political authority and the efficient bureaucracy needed to transform the tribes, this fundamental flaw in Jeffersonian optimism would have prevented its accomplishment. Though enthusiastic in his principles, the Jeffersonian could be phlegmatic in action. Believing that the goodness of nature would fulfill itself without undue interference, Jeffersonian philanthropy classified the incorporation of the Indian as part of this natural process.

2

Benevolence, the Jeffersonians failed to realize, would not compensate for the poverty of policy. Though their very benevolence demanded that the Indian be granted the honor of incorporation, its tendency to spill over into sentimentality revealed its shortcomings. Jeffersonians knew the end sought, but they confused the means required with a mere manifestation of goodwill. Still, they could not be faulted for their good intentions. "The Indians, on all occasions," instructed Henry Knox, "should be treated with entire justice and humanity." "Perfect candour" must be used in dealings with the natives, insisted Pickering. Dearborn favored "a spirit of friendship and harmony," instructing the government factor at Detroit to be at all times "temperate, prudent, and conciliatory." "We ought not," he said on another occasion, "to deviate from the principles of strict integrity in any of our dealings with the Indian Nations." With a finer sense of the weakness of the native position, Crawford cautioned that the "appearance of force, or menace, should be sedulously avoided." His magnanimity went even further: "When we are judges in our own cause, and where the weakness of the other party does not admit of an appeal from our decision, delicacy, as well as proper sense of justice, should induce us to lean in favor of the claim adverse to ours."[8]

8. Henry Knox to Timothy Pickering, May 2, 1791, Pickering Papers LX, 3, Massachusetts Historical Society, Boston (microfilm); Pickering to Edward Price, Nov. 26, 1795, Letter Book of the Creek Trading House, 1795–1816 (M-4), Records of the Bureau of Indian Affairs (RG 75), National Archives, hereafter cited as Letter Book, Creek Trading House (M-4); Henry Dearborn to Thomas Peterkin, July 28, 1802, Letters Sent, Sec. War (M-15), Roll 1: 252; Dearborn to William Henry Harrison, Feb. 21, 1803, *ibid.*, 328–329; William H. Crawford to John Coffee *et al.*, May 20, 1816, *ibid.*, Roll 3: 354; Crawford to Andrew Jackson, June 19, 1816, *ibid.*, 383–384.

From an even deeper strain of sympathy, Pickering proclaimed: "A man must be destitute of humanity, of honesty, or of common sense who should send them away disgusted: He must want sensibility if he did not sympathize with them." So profound an empathy for the natives' condition opened the wellsprings of philanthropic action. McKenney voiced the central command of philanthropic sentiment: the Indian must not be left to suffer in his savage isolation. Nothing that the government can provide should be withheld. "Our Country! It is the assylum for the miserable of all the world! It cannot therefore be indifferent to the distress of any portion of those composing its own family." And "it is enough to know that the Indians are Men . . . like ourselves" to know the burden of familial obligation. McKenney translated the universality of his benevolence into a call for the Indian's imitation of the white man. Can the Indian be denied "the knowledge out of which we derive our blessings, our comforts"? Shall he be permitted to live by the "impulses of nature" with an "uncertain subsistence, covered only with the skins of beasts" and "left alone to listen to the roar of the elements . . . , ignorant of all the vast concerns of the future"? "Why," McKenney hammered his point home, "should we enjoy all that has reference to the perfection of our nature, and our Brothers . . . be left to struggle on amidst clouds and darkness, and suffering, with a dread uncertainty resting on all the future?"[9] Philanthropic sympathy encompassed all in its universalist determination to form the world and the Indian in its own image.

One could certainly expect results from a benevolence so fervently held, but the red men's mental abilities added to the philanthropist's expectation of success. Jefferson believed that the "proofs of genius given by the Indians of N. America, place them on a level with Whites in the same uncultivated state." Pickering made the Indians' "original powers" the equal of white men's, and McKenney tipped the balance of talent in favor of the Indians. John Filson called them "a very understanding people, quick of apprehension, sudden in execution, subtle in business, exquisite in invention, and industrious in action."[10] All the threads in humanitarian

9. Timothy Pickering to George Washington, Dec. 31, 1790, Pickering Papers, LXI, 119; Thomas L. McKenney to Elias Cornelius, July 26, 1817, Letters Sent by the Superintendent of Indian Trade, 1807–1823 (M-16), Roll 4: 374–375; McKenney to P. Milledoler, Aug. 9, 1820, *ibid.*, Roll 6: 30–31.

10. Jefferson to Chastellux, June 7, 1785, Boyd, ed., *Jefferson Papers*, VIII, 185; Timothy Pickering to Iroquois Council, Oct. 13, 1791, Pickering Papers, LX, 224; Thomas L. McKenney, *Sketches of a Tour to the Lakes, of the character and customs of the Chippeway Indians, and of incidents connected with the Treaty of Fond du Lac* (Baltimore, 1827), 428; Filson, *Kentucke*, 100.

thought combined to grant the Indian more than sufficient talent
to take his place in a civilized order.

3

In the extensive discussion of the nature of the civilizing process,
the major division occurred between the interests of secular education and religious conversion. Neither side proposed to exclude the
other. For the Jeffersonian age, the first impulse toward the improvement of the native condition came from the secular progressivism of the Enlightenment, but as the movement gained force, prose-
lytizing religion assumed the major role. In part the transition demonstrated that the crisis of American Indian affairs spanned the
rationalist and romantic eras; yet it also revealed an essential unity
in spirit. Though one may have been clinical and secular and the
other enthusiastic and evangelical, both were meliorist and progressive, and both proposed a change in the Indian character. Since
no fundamental argument arose between the secular and religious
approaches to the Indian, the question concerned the order of the
civilizing process—timing, not substance.

Jefferson took a strong position on the secular side. Conceiving of
civilizing the native as part of the universal movement of humanity,
he tended to think that amelioration adumbrated the larger progressivist scheme. The movement proceeded from a primitive condition to a complex society with a religious component. The best
system of improvement, he thought, should begin with the acquisition of domestic animals and develop through farming, the household arts, separate property, money, the knowledge of arithmetic,
and writing; then would follow the reading of printed books, first
of the popular sort and finally those on religion as distinguished
from morality. For all his secularist inclinations, Jefferson put religion in the culminating stage of human development. He objected most strongly to the practice of converting the Indians first
and then attempting to civilize them.[11]

A solid consensus backed Jefferson's opinion. The transformation
of the tribesmen should begin with the simplest rudimentary skills

---

11. Jefferson to Benjamin Smith Barton, Apr. 3, 1814, Jefferson Papers, Lib.
of Congress (microfilm); Jefferson to James Pemberton, Nov. 16, 1807, Lipscomb and Bergh, eds., *Writings of Jefferson*, XI, 395; Jefferson to Pemberton,
June 21, 1808, *ibid.*, XII, 75; Jefferson to James Jay, Apr. 7, 1809, *ibid.*, 270–
271. Jefferson entitled the collection of Bible texts he brought together in 1803
the "Philosophy of Jesus of Nazareth" and subheaded it: "Being an abridg-
ment of the New Testament for the use of the Indians, unembarrassed with
matters of fact or faith beyond the level of their comprehensions." See Henry S.
Randall, *The Life of Thomas Jefferson* (New York, 1858), III, 654–656.

and should only increase in complexity and sophistication as they proved able to absorb new patterns of behavior and new intellectual formulations. Not necessarily antireligious, the position reflected the Protestant affinity for ideas, but also it probably indicated secularist opposition to evangelical enthusiasm. A succession of commentators on the Indian condition and the practicability of changing it opposed the inculcation of formal religion in the first stages. Adair, Filson, Knox, Pickering, and Hawkins all made positive statements on the subject. McKenney capsuled the argument in 1822: "Religious observances, and the ceremonies of the church, are all excellent, and should form part of every system for the conversion of the savage into the civilized man and Christian; but they are not sufficient, of themselves, to accomplish this great end."[12]

Of the various religious groups promoting civilization among the tribes, the Quakers had perhaps the highest reputation. Representing one of the least worldly versions of Christianity, they had earned the good opinion of both Indians and whites by their honesty and also by their low-keyed emphasis on teaching the natives the practical arts of survival in the white man's world. Wrote Pickering in praise of Quaker missionaries: "Their object is not to teach peculiar doctrines but useful practices, to instruct the Indians in husbandry and the plain mechanical arts and manufactures directly connected with it. This is beginning at the right end and if so much can be accomplished, their further improvement will follow of course."[13] Practicality and disinterestedness, it seemed, went together; ostentatious religious convictions foisted on the Indians by overly eager missionaries appeared self-serving.

Of course, all missionaries stressed religion. Many did more than link Christianity with civilization or merely give religion a certain priority over secular affairs. They held that Christianity itself included civilization. To be Christian was putatively to be civilized.

12. Adair, *History of American Indians*, 459–460; Filson, *Kentucke*, 103; Henry Knox to George Washington, July 7, 1789, *American State Papers, Indian Affairs*, I, 53–54; Timothy Pickering to Samuel Kirkland, Dec. 4, 1791, Pickering Papers, LXI, 304–305A; Augustus John Foster, *Jeffersonian America: Notes on the United States of America . . .* , ed. Richard Beale Davis (San Marino, Calif., 1954), 24–25; Thomas L. McKenney, Circular, May 28, 1822, *Missionary Herald*, XVIII (1822), 224.

13. Timothy Pickering to Jaspar Parrish, Feb. 15, 1796, Letters Received, Sec. War (M-271), Roll 1: 783; Pickering to Arthur St. Clair, May 31, 1796, *ibid.*, 785; Jefferson to Thomas Ellicot *et al.*, Nov. 13, 1807, Lipscomb and Bergh, eds., *Writings of Jefferson*, XVI, 289; Clinton, "Private Canal Journal, 1810," in William W. Campbell, ed., *The Life and Writings of De Witt Clinton* (New York, 1849), 188–189.

"True civilization is found only in Christian countries; and no where, but as the *result* of Christianity; of Christianity, too, planted in the first instance, by missionary enterprise." Cyrus Kingsbury confirmed this message and directed it to more practical matters. He contended "that the plain and simple, yet powerful truths of the gospel addressed to the hearts and consciences of the heathen, is the most direct way to civilize, as well as christianise them."[14] This unity between Christianity and civilization derived from the philanthropic determination that the Indian should accept the white man's society totally. The missionary mind left no room for selective cultural change; it clothed civilization in the message of conversion.

Aside from theory, the civilizing program did seem to bring results to the degree that the tribes became Christian. The Indians "appear to advance," wrote the missionaries at Brainerd, "just in proportion to their knowledge of the Gospel." Consequently, resistance to the exhortations of the missionary became the mark of savagery. A weakening of the tribal bond and a strengthening of the family tie accompanied conversion. In the same process, Christian Indians showed themselves more proficient in the arts of civilization. Loyalty to the tribal order represented social stagnation, mechanical incompetence, and eventually personal disintegration. Conversion held the key to progress. "Those . . . who come to Christ and join the church," said David Zeisberger, "turn to agriculture and raising stock, keeping cattle, hogs and fowls."[15] Most observers saw the transmission of civilization in a Christian context.

Yet this centrality of religion in the civilizing scheme did not necessarily hand over Indian relations to fanatic destroyers of heathendom. Samuel Worcester described the ideal missionaries as persons of "sagacious observation, comprehensive views and of sound judgment, not visionary theorists, but practical men, capable of collecting and embodying facts, of directing their inquiries judiciously

14. *Missionary Herald*, XXI (1825), 88; Cyrus Kingsbury to James Barbour, Feb. 1826, Letters Received by the Office of Indian Affairs, 1824–1881 (M-234), Schools, Roll 773: 227; "Extract from the George C. Sibley Journal," Donald Jackson, ed., *The Journals of Zebulon Montgomery Pike, with Letters and Related Documents* (Norman, 1966), II, 372–373.
15. "Extracts from the Brainerd Journal," *Missionary Herald*, XVII (1821), 73; Hulbert and Schwarze, eds., "Zeisberger's History," Ohio Archaeol. and Hist. Soc., *Pubs.*, XIX (1910), 14. See also Samuel Worcester to Cyrus Kingsbury, Nov. 19, 1817, American Board of Commissioners for Foreign Missions Papers, 1.01.I: 74, Houghton Library, Harvard University, Cambridge, Mass., hereafter cited as ABC 1.01.I: Jeremiah Evarts to Worcester, May 18, 1818, *Panoplist*, XIV (1818), 339; Cephas Washburn to James Barbour, Oct. 1, 1825, Letters Received, Off. Indian Affairs (M-234), Schools, Roll 772: 747–748.

in regard to Indian customs, dispositions, manners, and languages, and conveying their inquiries into solid results, and of consulting and securing the confidence extensively of the people both white and red."[16] The missionaries generally either thought civilization subsumed within Christianity or at least communicated best through Christianity, but they were as much devoted to civilizing the Indians as those few secularists who saw no use for religion.

The obvious advantages derived from missionary dedication and organizing skill convinced governmental authorities of the usefulness of religion. Despite a persistent tendency to quibble over means, the missionary agencies remained the only organized instruments capable of furthering the work of civilization. McKenney understood this better than most; hence his eagerness to harness the missionary energy to the philanthropic cause. He laid down policy explicitly for the government agent with the Osage: "There can be no doubt but the work of Indian reformation is in close necessary connexion with their improvement in moral and religious instruction, and no agent will be considered as fulfilling his duties who shall not second the labors of those who are under the government Sanction engaged in this great work." Since the secular and spiritual interests ultimately sought the same object, by the second decade of the nineteenth century they formed a firm alliance to bring the Indian within civilized society.[17]

The government's role became largely supervisory; the missionary organizations carried on the actual program.[18] The Indian office in the War Department required periodic reports, and agents among the tribes assisted with advice and the distribution of money for the erection of buildings at the mission stations. Eventually, the missionaries became dependent on the government for their physical plant. The government made a definite proposal to the missionary organizations in 1819. It would pay two-thirds of the building costs; payments would begin only after construction had commenced, and one-fourth would be withheld until the completion of the structures. Annual payments for the support of the approved schools

16. Samuel Worcester to William Jenkins, Sept. 25, 1815, ABC 1.01.I: 27.

17. Thomas L. McKenney to Benton Pixley, Mar. 26, 1825, Letters Sent, Off. Indian Affairs (M-21), Roll 1: 427. See also entry of Nov. 11, 1775, Worthington C. Ford *et al.*, eds., *Journals of the Continental Congress, 1774–1789* (Washington, D.C., 1904–1937), III, 351; Henry Knox to Benjamin Lincoln *et al.*, Aug. 29, 1789, *American State Papers, Indian Affairs*, I, 66; Henry Dearborn to Henry Drinker, May 22, 1801, Letters Sent, Sec. War (M-15), Roll 1: 51; Dearborn to William Findley, Feb. 25, 1802, *ibid.*, 170; John C. Calhoun to Elias Cornelius, July 18, 1818, *ibid.*, Roll 4: 185.

18. For a list of missionary establishments, see *Missionary Herald*, XXI (1825), 2–8.

would be made in proportion to the number of pupils and the president's evaluation of their progress. Thus the alliance of philanthropy went beyond common sympathy for the tribesmen and the scattered encouragement and aid that had come from the first four national administrations. Government and religion came together in an effort to formalize the white man's humanitarian commitment. The public authority provided initiative, direction, and physical resources, and the private organizations, though they gave much money also, supplied mainly the teachers who made actual contact with the Indians.[19]

The discussion over the nature of the civilizing process and the order of its development revealed the unity of the white man's culture. At base he had only one thing to offer the Indian: the full complement of his own way of life. Arguments between enlightened secularist forces and the religious missionary interest crippled neither, and until removal they operated as one. Government, representing largely the secular side, came to the point of giving over its responsibilities to religion. For their part, the missionaries accepted the role eagerly and went on to perform the basic task of teaching the natives the skills of civilized existence. In theory and then in the civilizing program, the philanthropist brought the full force of his society to the transformation of the Indian.

4

After the appropriation of 1819, the civilizing program was given barely a decade before its failure to effect incorporation led to removal. In the decade of the 1820s, the government partially subsidized close to forty schools, most of them in the Indian country but some in the white man's domain. The American Board of Commissioners for Foreign Missions, a Congregational and Presbyterian organization with headquarters in Boston, supported the largest number—ten among the Choctaws alone. At one time, approximately two thousand Indian youths attended the various institutions. The effort was formidable in size, and it yielded some notable results.[20] Beginning late, however, and attempting to survive in an

19. John C. Calhoun, Circular, Feb. 20, 1820, Letters Sent, Sec. War (M-15), Roll 4: 378–380.
20. Thomas L. McKenney to John C. Calhoun, Aug. 14, 1819, Letters Received, Sec. War (M-271), Roll 2: 1284–1287; Cyrus Kingsbury, "An Exhibit of the State of the Indian Schools in the Choctaw Nation for the Year Ending 30th Sept.–1830," Letters Received, Off. Indian Affairs (M-234), Schools, Roll 774: 481; McKenney to James Barbour, Nov. 15, 1825, Letters Sent, Off. Indian Affairs (M-21), Roll 2: 237; McKenney to Barbour, Nov. 20, 1826, *ibid.*, Roll 3: 232; McKenney, *Memoirs, Official and Personal*, 35–36.

atmosphere of increasing tension in Indian-white relations, it seemed only a last burst of benevolent energy.

Traditionally, missionaries carried the message of civilization into the Indian country by establishing for the tribesmen's benefit small replicas of civilization: patriarchal families, cultivated fields, workshops, among other evidences of civilized life. The traditional method persisted. The representatives of civilization, for the most part, worked their changes on native society within the tribal enclave. The practice seemed to place the philanthropist at an undue disadvantage; he confronted native society at its point of greatest strength. The obvious alternative, separating the Indian from his people and transporting him to the white man's settlements for an education, presented insurmountable problems. A combination of geography and numbers required that the natives be transformed as a society, and for this the white man went to the tribes. This, after all, merely repeated the larger process of Indian-white relations. Civilization always represented the positive, aggressive force. The Indian either generally accepted what civilization offered him or he receded before its advance; sometimes he did both.

The relative fixity of native society, which led to the acceptance of the principle that the Indian must be educated on his own ground, impelled Cyrus Kingsbury to propose that the missionaries do more than establish schools in the Indian country where the native youth could be given formal training. He saw the dangers of counter pressure from the villages, still largely unchanged by the white man's ways. Native children, with only the beginnings of a civilized education, would be sent back to a largely hostile environment. Kingsbury favored sending missionaries into the villages themselves "to teach at their own houses, those who will not be instructed at the schools."[21] The complexity of the native social order, and the internal strength it continued to display in the most trying times, allowed it to retreat before the philanthropic attack, build new defenses, and go on cultivating at least some of the old ways.

The accepted expedient, consequently, called for missionary schools near the centers of Indian population that would give the younger generation the semblances of an education and an introduction to the work habits that lay at the root of the white man's worldly success. McKenney stated the practical reasons. It would be

---

21. Cyrus Kingsbury to James Barbour, Oct. 21, 1826, Letters Received, Off. Indian Affairs (M-234), Schools, Roll 773: 305–306.

half as expensive as transporting the native pupils to schools in the settled areas. The money expended, part of it the Indian's own from annuities and land sales, would be spent within the tribal economy and would thus supply the resources for future progress. Furthermore, the success of education within the tribe would act as a leaven to influence a broader transformation of native society. For the same reasons, McKenney also favored the establishment of institutions of higher learning within the Indian territory. He understood that, in the course of learning, the native youths would require the security of familiar surroundings. Moreover, he expected enough difficulty in instilling the discipline of school life without imposing the burden of total separation from the past. In the Indian country, the student body would be homogeneous, whereas at schools outside, the Indians would be thrown in with white pupils with whom they would be ill equipped to compete. Within their own territory, supposedly, they would be less susceptible to the temptations of vice and more easily led to the gradual acceptance of civilized ways.[22]

A rough practicality underlaid the educational method. The Indian should emerge from the process as a copy of the youthful white scholar, hence the philanthropic concern to transmit the substance of a formal civilized education. But the vagueness of much philanthropic thinking permitted a general recognition of the limitations of the Indian's situation. Thus Kingsbury would have been content "to form these children to habits of industry." Similarly, McKenney hoped that a missionary education would make the natives familiar with the "excellent principles of our Government; the ties which unite and bind society together, with the great advantages of that state over that of the savage; or impress them with the importance of the observance of those great moral lessons, in the practice of which results so much security and happiness to man."[23] The imprecision of these dictums provided room for maneuvering and finally for an effort to implement them that paid considerable attention to the Indian's immediate needs.

Education seldom went beyond reading, writing, and simple

22. "Sketch of a Plan for Instructing the Indians," *Panoplist*, XII (1816), 150–152; Thomas L. McKenney to John C. Calhoun, Aug. 14, 1819, Letters Received, Sec. War (M-271), Roll 2: 1291–1292; McKenney to William Ward, July 18, 1825, Letters Sent, Off. Indian Affairs (M-21), Roll 2: 95; McKenney to Cyrus Kingsbury, Aug. 3, 1825, *ibid.*, 111; Jeremiah Evarts to Hugh Wilson, May 5, 1828, ABC 1.01.VIII: 281; McKenney to Levi Colbert, June 11, 1829, Letters Sent, Off. Indian Affairs (M-21), Roll 6: 9.

23. Cyrus Kingsbury to John C. Calhoun, May 15, 1818, Letters Received, Sec. War (M-271), Roll 2: 716–721; Thomas L. McKenney to Isaac Thomas, Dec. 14, 1816, Letters Sent, Supt. Indian Trade (M-16), Roll 4: 207–209.

arithmetic, with as much weight as possible on farming skills. "In a word," declared Timothy Pickering in 1791, "bring them up precisely in the manner in which our substantial farmers educate their own sons." The ideal remained the white man, but the level of projected literacy dropped significantly in order to increase the practical possibilities. In a different vein but for similar reasons, McKenney recommended a sensible, if somewhat Spartan, schooling. "Nothing is so ridiculous," he wrote, "as to make a *beau-monde* out of a school boy. His eyes ought never to be attracted by the glitter of a fine coat, or a pair of gewgaw trousers, nor a gay hat— and especially Indian boys, who have new tastes to be formed in regard to these matters, for you know they are bred up to the love of finery and feathers. Whilst these extrinsic ornaments will be avoided on the one hand, good, and suitable, and comfortable clothes, will be provided on the other."[24] Altogether, in mind and temperament, philanthropists expected the Indian to finish his scholarly sojourn with the middling mental accomplishments and unpretentious manners of an American farmer.

The missionaries did want the native character to be absorbed completely in the educational process. As a result, attendance and order constituted the most difficult problems. Kingsbury described the regimen at Elliot, one of the American Board schools for the Choctaws. Sessions occupied six hours a day and in winter five and a half. The boys worked four hours in summer and two hours in winter. Students rose a little after daylight with breakfast of coffee (three-fourths rye), corn bread, meat, and potatoes. A work period followed the meal, and school began at nine. A similar schedule completed the day. Though rigid by Indian standards, it was the usual for the missionaries. They employed the Lancastrian system, using the brighter students to teach the slower, which, according to Kingsbury, had been markedly successful. Within a year, of forty-four pupils, thirty-six could read from the Bible, six could do simple arithmetic, six knew English grammar, and two of the most favored could handle more complicated arithmetic.[25] The system

24. Timothy Pickering to George Washington, Jan. 8, 1791, Pickering Papers, LXI, 164–165A; Thomas L. McKenney to James L. McDonald, Feb. 5, 1827, Letters Sent, Off. Indian Affairs (M-21), Roll 3: 363.

25. John C. Calhoun to Stephen N. Roman, Apr. 1, 1820, Letters Sent, Sec. War (M-15), Roll 4: 694–697. See also "Plan of Rev. Gabriel Richard for Educating the Indians," Jan. 20, 1809, Clarence E. Carter, ed., *The Territorial Papers of the United States* (Washington, D.C., 1934–), X, 262–266; Calhoun to Joseph Lancaster, May 16, 1820, Letters Sent, Sec. War (M-15), Roll 4: 426–427; Christopher Vandeventer, Circular, Aug. 29, 1821, *ibid.*, 151.

proved mildly effective, though it never solved the problem of discipline, nor did it complete the process of transformation.

In time the schools grew too large, in some cases to more than a hundred students, and the problems of discipline and attendance became more acute. Results seemed less notable with greater numbers, and the American Board made an effort to reduce school size. Both Evarts and Kingsbury, with Calhoun's approval, established fifty students as an acceptable number. Cost would be less, perhaps by half, if a school accommodated approximately twenty Indian youths as boarders and drew the rest from the villages on a daily basis. As a consequence, an attempt to tighten the missionary program in order to retain discipline allowed some of the Indians to preserve tribal associations.[26]

The tug of the old order remained strong. Though life within the tribe afforded the native students the security needed for successful learning, it became increasingly clear that at some stage the transition of the Indian from one society to another would require a definite separation. Furthermore, as the missionaries saw it, the problem went beyond the reluctance of the natives to leave a healthy and satisfying society. The danger lay in the decay of that system and the effects its eventual collapse would have on the young Indians. Instead of absorbing the constructive elements of the civilized world, the younger generation seemed inclined to follow the older tribesmen in addiction to the white man's vices and in the despair of a declining culture.

Consequently, the pressure mounted to remove the Indian students from the failing atmosphere of the tribal environment. As early as 1816, Kingsbury advocated just such a scheme. "It appeared obvious," he wrote, "that the children should be removed as much as possible from the society of the natives, and placed where they would have the influence of example, as well as precept. This can only be done by forming the school into one great Missionary family, where they would be boarded by the Missionary and teachers, be entirely under their direction, and have their pious orderly and industrious example constantly before them." Kingsbury proposed separating the students from the tribe while still maintaining the Indian school in close proximity. A more positive solution called for the establishment in the civilized areas of schools where

26. Cyrus Kingsbury to John C. Calhoun, Nov. 18, 1822, Letters Received, Sec. War (M-271), Roll 4: 163–165; Calhoun to Kingsbury, Dec. 14, 1822, Letters Sent, Sec. War (M-15), Roll 5: 369; Daniel S. Butrick to Jeremiah Evarts, Oct. 17, 1824, ABC 18.3.1.IV: 3–4.

the Indians could acquire mainly formal education. The Kentucky Baptist Society supported one of the more noted of such institutions. The Baptists of Illinois initiated similar enterprises, as did the Catholic bishop of New Orleans at Florissant near St. Louis. The American Board supported the most prestigious of the lot at Cornwall, Connecticut. Wedded to the idea of educating the Indian on his own ground and doubtful that schools located in the white man's country could be controlled, the government at first hesitated to contribute to them. When the evidence showed, however, that these schools worked well, they received government money. But more important, the tribesmen themselves, the chiefs and half bloods especially, asked for institutions that would provide their children with education superior to the elementary fare available at the missionary schools in the Indian country.[27]

Soon the justification for schools in the white settlements became clear. The Choctaws had been eager to support the academy established in 1825 by Colonel Richard M. Johnson at his home near Blue Spring, Kentucky. The more prominent Indians wanted advanced education for their offspring, but they had also become dissatisfied with the menial regimen that the missionaries seemed to equate with civilization. Situated in the midst of the white man's world, the Choctaw Academy gave the Indians the opportunity to cultivate the refinements of gentlemen.[28] It also provided an opportunity for

27. Cyrus Kingsbury to Samuel Worcester, Nov. 28, 1816, ABC 18.3.1.III: 23; Thomas L. McKenney to John McKee *et al.*, Dec. 29, 1817, Letters Sent, Supt. Indian Trade (M-16), Roll 4: 471–474; Worcester to Ard Hoyt, Nov. 11, 1818, ABC 1.01.III: 99; John C. Calhoun to William Staughton, Mar. 9, 1820, Letters Sent, Sec. War (M-15), Roll 4: 477; Calhoun to Robert Bell, Dec. 18, 1821, *ibid.*, Roll 5: 207; S. P. Van Duickenborne to Calhoun [Oct. 1823?], Letters Received, Sec. War (M-271), Roll 4: 817; Stephen Van Rensselaer *et al.* to Congress, Mar. 3, 1824, *American State Papers, Indian Affairs*, II, 447; John Ridge to Albert Gallatin, Mar. 10, 1826, Gallatin Papers, Box 64–3, folder 42, New-York Historical Society; Cyrus Kingsbury to James Barbour, June 25, 1825, Letters Received, Off. Indian Affairs (M-234), Schools, Roll 773: 748–750.

28. Cyrus Kingsbury to James Barbour, July 6, 1825, Letters Received, Off. Indian Affairs (M-234), Schools, Roll 772: 562–568; Thomas L. McKenney to William Ward, Aug. 14, 1828, Letters Sent, Off. Indian Affairs (M-21), Roll 5: 86–87; John C. Calhoun to Richard M. Johnson, Mar. 3, 1821, Letters Sent, Sec. War (M-15), Roll 5: 61; McKenney to Kingsbury, Oct. 20, 1825, Letters Sent, Off. Indian Affairs (M-21), Roll 2: 196–197; McKenney to David Folsom, May 9, 1826, *ibid.*, Roll 3: 66–67; Kingsbury to McKenney, June 5, 1826, Letters Received, Off. Indian Affairs (M-234), Schools, Roll 773: 243. See also Shelly D. Rousse, "Colonel Dick Johnson's Choctaw Academy: A Forgotten Educational Experiment," *Ohio Archaeological and Historical Quarterly*, XXV (1916), 88–117. The school began with an academic program, but added practical training in 1832 and farming in 1837.

mixing students from the various tribes. Though begun by the Choctaws, it was soon attended by Creeks, Potawatomies, Miamis, and Chickasaws. Mixing cultivated "friendship among those who were once hostile to each other, but as the one cannot understand the language of the other, it became necessary that they converce altogether in english." More important, they lived in closer contact with white men. "Removed from the bad example of Wild Indians in their drunken revelry, there the native talent can be Cultivated, surrounded by the first families in the West." The original plans called for the admission of white students who would live by the same rules as the Indians, but none ever enrolled. In order to diversify further the influences on the natives, the school laid plans to board them with white families in the neighborhood. But by removing the prominent young natives from the tribal environment, the school had already done much to expand their experience.[29]

The academy represented a promising effort to further the philanthropic program. It proved the Indians capable of breaking out of their traditional system and of successfully dealing with the more sophisticated portions of the white man's world. It demonstrated their willingness to train a leadership class in the ways of civilization and to do it not only under the influence of whites but also in company with Indians of other tribes. Moreover, the school was in many ways an Indian project. Of course, Colonel Johnson had done much to promote the idea among them, as had other interests wanting a crack at tribal money, but the fact remained that the Choctaws persisted over government and missionary reluctance and that they financed the project in part with their own funds. Most philanthropists saw it as a harbinger of good things to come.

The government also demonstrated its flexibility by agreeing to place individual students in schools such as Princeton and Dartmouth and to pay living expenses and tuition of others at less well-known institutions in the white man's country. This special consideration came as much from the need to conciliate the leaders of the tribes as it did from the desire to educate the tribesmen. But despite the variety of methods, the government and the major

29. Thomas Henderson to James Barbour, Apr. 30, 1827, Letters Received, Off. Indian Affairs (M-234), Schools, Roll 773: 648–651; Henderson to Barbour, Nov. 1, 1827, *ibid.*, 679; Levi Colbert to Barbour, Mar. 10, 1828, *ibid.*, 945–946; John Lipton to Barbour, June 2, 1827, *ibid.*, 848–850; William Staughton to Henderson, Dec. 12, 1825, *ibid.*, Roll 772: 683; Trustees to J. T. Johnson *et al.*, May 1, 1826, *ibid.*, Roll 773: 127–128.

philanthropic agencies applied the greater part of their resources to civilizing the Indians within their own territory.[30]

5

When missionaries dealt with Indian languages, they encountered the problem of cultural persistence. The total annihilation of the tribal character left no room for the preservation of its vestiges in the native languages. Indeed, a primary sign that the tribesmen had been metamorphosed into civilized men would be the abandonment of their native tongues. But the problems of transition from one order of life to another required at some point the use of the native speech and hence its preservation. Once again, methodology forced the philanthropist to deal with the vexing problems of cultural change.

The simplicity of the humanitarian object supplied an obvious answer to the language question. "I have long believed," wrote McKenney, "the key to the civilization of our aborigines, to be the knowledge of our Christian language—but especially the *English.* . . . It is this which, after all, is to effect the change in the character and destiny of these people. It is the lever by which they are to elevate themselves into intellectual and moral distinction." Pickering had been at least as decisive. He wanted only English taught in the schools. "The *Indian* tongue," he intoned, "is the great obstacle to the civilization of the Indians. The sooner it is removed the better." As usual, the philanthropic argument was theoretically consistent. Since the Indians could be offered no alternative to incorporation, their languages served no useful purpose. "They should be made acquainted as early as possible," wrote a missionary among the Seneca, "with the language of that community with which they will in time, in all probability be amalgamated." McKenney stated the case more subtly. Taught to read in his own

30. Entry of July 31, 1781, Ford, ed., *Journals of the Continental Congress,* XXI, 819–820; Henry Knox to Timothy Pickering, May 2, 1771, *American State Papers, Indian Affairs,* I, 166; George Graham to Philip E. Thomas, Mar. 14, 1806, Letters Sent, Sec. War (M-15), Roll 3: 309; Henry Dearborn to George Colbert, Apr. 17, 1807, *ibid.,* Roll 13: 307; Dearborn to Capt. Hendricks, Jan. 30, 1809, *ibid.,* Roll 2: 430; Samuel Worcester to John C. Calhoun, Nov. 13, 1819, ABC 1.01.III: 332; Thomas L. McKenney to James Barbour, Dec. 1, 1827, Letters Sent, Off. Indian Affairs, Roll 4: 162–163; John H. Eaton to David Folsom, Dec. 2, 1830, Letters Received, Off. Indian Affairs (M-234), Schools, Roll 774: 325. Isaac McCoy arranged for a number of his charges to be sent east for advanced training; see McCoy to William Staughton, July 11, 1825, and McCoy to Lewis Cass, July 1, 1826, Isaac McCoy Papers, Kansas State Historical Society, Topeka (microfilm).

tongue, the Indian would be "bounded by the limits which are embraced in translated works." But if taught English, he would immediately be put in "possession of the mighty field which our language embraces. He can read our laws, understand whatever is written in English, and all this may be acquired in the same time that it would take to learn him to read his own language." Humanitarians saw no alternative to the immediate indoctrination of the Indian in spoken and written English. "Their whole character, inside and out; language, and morals, must be changed."[31]

In practice, the missionaries' confidence in their own way, plus their assumption that the Indian manner would change so quickly that it would be pointless to either preserve or learn the native languages, put them at a serious disadvantage. Interpreters served well enough for teaching farming and home manufactures, but they failed in communicating the abstruse details of Christian theology or the complexities of secular learning. Nearly all instruction given the Indians passed through an interpreter, a necessity that, reported the editors of the *Missionary Herald* in 1830, "often embarrasses the missionary and confines his labors within narrow limits." Some years before, Pickering had commented on Samuel Kirkland's failure to convince the Oneidas of the "mysteries of the gospel." After a ministry of twenty years, said Pickering, not one in twenty of the natives appeared to have any idea of his message. The problem was language. For all his years among the Indians, Kirkland could not make himself understood once he got beyond the ordinary occurrences of the day. John Gambold, the Moravian missionary among the Cherokees, frankly admitted that he had never been able to learn the native language. He contended that even those who married into the tribe found it difficult. As a result of his ignorance of the language, he possessed only a limited knowledge of tribal customs. "After 19 years Residence in this Country I have attained so little of the Language, that I can hardly purchase a Venison ham from an Indian, without an Interpreter." Such brazen delinquency derived from the basic assumption on

31. Thomas L. McKenney to John Pickering, Apr. 18, 1826, Letters Sent, Off. Indian Affairs (M-21), Roll 3: 39; McKenney to Lewis Cass *et al.*, July 7, 1817, Letters Sent, Supt. Indian Trade (M-16), Roll 4: 369; Timothy Pickering, "A Plan . . . for the Five Nations . . . ," Pickering Papers, LXII, 17–18; Thomson S. Harris and James Young to John C. Calhoun, Oct. 29, 1822, Letters Received, Sec. War (M-271), Roll 4: 126–130; McKenney to Benjamin Mortimer, Mar. 28, 1822, Letters Received by the Superintendent of Indian Trade, 1806–1824 (M-T58), Roll 1; McKenney to Cyrus Kingsbury, Apr. 10, 1826, Letters Sent, Off. Indian Affairs (M-21), Roll 3: 20.

which Gambold proceeded in his missionary activity. He proposed to civilize the Indians by teaching them English; the cultivation of the native tongue by either himself or the Indians could only be a sign that he had failed.[32]

Samuel Worcester established a positive policy for the American Board of Commissioners in 1815. The board sent its missionaries into the Indian country with no means of communication save English, which few of the Indians could understand. Guided by what he considered Gideon Blackburn's great success in teaching some five hundred native children to read English, he recommended the establishment of schools among the Choctaws to teach English immediately. Though ignorant of the Indian tongue, he instructed the missionaries to communicate what they could of "divine truth and of civilization to the parents." Also, he saw no point in preserving a language already in decline by translating the scriptures into it. Knowledge of the Indian languages, he told prospective missionaries, held little value for the work of civilizing the tribes.[33]

Soon after the beginning of the missionary program, the tactical difficulties of working only in English became apparent. Merely getting the students' attention presented formidable problems. The influence of the missionaries could be no more than a fraction of the native's overall experience; he spoke his own language with his family and companions. Because Indians carried on social intercourse without writing, the missionaries found it easier to teach written than spoken English. The young showed sufficient wit to adopt a new mode of expression that did not compete with the predominantly oral experience of Indian society. Spoken English could be taught only by keeping the students at school for three or four years, a longer period than most of the Indian youths could endure or their families would permit.[34]

The Cherokees made a further contribution to the missionaries'

32. *Missionary Herald*, XXII (1826), 352–353, XXVI (1830), 214; Timothy Pickering to Jeremy Belknap, June 16, 1796, Pickering Papers, VI, 187–188; John Gambold to Peter S. Du Ponceau, Vocabulary and Miscellaneous Papers, LXXXV, 39, Lib., Am. Phil. Soc., Philadelphia; Gambold to Thomas L. McKenney, Aug. 30, 1824, Letters Received, Off. Indian Affairs (M-234), Schools, Roll 772: 90–92. Isaac McCoy admitted that neither he, his wife, nor his chief assistant had ever learned Potawatomie very well, though he conceded the need to do so; see McCoy to James Loring, Oct. 5, 1824, Isaac McCoy Papers.

33. Samuel Worcester to Jeremiah Evarts, July 1, 1815, ABC 1.01.I: 22–24; Worcester to Ard Hoyt, Jan. 15, 1817, *ibid.*, 94–95.

34. Cyrus Kingsbury to John C. Calhoun, Oct. 16, 1823, Letters Received, Sec. War (M-271), Roll 4: 687; "Memoranda relative to the Cherokee Mission," Apr. and May 1822, ABC 18.3.1.II: 154.

dilemma. When Sequoya came forth with a method for writing his tribal language, they could no longer plead that English, being the only written mode for communicating civilization, must displace all native vehicles for expression. Of course, the missionaries saw language as more than a means for bringing civilization to the Indian: it was part of the very tissue of civilization. An apparently workable system of Indian writing encroached on the exclusivity of English as the necessary precondition for civilized life. Many philanthropists, consequently, kept a distinct reserve in their reaction to Sequoya's invention. The government gave him a formal reward in 1828, but McKenney remained hostile to the idea as did the American Board officials. Finally, however, they accommodated their opinions to an accomplished fact; the Indians intended to go into the printing business. Besides, the men in the field had been forced very early to make concessions to the natives' own way of doing things.[35]

The nature of the task before them compelled the missionaries to learn the Indian languages. Indeed, from the very beginning of the American Board program, Worcester had planned that at least one missionary at each station should become proficient in the tribal language, though he persisted in requiring that classes be conducted in English. The missionaries had always realized that the children and the adults constituted different problems. Although they pinned their hopes on the younger generation, they were sufficiently confident in the merit of their message to think that it would affect every strata of native society. Hence they made a significant distinction in method. The elder generation would be addressed in the native tongue. The philanthropic expectation of a total and immediate alteration rested mainly on the more susceptible chil-

35. "Memoranda relative to the Cherokee Mission," Apr. and May 1822, ABC 18.3.1.II: 154; Thomas L. McKenney to William Chamberlain, July 25, 1825, Letters Sent, Off. Indian Affairs (M-21), Roll 2: 103; *Missionary Herald*, XXII (1826), 47–49; "Articles of a Convention . . . ," D. S. Butrick to Jeremiah Evarts, Mar. 26, 1829, ABC 18.3.1.IV: 34. See also Berkhofer, *Salvation and the Savage*, 101–106; Isaac McCoy to Lewis Cass, May 6, 1828, Letters Sent, Off. Indian Affairs (M-21), Roll 4: 433; McKenney to E. Whittlesey, Jan. 21, 1829, *ibid.*, Roll 5: 276–277; McKenney to Thomas Henderson, Jan. 30, 1829, *ibid.*, 285. The importance of Cherokee writing is open to question. The major language of the *Cherokee Phoenix* (New Echota, Ga.) was English. It usually printed about 3 columns in Cherokee and about 17 in English. Cherokee being a more economical language, the disparity is not as great as a perusal of the paper makes it appear. But the reader has the impression that the important material was printed in English. See Thurman Wilkins, *Cherokee Tragedy: The Story of the Ridge Family and the Decimation of a People* (New York, 1970), 193.

dren. Experience proved to the missionaries that they could demand only a slower and less pervasive change in the older people.[36]

With the advent of Sequoya's wonderful achievement and the gradual intensification in the 1820s of loyalty among the southern Indians to the newly vitalized tribal state, the missionaries saw a particular need to use the Indian languages. Kingsbury, among the Choctaws, was especially attuned to the trend in favor of the native tongues. He did not abandon English; proficiency in it remained the principal object of the educational program. But he encouraged Cyrus Byington at the Mayhew station to cultivate spoken and written Choctaw and to prepare books in that tongue for the schools and for church services. Missionaries at the other Choctaw stations learned the tribal language, as did a number at the Cherokee missions of the American Board. By the end of the decade, the effort to eliminate the native tongue had failed. In 1830 Jeremiah Evarts opposed the establishment of a boarding school among the Chippewas unless books could be found in their language and missionaries could be trained to conduct services in Chippewa. Some initial preaching in English through an interpreter might be acceptable, he thought, but success would come only if the missionaries communicated in the Indian language.[37]

In seeking to eliminate the tribal languages, philanthropists had stimulated a movement among the Indians to restore their native tongues. But this irony could not be explained merely as a response to a direct attack by a foreign culture. The Cherokees in particular reacted, but the manner in which they chose to do so paid tribute in part to the success of the civilizing program. The Indians elected,

36. Samuel Worcester to Ard Hoyt, Cyrus Kingsbury, and Daniel Butrick *et al.*, Mar. 14, 1818, ABC 1.01.III: 36; *Panoplist*, XVI (1820), 561; Alfred Finney and Cephas Washburn to Jeremiah Evarts, Sept. 7, 1822, *Missionary Herald*, XVIII (1822), 382–383. See also Kingsbury to James Barbour, Feb. 1826, Letters Received, Off. Indian Affairs (M-234), Schools, Roll 773: 228–229. McKenney objected in an answer to Kingsbury (Apr. 10, 1826, Letters Sent, Off. Indian Affairs [M-21], Roll 3: 20) that he wanted no concessions to the Choctaw language. Kingsbury replied that there was no basic change in the policy to teach English first in the schools; the native language was for the adults only. See Kingsbury to McKenney, June 5, 1826, Letters Received, Off. Indian Affairs (M-234), Schools, Roll 773: 233–236.

37. Cyrus Kingsbury, "Elliot Journal," *Missionary Herald*, XIX (1823), 114–115; Kingsbury to Calhoun, Oct. 16, 1823, Letters Received, Sec. War (M-271), Roll 4: 687–688; Kingsbury to James Barbour, Oct. 28, 1825, Letters Received, Off. Indian Affairs (M-234), Schools, Roll 772: 584; Kingsbury to Barbour, Oct. 21, 1826, *ibid.*, Roll 773: 305–306; Kingsbury to McKenney, Feb. 15, 1830, *ibid.*, Roll 774: 472–473; Jeremiah Evarts to J. D. Stevens, Nov. 23, 1830, ABC 1.01.X: 379–380.

not to return to their traditional oral society, but to engraft an essential element of the white man's mode of communication onto their ancient language. In this case, the medium proved more significant than the content. The acceptance of written communication constituted an important step in the native movement toward civilization.

The missionaries probably understood this only dimly; realizing that they had no chance against the tribal reawakening for which they were partially responsible, the missionaries compromised— mainly for tactical reasons—though McKenney, who had done so much to keep the flame of philanthropy burning, refused any concessions. He remained convinced that the amelioration of the Indians required but one step of major importance: the prompt abandonment of all the elements of savagery. Correct in conceiving English essential to the obliteration of the Indian's tribal mode of life, he failed to perceive the complexity of the process of transition. The missionaries compromised, but they persisted in their ultimate determination to change the Indian's way of life. The need to change their plans did not affect their optimistic evaluation of the natives' progress. Demanding a transition so complete, philanthropists generally found it easy to see every small accomplishment as a contribution to the greater end.

6

The civilizing program did, in fact, meet with considerable success. The substantial mixed blood population was already strongly influenced by the white man's ways. Farming, grazing, and home manufactures had caught on in most of the tribes. A small cadre of Indian youth learned to read and write English. The white man's religion became an issue in tribal affairs. More and more Indians seemed to behave like white men and even to think like white men. Of course, such signs did not tell everything about the internal condition of native society or about the possibilities for incorporation, but they did confirm in a practical way what had been predicted theoretically.

Much of Jefferson's information on the condition of the Indians came from his confidant, Benjamin Hawkins, who went into the Indian country to stay in the 1790s. Until his death in 1816, Hawkins served as agent for the Creeks and as one of the foremost secular advocates of the civilizing policy. He promoted an intensely practical program for the Creeks with an object equally as grandiose as that supported by the missionaries. In order to be civilized, he counseled the Indians to cease wandering, abandon the hunting economy, fence, plow, and plant their fields, and acquire the skills for domestic industry. He also envisioned a complete revamping of the tribal political order, a more tightly defined public authority with more power for the chiefs, and a national council under the direction of the agent. Beginning with very specific objects, he intended the final overthrow of tribal society.[38] Hawkins possessed a quiet assurance that his program would be successful, although the demands he made upon native society cut deep and generated animosity that rose to the surface in the Creek War at the end of his career. In the meantime, however, he worked busily at making over the Indian in the image of the white man. His usual report indicated slow but regular progress: "Success finally is no longer doubtful," he wrote in 1803. He predicted no apocalypse, but he always seemed fully convinced that the native would soon be civilized.[39] From so confident a correspondent, Jefferson took his own sanguine opinions of the Indian's future.

Once the more fully organized and more ideologically thorough programs of the missionary societies replaced the desultory efforts of the 1790s and the first one and a half decades of the nineteenth century, the philanthropists tended to expect more immediate results. The conditions among the natives lent credence to these anticipations. The progress made seemed indicative of even greater advances to come, and the complete transformation demanded by the notion of Christian conversion supplied the basis for a final resolution for the philanthropic enterprise. With the end apparently in easy reach, the meliorist rhetoric became more expansive. The realistic letdown, always near in the 1820s, proved all the more painful for the level of enthusiasm that had preceded it. The program of specific improvements continued and met with the usual successes, but the process of internal disintegration and nationalist consolida-

38. Benjamin Hawkins, "A Sketch of the Creek Country, in the Years 1798 and 1799," Georgia Historical Society, *Collections*, III (1848), 27, 30, 68–80; Hawkins, "General View," Dec. 8, 1801, *American State Papers, Indian Affairs*, I, 646–648; Hawkins to James McHenry, Jan. 6, 1797, *Letters of Benjamin Hawkins, 1796–1806* (Ga. Hist. Soc., *Colls.*, IX [Savannah, 1916]), 57–58, hereafter cited as *Letters of Hawkins*.

39. Benjamin Hawkins to Thomas Jefferson, July 23, 1800, Jefferson Papers; Hawkins, "General View," Dec. 8, 1801, *American State Papers, Indian Affairs*, I, 647; Hawkins to Jefferson, July 11, 1803, Jefferson Papers; Hawkins to John Milledge, Aug. 11, 1805, Benjamin Hawkins Papers, Department of Archives and History, Atlanta; letter from Hawkins, dated Aug. 5, 1808, in the *Republican and Savannah Evening Ledger*, Aug. 27, 1808, quoted in Merritt B. Pound, *Benjamin Hawkins—Indian Agent* (Athens, Ga., 1951), 147.

tion of the new Indian states also became apparent. Still, the characteristic reaction until the mid-1820s remained hopeful.

In 1827 the *Missionary Herald* recorded the signs of gradual improvement among the Cherokees by merely listing the increases in domestic animals, implements of manufacture and agriculture, schools, and ferries from 1810 to the time of writing. The jump was substantial in each category, and in some the numbers had doubled. From the Chickasaws a report in 1824 noted the important class differences between the half bloods and chiefs and the more lowly, full-blood Indians. The leaders now looked more like white men, and even the ordinary tribesmen had made substantial progress. Such savage customs as infanticide, witch-hunting, and suicide had been abandoned. Almost all families had settled down in permanent houses and cultivated small farms with stocks of cattle. By 1830 Jeremiah Evarts could defend the philanthropic program in the argument over removal by citing the notable improvements among the Cherokees. Most wore civilized clothing; the women grew the raw materials and did the spinning and weaving. He knew of no Cherokee family dependent on game for its food. The tribesmen lived in a variety of houses, mostly log cabins, poorly furnished. A modest number could read and write English; a majority could both read and write the Cherokee language. Moreover, the establishment of a formal political order showed positive signs of progress. John Johnston reported "slow but steady progress" among the Ohio tribes. Of the Seneca, he noted that "they labour more steadily, have better houses and farms, and appear more like white people in their dress and manners."[40]

The decline in drunkenness, one of the common evidences of improvement, revealed the complexity of the process of change. The missionaries and agents were happy when they saw a new development in tribal habits, but they knew that nothing would be accomplished if civilized vices replaced primitive obscurantism. As dedicated reformers, they wished to eradicate not only the last remains of savage existence but also whatever signs they found of

40. *Missionary Herald*, XXIII (1827), 116; *Cherokee Phoenix* (New Echota, Ga.), May 6, 1828; John C. Stuart to Thomas L. McKenney, Sept. 27, 1824, Letters Received, Off. Indian Affairs (M-234), Schools, Roll 772: 391–392; Samuel A. Worcester to William S. Coodey, Mar. 15, 1830, in Robert Sparks Walker, *Torchlights to the Cherokees: The Brainerd Mission* (New York, 1931), 250–255; John Johnston, "Account of the Present State of the Indian Tribes Inhabiting Ohio . . . ," Am. Antiq. Soc., *Archaeologia Americana*, I, 274, 276–277. See also John Ridge to Albert Gallatin, Mar. 10, 1826, Gallatin Papers, Box 64–3, fol. 42.

civilization's fall from grace. From the beginning, therefore, humanitarians fought as strongly against the advance of civilized vices as they did against the persistence of savage customs. They drew no significant distinctions between the disorder in the life of the wilderness and that in the lives of whites who did not adhere to the moral code of the missionaries.[41]

Missionaries and government officials especially welcomed any promising evaluation of the civilizing program obtained from the tribesmen, since the opinion would itself be evidence of progress. The Indians lived closer to the center of change, and even in the turmoil of their culture, they maintained an area of privity that white men recognized as offering a unique perception of their own future. In addition, evidences of native cooperation in the program played an important part in countering the tendency to place too much stress on the disintegration of native society. Indians actually supporting the program by farming the land or sending their children to the missionary schools were welcome sights; above all, the leadership's decision to spend tribal funds for establishing schools instead of squandering them on frivolities constituted reassuring evidence of progress.[42]

When the various lines of Indian-white relations converged in the crisis of the 1820s, philanthropists inflated their rhetoric even more and played thoughtlessly on the coming success. The doubts had long since been uncovered, emerging with more frequency as the pressure on the Indian to move became more intense. At the same time, humanitarians seemed determined to convince the world and perhaps themselves that the civilizing program had brought incorporation into sight. From the field came encouraging news of progress. The missionaries to the western Cherokees at Dwight announced in 1822 that "the results, which have already followed the efforts for their improvement are sufficient proof that the hope of complete success is not chimerical." The next year the hopeful tone persisted. Each day's experience strengthened the conviction, the

41. Cyrus Kingsbury to John C. Calhoun, Jan. 15, 1823, Letters Received, Sec. War (M-271), Roll 4: 708; Jeremiah Evarts to Calhoun, July 27, 1826, Letters Received, Off. Indian Affairs (M-234), Schools, Roll 772: 65–66; Kingsbury to Thomas L. McKenney, *ibid.*, Roll 774: 464–470.

42. Speech of Hopoie Mico to Benjamin Hawkins, July 15, 1806, *Letters of Hawkins*, 443; John C. Calhoun to John McKee, Aug. 12, 1820, Letters Sent, Sec. War (M-15), Roll 5: 9; Thomas L. McKenney to Calhoun, Jan. 1821, Letters Sent, Supt. Indian Trade (M-16), Roll 6: 306; Calhoun to William Ward, Oct. 2, 1821, Letters Sent, Sec. War (M-15), Roll 5: 162; McKenney to Chiefs of Chickasaw, Feb. 16, 1829, Letters Sent, Off. Indian Affairs (M-21), Roll 5: 306–308.

mission station reported, that the plan for native reform was practical, that the only means required were those "within the reach of an enlightened and benevolent community" to make the Indians "as happy as enlightened and as moral as any part of the United States or any part of the christian world." In 1824 just an inkling of doubt seeped into the missionaries' rosy world, but they seemed to have little difficulty in brushing it aside. Civilizing all the Indians within the jurisdiction of the United States would be "the work of years and must incur no little expense"; yet it would certainly be accomplished once the program began efficient operation. "Under the foster hand of the general government," the Indians *"will, ere long* become such a portion of our population."[43]

Within the government, McKenney held the most enthusiastic opinions about the coming success. He filled his correspondence with his confidence that the Indian would soon be transformed. "Yes—Happy Osages!" he wrote to that primitive western tribe in 1820, "the days of your gloom are about to close. Already does the light gleam across, and fringe the skirts of the clouds which have so long hung over you." The season for doubting had ended. Those who had taken the time to examine the problem could not question the possibility of introducing "into the aboriginal Intellect the lessons of civilization." If there was a problem, it concerned merely the choice of means. "There needs nothing, thoroughly to reform the Indians, as a race, but a system adequate in extent, and power; in means, and in energy, to civilize the whole (I mean the rising generation, of course) *in a single generation."* He found no "insuperable difficulties," he repeated many times; it was only necessary to pursue the present program to effect "a complete reformation of the principles and pursuits of the American Indian." Having taken the highest ground, as he well might considering the intellectual and emotional investment he had put into the philanthropic program, he became that much more susceptible to the doubts that soon settled over an important segment of the humanitarian mind.[44]

43. Alfred Finney and Cephas Washburn to John C. Calhoun, Oct. 1, 1822, Letters Received, Sec. War (M-271), Roll 3: 106; Finney and Washburn to Calhoun, Oct. 1823, *ibid.*, Roll 4: 562–564; Finney and Washburn to Calhoun, Oct. 1, 1824, Letters Received, Off. Indian Affairs (M-234), Schools, Roll 772: 85–86.

44. Thomas L. McKenney to P. Milledoler, Aug. 9, 1820, Letters Sent, Supt. Indian Trade (M-16), Roll 6: 31; McKenney to Bishop McEndree, Mar. 13, 1820, *ibid.*, Roll 5: 423; McKenney to E. Whittlesey, Jan. 9, 829, Letters Sent, Off. Indian Affairs, Roll 5: 276–277; McKenney to John C. Calhoun, Nov. 24, 1824, *ibid.*, Roll 1: 238.

At times even the natural tentativeness of any human situation seemed crabbed before the putative accomplishments of the philanthropic plan. Predictions of the future came easily when evidence could be found that the Indian would soon be incorporated, but it was daring indeed to proclaim success to a world that need only look about to discover the truth. Hawkins might only be considered garrulous or perhaps premature when he announced in 1798 that "the Cherokees are no longer to be called Savages, they are a decent orderly set of people." But McKenney reached the limit of his optimism by contending in 1825 of the same tribe: "They may be considered as a civilized people."[45] Doubtless this consistent strain of optimism grew out of the very nature of humanitarian thought. It tended to ignore the failures and exaggerate the successes.

7

In so far as educating the Indians and teaching them farming might form the basis for incorporation, the philanthropists had adopted a sensible scheme. They could hardly have been expected to discern that civilization and incorporation represented very different phenomena. The more the southern tribes chose civilization, the less were the possibilities for their incorporation. Furthermore, the parsimony of the government and the episodic direction given to the program could be set down to the character of the age. What more could be expected from a loosely organized political order with a visceral conviction that great ends would be consummated from only limited means? Precisely this vague optimism that nature would fulfill its destiny in civilizing the Indians posed insuperable obstacles to the bureaucratic implementation of the plan. It proved strong enough to throttle any hesitations but too lacking in programmatic detail to insure success.

Yet the plausibility of the scheme could not be denied. A New World in the throes of dynamic proliferation provided the setting for the natives' translation into the white man's image. The benignity of the natural order accounted for both the need to accomplish so laudable an end and the affirmation of the Indians' capacity to achieve it. Even apparent historic antagonisms seemed to vanish before the imperatives of philanthropy. Secular and re-

---

45. Benjamin Hawkins to George Washington, Nov. 4, 1798 (typed transcript), Hawkins Papers; Thomas L. McKenney to James Barbour, Dec. 13, 1825, Letters Sent, Off. Indian Affairs (M-21), Roll 2: 300; Isaac McCoy, *Remarks on the Practicability of Indian Reform, Embracing Their Colonization*, 2d ed. (New York, 1829), 28.

ligious humanitarianism contrived a judicious combination for bringing the native within the compass of civilization. Jeffersonianism had but a fleeting doubt before it rushed into alliance with the evangelical and the more staid church organizations to give the tribesmen both Christianity and civilization. When all had been said, few could conceive of the one without the other. The conception of the transference of civilization to the Indian in a simple, one-to-one transaction almost came to grief on the question of Indian languages, but the missionaries solved even that difficult problem. All roads led to the grand reconciliation of Jeffersonian optimism, at its height just at the moment of precipitate collapse.

Eventually, the doubt so evident in the hollowness and uncritical naïveté of the optimistic rhetoric demanded an accounting, which came in the 1820s with the scheme for removal and the continuation of the civilizing program west of the Mississippi. But from the beginning the philanthropic mind, in great measure unconsciously, had formulated a basic method for dealing with the threat of failure. Jeffersonians may have been visionary, but they were also men of affairs busily about the process of conquering the continent. They knew something about the needs of the moment, even if they continued faithfully to anticipate a spectacular future. These immediate necessities, the slowness of cultural transference, the constant erosion of the stability of native society, and the uncontrollable force of the frontier settlements, fed the repeated crises of Indian-white relations and demanded of philanthropy a more subtle plan for the native's future. As a consequence, manipulation, the habit of working by indirection, became as characteristic of the humanitarian scheme as the straightforward evangelism of the missionary organizations.

Chapter VI

Manipulation

In attempting to civilize the Indian, government agents and missionaries encountered both the ineffectuality of their own idealism and the formidable cultural resistance of the native populations. As a result, Jeffersonian reformers, sensing the possibility of failure, told the Indian only what he needed to know. In principle, they advocated a rational presentation of civilized manners to the native society with every anticipation of acceptance; but realistically, they sensed that the processes of cultural transfer would not follow neat lines of development. Faced with a persistent lag between anticipation and actuality, their philanthropy became increasingly manipulative. Idealism and environmentalism assumed a prompt transformation of aboriginal society, but the tribes, despite an avid appetite for certain elements from the white man's world, manifested a perverse tendency to retain a substantial portion of their Indian way of life. When the native failed to recognize his true interest in the benefits offered by civilization, he could not be allowed to follow his own misguided path to oblivion. In keeping with humanitarian responsibility, the philanthropists arranged the process of amelioration so that the Indian would act in his own best interests, even though contrary to his inclinations. If the Indian could not be introduced into civilization through the formal procedures of presentation and conversion, then he would have to be slipped in through adroit manipulation.

Since the reformer always believed that he knew best, manipulation involved no qualification of altruism. His affection for the tribal order did not inhibit his determination to transform it into civilized society. The doctrine of progressive change assumed a development from savagery to civilization; for the philanthropist the ultimate altruism was to aid this process, and for the Indian the final prudence was to acquiesce in its unfolding. The reformer became the agent of progress, the aborigine his primary subject. Imperceptibly, amelioration lent itself to manipulation, to the subtle and partly corrosive transformation of the Indian into the white man's image of himself.

Jeffersonian altruism knew the uses of power. Alternating between overbearing menace and ingratiating supervision, it never allowed the Indian to forget his weakness. Should he too readily take benevolent interest as concession to his independence, the proliferating force of civilization would remind him that he survived at the white man's sufferance. "The principles," wrote Jefferson, "on which our conduct towards the Indians should be founded are justice and fear."[1] He defined justice according to the imperatives of progressive improvement: it concerned the ends of philanthropy. And he made fear its motive force. Through the constant reiteration of these themes in his communications with the tribes, Jefferson intended to imbed in the native mind a conviction of the white man's strength and the impotence of savagery to survive.

He used the special locutions he believed characteristic of the native languages to warn the Indians repeatedly that the white people were as numerous as the "leaves of the trees" or the "stars in the heavens," that they were all "gun men," and that the Indians must be fully apprised of their superiority. He always mixed these cautions with reassurances of goodwill and hope for a bright future, though the message could not have been lost on the Indians. As a concrete form of intimidation, visiting tribal delegations would be shown the vast resources of the white man's world. The government instructed its agents residing in the Indian country to impress upon the natives the preponderant power of the white man and the ineffectuality of the Indian capacity for war. "The difference between the strength and resources of the United States," wrote William H. Crawford to the commissioners on the way to a treaty with the northwestern Indians in 1816, "compared with the whole body of Indians, must convince the reflecting part of their warriors, that apprehension of Indian aggression can never enter into the views of the President in negotiating with them. Nothing could be more fatal to the Indian race." Sometimes bluntly, but sometimes also

1. Jefferson to Benjamin Hawkins, Aug. 13, 1786, Boyd, ed., *Jefferson Papers*, X, 240; Hawkins to Henry Dearborn, Nov. 14, 1801, Letters Received, Sec. War (M-271), Roll 1: 31.

with a delicate attention to the Indian's sensibility, the white man tried to convince the tribesman of his inferiority.[2]

The threat of coercion always lurked in the background of Indian-white relations. The government drove hard bargains for tribal lands and usually obtained them at its own convenience, for what it wished to give, and with the understanding that it might not always be possible to retain the Indian's goodwill. The tribesman either owed money that he could not pay or needed some commodity for which the white man knew he would pay a high price. In the overall balance of the relationship, the native worked at a disadvantage. Civilized man confronted the Indian as a conqueror, outraged creditor, or prospective buyer with full control of the market. And he always demanded respect for his ascendant power on the continent. The white man established the terms of contact between the two societies. Describing the relationship frankly, Edmund P. Gaines wrote that "every effort in the work of civilization, to be effectual, must accord with the immutable principles of justice. The savage must be taught and compelled to do that which is right, and to abstain from doing that which is wrong. The poisonous cup of barbarism cannot be taken from the lips of the savage by the mild voice of reason alone; the strong mandate of justice must be resorted to, and enforced."[3]

In practice, the white man sometimes moderated the assertion of his power without abandoning his ultimate object. Even the Indian in decline retained a modicum of pride, and the philanthropists willingly conceded him the forms of independence, if only to achieve their ends more quickly. In the same sense, the government recognized the tribes in interminable negotiations over alliance in war and land cession in peace. Humanitarian treatment of the natives covered the full range of human sensitivity: reason, parental guidance, solicitous concern, occasionally condescension, and a variety

2. Saul K. Padover, ed., *The Complete Jefferson* . . . (New York, 1943), 464, 474, 497–498; Richardson, ed., *Papers of the Presidents,* I, 340–342; Henry Dearborn to DeWitt Clinton, Dec. 30, 1803, Letters Sent, Sec. War (M-15), Roll 1: 406–407; Foster, *Jeffersonian America,* ed. Davis, 42; William H. Crawford to Benjamin Parke *et al.,* May 3, 1816, Letters Sent, Sec. War (M-15), Roll 3: 338–339; Benjamin Hawkins to Andrew Pickins *et al.,* June 20, 1785 (typed transcript), Hawkins Papers, Ga. Dept. of Archives and History.

3. Padover, ed., *Complete Jefferson,* 474; William H. Crawford to William Cocke, June 26, 1816, Letters Sent, Sec. War (M-15), Roll 3: 387; Henry Dearborn to Return J. Meigs, June 21, 1804, *ibid.,* Roll 2: 6; Dearborn to Hawkins, May 24, 1803, *ibid.,* Roll 1: 350–351; Thomas L. McKenney to James Barbour, Dec. 26, 1827, Letters Sent, Off. Indian Affairs (M-21), Roll 4: 209; Edmund P. Gaines to the secretary of war, Dec. 4, 1817, *American State Papers, Indian Affairs,* II, 161.

of other attitudes. The form, however, did not make the substance. Savagery made the Indian inferior in the white man's eyes; any gesture of benevolence toward the native carried with it the possibility of infantilization. Though the philanthropic attitude publicly assumed the sovereignty of the tribal organism, the reality of Indian-white interchange called for the tribesman's gradual psychic subjection.

Many efforts to convince the Indian that his interest lay in conforming to the white man's plan exuded an air of scarcely concealed exasperation. "Would it not please you," said Timothy Pickering to the Iroquois, "to have as many necessaries and good things as they know? and instead of decreasing, or becoming fewer and fewer, do you not wish to increase your numbers, and to grow stronger and stronger? I think I need not wait for your answer: you are men of understanding." Or Henry Dearborn, demanding a landed reimbursement from the Creeks for services rendered, could append to the agent's instructions: "I see no good reason why they should refuse it."[4] In a white man's world, reason and interest were on the white man's side.

More often than reason, the agents of humanitarianism employed parental guidance. Because he doubted the native's sense of responsibility, Calhoun favored paying tribal annuities directly to the independent philanthropic agencies rather than risk an intermediate stop in Indian hands. For similar reasons, Hawkins opposed one of the prime items in the civilizing program, the individual possession of land. He had no confidence in the native's ability to retain ownership in the face of the wiles of the speculator and the temptations of civilization. From his own considerable experience, Pickering doubted the strength of the tribes themselves to maintain their boundaries against the persistence of private interests. He tried to impress on the Iroquois their weakness in negotiations, using examples of their past embarrassments, and he issued a list of instructions to them for treating with the whites.[5]

Such goodwill invariably came mixed with condescension. The Indians' "imperfect state of society," wrote Crawford to Andrew Jackson, their inability to make individual warriors conform to

4. Pickering to Council of the Six Nations, July 5, 1791, Pickering Papers, LX, 84; Henry Dearborn to Benjamin Hawkins, Feb. 19, 1803, Letters Sent, Sec. War (M-15), Roll 1: 325–326.

5. John C. Calhoun to Philip E. Thomas, June 14, 1820, Letters Sent, Sec. War (M-15), Roll 4: 446; Benjamin Hawkins to Henry Dearborn, Sept. 6, 1801, Letters Received, Sec. War (M-271), Roll 1: 27; Timothy Pickering to Iroquois Council, Oct. 13, 1794, Pickering Papers, LX, 224–228, Mass. Hist. Soc. (microfilm).

tribal policy, frequently made it necessary to "depart from the usages established between civilized states," though we ought, he added, to avoid carrying this principle beyond necessary circumstances. In any case, both Calhoun and Jackson spoke against negotiating with the tribes as though they possessed sovereign powers. And the fiction of sovereignty notwithstanding, Indian-white relations required the constant lubrication of presents. The white man knew well enough that dealing with aborigines was not the same as dealing with civilized men; it required a special set of definitions, always manipulative and sometimes openly coercive.[6]

The language of Indian-white relations reflected the Indian's tributary position. The tribes, having "ceased to be an object of terror," in Calhoun's words, "have become that of commiseration." Jefferson probably spent more time cultivating the art of commiserating with them than anyone else in the late eighteenth and early nineteenth centuries. He always employed a conciliatory tone, but it held a note of realistic necessity. There could be no doubt that the Indian's situation was precarious, that he faced the stark choice of civilization or destruction. Jefferson conveyed this message through a contrived form of linguistic primitivism. He spoke to the Indians in the manner adopted by whites at Indian negotiations, imitating the simple rhythms supposedly characteristic of native eloquence. But the additional ingredient of crisis led to a coddling, superficially ingratiating tendency to infantilize the Indian. The language purported to be childlike in its primitive simplicity, the principal form of address being "Children." Jefferson gave the impression of a slightly exasperated patriarch who, knowing the cruelty of the real world and the vulnerability of his charges, tried desperately to shield them from the destruction he was certain would be inevitable if they were left to their own devices. Basically, he had no confidence in the Indian's capacity to make his own way. The responsibility for his future lay with the white man. Confronted with the overwhelming competence of civilization, the Indian could only be considered a child.[7]

Like Jefferson, McKenney refused to accept the natives on an equal footing. Constantly faced with recalcitrant tribes that seemed incapable of recognizing the requirements of their situation, he

6. William H. Crawford to Andrew Jackson, May 21, 1816, Letters Sent, Sec. War (M-15), Roll 3: 357–358; John C. Calhoun to Jackson, Nov. 16, 1821, *ibid.*, Roll 5: 191; Weld, *Travels through the States*, 360–361; Calhoun to Lewis McLane, Jan. 22, 1825, Letters Sent, Off. Indian Affairs (M-21), Roll 1: 318.

7. Padover, ed., *Complete Jefferson*, chap. 12; Foster, *Jeffersonian America*, ed. Davis, 22.

more and more adopted the methods of manipulation. He retained a deep sympathy for Indians, but the day-to-day effort to rearrange the native world drove him to the role of arbitrary overseer. To be sure, he did no more than the implications of philanthropic superiority required. He saw a childlike Indian for whom he would provide guidance and, if this should prove ineffectual, gentle and perhaps clandestine assistance toward maturity.

When intertribal conflict seemed likely to spill over onto the frontier in 1821, affecting the white settlers and interfering with the progress of the civilizing scheme, McKenney wrote to the Senate: "Our Indians stand pretty much in the relation to the Government as do our children to us. They are equally dependent; and need, not unfrequently, the exercise of parental authority to detach them from those ways which might involve both their peace and their lives. It would not be considered just for our children to be let alone to settle their quarrels in their own way; but rather that superior power be interposed for the adjustment of their differences for them." In time the infantile phrasing became a familiar motif in McKenney's discussions of Indian affairs. "Indians are children," he wrote when informed that the Creeks had squandered money paid them in exchange for land, "and require to be nursed, and counselled, and directed as such." Henceforth, payment should be made in goods. On hearing a complaint that the tribes intended to divert funds previously spent on schools to less useful purposes, he replied irately: "It will not be sanctioned. Indians, I have found out, are only children, and can be properly managed, only, by being treated as such. It requires care, and a knowledge of their character to guide them—but they can be guided." The philanthropic conception itself supplied the sanction for such overbearing patronization. Reacting like a spurned father, McKenney revealed the deeply felt stewardship of humanitarianism. The Indians were "nothing but children, and . . . nothing would be so good for them as to treat them as such—provided the object of the treatment was to improve their condition; and those who undertook their guardianship were qualified, both as it regards the *power,* and the *will,* to advance their happiness."[8]

8. Thomas L. McKenney to the Senate, Dec. 27, 1821, *American State Papers, Indian Affairs,* II, 264; McKenney to John Cocke, Jan. 23, 1827, Letters Sent, Off. Indian Affairs (M-21), Roll 3: 328; McKenney to Thomas C. Stuart, Apr. 14, 1828, *ibid.,* Roll 4: 406; McKenney to Heman Lincoln, Sept. 28, 1829, *ibid.,* Roll 6: 100. See also Henry Dearborn to William Henry Harrison, May 24, 1805, Letters Sent, Sec. War (M-15), Roll 2: 78–79; Return J. Meigs to William H. Crawford, Aug. 19, 1816, *American State Papers, Indian Affairs,* II, 114; Lela Barnes, ed., "Journal of Isaac McCoy for the Exploring Expedition of 1828," *Kansas Historical Quarterly,* V (1936), 250.

2

The distribution of civilized goods among the Indian tribes formed part of the indirect process of acculturation. In order to speed the process and to shield the natives against the deleterious consequences that accompanied the trade, the government required licenses for Indian traders and established a system of factories in 1796. Of course, the government found far-reaching political reasons for controlling commerce in the wilderness. International politics in the New World required an influence among the tribes; the continuous expansion of settlement dictated the need to cultivate peace with the native inhabitants. Furnishing the Indians with a steady, inexpensive supply of civilized products served the ends of both politics and philanthropy.

While McKenney occupied the office of superintendent of Indian trade, with the principal function of directing the government factories, he used the position to promote the civilizing program. Though only a minor functionary, he seems to have been permitted considerable latitude in the exercise of his office. Under his guidance, the factories supplied the Indians with the articles necessary for security against the elements, as well as farming tools and exhortations to abandon hunting. They also attempted to foster among the tribes a high opinion of the white man's goodwill. Except for the operations of the factories, maintained McKenney, "savagism would characterise, and deform [the native tribes]; and desolation would brood over minds, over which civilization and social life, and the principles of improvement, have a fixed and permanent controul." The factors introduced into the Indian country articles that otherwise would not have been available. Divorced from the destructive consequences of the profit motive, government factories, in Dearborn's words, inculcated in the native mind the "propriety and usefulness of a gradual introduction of the arts of civilization." McKenney stressed the importance of the factor's subtle influence on the tribes. "Our intercourse with the Indians[,] it is desireable[,] should be conducted by men whose examples of goodness and practical industry shall be uniform in order that such lessons may be carried in amongst these unfortunate people for their observation and imitation."[9]

9. Thomas L. McKenney to Isaac Thomas, Dec. 14, 1816, Letters Sent, Supt. Indian Trade (M-16), Roll 4: 202–206; McKenney to John C. Calhoun, Aug. 19, 1818, Letters Received, Sec. War (M-271), Roll 2: 675–699; Henry Dearborn to Peter Chouteau, July 17, 1804, Letters Sent, Sec. War (M-15), Roll 2: 10; McKenney to Josiah Butler, Mar. 31, 1820, Letters Sent, Supt. Indian Trade (M-16), Roll 6: 425.

Soon after giving the principal role in civilizing the Indians to independent charitable and missionary organizations, the government abandoned the factory system. The trading interests opposed it, and there was serious doubt that it had yielded important results. Fittingly, however, after a short retirement McKenney accepted a position in the War Department, where he handled Indian affairs and the civilizing plan directly rather than through the remote influence of the trading office.[10]

The War Department had long recognized the need to place the implements of civilization in the Indians' hands. Almost anything practical would do, as long as it was not obviously destructive and aided the tribes in learning agriculture and the basics of the white man's life. As Alexander James Dallas explained in 1815, "The establishment of a new Indian agency in the Illinois country would restore harmony in the area and help in ameliorating the situation of the Indians . . . , by facilitating the attainment of those articles, indispensably necessary in the first stages of civilization." Incidental items such as clothing were often supplied generously— sixteen suits to the Chickasaws and fifty for the Choctaws in 1794, plus blankets, hats, shirting, and the homespun that the Indians coveted. But the philanthropic plan favored farming implements. In 1800 Hawkins merely intimated the need for such articles and the War Department spent a thousand dollars on hoes and axes for the Choctaws and requested another thousand the next year for the neighboring tribes.[11]

Later, with the development of the complicated system of Indian

10. Ora Brooks Peake, *A History of the United States Indian Factory System, 1795–1822* (Denver, 1954), 3, 8; Francis Paul Prucha, *American Indian Policy in the Formative Years: The Indian Trade and Intercourse Acts, 1790–1834* (Cambridge, Mass., 1962), 84–93. See also Herman J. Viola, "Thomas L. McKenney and the Administration of Indian Affairs, 1824–30" (Ph.D. diss., Indiana University, 1970), 31–34.

11. Alexander J. Dallas to James Madison, July 7, 1815, Letters Sent, Sec. War (M-15), Roll 3: 241–243; Tench Coxe to Tench Francis, July 15, 1794, Letters of Tench Coxe, Commissioner of Revenue, Relating to the Procurement of Military, Naval, and Indian Supplies, 1794–1796 (M-74), 77, Records of the Bureau of Indian Affairs (RG 75), National Archives, hereafter cited as Letters of Coxe (M-74); Jonathan Halstead to Henry Dearborn, Oct. 9, 1802, Letter Book, Creek Trading House (M-4), 231; Dearborn to Israel Whelan, Mar. 4, 1802, Letters Sent, Sec. War (M-15), Roll 1: 176–177; John Sibley to Dearborn, 1807, Letters Received, Sec. War (M-271), Roll 1: 448–451; Samuel Dexter to Benjamin Hawkins, Nov. 26, 1800, Letters Sent, Sec. War (M-15), Roll 1: 4; William H. Crawford to Chickasaws, June 6, 1816, *ibid.*, Roll 3: 373; Thomas L. McKenney to William Clark, Aug. 23, 1824, Letters Sent, Off. Indian Affairs (M-21), Roll 1: 183; Dearborn to William Cooke, Nov. 4, 1803, Letters Sent, Sec. War (M-15), Roll 1: 387; George Graham to John Mason, June 20, 1815, *ibid.*, 229–230.

annuities, the tribes had merely to request the needed supplies. Believing that the Indians wasted the money given them, the government tried not to deal in cash. Almost any species of goods would be better, even frivolities, but the agencies and missionary stations favored the distribution of tools. McKenney claimed that traders eager to sell whiskey "put up" the Wyandots to demand specie for their annuity in 1819. "Their annuity grounds thronged by the avaricious and speculating traders, soon displayed a scene of riot and drunkeness and murder which resulted in a total loss to the Indians of all value from that year's annuity. They *felt* in their Nakedness and wants, how this had happened, and requested of the Government that their annuities might in future be sent them in usefull articles for farming and the like."[12] Although the government frequently discharged its obligations by paying the Indians in cash, agents and missionaries encouraged the tribes to use their annuities to further their progress toward civilization.

The government made efforts to tailor goods specifically for the native taste. European manufacturers had long since developed a special line of merchandise for the primitive New World trade. Agents of the government received instructions to be mindful of Indian desires as well as needs. The policy had a practical basis, since the government believed that expensive, durable goods would be wasted on primitive men still largely improvident. Such statements as "these articles are to be of the quality usually furnished to this description of people in the way of Trade" described materials ordered for the Indians. "Our Copper Kettles," wrote the factor at Michilimackinac, "will not sell for much more than first cost, they are to be sure well made, strong and heavy, well calculated for the use of white people; but they are too thick, too heavy in proportion to their size; in short, they are too good for Indians; which brings them so high that they cannot afford to purchase them; or rather they think they cannot, having been in the habit of using Kettles of the same size that would not weigh half as much, and would of course cost much less." Other articles unsuited to the native preference in design and price sold poorly in the factories. Heavy and expensive earbobs, arm and wrist bracelets, brooches, and crosses all lay on the shelves unsold. The cheaper and better steel traps and such tools as ice chisels retailed by the Canadian traders often undersold the factory articles. Moreover, the natives knew good powder from bad, and the factors tried to

12. McKenney to Alexander Armstrong, Aug. 15, 1821, Letters Sent, Supt. Indian Trade (M-16), Roll 6: 249.

keep their supply of high quality.[13] Civilizing the Indians, even doing business with them, required a perception of their peculiarities in taste and of the level of acculturation they had reached as a result, in part, of that very trade.

The native's apparent independence in business transactions, however, masked his real subordination to civilization. Indeed, the government made some effort to stop the practice of gift giving on the ground that it led to dependence and was unhealthy for the tribes' development. But McKenney probably voiced the more typical reaction when he told Calhoun that "a nation of savages no matter how hostile their spirit, nor how war loving they may be, may be kept quiet at all times, in the exact proportion as they are made to Depend on those, against whom they may indulge a spirit of hostility, for their commercial privileges."[14] Realism dictated that the Indians should enjoy the benefits of civilization and that they should be kept closely bound to their source of supply.

A slightly different version of the dependence theme arose from the policy of sending white mechanics into the Indians' country to keep their newly acquired tools in good repair and to teach the necessary practical arts to the younger tribesmen. By spreading as much technical knowledge as possible through the forests, the government kept the tribesmen peaceful and friendly and also advanced them that much further toward civilization. The very act of replacing homegrown utensils with those of a strange culture created a condition of dependence for the recipients, though the attempt to teach the necessary proficiencies in handling the tools showed a desire to see the native stand on his own feet. The tribes always required the services of a blacksmith, in residence if possible. Farmers living near the native villages also helped to demonstrate the desirability of tilling the ground. Hawkins, with his enlarged view of the possibilities for civilization, recommended the use of army personnel on the frontier, wheelwrights, halters, tinners, printers, potters, tanners, saddlers, and shoemakers, to train the Indians.

---

13. John Armstrong to John Mason, Feb. 15, 1814, Letters Sent, Sec. War (M-15), Roll 3: 174; Joseph B. Varnum to Mason, Sept. 30, 1810, Letters Received, Supt. Indian Trade (M-T58), Roll 1; Mason to E. L. Dupont de Nemours and Co., Dec. 28, 1807, Letters Sent, Supt. Indian Trade (M-16), Roll 1: 21.

14. Thomas L. McKenney to John C. Calhoun, May 9, 1818, Letters Sent, Supt. Indian Trade (M-16), Roll 5: 32; Timothy Pickering to Council of the Six Nations, July 5, 1791, Pickering Papers, LX, 84–84A; Henry Dearborn to William Wells, Mar. 10, 1808, Letters Sent, Sec. War (M-15), Roll 2: 362.

Indeed, training the Indians became a common philanthropic method. The Quakers stated simply what they expected of one of their agents among the Senecas: "Our mind was he should not do all the work for them, but rather teach their young men to do it for themselves, so that when he should go away, they might be able to do their own smith work." Halliday Jackson recorded that the Quaker families living close to the native villages "had opportunities of instruction and encouraging them in habits more assimilated to civilized life. The Indian women, also, made frequent visits to them and by observing their industry, economy, and superior mode of living, an inclination began soon to manifest itself, even among these uncultivated females of the wilderness, to imitate the more useful and rational economy of our women Friends." The danger persisted, however, that the Indians would settle down to the luxury of technical services rendered by white mechanics and paid for by government annuities. Still worse, the possibility always existed that the increasing dependence on the white man's goods, intended by the civilizing plan, would retard the expected emergence of an independent civilized Indian.[15]

But lacking full confidence that a simple, rational explanation would convince the Indians of the requirements of the times or that formal methods of instruction would civilize them, philanthropists often tried subtle indirection. Jedidiah Morse, with his idea for "Education Families," presented the most coherent such plan. He contended that by exposure to civilization the Indians would gradually absorb the white man's manners and learn the simple procedures of agricultural life. In a more formal variant of the Quaker method, he advocated the establishment of farmers in the Indian country so that these natural processes of imitation would take their course:

15. Henry Dearborn to Return J. Meigs, Oct. 20, 1801, Letters Sent, Sec. War (M-15), Roll 1: 111; Samuel Dexter to Israel Chapin, Feb. 17, 1801, *ibid.*, 23; Dearborn to Israel Whelan, May 6, 1803, *ibid.*, 346; to William Clark, Aug. 17, 1807, *ibid.*, Roll 2: 328; William H. Crawford to Lewis Cass, July 2, 1816, *ibid.*, Roll 3: 391; Philomen Hawkins to Crawford, Nov. 8, 1816, Letters Received, Sec. War (M-271), Roll 1: 1134–1135. See also Henry Drinker *et al.* to Dearborn, Dec. 31, 1801, *ibid.*, 773–774; Halliday Jackson, *Civilization of the Indian Natives* . . . (Philadelphia, 1830), 50–51; Dearborn to Meigs, July 10, 1801, Letters Sent, Sec. War (M-15), Roll 1: 88; Dearborn to Callender Irvine, Aug. 6, 1802, *ibid.*, 261; Crawford to Indian Agents, Sept. 23, 1816, *ibid.*, Roll 3: 431–432; Meigs to Crawford, Nov. 4, 1816, Letters Received, Sec. War (M-271), Roll 1: 1259–1261; John McKee to Crawford, Nov. 18, 1816, *ibid.*, 1200–1201; Thomas L. McKenney to John Crowell, Apr. 7, 1824, Letters Sent, Off. Indian Affairs (M-21), Roll 1: 29.

Let him cultivate, in the vicinity of the village, with the consent of the nation, a small farm, and keep a small stock of horses, oxen, and cows. It should be understood among the Indians, that the farming establishment is solely for the benefit of the Agent. Should it be known among them, that the object was to learn them to cultivate the soil, as the whites do, they would most certainly object to it; but if this is not known, they will soon see the advantages of employing the plough, harrow, etc. etc. and be induced to imitate our examples, and thus get on the road which leads to civilization, before they are aware of it.[16]

Morse revealed a basic facet of philanthropy, but he also emptied humanitarian optimism of any trace of sentimentality.

Likewise, the white man carried his notions of enterprise to the Indian, exploiting the land and inducing the tribes to follow suit. The basic skills of carding and spinning accompanied the planting of cotton, and in some instances the Indians learned to bring the process to the weaving stage. Besides such light manufactures, saw-mills and gins appeared in the Indian country. White men under contract with the tribes, often the natives themselves, extracted minerals such as saltpeter, plaster of paris, iron, and tin from Indian land. In many indirect ways, civilization infiltrated the Indian's primitive domain, supplying him with new desires and the means to satisfy them, quietly persuading large segments of the tribes to change their manner of life.[17]

After acquiring the lands along the Mississippi and then purchasing New Orleans and Louisiana, the government negotiated with the tribes for the right to build roads across their territory. Although

16. Morse, *Report on Indian Affairs*, 58–59. Morse was quoting with approval an answer to one of his questions by a Major Marston at Fort Armstrong.

17. Benjamin Hawkins to ———, Mar. 4, 1797, Hawkins Papers; Henry Dearborn to Return J. Meigs, May 15, 1801, Letters Sent, Sec. War (M-15), Roll 1: 45; Dearborn to Samuel Mitchell, Oct. 8, 1802, *ibid.*, 282; William Eustis to Silas Dinsmoor, Oct. 23, 1810, *ibid.*, Roll 3: 51; John Mason to Hawkins, Sept. 22, 1812, Letters Sent, Supt. Indian Trade (M-16), Roll 3: 63; Hawkins to John Armstrong, Letters Received, Sec. War (M-271), Roll 1: 765; Armstrong to John McKee, July 28, 1814, Letters Sent, Sec. War (M-15), Roll 3: 176; John Ridge to Albert Gallatin, Mar. 10, 1826, Gallatin Papers, Box 64–3, fol. 42, N.-Y. Hist. Soc. See also McKee to William H. Crawford, Apr. 1, 1816, Letters Received, Sec. War (M-271), Roll 1: 1187–1188; Crawford to McKee, Sept. 13, 1816, Letters Sent, Sec. War (M-15), Roll 3: 422; Crawford to McKee, Sept. 23, 1816, *ibid.*, 431; John C. Calhoun to Arkansas Cherokee Delegation, Feb. 12, 1823, *ibid.*, Roll 5: 355; Thomas L. McKenney to E. W. DuVal, Apr. 18, 1825, Letters Sent, Off. Indian Affairs (M-21), Roll 1: 452. Also Eustis to Meigs, Apr. 28, 1812, Letters Sent, Sec. War (M-15), Roll 3: 127; Eustis to Meigs, Sept. 12, 1812, *ibid.*, 150; Lewis Cass to Calhoun, Mar. 10, 1820, Letters Received, Sec. War (M-271), Roll 3: 54–57; Eustis to Elias Earle, May 14, 1812, Letters Sent, Sec. War (M-15), Roll 3: 129; James Monroe to Earle, Feb. 3, 1815, *ibid.*, 193–194.

these roads had immediate strategic value, the government also saw them as part of the general policy of invading the preserve of savagery. Indeed, scarcely any aspect of the relations between the two societies could not be connected with the plan to replace savagery with civilization. Henry Dearborn proposed an imaginative scheme for the use of the route from Nashville to Natchez through the Chickasaw and Choctaw country. He planned to erect public houses run by a white man and an Indian in partnership every twenty or thirty miles along the way,

so that there shall be one discreet prudent Indian with each white man at the several places . . . the white man to have a lease of a few hundred acres of Land for the purpose of raising Stock, Corn etc. etc. sufficient for supplying travellers, and the profits of the business to be shared between the White man and the Indian in an equitable manner, the United States will engage on their part to assist in put[t]ing up a small house and Stables at the several places which may be agreed on. All subsequent expenses to be defrayed by the white man. Such an arrangement would be of great advantage to the Chickasaws, by affording many of them opportunities of acquiring the arts of Civilization, such as agriculture, domestic manufactures, and the mechanic arts, at the same time they would be receiving handsome profits from the public houses.[18]

However unrealistic, since the Indians generally opposed even the building of the roads and succumbed only under heavy government pressure, this ingenious innovation illustrated the strength of the philanthropic impulse to affect even a normal effort to link the parts of the rising American nation.

Although in this instance the government found difficulty in introducing white men into the Indian territory, the tribesmen formed a constant stream of visitors to civilization. The Washington authorities welcomed these native delegations for diplomatic reasons, hoping to bring them to the American side against the Spaniards and the British and to maintain peace between the Indians and the frontiersmen. But they also intended to give the tribesmen a view of the white world that would color the future relations of the two societies. Besides visiting Washington, where the president would greet them with ceremony, they were often sent at government expense on a tour of Baltimore, Philadelphia, and New York. Welcomed with much enthusiasm by the crowds and by society in the various towns, the Indians enjoyed these visitations. The heavy expense and the possibility of undermining the authority of the agents in the Indian country led the War Depart-

18. Henry Dearborn to Samuel Mitchill, July 9, 1803, Letters Sent, Sec. War (M-15), Roll 1: 359–360; Dearborn to W. C. C. Claiborne, July 9, 1803, *ibid.*, 362.

ment to discourage them. The natives themselves risked disease and death in a strange environment—or sometimes merely the embarrassments of notoriety, drunkenness, and unpaid bills. Government officials were often ignorant of the proper form for these conferences: more than once they entertained visiting tribesmen in a style beyond their proper station; communication always proved difficult when interpreters could not be found; they arranged formal meetings with more surmise than accurate knowledge. But native delegations continued to arrive at the seats of civilized authority to be impressed by the numbers and power in the white man's world and to carry back with them a new insight into the manner in which their own way of life would soon be changed.[19]

In the broadest sense, then, philanthropists seemed to believe that all contact between white and Indian would lead to the transmittal of civilization. They knew well enough that some aspects of Indian-white relations, especially the influences of vice-ridden frontiersmen, would have destructive consequences, but they explained these as incidental tendencies. Their great faith in their own way of life made it easy for them to overlook the negative impact of the civilizing process. But more significant, they perceived that direct appeals to the tribes might not yield a quick enough response, and so they adopted indirect means to reach the Indians. Hence benevolence often led to deception. More consciously, philanthropists saw the possible usefulness of certain members of the tribal society who might be particularly susceptible to civilized influence.

3

Philanthropists concentrated their attack on the weakest elements in the native's social defense: half bloods, women, and children. Rely-

19. Tench Coxe to Tench Francis, June 11, 1794, Letters of Coxe (M-74), 16; Samuel Dexter to Benjamin Hawkins, Nov. 26, 1800, Letters Sent, Sec. War (M-15), Roll 1: 3–4; Henry Dearborn to Return J. Meigs, July 10, 1801, *ibid.*, 88–89; Dearborn to Ezra Lunt, Nov. 2, 1801, *ibid.*, 114–115; Dearborn to William Henry Harrison *et al.*, Jan. 14, 1802, *ibid.*, 145–146; entry of July 11, 1794, Charles Francis Adams, ed., *Memoirs of John Quincy Adams, Comprising Portions of His Diary from 1795 to 1848* (Philadelphia, 1874–1877), I, 34–35. See also Dexter to David Henley, Nov. 19, 1800, Letters Sent, Sec. War (M-15), Roll 1: 1–2; Dearborn to Meigs, Nov. 20, 1801, *ibid.*, 123–124; Pierre Chouteau to Harrison, May 22, 1805, Logan Esarey, ed., *Messages and Letters of William Henry Harrison*, Governors' Messages and Papers Series (*Indiana Historical Collections*, VII, IX [Indianapolis, 1922]), I, 128–129, hereafter cited as Esarey, ed., *Messages of Harrison*, I; George Graham to Joseph Anderson, June 14, 1816, Letters Sent, Sec. War (M-15), Roll 3: 378; John C. Calhoun to William Clark, Mar. 13, 1822, *ibid.*, Roll 5: 228; Jackson, ed., *Journals of Pike*, II, 371–372; Katharine C. Turner, *Red Men Calling on the Great White Father* (Norman, 1951).

ing on the relative openness of the tribes, their hospitable inclination to accept white men into their domain, the civilizing plan stressed the role of the white man who would settle in the native country and gain prestige and influence over the tribal authorities. Presumably, such whites would intermarry and leave a progeny of mixed bloods who could then be expected to play an important part in communicating civilization. Also, the lesson had been learned early that dealing directly with the tribal leadership and the male warrior class seldom yielded results. The men in the field recommended a reliance on overworked and oppressed women, who might be open to proposals for improving their lot. Besides, teaching them spinning, weaving, and home manufactures would increase the efficiency of the tribal economy. Yet these measures never replaced the major drive to educate the children so that the next generation would take its place in the civilized world. This selective procedure worked well enough when the tribe seemed acquiescent in changing its way of life, but sometimes, particularly in the use of the mixed bloods, it became a way of maneuvering an unwilling society into the web of civilization by choosing its least resistant or most compromised segment.

The mixed bloods played an ambiguous part in Indian-white relations. The offspring usually of white men and Indian women, raised in the native way but with some fatherly influence, they became important instruments in opening the tribes to civilization. Traders who spent much time in the Indian country, Scotsmen among the Cherokees and Creeks in the 1790s particularly, tory stragglers from the Revolution, itinerant artisans, fugitives from civilized justice, and white captives, male and female, who chose to marry and remain with the Indians, all left their seed among the tribes and inevitably some part of their own cultural heritage. Native hospitality required strangers to accept Indian ways. The influence of half bloods rested first on their identification with the tribal interest but also on their capacity to convince the whites that they retained important remnants of civilized loyalty and hence could bridge the gap between the two societies. This equivocal position made the mixed bloods useful to both sides, but caught in the middle, they frequently suffered for their efforts. Alexander McGillivray, the son of a Scottish trader, led the Creeks just after the Revolution by defending their independence against the Americans. But during the Creek War, Indians attacked his relatives at Fort Mimms, and later white men drove them from their lands in Mississippi. They remained loyal to the Indian nation, for which the white settlers demanded a price, but they had taken to farming and grazing and acting like white men, which turned the natives against them. In the 1820s mixed bloods defended the sovereignty of the Indian nations because they knew the white man's ways and could deal with the government on its own terms and because, like civilized men, they owned property that they wished to retain.[20]

But aside from the vagaries of tribal politics and the difficulties of a mixed population astride two cultures, philanthropists took the presence of mixed bloods in the tribes as a harbinger of good things to come. They could not know that removal would become a humanitarian policy and that these apparent evidences of success would become its major opponents in the tribes; it was enough that changes, biological and environmental, took place in native society. Moreover, amalgamation remained the consummation of philanthropy, and as Timothy Flint noted, this could not be expected without "crossing the breed." He went on to explain that "wherever there are half-breeds . . . , there is generally a faction, a party; and this race finds it convenient to espouse the interests of civilization and christianity. The full-blooded chiefs and Indians are generally partisans for the customs of the old time, and for the ancient religion." Half bloods represented progress.[21]

By singling out the native children to receive civilized training, the missionaries chose an element in tribal society with even more subversive potential than the mixed bloods. Although the educational program still appealed directly and rationally to the younger natives, its special emphasis on youth had profound manipulative connotations. The children would be less imbued with tribal prejudices, more pliable to the pressures of the civilizing plan. Mature Indians had already proved to be difficult subjects, not only because they possessed a viable culture but because so many seemed to decline under white influence. Civilization could be given to healthy Indians or to their receptive offspring, but not to the disoriented wrecks so prevalent in tribes closely associated with civilization. By centering their efforts on the children, the missionaries picked the

20. Talk of Creek Chief William McIntosh, Nov. 5, 1805, Letters Sent, Sec. War (M-15), Roll 2: 151–152; Statement of Return J. Meigs, Feb. 23, 1819, Letters Received, Sec. War (M-271), Roll 1: 1529; John Ridge to Albert Gallatin, Mar. 10, 1826, Gallatin Papers, Box 64–3, fol. 42. See also Lauchlin Durant *et al.* to James Madison, May 29, 1815, Letters Received, Sec. War (M-271), Roll 1: 838–840; Benjamin Hawkins to William H. Crawford, Jan. 19, 1816, *ibid.*, Roll 1: 1100–1102.

21. Flint, *Recollections*, 147. See also Henry Thompson Malone, *Cherokees of the Old South: A People in Transition* (Athens, Ga., 1956), 53–54; Berkhofer, *Salvation and the Savage*, 113–114.

shortest path to Indian society and also solved the problem of trying to civilize natives who disintegrated in proportion to the goodwill accorded them.

Gideon Blackburn, one of the first missionaries into the southern
Indian country, recorded his own experience among the Cherokees.
"I have concluded," he wrote, "that after the habits are formed,
the only way to reduce them is by the influence of the children. To
this point I have, therefore, bent my whole force." As a manipulative
strategy for ultimately converting the tribes, Blackburn's plan had
merit. A more subtle, yet more naive, statement came from one of
the American Board mission stations: "As it is a well known principle of human nature that parents consider a favor conferred on their
children in the same light as if it were conferred upon themselves,
it is, therefore plain that, becoming in some measure familiar with
the children and gaining their affections, the instructor is furnished
with a great moral power for removing the prejudices, conciliating
the esteem, and securing the attention of the parents to the truth
of God's word." Directing the civilized message to the younger
generation revealed a perception of the limits of meliorism, but it
also smacked of disdain for the good sense of the mature Indian
population.[22]

As the tribes declined under the assault of a foreign culture, the
children seemed more and more the only hope for the future. Some
of the Indians, recognizing the threat to their own world, lost confidence and looked to the younger members of the tribes to save the
future, thus abetting the white man's scheme. A Seneca chief answered the proposal of two New York speculators for the sale of
tribal lands by lamenting the Indians' present condition and also
by recording his hope that the youth might still be capable of
achieving civilization:

When I look back upon our ancestors, I see nothing to admire—nothing
I should follow—nothing that induces me to live as they did. On the
contrary, to enjoy life, I find we must change our Situations. We who
are present have families and children and we have a respect for our
children. We wish them to be enlightened and instructed, if we have not
been. By this means their eyes will be opened. They will see the light, if
we have not. We are getting old and cannot receive the instruction we
want our children to receive: our children will know how to do business
after we are dead and gone, and are under the dust, and they will bless
us for giving them instruction which their Fathers had been deprived of.

22. Gideon Blackburn, "An Account of the origin and progress of the Mission
to the Cherokee Indians . . . , Letter III," *Panoplist*, III (1808), 322; Report
on the Station at Candy's Creek, Apr. 1828, ABC 18.3.1.V: 6.

Cyrus Kingsbury, the American Board missionary to the Choctaws, carried on the theme of decline and hence the need for manipulating the younger generation by noting the difficulties of bringing instruction to the adults. Competent interpreters could not be found, and the missionaries had no trained men for such work. As a result "the Choctaws still continue the slaves of ignorance, vice, and superstition." Each year many Indians suffered because of witchcraft. Furthermore, the tribe had been debauched by unscrupulous whites who, in defiance of the law, kept the natives supplied with whiskey. In despair at their inability to cure their own intemperance or to suppress the trade, "many of them say they wish their children to be at school that they may learn better things."[23] In this situation, the missionaries found it easy to begin the process of transformation with the children, sometimes with the acquiescence of the older generation but more often as part of the philanthropic tendency to maneuver the tribes into civilization by any means available.

Part of the difficulty in converting the mature tribesmen stemmed from the cult of the warrior, which caused the male Indian to shun most activity that the white man would have classified as work. Hunting, the maintenance of personal prestige, and the leisurely deliberations of the tribal council fulfilled his role. By any civilized criteria, the woman was the drudge of native society. She performed all the menial functions that kept ordinary existence intact, and by cultivating the soil, she compensated for the sparse return from her husband's hunting. The philanthropist convinced himself that she yearned for liberation, to be treated in effect, like any self-respecting white woman. Besides the children, therefore, the female of the tribes seemed an admirable subject for the reception of civilization.

Benjamin Hawkins made a persuasive case for using Indian women. Early in his years among the Creeks, he visited the old men and the women of the tribe, inquired about their problems, and asked what he might do to make their lot easier. "I was the first," he reported, "who thought it worth the while to examine into the situation of the women. I had addressed myself to them and talked freely and kindly to them, and they were sure I meant

23. Address of the Seneca Chief Pollard, July 10, 1819, Letters Received, Sec. War (M-271), Roll 2: 1481–1482; Cyrus Kingsbury to John C. Calhoun, Dec. 21, 1820, *ibid.*, Roll 3: 403–404. See also William F. Vaill to Calhoun, Oct. 30, 1821, *ibid.*, Roll 4: 221–226; Alfred Finney and Cephas Washburn to Calhoun, Oct. 1, 1822, *ibid.*, 101–106; J. L. Hudson to Calhoun, Oct. 1822, *ibid.*, 135–137; Gallatin, "Synopsis of the Indian Tribes," Am. Antiq. Soc., *Archaeologia Americana*, II (1836), 159.

to better their condition." He proposed to teach them spinning and
weaving, to change the basis of the tribal economy, and hence to
bring the warriors along into a more efficient and beneficent way of
life. He made a brash beginning and lost the confidence of the male
leadership, but he remained hopeful that they would agree in the
end. "The chiefs, who were apprehensive, at first, that, if their
women could clothe and feed themselves by their own exertions
they would become independent of the degraded state of connexion
between them, have had proofs that the link is more firm in proportion, as the women are more useful, and occupied in domestic
concerns."[24] Since he wished to imbue the native with habits of
work, why not begin where success could be expected? Indian
women possessed the discipline necessary for acquiring new
skills. Rather than totally changing their social role, they would
merely add some of the household arts that civilization found so re-
warding. The end would still be the overturn of tribal society, but
to accomplish this upheaval, it would be necessary to utilize all
those elements in the native world that might contribute to its
destruction.

The indirect method produced striking results. The women took
to home manufactures, and the Indian braves, reluctantly at first,
found themselves drawn into new arrangements. Many became more
"accustomed to work" and better farmers after watching the mixed
bloods and the women become more and more like the whites. John
Ridge repeated an anecdote that illustrated the acuteness of the
philanthropic insight. It concerned a Cherokee chief who had op-

24. Benjamin Hawkins to ———, Mar. 4, 1797, Hawkins Papers; Report to
Congress by Thomas Jefferson, Dec. 8, 1801, *American State Papers, Indian
Affairs*, I, 647. Sometimes Hawkins's too clever use of women to have his way
with the Creeks revealed the extent to which he proposed to overthrow native
manners. A pertinent anecdote was told by Foster, *Jeffersonian America*, ed.
Davis, 25–26: "Colonel Hawkins has employed the females a good deal in his
plans of civilization. These were formerly treated like beasts of burthen but now
many of them ride and meet with great respect. Thirteen, some years ago, in
allusion to the thirteen United States, came on horseback in a kind of riding
habit with switches in their hands to wait on the Colonel, who when they came
up desired some of the men present to help them off, which however they declined as a thing beneath their dignity to do. On this Colonel Hawkins went up
himself and lifted off the lady nearest him, when the rest all remained seated
till their men were shamed into doing the same service for the others. He added
that formerly women were obliged to leave the pathway when they met any of
the men but by his example the men will now show their respect to the women
and the women expect it." See also entry for Jan. 26, 1797, *Letters of Hawkins*,
65; Hawkins to James McHenry, Nov. 19, 1797, *ibid.*, 240; Richard Thomas to
Henry Gaither, Jan. 28, 1798, *ibid.*, 478; Hawkins to McHenry, Feb. 23, 1798,
ibid., 293.

posed the efforts of the agent Silas Dinsmoor. When the time arrived for his yearly hunt, which would keep him away for six "Moons," he requested the agent to refrain from speaking to his family about the civilizing program. But Dinsmoor recognized a higher duty and prevailed upon the chief's wife and daughters to spin and weave in his absence. On his return, the Indian found that the product of the women's industry yielded more than the entire catch from his hunt. "Pleasantly disappointed, he immediately came to the Agent and accused him of making his women better Hunters and requested a plough, which was given to him, and from that time he became a farmer." Philanthropy may have not only turned some hunters into farmers but also affected the basic arrangements of native family life. Ridge went on to reveal how deeply the reforming edge had cut into the native psyche. To such a state had the relations between Indian men and women finally come: "In our Country females aspire to gain sober men for husbands and Mankind must yield to the tender sex. Woman civilizes man or makes him barbarous at her pleasure. If Ladies gave us universally the smiles of approbation in our extravagancies, we would be extravagant—if in murder, we would delight to kill—if in cruelty we would be cruel."[25] The first probing effort to convert the Indian women, by Ridge's interpretation, seemed to sink native society into a flaccid imitation of the white man's sentimentality.

4

The land held a central place in the Jeffersonian design for the Indian's future. The tribes claimed it, and white men wanted it. The government wished ultimately to distribute the Indian's vast acres among the members of civilized society, and it consequently intended to take most of the land away from the Indians. Philanthropists found as much significance in divesting the Indian of his tribal property as in the final consignment of the land to civilized use. Since the tribal possession of these surplus acres constituted one of the major signs of savagery, the abandonment of the land was a positive step toward civilization. Simply stated, the philanthropic program abetted the white man's desire for the land, proving once again that civilization closed its ranks in the face of savagism. Without the land the Indian would soon enter civilization; with it he would remain a savage.

Both tradition and theory dictated that lands should be purchased

25. Choctaw Treaty, Dec. 15, 1801, *American State Papers, Indian Affairs*, I, 662; John Ridge to Albert Gallatin, Gallatin Papers, Box 64–3, fol. 42.

from the Indians. Although common opinion from Vattel to Jefferson refused to grant a primitive people sovereignty over land they did not cultivate, it·did require that their right to its use should be formally purchased. Practically, there was no alternative. The mode of Indian land occupation demanded a formal system of liquidation. From the beginning the English either conquered the territory or arranged for the steady advance of their settlements by treating the Indians with the forms of sovereign power and by offering money or goods in return for each plot of ground.[26]

The rhetoric of Indian negotiators, as a consequence, dripped with assurances that the Indians possessed full right to retain their lands as long as they wished. They held an unimpeachable title, and the government would not and could not force them to sell. The government repeatedly gave blanket guarantees to the tribes recognizing the legitimacy of their possession. And even when the inevitable moment arrived that white men wanted the land for new settlements, a certain formal delicacy usually characterized the proceedings. The government initiated negotiations and distributed gifts and whiskey to facilitate the discussions. Once boundaries and price (usually not more than a penny an acre) had been set, the negotiators gave new assurances for the Indian's future security.[27]

Yet the truth of the matter could be gleaned from any long-run view of the white man's actions. Not for a moment would savagery impede the progress of civilization, not for the Puritans

26. Wilcomb E. Washburn, "The Moral and Legal Justifications for Dispossessing the Indians," in James Morton Smith, ed., *Seventeenth Century America: Essays in Colonial History* (Chapel Hill, 1959), 15–32; Prucha, *American Indian Policy*, 139–144; Vaughan, *New England Frontier*, 104–109. See also Thomas Jefferson to William Short and William Carmichael, May 31, 1793, Lipscomb and Bergh, eds., *Writings of Jefferson*, IX, 101–104; Jefferson to William Henry Harrison, Feb. 27, 1803, *ibid.*, X, 371; "Heads of Conversation with Mr. Hammond," *ibid.*, XVII, 333; Jefferson, "Vindication of Virginia's Claim Against the Proposed Colony of Vandalia," Boyd, ed., *Jefferson Papers*, VI, 656. Jefferson believed that Virginia had obtained its lands from the Indians largely by purchase; see letter to St. George Tucker, May 9, 1798, quoted in Robinson, "Indian Policy in Colonial Virginia," 78–79.

27. Henry Dearborn to Cherokee Delegation, July 8, 1801, Letters Sent, Sec. War (M-15), Roll 1: 77; Dearborn to Black Hoof and Shawnee Delegation, Feb. 10, 1802, *ibid.*, 155; Dearborn to Chiefs and Warriors of the Osage, July 18, 1804, *ibid.*, Roll 2: 12; Jefferson to Dearborn, Sept. 2, 1807, Lipscomb and Bergh, eds., *Writings of Jefferson*, XI, 354–355; William Eustis to James Neeley, Mar. 29, 1811, Letters Sent, Sec. War (M-15), Roll 3: 72; William H. Crawford to William Cocke, Mar. 19, 1816, *ibid.*, 315; Crawford to Benjamin Parke *et al.*, May 3, 1816, *ibid.*, 339; Red Jacket in Council, July 9, 1819, Letters Received, Sec. War (M-271), Roll 2: 1472–1473. See also Dearborn to Silas Dinsmore, Oct. 25, 1804, Letters Sent, Sec. War (M-15), Roll 2: 20; Dearborn to Charles Jouett, Apr. 2, 1805, *ibid.*, 62–63.

or the Quakers, certainly not for the frontier society, and most emphatically not for the philanthropists who had planned the Indian's future so carefully. Precisely because Jefferson and those who carried on his policy had thought out the problem of Indian-white relations, they knew that in the end the Indian must give up the land. Such extensive acreage fostered the savage condition. The Indian was uncivilized, that is undisciplined, disordered in his manner of life, because he lived irresponsibly from the fat of the land. Civilization required a direct relation between the individual and the soil. It marked off the bounds of earthly endeavor by limiting the Indian's property to the amount he could cultivate with the work habits acquired from the white man. Since the process of transition from savagery to civilization would be gradual, the land must be surrendered at a rate corresponding to the alteration in the Indian's way of life, although taking it might accelerate the move into civilization. Without the largess of the untouched wilderness, the Indian would be forced to take his living from the ground by farming. Hence the symmetry of the process: the ultimate good of the native demanded the adoption of civilization; the end could not be achieved lest he surrendered the land; and the white man stood ready to accept it from him.

Jefferson was only slightly ingenuous when he told Little Turtle: "I have . . . always believed it an act of friendship to our red brethren whenever they wished to sell a portion of their lands, to be ready to buy whether we wanted them or not, because the price enables them to improve the lands they retain, and turning their industry from hunting to agriculture, the same exertions will support them more plentifully." He had in mind a kind of friendship that in his deepest thoughts he doubted the Indians would understand—a friendship of serene objectivity, one that only the highest policy could comprehend. Jefferson found a perfect congruence of interest between the two societies. The Indians would never be asked to give up more than the circumstances of their gradual transformation required; the white man would never request more land than the orderly advance of civilized life across the continent demanded. The interrelation of the two factors had the purity of a metaphysic; progress as a transcendent necessity seemed to reconcile all existential disparities.[28]

28. Jefferson's views are conveniently available in Padover, ed., *Complete Jefferson*, 461, 464, 474, 497–498; Jefferson to James Jackson, Feb. 16, 1803, Jefferson Papers, Lib. of Congress (microfilm); Jefferson, Message of Jan. 18, 1803, Richardson, ed., *Papers of the Presidents*, I, 352.

In Jefferson's tone, in the frequency with which he implored the Indians to move toward civilization, and in the edge of desperation that sharpened his rhetoric, he revealed his own inner misgivings. The frontier seemed so difficult to control. The lust for land that drove intruders into the Indian country, the pervasive policy of territorial aggrandizement that seemed basic to the existence of the new state governments, all added to the crisis of the Jeffersonian plan. Besides, the Indians themselves began to suspect that their interests did not lie in gratifying the white man's land hunger. While cultural change seemed excruciatingly slow, even its limited success made the natives more eager to retain their land. But Jefferson knew that their survival rested on their willingness to give it up. Imperceptibly, circumstances forced him into the dilemma of arranging for the successful consummation of the civilizing plan while recognizing that events on the frontier beyond his control worked directly against it.

As a result, deception became characteristic of philanthropy. Determined to change the very character of the Indian, it paid little attention to the natives' conception of the future. Though the humanitarian intended to help the indigent savage, from the very nature of the ameliorative process he found it necessary to do certain things to him. Men like Calhoun, Crawford, and Cass could be brutally frank in appraising the Indian's situation and informing him of it. Philanthropists justified taking the land on the basis of such realism, and later the removal policy sprang from a similar argument. But the long experience of Indian-white relations also afforded many examples of the white man's dishonest treatment of the tribes. Heckewelder told of the first meeting of the Dutch settlers and the Indians. After arriving and making themselves familiar with the ground, the white men requested a piece of land on which to settle. They indicated the extent they would require by spreading a bullock hide. The Indians readily granted the request. Then the whites proceeded to cut the hide into a thin rope that they used to encompass a much larger area. Having ample territory, the Indians acquiesced in the European's crude artifice. The anecdote illustrated, as did such incidents as the Walking Purchase of 1737, the white man's habit of employing ruse to have his way with the tribesman, but it did not fully summarize the white man's attitude toward the Indian.[29] Certainly, it contrasted

29. Enclosure, Heckewelder to Samuel Miller, Feb. 26, 1801, Samuel Miller Collection, Vol. I, N.-Y. Hist. Soc.; Boyd, ed., *Indian Treaties*, xxviii.

with philanthropic goodwill. Blatant trickery seldom characterized Jeffersonian policy, but as time went on subtle manipulation did become common.

Jefferson's most compromising proposal came in a letter to William Henry Harrison in 1803. He suggested that the governor, in order "to promote this disposition to exchange lands," cultivate the Indian relationship with the government factories and "be glad to see the good and influential individuals among them run into debt, because we observe that when these debts get beyond what the individual can pay, they become willing to lop them off by a cession of lands." The previous year he had incorporated the same idea into a memorandum concerning Indian boundaries.[30] In this one instance, a Jeffersonian proposal went over the edge of patriarchal manipulation and became outright deception, demonstrating how close the assertion of civilized superiority could come to reprehensible coercion.

At about the same time, the government wanted to obtain land along the Mississippi to counter the Spanish threat and, after the purchase of Louisiana, to establish a contiguous line of settlements between the American possessions. Conveniently, the Choctaws had run up a debt with the British trading house of Panton and Leslie. The company wanted land, but Jefferson would not permit it to acquire American territory. He proposed instead that the United States assume the debt and accept the land from the Indians in payment. The government did not get the territory on the Mississippi originally asked for, but in 1805 it did obtain another cession, thus exploiting the natives' weakness in dealing with civilized economics.[31]

Yet government policy did not hold to a consistent pattern. In 1805 Harrison recommended the passage of a law to protect the Kaskaskia Indians against designing whites who had lured them into debt and had then threatened suit if they did not prevail upon the governor to assume payment. Both John Mason and Thomas L. McKenney in the office of superintendent of Indian trade cautioned

30. Jefferson to Harrison, Feb. 27, 1803, Lipscomb and Bergh, eds., *Writings of Jefferson*, X, 369–370; "Hints on the Subject of Indian Boundaries . . . ," *ibid.*, XVII, 374.

31. Padover, ed., *Complete Jefferson*, 464–465, 471–472; Richardson, ed., *Papers of the Presidents*, I, 422–423. See also Henry Dearborn to W. C. C. Claiborne, June 11, 1802, Letters Sent, Sec. War (M-15), Roll 1: 226–227; Dearborn to Silas Dinsmore, Jan. 7, 1804, *ibid.*, 418–419; Dearborn to James Robertson and Dinsmore, Mar. 20, 1805, *ibid.*, Roll 2: 47–48; Dearborn to James Wilkinson, Apr. 16, 1803, Carter, ed., *Territorial Papers*, V, 213–214.

factors not to permit the natives to run up accounts. "It has occurred to me," wrote McKenney, "that you might represent to a
few of the influential Chiefs, who appear themselves to be the
largest debtors, that they would be promoting the ability of the
factory to serve them and their nation by being themselves punctual
in paying their accounts; that it would be also reputable to them
as Chiefs, and especially so, were they to stir up those of their tribe
who are debtors, to be punctual also." McKenney used the factory
system to promote civilization, and he did not hold a high opinion
of tribal autonomy, but he would not go beyond the bounds of
ordinary honesty in dealing with the Indians.[32]

By civilized standards, bribery of the chiefs constituted a more
reprehensible yet more direct manner of influencing the tribes. The
practice doubtless originated in the native tradition of gift giving
and in the requirements of status within the tribal organization.
The whites had always followed the native practice, but with the
increasing sophistication of the tribal leadership and the heavy
pressure for them to conform to government policy, the acceptance
of gifts became indistinguishable from disloyalty and corruption.
Chiefs took money to change their positions in the tribal council,
frequently contrary to their own beliefs and against the common
opinion of the tribe. And in certain crucial instances, the government paid money in order to obtain a prestigious signature on a
desired land cession. In 1825 the Creeks murdered their chief,
William McIntosh, for ceding land. He had accepted payment from
the government for arranging a treaty with the Creeks, and he
had previously acted as an intermediary for a similar transaction
with the Cherokees, for which he also received compensation.[33] Before the Indians had learned enough of the white man's lessons to
realize the value of their possessions, bribery had a certain utility
in the civilizing process, but once the tribes came to consider it in
the light of civilized morality, it became a form of aggression rather
than manipulation.

On the whole, government officials favored bribery as an instrument for forming the natives to the white man's design. Policy

32. Harrison to Henry Dearborn, Nov. 29, 1805, Esarey, ed., *Letters of
Harrison*, I, 176; Arthur St. Clair to Henry Knox, May 1, 1790, William Henry
Smith, ed., *The St. Clair Papers . . .* (Cincinnati, 1882), II, 139; John Mason
to George S. Gaines, Aug. 28, 1810, Letters Sent, Supt. Indian Trade (M-16),
Roll 2: 187; Thomas L. McKenney to Gaines, Sept. 23, 1819, *ibid.*, Roll 5: 321.

33. R. S. Cotterill, *The Southern Indians: The Story of the Civilized Tribes
before Removal* (Norman, 1954), 217–222.

called for the distribution of gifts to carefully selected chiefs and not indiscriminately among the tribes. The government usually allocated a moderate sum to negotiators to "act in such cases, as circumstances may require." Or occasionally, agents openly distributed gifts to cooperative chiefs in the hope that their friendship would be secure for the future. Dearborn, Calhoun, and Cass all frankly acknowledged the need of these practices.[34]

Some government officials opposed bribery. Hawkins insisted that, in his dealings with the Creeks, he operated "on them by principle and not by bribery." James Barbour peremptorily refused to offer gratuities for a treaty with the Creeks. Whatever the "usages of Government," he maintained, the sum "given as the price of the land should appear on the face of the treaty." Because he would not deal with the tribes as sovereign entities, Andrew Jackson also opposed bribery. It had come to the point, he said, that nothing could be done with the Indians without first corrupting their chiefs. He considered it inhumane and "inconsistent with the virtue, and principles of our Government." The most prescient opinion on the usefulness of bribery, however, had been expressed by Timothy Pickering in 1791:

For, with a few exceptions it appears to me, that the leading Chiefs are as corrupt as the ministers of any court in Europe. Yet bribery would be less efficacious for whatever might be their engagements, as their importance depends wholly on their popularity, and all their power consists in the arts of persuasion: they can accomplish nothing—they dare undertake nothing which is obviously against the interest of their nation. That they should be thus corrupt is not surprising. For a century past, rival powers have aimed at engaging the friendship of the Chiefs and of their nations. The means—presents of cloaths, money and trinkets. The principal Chiefs have very much subsisted [?] by *private presents* —in other words— by *bribes*. And bribery has been the more generally practised, because it was so easy to practise—small sums being equal to the highest views of the Greatest Chiefs. I therefore consider the influence of any white man

34. Nathan Dane *et al.*, "Report of committee on Indian Affairs," Aug. 9, 1787, Ford *et al.*, eds., *Journals of Continental Congress*, XXXIII, 479–480; Henry Dearborn to James Robertson, July 3, 1805, Letters Sent, Sec. War (M-15), Roll 2: 88; Dearborn to Return J. Meigs, Jan. 8, 1806, *ibid.*, 153; Francis Paul Prucha and Donald F. Carmony, eds., "A Memorandum of Lewis Cass . . . ," *Wisconsin Magazine of History*, LII (1968), 35–50; Lewis Cass to George Graham, July 3, 1817, *American State Papers, Indian Affairs*, II, 137; John C. Calhoun to Isaac Shelby and Andrew Jackson, May 2, 1818, Letters Received, Sec. War (M-271), Roll 2: 954–955; Calhoun to Shelby, July 30, 1818 Letters Sent, Sec. War (M-15), Roll 4: 195–196. See also Cotterill, *Southern Indians*, 153; Malone, *Cherokees of the Old South*, 66–67, 196n.

over any particular chief or chiefs—if it has been acquired by bribery, not worth a rush."[35]

The ineffectiveness of bribery, because the corrupted chiefs could not control their people, became even more apparent in later years. But the policy remained part of the governmental means of influencing the tribes, a legacy of the habit of manipulation.

5

When Jefferson spoke of incorporating the Indian, he had in mind not only social union with the white man but also biological amalgamation. More than once he told the Indians: "Your blood will mix with ours; and will spread, with ours, over this great island." He wrote to Hawkins, in language that broadly assumed the desirability of an eventual racial union: "The ultimate point of rest and happiness for them is to let our settlements and theirs meet and blend together, to intermix, and become one people. Incorporating themselves with us as citizens of the United States, this is what the natural progress of things will of course, bring on, and it will be better to promote than retard it." Intermarriage might be specifically promoted, but more likely it would follow the course of nature, reflecting and accelerating the union of the two societies.[36]

Intermixing on a scale that might have produced a blending of white and red never took place. Jeffersonian opinion almost universally recommended the policy, but philanthropists tended to live at a comfortable distance from the point of contact between the two societies. The mechanism of cultural transference required that whites go into the Indian country to deliver their message. Their numbers remained small. Though marriages between whites and natives occurred regularly, they never reached a mass scale. When the whites did move into the Indian territory en masse, conflict resulted instead of the peaceful amalgamation that had been hoped for. Under the circumstances, racial mixture could not have solved the problem of Indian-white relations, though it seemed to most

35. Hawkins to David D. Mitchell, Nov. 16, 1812, Hawkins Papers; James Barbour to Thomas H. Benton and Louis McLane, May 15, 1826, *American State Papers, Indian Affairs,* II, 665; Andrew Jackson to John C. Calhoun, Aug. 24, 1819, Letters Received, Sec. War (M-271), Roll 2: 1181–1182. For evidence that Jackson did not always act the way he talked, see Wilkins, *Cherokee Tragedy,* 94–96. Pickering to Henry Knox, Aug. 10, 1791, Pickering Papers, LX, 115½–116.

36. Padover, ed., *Complete Jefferson,* 503, 505–506, 509; Jefferson to Benjamin Hawkins, Feb. 18, 1803, Lipscomb and Bergh, eds., *Writings of Jefferson,* X, 363.

observers the best evidence of the gradual intermeshing of the savage with civilization.

The marriage of John Rolfe and Pocahontas constituted the great archetype of Indian-white conjugal union. Without accepting the kind of cosmic symbolism seen by Vachel Lindsay in his "Our Mother, Pocahontas," Jeffersonian writers generally approved the alliance and regretted only that this initial transaction had not become a widespread practice. An early interpretation worried about an Indian princess marrying beneath her station, but there had never been much concern for Rolfe's racial integrity in mingling his blood with an Indian's. Proverbially, Virginians proudly claimed an ancestral link with the Indian maid. John Randolph considered his reputed connection a bright star in his family's past. Even Jefferson, though he was little inclined to celebrate the virtues of his forebears, spoke approvingly of a remote ancestral association with the Indian princess. He told Samuel Whitcomb, who visited him in 1824, that once in conversation with an Indian chief he had proudly informed the native that both his daughters had married descendants of Pocahontas. Samuel Stanhope Smith spoke of two youths at the College of New Jersey "of one of the first families in the state of Virginia" who were fourth-generation descendants of Pocahontas, "a high spirited and generous woman." Environmental conditioning had altered what remained of their Indian appearance, but one retained the "dark and vivid eye that has distinguished the whole family, and rendered some of them remarkably beautiful."[37]

Authorities took few steps to foster intermarriage. The British announced in 1719 that they would give ten pounds and fifty acres in Nova Scotia to any Englishman who would marry an Indian girl or any English girl who would marry an Indian man. Only a few claimed the bounty. In 1784 Patrick Henry introduced a bill in the Virginia House of Delegates allowing for free education, tax relief, and bounties for children to anyone who would marry an Indian. It would have been difficult to promote intermarriage as a positive

37. Stith, *History of First Discovery of Virginia*, 142; "Copy of an Interview with Thomas Jefferson by My Father, the Late Samuel Whitcomb, Formerly of Dorchester, Mass., June 1, 1824," Jefferson Papers, Alderman Lib., Univ. of Va., Charlottesville; Smith, *Essay on Variety*, 19–20. Benjamin Latrobe read a paper before the American Philosophical Society, Feb. 18, 1803, entitled, "Account of the descendants of Pocahontas, daughter of Powhatan, king or chief of the tribe of Powhatan, who inhabited the country about the falls of the James River, Va.," Am. Phil. Soc., *Procs.*, XXII (1885), 333. Richard Beale Davis, *Intellectual Life in Jefferson's Virginia, 1790–1830* (Chapel Hill, 1964), 313–319.

policy. Philanthropists encouraged it, but they probably did no more than follow the practice of life on the frontier, where it remained a common phenomenon.[38]

The French reputation for Indian diplomacy and for success in bringing civilization into the wilderness stemmed in part from their willingness to mix freely with the tribes. The English trader, however, maintained a reputation of sorts. Henry M. Brackenridge recorded a conversation with an Arikara: "Seeing the chief one day in a thoughtful mood, I asked him what was the matter—'I was wondering' said he 'whether you white people have any women amongst you.' I assured him in the affirmative. 'Then' said he, 'why is it that your people are so fond of our women, one might suppose they had never seen any before?'" In a more serious vein, Zebulon Pike said of the trading population at Prairie du Chien: "Their mode of living had obliged them to have transient connexion with the Indian women; and what was at first policy is now so confirmed by habit and inclination, that it is become (with a few exceptions) the ruling practice of all the traders; and, in fact, almost one half of the inhabitants under 20 years have the blood of the aborigines in their veins." The many half bloods in important tribal positions furnished evidence enough of the traders' willingness to intermix. Sir William Johnson, Lachlan McGillivray, William Wells, and Timothy Barnard were but a few who fathered children by native women.[39]

Conceived of as an instrument of civilization, intermarriage had few racial obstacles to surmount. A Virginia correspondent of the *Analectic Magazine* set the issue to rest in 1818. "Differences of colour in the human race," he wrote with respect to Indian-white amalgamation, "does not excite so unconquerable an aversion as the owners of negro slaves imagine." Of course, proposals for intermarriage with the Indians had a long history among the Virginians. Robert Beverley cited a long list of misfortunes that might have

38. Edmund S. Morgan, "The American Indian: Incorrigible Individualist," in *The Mirror of the Indian* . . . (Providence, 1958), 10; Robert McColley, *Slavery and Jeffersonian Virginia* (Urbana, 1964), 138; Imlay, *Topographical Description*, 296.

39. Flint, *Recollections*, 163–164; H. M. Brackenridge, *Views of Louisiana; Together with a Journal of a Voyage up the Missouri River, in 1811* (Ann Arbor, 1966 [orig. publ., Pittsburgh, 1814]), 258; Jackson, ed., *Journals of Pike*, I, 198; Benjamin Bissell, *The American Indian in English Literature of the Eighteenth Century* (New Haven, 1925), 37–38, n. 2; Joseph A. Parsons, "Civilizing the Indians of the Old Northwest, 1800–1810," *Indiana Magazine of History*, LVI (1960), 208; Deposition of Abram Mordecai, Jan. 10, 1825, Timothy Barnard Papers, Dept. of Archives and History, Atlanta, Ga.

been avoided had the two peoples intermarried early. Wars would not have been the usual method of Indian-white intercourse, and those Indian tribes now decimated would be thriving in health and vigor, but more important, "in all Likelihood, many, if not most, of the *Indians* would have been converted to Christianity by this kind Method." William Byrd made an even stronger case for intermarriage. If the colonists had really been serious about civilizing the Indians, he wrote, no more opportune method could be found than a general physical union. "For, after all that can be said, a sprightly Lover is the most prevailing Missionary that can be sent amongst these, or any other Infidels." Benjamin Rush later added a further item to the advantages of intermarriage. Not only would the natives benefit by the acquisition of civilized ways, but intermixture might improve the intellectual capacity of the race. "The mulatto has been remarked, in all countries, to exceed, in sagacity, his white and black parent. The same remark has been made of the offspring of the European, and North American Indian."[40]

The theme persisted and, if anything, became more closely allied with the civilizing plan. Morse, for example, though he favored intermarriage, had doubts about its feasibility until a sufficient number of Indians had been educated. He agreed that many white men of respectable talents had already married native women. He thought that more than half the Cherokees and substantial numbers of the other southern tribes who had been in contact with the whites were of mixed blood. Whatever obstacles still remained would be removed by an effective education program among the tribes. Once accomplished, *"then* let intermarriage with them become general, and the end which the Government has in view will be completely attained. They would then be literally of one blood with us, be merged in the nation, and saved from extinction." The American Board also saw the uses of intermarriage. Milo Hoyt, the son of one of its missionaries, married one of the native converts and proposed, with the blessing of his superiors, to establish himself in the Indian country and become the leaven for the gradual transformation of the tribes.[41]

In the right place and between the right people, intermarriage

40. "Reflections on the Institutions of the Cherokee Indians," *Analectic Mag.,* XII (1818), 54; Beverley, *History and Present State of Virginia,* ed. Wright, 38–39; W. K. Boyd, ed., *Byrd's Histories of the Dividing Line,* 3–4, 120–122; Rush, "On the Influence of Physical Causes," in *Sixteen Introductory Lectures,* 117.

41. Morse, *Report on Indian Affairs,* 73–75; *Panoplist,* XVI (1820), 558. See also William H. Crawford to the Senate, Mar. 13, 1916, *American State Papers, Indian Affairs,* II, 28.

could be a very good thing indeed—but not always. The famous incidents at the mission school in Cornwall, Connecticut, added new meaning to the question. Two full-blood Cherokees married white girls, and the town uproar forced the American Board, otherwise in favor of intermarriage, to repudiate the practice and finally to close the school. But the case was clear. Intermarriage took place between white men and Indian women. Hence the subtle defenses of civilized superiority would be maintained, the father presumably would bring into the wilderness the ways of civilization. The most publicized unions between white female and Indian male had taken place in captivity, which meant the subjection of the white and the preservation of savagery. As a means of fostering civilization, intermarriage had to be part of the white man's expanding way of life. The surrender of his women to the savage scarcely conformed to the necessary pattern. Of course, neither of the two young men from Cornwall, John Ridge and Elias Boudinot, could be called savages, yet they came from an alien people still under the tuition of the white man's society. They could not qualify as equals in Connecticut.[42]

The doctrine that savagery would persist and even spread unless civilization opposed it cast some doubt on the utility of intermarriage. The facts were plain. Traders and other likely prospects established their connections with native women in the Indian

42. Daniel S. Butrick to Jeremiah Evarts, Nov. 21, 1824, ABC 18.3.1.IV: 1; Catalogue of the Foreign Mission School, letter of June 17, 1825, signed by Lyman Beecher *et al.*, ABC, North American Indians, Miscellaneous, Vol. I, doc. 75; Butrick to ———, Sept. 27, 1825, ABC 18.3.1.IV: 1–4. Hermann Vaill, an American Board missionary related by marriage to Harriet Gold (the wife of Elias Boudinot), protested that he favored intermarriage as a matter of principle but opposed this marriage because he feared that it would have an adverse effect on the Cornwall school. He explicitly denied that his opposition carried any racial connotations, but saw fit to add in a letter admonishing Harriet: "[I] hope that you will be the instrument for accomplishing much in behalf of that People whom I suppose you now consider as *your Nation*." There was apparently some concern in his mind that in becoming part of the Indian nation, the girl would abandon the effort to civilize the Cherokees. Hermann Vaill to Harriet Gold, Mar. 3, 1826, Aug. 22, 1823, and June 29, 1825, and Vaill to Mary W. Brinsmade, Aug. 2, 1825, Vaill Collection (microfilm), Yale University. For an account stressing racial tension, see Wilkins, *Cherokee Tragedy*, chap. 6. *Niles' Weekly Register*, XXVIII (1825), 298, defended the Gold-Boudinot marriage, referred to the frequent boasts of whites with Indian blood, and hoped that Harriet Gold would "teach the Indians to make butter and cheese—how to spin, make clothes, etc. and become the parent of children, taught by her to read and write, and think and reflect on things of deep interest to them and all the human family." According to the *Cherokee Phoenix* (New Echota, Ga.), May 24, 1828, in 1825 there were 147 white men and 73 white women married to Cherokees in a total population of 13,563.

country. Frequently men of a primitive cast and unsettled habits, they manifested little interest in the issue of their relationships. Moreover, in the Indian family, children followed the lineage of the mother. These circumstances, together with the persistent rumors that civilization tended to crumble in the primeval forest, worked to counter the faith in intermarriage as an instrument of civilization. The actions of the Indians themselves also became important. Especially in the South, after civilization had made significant advances, loyalty to the tribal nation took on new meaning. The Indians rejected civilized ways that required its abandonment. In these circumstances, intermarriage no longer served philanthropic purposes.[43]

Hawkins's experience illustrated both sides of the intermarriage problem. When he entered the Indian country in the 1790s, he held a high opinion of intermarriage, and he intended to promote it at his agency as an important part of the civilizing plan. But he quickly found that it did not necessarily raise the level of Creek society. Some of the artisans at the agency married Creek women and, by Hawkins's account, soon found themselves under the tyranny of balky squaws and with no control over their children. Besides, the Indians held them in contempt for their inability to control their wives. Nothing in the situation aided the spread of civilization. Hawkins had married a white woman, and he decreed that his retainers should follow his lead. He forbade intermarriage at the Creek agency. Once the civilizing program had produced some results, however, he changed his mind. The native women, he reported, "have recently made propositions to me to submit themselves and children to be governed by white men if I will rescind the order. I have some young girls of good families raised under my own roof to usefulness, with whom I shall begin the experiment a new with the smiths and strikers in the public service or such young men as I can get to marry them, and settle out on farms at such places as I shall direct."[44]

The spell of intermarriage as a means of civilization or as the end of the civilizing process remained sufficiently strong to overcome most hesitations about its utility. Consumed by the need for human unity, expressed in one sense as civilizing the native, philanthropists

43. Harriss, ed., *Lawson's History of North Carolina*, 195–196; Ninian Edwards to William H. Crawford, Nov. 1815, *American State Papers, Indian Affairs*, II, 64; Creek Laws, June 12, 1818, Letters Received, Sec. War (M-271), Roll 2: 773–774; John Ridge to Gallatin, Gallatin Papers, Box 64–3, fol. 42.
44. Benjamin Hawkins to Thomas Jefferson, July 11, 1803, Jefferson Papers.

continued to hope for the absorption of the Indian as a physical entity. There could be no greater victory for civilization and progress. As an indirect way of bringing the two societies together, intermarriage seemed the most natural and least manipulative method of all.

6

An irony always lay at the heart of philanthropic optimism. Even the signs of realism in Jeffersonian thought became in actuality manifestations of humanitarian naïveté. The Indian could certainly be cajoled, cozened, and bamboozled into a position somewhat closer to civilization, and because he faced annihilation as an alternative, one might well overlook the superciliousness of such manipulation. Yet with the end of the process in racial amalgamation only a distant hope, the irony in Jeffersonian philanthropy became more poignant. The intensive use of manipulation could not compensate for the limited results obtained from the direct program of civilization. The amalgamation of the two societies never took place.

In part the problem could be attributed to a lapse in logic. It did not follow from the Indian's adoption of some of the white man's ways, farming, home manufacture, and political organization, that he would then automatically be melded with the white into one society. The civilized native should have ceased being an Indian, but he did so only in part; native society changed drastically, but it remained discernible as native society. It did not disappear within the enveloping folds of the white man's world. Because the philanthropist doubted that a straight presentation of the advantages of civilization would convince the Indian to commit cultural suicide, he accompanied his missionary activity with a plethora of strategems designed to accomplish his end without the Indian's conscious assent. The Indian accommodated him in little ways, but he never took the final step into cultural and racial oblivion.

Manipulated, coddled, and trampled upon, the Indian proved less able to meet the demands of progress. Philanthropy was premised on the Indian's willing acceptance of civilization, but the policy of indirection supposed either his lack of capacity or his refusal to do so. Humanitarians looked forward to the time when the tribesman would take his place in the civilized world in full possession of the self-esteem and autonomy so prized by white men. Yet in resorting to a policy that began by denying the Indian the opportunity to make his own way in the world, they not only contributed

to the breakdown of the tribal order but created a native population constitutionally incapable of making the transition to civilization. Finally, philanthropic manipulation made enemies of the new
leadership that came forward in many of the tribes after the War of
1812. Most Indians had a very clear idea of the identity of their
enemies, but philanthropic policy often made it difficult for them
to distinguish their friends. Whatever realistic hope could be held
out for incorporation, it required the maintenance of friendship
and trust between the two peoples. The objective difficulties of
Indian-white relations allowed little enough room for either; manipulation did much to eliminate them entirely.

The policy of indirection was more than a reaction to the failure
of the civilizing plan. It could be seen as closely allied to the white
man's effort to conquer the native tribes. Stubborn Indians who
stood in the way of progress would ultimately be forced to yield.
But for all the vast resources expended in destroying the tribes
militarily, the government and its philanthropic allies also invested
considerable energy in maneuvering them into a condition congenial to American policy. And yet there were real differences between open warfare and even the worst sort of intimidation. In the
1790s the civilizing program was initiated as an alternative to frontier conflict. Philanthropists supported war when necessary, but
they conceived of it as evidence of the failure of their program. For
all its defects, manipulation could not be separated from the larger
civilizing effort; at least it held out some hope for success. Open conflict represented the antithesis of civilized life.

Illusions

Chapter VII

Violence

I

Late in the afternoon of July 11, 1782, about a mile from the Delaware village on the Tymachee in Ohio, Dr. John D. Knight sat horror-struck at the scene before him. His Indian captors had forced him to view the systematic annihilation of his commanding officer, Colonel William Crawford. The Indians—Delaware with a sprinkling of Wyandot—under the command of the war chiefs, Captain Pipe and Wingenund, had routed Crawford's force and had taken a number of captives, some of whom they proposed to torture. According to Knight, the Indians singled out Crawford for special treatment; they inflicted on him the painful refinements of many centuries of savage violence. Let Knight describe the scene:

When we went to the fire the Col. was stripped naked, ordered to sit down by the fire and then they beat him with sticks and their fists. Presently after I was treated in the same manner. They then tied a rope to the foot of a post about fifteen feet high, bound the Col's hands behind his back and fastened the rope to the ligature between his wrists. The rope was long enough for him to sit down or walk round the post once or twice and return the same way. The Col. then called to [Simon] Girty and asked if they intended to burn him? Girty answered, yes. The Col. said he would take it all patiently. Upon this Captain Pipe, a Delaware chief, made a speech to the Indians, viz.: about thirty or forty men, sixty or seventy squaws and boys.

When the speech was finished they all yelled a hideous and hearty assent to what had been said. The Indian men then took up their guns and shot powder into the Colonel's body, from his feet as far up as his neck. I think not less than seventy loads were discharged upon his naked body. They then crowded about him, and to the best of my observation, cut off his ears; when the throng was dispersed a little I saw the blood running from both sides of his head in consequence thereof.

The fire was about six or seven yards from the post to which the Colonel was tied; it was made of small hickory poles, burnt quite through in the middle, each end of the poles remaining about six feet in length.

Three or four Indians by turns would take up, individually, one of these burning pieces of wood and apply it to his naked body, already burnt black with the powder. These tormentors presented themselves on every side of him with the burning faggots and poles. Some of the squaws took broad boards, upon which they would carry a quantity of burning coals and hot embers and throw on him, so that in a short time he had nothing but coals of fire and hot ashes to walk upon. . . .

Col. Crawford at this period of his sufferings besought the Almighty to have mercy on his soul, spoke very low, and bore his torments with the most manly fortitude. He continued in all the extremities of pain for an hour and three-quarters or two hours longer, as near as I can judge, when at last being almost exhausted, he lay down on his belly; they then scalped him and repeatedly threw the scalp in my face, telling me "that was my great captain." An old squaw (whose appearance every way answered the ideas people entertain of the Devil,) got a board, took a parcel of coals and ashes and laid them on his back and head, after he had been scalped, he then raised himself upon his feet and began to walk round the post; they next put a burning stick to him as usual, but he seemed more insensible of pain than before.

At this point, the Indians took Knight from the scene, and he did not see Crawford's last moments. Simon Girty reported that "they roasted him by a slow fire."[1]

Knight's description of Crawford's torture brought to perfection the white man's conception of the native art of ritual murder. The account, though superficially painting the savages in flaming orgy over the dissolving form of Crawford, showed the workmanlike precision with which they went at their business. They knew what they were about, not only for killing their victim but also for the purpose of draining every particle of violence from the scene, by which the tribe exorcised the injuries it had received in war. This ritualistic pursuit of vengeance particularly fascinated and outraged civilized observers. The Indians seemed fiendish in their single-minded

1. H. H. Brackenridge, ed., *Indian Atrocities. Narratives of the Perils and Sufferings of Dr. Knight and John Slover, among the Indians, during the Revolutionary War* . . . (Cincinnati, 1867), 22–25. See also C. W. Butterfield, *An Historical Account of the Expedition against Sandusky under Col. William Crawford in 1782* . . . (Cincinnati, 1873), chap. 20; Nathaniel Knowles, "The Torture of Captives by the Indians of Eastern North America," Am. Phil. Soc., *Procs.*, LXXXII (1940), 151–225, offers a thorough survey of the uses of torture by the eastern Indians. He finds, especially among the Iroquois, that it was an important functional element in their culture. Among the southeastern Indians, this does not seem to have been the case. Torture was practiced, but it was derivative and nonfunctional. The use of the stake, for example, was an adaptation from European methods. Knowles makes passing mention of the Crawford incident (p. 178), but has him a British officer tortured by the Shawnees; see also Wendel S. Hadlock, "War among the Northeastern Woodland Indians," *Am. Anthro.*, N.S., XLIX (1947), 204–221.

cultivation of human agony. By its side the white man's violent response lacked the symmetry, the artistic finality, of the native's performance. Europe had bequeathed a long tradition of violence, and some of it, as in public executions, had served a social function, but the white man's behavior in wilderness warfare gave more evidence of civilization's decline than of his capacity to defend civilized order. By striking out with indiscriminate rage at his savage enemy, the frontiersman demonstrated that the Indian in his desperate struggle for survival was yet capable of making the white man abandon his claims to cultural superiority. Whether taken from the point of view of the Indian or the white, frontier violence held its place as the antithesis of civilization. It worked against both the Indian's chance to attain civilization and the white man's to maintain its integrity.

Witness the massacre of Moravian Indians at Gnadenhutten in Ohio—an incident that occurred the same year but before Crawford's death and that the Indians cited as an excuse for killing him. Early in 1782 the northwestern frontier came under intermittent harassment by the tribes. A number of incidents had occurred before the whites sent out the expedition that ended at Gnadenhutten. On February 8 the tribesmen murdered John Fink near Buchanan, Ohio, and a short time after, they took Mrs. Robert Wallace and her three children captive near Raccoon Creek. The mother and her infant were tomahawked and scalped on the way back to the Indian country. One son died while with the Indians, and the other remained captive for over two years. John Carpenter fell into the hands of Indians, two of whom he claimed were Moravians, but managed his escape. Within sight of the fort at Buchanan on March 8, 1782, the warriors wounded William White in the hip, scalped and mutilated him, before taking Timothy Dorman and his wife prisoner.

In the wake of these atrocities, Colonel David Williamson, soon after to be Crawford's second in command, led the militia of Washington County, Pennsylvania, in a foray into the western territory. The Moravian historian George Henry Loskiel described the slaughter of the Christian Indians at Gnadenhutten by Williamson and his men:

When the day of their execution arrived, namely the 8th of March, two houses were fixed upon, one for the Brethren and another for the Sisters and children, to which the wanton murderers gave the name of slaughter-houses. Some of them went to the Indian Brethren and showed great impatience, that the execution had not yet begun, to which the Brethren replied, that they were ready to die, having commended their immortal souls to God, who had given them that divine assurance in their hearts, that they should come unto him, and be with him for ever.

Immediately after this declaration the carnage commenced. The poor innocent people, men, women, and children were led, bound two and two together with ropes, into the above-mentioned slaughter-houses and there scalped and murdered.

According to the testimony of the murderers themselves, they behaved with uncommon patience and went to meet death with chearful resignation. . . . Brother Abraham was the first victim. A Sister, called Christina, who had formerly lived with the Sisters in Bethlehem, and spoke English and German well, fell on her knees before the captain of the gang and begged her life, but was told, that he could not help her.

Thus ninety-six persons magnified the name of the Lord, by patiently meeting a cruel death. Sixty-two were grown persons, among whom were five of the most valuable assistants, and thirty-four children.

Only two youths, each between fifteen and sixteen years old, escaped almost miraculously from the hands of the murderers. One of them, seeing that they were in earnest, was so fortunate as to disengage himself from his bonds, then slipping unobserved from the crowd, crept through a narrow window, into the cellar of that house in which the Sisters were executed. Their blood soon penetrated through the flooring, and according to his account, ran in streams into the cellar, by which it appears probable, that most, if not all of them, were not merely scalped, but killed with hatchets or swords. The lad remained concealed till night, providentially not one coming down to search the cellar, when having with much difficulty climbed up the wall to the window, he crept through and escaped into a neighboring thicket. The other youth's name was Thomas. The murderers struck him only one blow on the head, took his scalp, and left him. But after some time he recovered his senses and saw himself surrounded by bleeding corpses. Among these he observed one Brother, called Abel, moving and endeavoring to raise himself up. But he remained lying as still as though he had been dead, and this caution proved the means of his deliverance: for soon after, one of the murderers coming in, and observing Abel's motions, killed him outright with two or three blows. Thomas lay quiet till dark, though suffering the most exquisite torment. He then ventured to creep towards the door, and observing nobody in the neighborhood, got out and escaped into the wood, where he concealed himself during the night. These two youths met afterwards in the wood, and God preserved them from harm on their journey to Sandusky, though they purposely took a long circuit, and suffered great hardships and danger. But before they left the neighborhood of Gnadenhuetten they observed the murderers from behind the thicket making merry after their successful enterprise, and at last setting fire to the two slaughter-houses filled with corpses.[2]

2. George Henry Loskiel, *History of the Mission of the United Brethren among the Indians in North America*, trans. Christian Ignatius La Trobe (London, 1794), Pt. III, 180–181; C. W. Butterfield, *Expedition against Sandusky*, 33–35; C. W. Butterfield, ed., *Washington-Irvine Correspondence: The Official Letters which Passed between Washington and Brig.-Gen. William*

Humanitarians found it difficult to retain their belief in the smooth transfer of civilization from white to Indian in the face of such portrayals of reciprocal violence. Environmentalism supposed an entirely positive and dynamic relationship between the two societies, but the description of mutual destruction contained in much Jeffersonian literature conveyed a picture of static opposition between two irreconcilable enemies. The reality of white and Indian violence on the frontier held less significance than the pictorial disjunction between savagery and civilization so vividly implied in the white man's fixation with the macabre details of frontier conflict. The opposition to incorporation may have been fostered by other equally deep-seated reasons, but it certainly drew strength from the conviction that a person as violent as the Indian seemed to be could not take part in civilized life. In any event, the intemperate cultivation of frontier violence as virtually a literary genre illustrated the intensity with which even well-disposed men felt the opposition between the two societies.

2

Violence could be considered no more characteristic of Indian-white relations on the frontier than trade and the various forms of peaceful intercourse. Nevertheless, it had a way of catching the white man's imagination, of riveting his attention to the least laudable aspects of frontier life. By concentrating on the more gruesome episodes of Indian-white warfare, the civilized observer became deeply impressed by the division between civilization and savagery. As the noble savage theme had eased the transition from one to the other, the obverse image of the vicious savage accentuated the divergence between the two conceptions of humanity. Even the culturally disintegrated Indian, no matter how pathetic his condition, offered slim hope that he might absorb some of the blessings of civilization. The primitive hunter bent on preserving the old ways claimed virtue enough to support a hope for his ultimate conversion. But the violent savage, indulging as a matter of course the unspeakable propensities of man before civilization had ordered his life in a more peaceful mode, cut himself off from the processes

Irvine and between Irvine and Others concerning Military Affairs in the West from 1781 to 1783 (Madison, 1882), 99–100n; see p. 237n for a description of the Gnadenhutten incident by Frederick Leinbach that parallels Loskiel's account. For the contention that the Gnadenhutten and Crawford affairs were connected, see Downes, *Council Fires on the Upper Ohio*, 271–274; Milo M. Quaife, "The Ohio Campaigns of 1782," *The Mississippi Valley Historical Review*, XVII (1930–1931), 519.

of amelioration. He was necessarily both uncivilized and un-civilizable.

After offering a typical description of native torture, Edmund Burke commented that such behavior demonstrated "to what in-conceivable degree of barbarity the passions of men let loose will carry them." Religion taught men compassion; civilization had "softened the ferocity of the human race." The traveler and trader John Long pictured the savage stimulated by his thirst for blood to cover immense distances in the forests, to endure inexpressible hardships, all to satisfy his grisly passion, and then to return ex-ultant from his expedition and relate in detail the agonies inflicted on the enemy. "The most dreadful acts of a maniac cannot exceed such cruelty: happy those, who enjoy the benefits of society, whose civilization, and whose laws protect them from such detestible out-rages." H. H. Brackenridge, having no high opinion of the Indian, directed his strictures at those philosophers (he likened them to young women who read romances and had no knowledge of life) who looked for perfect virtue in the "simplicity of the unrefined state." "All that is good and great in man," he wrote, "results from education; an uncivilized Indian is but a little way removed from a beast who, when incensed, can only tear and devour, but the savage applies the ingenuity of man to torture and inflict anguish." Indian violence and civilization occupied opposite poles of human existence. The philanthropic plan to transmit civilization through education faltered in the face of the Indian's persistent habit of indulging in a level of ferocity inconsistent with the white man's notion of humane civilization.[3]

Curiously, no precise connection can be made between the actual level of frontier conflict and the decision to transfer the civilizing effort west of the Mississippi. In fact, it appeared that the intensity of frontier war lessened as the evidence came in that the civilizing program could not be continued in the East. The defeat of the Indians during the War of 1812, the last important conflict in the East, only confirmed what had been made certain in the 1790s: the white man had established his hegemony over the frontier re-gions, and the Indian would either retreat or accommodate himself to civilization. But more significant, at the very time when the

3. [Edmund Burke], *An Account of the European Settlements in Amer-ica* . . . , new ed. (London, 1766) , I, 185; Long, *Voyages and Travels,* 76. Brackenridge is in Archibald Loudon, comp., *A Selection, of Some of the Most Interesting Narratives, of Outrages, Committed by the Indians, in Their Wars, with the White People* . . . (Harrisburg, 1888 [orig. publ., Carlisle, Pa., 1808–1811]) , I, v.

Indian, convinced of the impossibility of victory, began busily adopting civilized ways or became so demoralized as to be incapable of offering violent resistance, the white man markedly increased his appetite for vicarious savage violence. The captivity narrative, for example, as a genre dedicated to the cultivation of quasi-fictional violence, began to flourish at the moment that the eastern Indians had stopped behaving in the manner it described. Furthermore, it continued to be an important source of the folklore of Indian-white conflict throughout the period of philanthropic disillusion with the civilization program. As the Indian supposedly showed less and less capacity for entering civilization, his public image, through the medium of the captivity narrative, became more and more violent. Whatever the reality, there can be no doubt that white men continued to believe in the disjunction between civilization and savagery, order and violence.[4]

Jefferson believed firmly that the two could be mixed only at the peril of civilization. Precisely at the point that the Indians gave up their vicious mode of war, they would be eligible for civilized life. The Cherokees began their admirable progress toward civilization only after the Revolution, when they ceased "murdering and scalping helpless women and children according to their cruel and cowardly principles of warfare." John Eaton, Jackson's secretary of war, in pointing out the Indians' failure to become civilized and in hinting at their incapacity to do so, noted that "if they have yielded the barbarous practice of burning prisoners at the stake, they have not even after the lapse of many years, and frequent association with the whites, surrendered the no less savage habit of considering women and children fit subjects for the Tomahawk and scalping knife." In his usual frenetic style, McKenney sketched the image of the savage that worked against the Indian's successful incorporation into the white man's society.

Which of us has not listened with sensations of horror to the nursery stories that are told of the Indian and his cruelties? In our infant mind,

4. Roy Harvey Pearce, "The Significances of the Captivity Narrative," *American Literature*, XIX (1947–1948), 6, dates the transition from the captivity narrative as matter-of-fact description and manifestation of God's providence to the "blood and thunder shocker" in the mid-18th century, which conforms with his contention that the image of the Indian was negative after that date; see Pearce, *Savages of America*, ix, 3–4, 41–42, 73–74. Certainly by the second and third decades of the 19th century, the captivity narrative as a genre portrayed the Indian mainly as a violent savage; see the two major anthologies that reprint narratives in the period: Loudon, comp., *Narratives of Outrages;* Samuel G. Drake, ed., *Indian Captivities or Life in the Wigwam . . .* (Auburn, N.Y., 1852).

he stood for the Moloch of our country. We have been made to hear his yell; and to our eyes have been presented his tall, gaunt form, with the skins of beasts dangling round his limbs, and his eyes like fire, eager to find some new victim on which to fasten himself, and glut his appetite for blood. We have been made to see the desperate onset: to hear the piercing war-cry, and the clash of arms, and the heavy, dead sound of the war-club, as it fell on the head of the victim . . . and then we have had disclosed to us the scene of carnage; and the Indian striding amidst the bodies of the slain; or beheld him seated over some favorite victim, with his fingers dripping with blood, and his face disclosing a ferocious smile, as he enjoyed the sight of the quivering limbs, and the agonies of the dying![5]

Bloodcurdling imaginings of this sort could not be easily ignored.

3

The conception of the Indian as synonymous with war and violence drew on a long tradition. Howard Mumford Jones has pointed to the similarities in the rhetoric used to describe savage war in America and that employed in accounts of the civil conflict in Ireland in the sixteenth century.[6] Bestiality seemed equally natural to the Irishman and the native American, and neither appeared susceptible to the taming of civilized manners. The Indian as warrior behaved in a manner consistent with his primitive condition. The absence of civilization, in this negative formulation, presumed a world of violence and savagery.

Consequently, Jeffersonian thought tended to view war as inherent in the savage condition. From civilization men learned to accommodate animosities—savage diplomacy brought war to an end, it did not prevent it. Jedidiah Morse spoke of the Indians' "taste for war which forms the chief ingredient of their character." DeWitt Clinton voiced the frequently heard opinion, from which he excepted the Iroquois only, that "with savages in general, this ferocious propensity was impelled by a blind fury, and was but little regulated by the dictates of skill and judgment." The Indian tribes, according to Clinton, engaged in interminable conflict that stunted their cultural progress and kept their numbers small. They utterly destroyed their enemies by eating their bodies, not because they

5. Jefferson, "Sketch of the Chief Incidents in the Life of Capt. Meriwether Lewis," Aug. 18, 1813, in Jackson, ed., *Letters of Lewis and Clark Expedition*, 587; Eaton to Forsyth, Oct. 14, 1829, Letters Sent, Off. Indian Affairs (M-21), Roll 6: 114; McKenney, *Memoirs, Official and Personal*, I, 233.

6. Jones, *O Strange New World*, 167–173: "Doubtless the Spaniards, the Portuguese and the French were equally brutal in a cruel and brutal age, but the doctrine that the only good Indian is a dead Indian first took shape, it would appear, in the doctrine that the only good wild Irishman is a dead wild Irishman."

had an appetite for such fare but in order to excite themselves to greater fury. Those unfortunate enough to be captured would be killed with "the most severe and protracted sufferings."[7]

James Adair, a particularly knowledgeable observer of Indian life, expressed more tentative opinions about the place of war in the primitive world. He concluded at one point that war resulted largely from conflict between two incompatible cultures. The Indians did not wage war on each other unless prompted to it by the white traders. And when they did fight each other, they killed few on either side. They showed their distaste for war, according to Adair, by purging themselves at its end in propitiation for the shedding of blood. Yet he also insisted that the tribesmen's natural belligerence required a firm hand from the white man. The native would interpret any sign of weakness as an invitation to aggression. "A mean submissive temper can never manage our Indian affairs." He seemed to detect a natural pugnacity in all primitive cultures. Without the advantages of improved intellectual powers and an acquaintance with the sciences, such societies

cannot well live without war; and being destitute of public faith to secure the lives of ambassadors in time of war, they have no sure method to reconcile their differences: consequently, when any casual thing draws them into a war, it grows every year more spiteful till it advances to a bitter enmity, so as to excite them to an implacable hatred to one another's very national names. Then they must go abroad to spill the enemy's blood, and to revenge crying blood. We must also consider, it is by scalps they get all their war titles, which distinguish them among the brave: and these they hold in as high esteem, as the most ambitious Roman general ever did a great triumph. By how much the deeper any society of people are sunk in ignorance, so much the more they value themselves on their bloody merit.[8]

Most observers believed that the Indians fought mainly for revenge. Other issues sometimes came into play: disputes over land, competition for hunting grounds, the need to augment a diminishing population through the adoption of captives, and even the quest for empire. But these emotionally extraneous motives, the results of rational calculation, did not fit the conception of savagery as inherently violent. "Excuse my telling you these things," the Oneida chief Good Peter addressed Timothy Pickering in 1791, "we do not fight for lands. After we have done fighting, we do not

7. [Morse], *History of America*, 48; Clinton, "Discourse Delivered before the New-York Historical Society," N.-Y. Hist. Soc., *Colls.*, II (1814), 54–56, 86.

8. Adair, *History of American Indians*, 151–152, 224, 274, 286–288, 367, 379–380, 388.

think we have the lands in our grasp. This is the rule of ancient times." Such evidence merely strengthened the white man's tendency to trace the Indian's violent inclinations to sources deep in his primitive being. Revenge had the sound of an indiscriminate savage reaction; it made war arise from causes intrinsic to the Indian character. Jonathan Carver wrote that "the passion of revenge, which is the distinguishing characteristic of these people, is the most general motive [for war]. Injuries are felt by them with exquisite sensibility, and vengeance pursued with unremitted ardor." John Heckewelder, a usually sympathetic observer of Indian life, admitted that "the worse that can be said of them is that the passion of revenge is so strong in their minds that it carried them beyond all bounds." But it was left to Albert Gallatin to treat the subject historically: "[The Iroquois] conquered only to destroy: and, it would seem, solely for the purpose of gratifying their thirst for blood. Towards the south and the west, they made a perfect desert of the whole country within five hundred miles of their seats. A much greater number of those Indians, who, since the commencement of the seventeenth century have perished by the sword in Canada and the United States, have been destroyed by that single nation than in all their wars with the Europeans."[9] Gallatin followed the account of native ferocity given by Cadwallader Colden, who had supplied some of the basic evidence for what the naturalist Thomas Nuttall called the native American's indiscriminate "thirst for revenge."

9. Good Peter to Pickering and Iroquois Council, July 14, 1791, Pickering Papers, LX, 104, Mass. Hist. Soc. (microfilm); Carver, *Three Years Travels,* 194; Heckewelder, "Account of the Indian Nations," Am. Phil. Soc., *Trans. of Hist. and Lit. Comm.,* I (1819), 328 (Heckewelder added: "But set this aside, and their character is noble and great"); Gallatin, "Synopsis of the Indian Tribes," Am. Antiq. Soc., *Archaeologia Americana,* II, 79–80; Cadwallader Colden, *The History of the Five Indian Nations Depending on the Province of New-York in America* (London, 1747), 27; Thomas Nuttall, *A Journal of Travels into the Arkansa Territory, during the Year 1819 . . .* (Ann Arbor, 1966 [orig. publ. Philadelphia, 1821]), 236. George S. Snyderman, *Behind the Tree of Peace: A Sociological Analysis of Iroquois Warfare* (Philadelphia, 1948), chap. 3, confirms the belief that revenge was closely associated with Iroquois warfare. He connects revenge with the notion of the blood feud, but notes that neither can be considered as a cause of Indian war. Rather, both were useful images through which the Indian viewed the fact of war, which was the result of a complex of causes—desire for land, prestige, need to increase population through adoptions. See Hadlock, "War among the Northeastern Woodland Indians," *Am. Anthro.,* N.S., XLIX (1947), 213–217. Also Rogers, *Concise Account of North America,* 212–213; Williams, *History of Vermont,* 142–144; [Morse], *History of America,* 35; Smith, *Essay on Variety,* 2d ed., 360–363; *Am. Museum,* V (1789), 147–149.

4

Civilized opinion found no difficulty in combining the disinterested
ferocity of savage torture with the uncontrolled frenzy of Indian
warfare. Revenge explained both the motives of the scientific tor-
turer and the impulse of the savage warrior. Revenge also helped to
explain why the Indian waged total war. Limited only by technological incapacity, native conflict affected all members of society.
Samuel Stanhope Smith contrasted the "cool policy," which he
thought motivated civilized conflict, with

> those furious, and deadly passions which inflame barbarian soldiers, and
> savage warriors. Being but a small proportion to the population of the
> country, the nation is but little affected by the individual fate of those
> who fall in battle. And armies are so constituted, that the loss of thousands
> of the common soldiery possesses but small interest in the sympathies of
> that class of society which chiefly influences the public measures, and
> gives the tone to the public feeling. If a few of better rank are slain in
> the field, their friends are consoled by the glory of their fall. But, among
> the savages of America, the same men who fight, decide the fate of the
> prisoners, and they do it with the same passions with which they fought.
> They have no reasons of state, which induce nations to make war without
> passion. Their wars are the consequences of recent injuries keenly felt.
> Their armies, although small, bear a large proportion to their entire pop-
> ulation. Every warrior stands in some relation of kindred to his whole
> tribe. . . . No artificial sentiments of glory serve to console the survi-
> vors. . . .[10]

The passionate totality of native warfare set it apart from the
comparatively disciplined activity of civilized conflict.

Many white men had long thought that the Indian waged war
for the purpose of destroying as many as possible of the opposing
side. In Adair's words, once the contest began, the Indians had no
sense of where to end it. "Their thirst for the blood of their reputed
enemies, is not to be quenched with a few drops—The more they
drink, the more it inflames their thirst. When they dip their finger
in human blood, they are restless till they plunge themselves in it."
In war the Indian killed at random, in order to exterminate the
enemy. Women, children, and warriors suffered the same fate.
"Even the foetal state is criminal . . . ," wrote Joseph Doddridge.
"It is not enough that the foetus should perish with the murdered
mother, it is torn from her pregnant womb and elevated on a stick
or pole, as a trophy of victory and an object of horror, to the survivors of the slain." The murdered children could not then grow

10. Smith, *Essay on Variety*, 2d ed., 399-400.

into warriors or the mothers of warriors. The battle must be won, and the enemy must be incapacitated for fighting any future battles.[11]

One of the more gruesome episodes in the history of Indian warfare had been the Iroquois conquest of the Hurons. From it the Five Nations acquired their reputation for military superiority. Whatever the real reasons for the conflict and for the decisive victory of the Iroquois, it constituted a startling sample of the violent propensities supposedly inherent in the primitive state. And it occurred, in the Jeffersonian view, without the influence of the whites. Indian set upon Indian. Surely the inherent viciousness of the natives had caused the conflict. Smith conjured a vision of violence and despair: the Iroquois crouch on the outskirts of a Huron village that lacks either ramparts or guards; at a favorable moment in the early morning, they spring upon the unsuspecting enemy.

Some, bearing flaming brands in their hands, fire the huts in various directions. Others burst open the ill barred doors with hideous yells, and attack the wretched inhabitants just waking from sleep and confounded with these frightful and diabolical sounds. At this moment little use is made of their fire arms. They rely chiefly on the murderous tomahawk. They sink it into the skulls of the defenceless, and mangle the limbs of those who attempt to make any resistance. Men, women, and children share the same fate, and are slaughtered without distinction. At length, some of the wretched victims, escaping from their burning habitations, maintain a desperate conflict with the victors in the area before their doors. Despair augments their force. With the fury of demons they rush upon their conquerors. They conflict, they mingle their tomahawks, with most frightful yells and screeches: all is despair, and rage; and, the flaming town shedding a dismal light upon this scene of darkness and horror, resembles what our imaginations have pictured most dreadful in hell.[12]

In the carnage that ensued, the Iroquois killed and mutilated with abandon. Finally, having sated the urge for blood, they took the

---

11. Adair, *History of American Indians*, 246; Doddridge, *Notes, on Settlement and Indian Wars*, 207–210.

12. Smith, *Essay on Variety*, 2d ed., 375–376. For evidence that the Iroquois-Huron conflict was tightly intertwined with the influence of the white man's technology and the fur trade, see George T. Hunt, *The Wars of the Iroquois: A Study in Intertribal Trade Relations* (Madison, 1940), 11–12, 87–100. Hunt's thesis is that the European influence made Indian war incomparably more violent than it had ever been before. In a review of the Hunt volume, *Am. Anthro.*, N.S., XLII (1940), 662–664, William N. Fenton commends the thesis that the Iroquois-Huron war was associated with the economic demands of European infiltration, but rejects a monistic economic interpretation. His overall proposition is that Indian society proved remarkably durable despite serious white inroads.

few survivors prisoner to endure a more horrid fate on the return to the victor's country.

These atrocities, saved by the Indians for the entertainment of the home village, interested white men as much as did descriptions of the warriors in the heat of conflict. Howard Mumford Jones records the various crimes attributed to the Indians during King Philip's War: "The contest was illustrated . . . by the raping and scalping of women, the cutting off of fingers and feet of men, the skinning of white captives, the ripping open the bellies of pregnant women, the cutting off of the penises of the males, and the wearing of the fingers of the white men as bracelets or necklaces." Adair thought the Indian treatment of prisoners "so shocking to humanity" that it defied description, a widely held opinion that in no way inhibited the vivid portrayal of torture scenes. The natives apparently cultivated torture as an art and as a communal spectacle that permitted noncombatants to partake of the bloody satisfactions of successful combat. For the victim, the Indians closely associated the endurance of pain with manhood. The warrior's anesthetized nervous system, it seemed, set him apart from the less stoical white man—though Colonel Crawford acquitted himself well enough and Simon Kenton reputedly ran the gauntlet no less than nine times.[13] Morse offered a synopsis of the white man's version of the native method:

They begin at the extremity of his body, and, gradually, approach the more vital parts. One plucks out his nails by the roots, one by one; another takes a finger into his mouth, and tears off the flesh with his teeth; a third thrusts the finger, mangled as it is, into the bowl of a pipe made red-hot, which he smokes like tobacco; then they pound his toes and fingers to pieces between two stones; they cut circles about his joints, and gashes in the fleshy parts of his limbs, which they sear immediately with red-hot irons, cutting, burning, and pinching them alternately; they pull of his flesh, thus mangled and roasted, bit by bit, devouring it with greediness, and smearing their faces with the blood, in an enthusiasm of horror and fury. When they have thus torn off the flesh, they twist the bare nerves and tendons about an iron, tearing and snapping them, whilst others are employed in pulling and extending his limbs in every way that can increase the torment. This continues, often, five or six hours; and sometimes, such is the strength of the savages, days together. Then they frequently unbind him, to give a breathing to their fury, to think what new torments they shall inflict, and to refresh the strength of the sufferer, who, wearied out with such a variety of unheard-of torments, often falls into so profound a sleep, that they are obliged to apply the fire to awake

13. Jones, *O Strange New World*, 59; Adair, *History of American Indians*, 388–389, 395–396. For an account of Kenton's ordeal, see Moore, *Frontier Mind*, 100–102.

him, and renew his sufferings. He is again fastened to the stake, and again they renew their cruelty; they stick him all over with small matches of wood that easily takes fire but burns slowly; they continually run sharp reeds into every part of his body; they drag out his teeth with pincers and thrust out his eyes; and, lastly, after having burned his flesh from the bones with slow fires; after having so mangled the body that it is all but one wound; after having mutilated his face in such a manner as to carry nothing human in it; after having peeled the skin from the head, and poured a heap of red-hot coals or boiling water, on the naked skull— they once more unbind the wretch; who, blind, and staggering with pain and weakness, assaulted and pelted on every side with clubs and stones, now up, now down, falling into their fires at every step, runs hither and thither, until one of the chiefs, whether out of compassion, or weary of cruelty, puts an end to his life with a club or dagger. The body is then put into a kettle, and this barbarous employment is succeeded by a feast as barbarous.[14]

The particulars of the description held less significance than the patent exaggeration. Even if the Indian had possessed the imagination to inflict such an array of tortures, no victim could have long endured them. The more bizarre the story, the better the Jeffersonian age liked it and the wider the implicit gulf between civilization and savagery.

No doubt, the truth of most of the accounts of Indian violence should be questioned.[15] The captivity narratives in particular contain many overdone, self-conscious, and obviously contrived descriptions of aboriginal ferocity. Yet violence did play an important part in tribal life; Indians inflicted pain with much less misgiving than did civilized men, and this deeply impressed white men. Violence from both sides had always been an important element in accounts of Indian-white relations. In the Jesuit Relations, a treasure-house of anthropological information, violence constituted a major Indian diversion.[16] The Jeffersonian period continued the general fascination with the subject. A constant flow of literature treated readers to a high level of stimulation. With time, the Indian increased his proficiency in inventing contrivances for the white prisoner's destruction. Writers gave vent to a single-minded attempt to convey to the reader the tribesman's utter lapse in humanity. As the antithesis of civilization, he became more a demonic force than a liv-

14. [Morse], *History of America*, 42–44, where the general scene is reminiscent of Knight's version of Crawford's torture; also Burke, *Account of European Settlements in America*, 182–184.

15. Stanley Pargellis, "The Problem of American Indian History," *Ethnohistory*, IV (1957), 117–120.

16. John H. Kennedy, *Jesuit and Savage in New France* (New Haven, 1950), 128–129.

ing person, a rampaging demiurge, not just a member of a primitive culture with deficient manners. Once the literature of the Jeffersonian age took up propaganda seriously, accuracy became irrelevant.

Some variations on the usual torture-at-the-stake procedure were truly spectacular feats for all concerned. One imaginative innovation called for the burial of the victim so that only his head showed above the ground and the infliction upon him of a variety of atrocities, culminating in burning until, as Timothy Flint put it, "his brain boiled" and "the pupils of his eyes burst from their sockets."[17] The pine-splinter method used on the famous Manheim twins (sixteen-year-old virgins) called for puncturing the body with numerous pitch-soaked splinters that the warriors then set afire.[18] Surely the most ingenious anatomical achievement prescribed an incision in the victim's abdomen from which the torturers extracted a loose end of his intestine, which they fastened to a tree; they then drove the unfortunate fellow in a circle, unraveling his insides. Additions of any number of bizarre anecdotes would not affect the basic fantasy of the many accounts of savage atrocity.[19]

Yet the violence of frontier war need not be exaggerated. Witness the cool matter-of-factness of Mrs. Elizabeth Hanson, who failed to silence one of her shrieking children for the convenience of her Indian captors. The savages "to ease themselves of the noise, and to prevent the danger of a discovery that might arise from it, immediately, before my face, knocked his brains out. I bore this as well as I could, not daring to appear disturbed or to show much uneasiness, lest they should do the same to the others." Mary Jemison, a famous captive who lived many years with the Senecas, described the scene along the Ohio in 1758. Passing a Shawnee town, charred heads, arms, legs, and miscellaneous fragments of white settlers who had just been burned could be seen hanging along the shore. "The fire was yet burning; and the whole appearances afforded a spectacle so shocking, that, even to this day, my blood almost curdles in my veins when I think of them!"[20]

17. Flint, *Indian Wars of the West*, 40–41. Flint's story follows closely an account by the sensational Peter Williamson. See Drake, ed., *Indian Captivities*, 152–153; Loudon, comp., *Narratives of Outrages*, I, 107–110.

18. *Am. Museum*, I (1787), 295–296; also James E. Seaver, *A Narrative of the Life of Mrs. Mary Jemison . . .* (New York, 1961 [orig. publ. Canandaigua, N.Y., 1824]), 28.

19. Seaver, *Life of Mary Jemison*, 81; Loudon, comp., *Narratives of Outrages*, II, 188.

20. Drake, ed., *Indian Captivities*, 115; Seaver, *Life of Mary Jemison*, 43.

With a disarming frankness that rings true despite the loaded prose of her interlocutor, John Seaver, Mrs. Jemison told of the training of her last husband.

> In early life, Hiokatoo showed signs of thirst for blood by attending only to the art of war, in the use of the tomahawk and scalping knife; and in practising cruelties upon every thing that chanced to fall into his hands, which was susceptible of pain. In that way he learned to use his implements of war effectually, and at the same time blunted all those fine feelings and tender sympathies that are naturally excited, by hearing or seeing, a fellow being in distress. He could inflict the most excruciating tortures upon his enemies, and prided himself upon his fortitude, in having performed the most barbarous ceremonies and tortures, without the least degree of pity or remorse. Thus qualified, when very young he was initiated into scenes of carnage, by being engaged in the wars that prevailed amongst the Indian tribes.[21]

As a young man, Hiokatoo took part in the torture of Crawford, apparently making good use of his early education. The descriptive embellishments of the Knight version of that incident pale before Mrs. Jemison's unadorned reportage.

Also, no fantasy-ridden portrayal of savage violence cut more deeply into the Indian's reserve of humanity than the charge of cannibalism. Some commentators denied the accusation; others made palliating distinctions over the circumstances in which Indians would eat human flesh. James Adair protested that they consumed only the heart of the enemy in order to inspire them with his courage, and at the same time, he denied that Indians were cannibals. An occasional account took pleasure in a bloody anecdote. John Long quoted the story of a Jesuit missionary who described an Indian woman feeding her children when her husband arrived with an English prisoner: "She immediately cut off his arm, and gave her children the streaming blood to drink," asserting at the priest's protestation that she wanted her children to be warriors "and therefore fed them with the food of men." A sergeant named Jordan wrote to his wife from the Northwest in 1812 and told of an incident that occurred immediately following his capture by "four damned yellow Indians." One of the natives agreed to spare his life because Jordan had once given him tobacco at Fort Wayne. But the savage went to the body of Captain Wells who lay nearby, "cut off his head and stuck it on a pole, while another took out his heart and divided it among the chiefs, and they ate it up raw."[22] The fact could not be disputed. Indians had eaten human flesh and thus had offended against the moral basis of human existence. No amount of explanation could quite cover the crime, nor would any fanciful description replace the accusation.

The natural affinity between the savage state and violence, whether the unreasoned onslaught of frontier war or the elaborately staged grand guignol of savage torture, widened the gulf between civilization and native society. The intensive cultivation of the subject, the submergence of the actualities of native violence in a formalized literary genre, demonstrated its pertinence for the white man's conception of the Indian. Yet at least until the end of the War of 1812, the setting of Indian violence also tended to unite the two societies. White men also engaged in war and they used Indian allies, sometimes reluctantly but always with the effect of raising the level of ferocity. Ironically, the Indian detracted from his own stature in the eyes of civilization by doing the white man's bidding. And to compound the matter, the white man interpreted his own atrocities as imitations of Indian savagery.

5

The lure of savagery has been noted by Roy Harvey Pearce. "For regularly an irony is remarked by tellers of tales on Indian haters: It is these men who have made the frontier safe for civilization; yet, to do so, they have had to become one of the very savages whom they would destroy." The precious gift of civilization quickly crumbled when men faced savage opposition; seldom did one find a white man capable of retaining his civilized ways undefiled when presented with the problem of survival in the forest. At the point of conflict, the white man could be given little chance of success unless he fought the Indian on his own terms, and this meant adopting methods that the Jeffersonian considered savage. Joseph Dodd-ridge stated the problem succinctly: "History, scarcely presents an example of a civilized nation, carrying on a war with barbarians, without adopting the mode of warfare of the barbarous nation."

22. McCulloh, *Researches, Philosophical and Antiquarian,* 77, 143n; Thwaites, ed., "James's Account of S. H. Long's Expedition," in *Early Western Travels,* XIV, 304–305; Foster, *Jeffersonian America,* ed. Davis, 39–40; Adair, *History of American Indians,* 135, 209; Hulbert and Schwarze, eds., "Zeisberger's History," Ohio Archæol. and Hist. Soc., *Pubs.,* XIX (1910), 107–108; Carver, *Three Years Travels,* 170, 197; Dexter, ed., *Extracts from the Itineraries of Ezra Stiles,* 401. See also Long, *Voyages and Travels,* 77; Esarey, ed., *Messages of Harrison,* II, 165.

The Indians themselves seemed to recognize the close affinity between the wilderness and war. Scaroyady, the Oneida chief, once told the British that they could not "live in the woods and stay neutral."[23] Thus as Indian and white became locked in conflict, the white man behaved more and more like the savage.

In part the problem arose because of the need to deal with the Indian in his own habitat and consequently to accommodate the ways of civilization to those of the forest. The frontiersman could not fight the Indian with the methods of European war. If the tribesman would not accept the white man's rules, the white man would have to accept his. The forest broke the lines of advance, relaxed discipline, and replaced order and preponderant force with cunning and stratagem. Anyone with a sense of reality favored an alteration in the system of European conflict in the face of a savage foe determined to defend his homeland in his own way. Even for those who conceded that savage rules should govern, the Indian remained a deadly enough adversary. The best of the white frontiersmen found difficulty in matching the native on his own ground.[24]

Accounts of the white man's atrocities filled the literature. Cited frequently to prove the unruly frontiersmen the real villain of Indian-white conflict, the stories drew heavily on the fear of the white man's fall from grace under the pressure of frontier necessity. Although civilization could be expected to produce its share of dark deeds, the special circumstances of frontier war tended to make the white man's violence derivative of the Indian's. Scalping,

---

23. Roy Harvey Pearce, "The Metaphysics of Indian-Hating," *Ethnohistory*, IV (1957), 29; Doddridge, *Notes, on Settlement and Indian Wars*, 208. Scaroyady is quoted by Julian P. Boyd, "Indian Affairs in Pennsylvania, 1736–1762," in *Indian Treaties*, xxxiii.

24. "Proposal to the Associators," Mar. 21, 1748, Labaree *et al.*, eds., *Franklin Papers*, III, 281; Franklin, "To the Printer of *The London Chronicle*," May 9, 1769, Smyth, ed., *Writings of Franklin*, V, 210–211; Jefferson to William Fleming, June 8, 1779, Boyd, ed., *Jefferson Papers*, II, 288–289; Jefferson to Harry Innes, Mar. 7, 1791, Lipscomb and Bergh, eds., *Writings of Jefferson*, VIII, 136; Williams, *History of Vermont*, 2d ed. (Burlington, Vt., 1809), I, 300; Moore, *Frontier Mind*, 63. A particularly frank proposal was printed in *Am. Museum*, XI (1792), 38: "But if money must be expended to kill Indians, offer to the whites and friendly Indians a large bounty upon Indian scalps; five, nay ten dollars a scalp. We shall soon see that country clear of savages. Start not at this proposal, as dishonourable. It is not dishonourable. If war must be carried on, by us, it is the most proper way of doing it; for it is the Indian way—and the laws of war urge for retaliation. It is shocking, it is monstrous, to send solid columns of men into the woods, to stand as marks to be shot at by an enemy in the grass. Offer bounties for scalps, and prompt the avarice of men in a war where no glory is to be obtained. Until the mode of war is changed, our men do not fight on equal terms."

for example, became characteristic of war in America. Both whites and Indians took scalps, and colonial authorities encouraged the practice by paying bounties for these trophies. Cotton Mather told of Hannah Dustan, who had been captured by Indians in 1697. With the help of her maid and a young captive, she murdered the sleeping Indians and brought in their scalps, for which the Massachusetts Assembly awarded her fifty pounds. An incident recorded by Benjamin Franklin rivaled Mrs. Dustan's exploits. One David Owens, a regular soldier who had deserted to the Indians during the Seven Years' War, returned in 1764 carrying five Indian scalps and accompanied by a white boy who had been an Indian captive.

The Account given by him and the Boy is, that they were with a Party of nine Indians, to wit, 5 men, 2 Women, and 2 Children, coming down [the] Susquehanah to fetch corn from their last Year's Planting Place; that they went ashore and encamp'd at Night and made a Fire by which they slept: that in the Night Owens made the White Boy get up from among the Indians and go to the other side of the Fire; and then taking up the Indian's Guns, he shot two of the Men immediately, and with his Hatchet dispatch'd another Man together with the Women and Children. Two Men only made their Escape. Owens scalp'd the 5 grown Persons, and bid the White Boy scalp the Children; but he declin'd it, so they were left.

Peter Collinson commented on this description: "What must the Five Indian Nations think of the White Men who vie with them in Cruelties."

Reportedly, Daniel Boone did not take scalps, but he was one of the few. A Pennsylvanian, off to fight the Indians in 1756, voiced a more typical intention: "I for my Part am determined to scalp all I lay my Hands on with unrelenting Rage and there are few in our Troops will show them more Mercy." The practice persisted in the years following. A correspondent of Henry Knox's reported with some surprise that a Kentucky contingent had committed no atrocities against the Indians in the Northwest and had even refrained from the "inveterate habit of scalping the dead."[25] On such a limited but symbolically weighty issue as scalping, the savage way had generally prevailed.

25. Cotton Mather, *Magnalia Christi Americana; or, The Ecclesiastical History of New-England* . . . (Hartford, 1820 [orig. publ. London, 1702]) , II, 550–552; Franklin to Peter Collinson, Apr. 12, 1764, Smyth, ed., *Writings of Franklin*, IV, 241–242, ed. note; John Bakeless, *Daniel Boone: Master of the Wilderness* (New York, 1939) , 163. Simon Kenton, a more typical woodsman, did take scalps. *Ibid.*, 194. Thomas Lloyd to ———, Jan. 30, 1756, Labaree *et al.*, eds., *Franklin Papers*, VI, 382; Charles Scott to Knox, June 28, 1791, *American State Papers, Indian Affairs*, I, 132.

But for evidence of the white man's descent into savagery, scalping could not compare with the story told of David Morgan who encountered two Indians outside a stockade on the Pennsylvania frontier. He clubbed one and killed the other with the victim's own knife before a rescue party arrived from the fort. They encountered the first Indian, who had now revived from Morgan's blow: "He saluted them with, How do do, broder, how do do, broder? but alas! poor savage, their brotherhood to him extended only to tomahawking, scalping, and, to gratify some peculiar feelings of their own, skinning them both; and they have made drum heads of their skins." Rumor had it that, after the battle at the Thames in 1813, Tecumseh's remains were skinned and the grisly souvenir used to cover numerous mementos in later years.[26]

Because he had formally abandoned civilization, the white savage occupied an important position apart from the miscellaneous horror stories told about him. Some became famous, like Mike Fink and Simon Girty, but others lived little noted on the borderland between savagery and civilization. One Alexander Outlaw, after the murder of Corn-tassel, entered a native town called Citico, "where he found a few helpless women and children, which he inhumanly murdered, exposing their private parts in the most shameful manner, heaving a young child, with both its arms broke, alive, at the breast of its dead mother." Outlaw, the report went, had "done everything in his power to drive the Indians to desperation." Equally barbarous, an unlikely frontier character with a patch over one eye and a piece out of his nose named Benjamin Harrison murdered seventeen Creeks at Carrs Bluff in 1795 and decapitated some of them with a broadax.[27]

Mary Jemison cited the case of Ebenezer Allen, a curious mixture of white savage and frontier entrepreneur, who joined the tribesmen in attacking the settlements. He had done a little trading between Philadelphia and the Seneca country during the Revolution, and he later sent his children to Philadelphia for their education, but he also joined some of the tory expeditions against the New York and Pennsylvania frontier, in compensation for which he received land from the Indians. His personal affairs matched

26. Letter, dated Westmoreland, Apr. 26, 1779, in *Affecting History of Manheim's Family*, 11–14; Woodward, *Woodward's Reminiscences*, 85. Wilkins, *Cherokee Tragedy*, 77, gives evidence of another skinning incident.

27. Joseph Martin to Henry Knox, Feb. 2, 1789, *American State Papers, Indian Affairs*, I, 48; Timothy Barnard to George Matthews, Oct. 9, 1795 (typed transcript), Timothy Barnard Papers, Ga. Dept. of Archives and History; Barnard to James Seagrove, Dec. 18, 1795, *ibid.*; Jacob Kingsbury to John Milledge, May 6, 1803, *ibid.*

the incongruity of his public life. At one time or another, he had four wives (three at once), two squaws and two white women. He attached one of the squaws to his household after murdering her elderly Indian husband—his second murder. Previously, he had drowned his partner in a millpond in order to obtain his share of the property. His behavior in frontier war, however, measured the extent of his decline.

At one time, when he was scouting with the indians in the Susquehannah country, he entered a house very early in the morning, where he found a man, his wife, and one child, in bed. The man, as he entered the door, instantly sprang on the floor, for the purpose of defending himself and little family; but Allen dispatched him at one blow. He then cut off his head and threw it bleeding into the bed with the terrified woman; took the little infant from his mother's breast, and holding it by its legs, dashed its head against the jamb, and left the unhappy widow and mother to mourn alone over her murdered family.

According to Mrs. Jemison, he later repented the crime.[28]

The flexibility of civilization permitted the white man to maintain the forms of civilized life and at the same time to act like a savage. When the tribes dared to oppose him, the white man responded with devastating force. In retaliation for the Indian massacres in 1622 and 1644, the Virginians followed a policy of extermination. The New Englanders reacted similarly to the Pequots. Later, in King Philip's War, the whites engaged in an orgy of brutality. Colden recorded that the great Frontenac himself had been tainted by Indian savagery in allowing the Christian Indians of Loretto to burn an Iroquois while the French inhabitants viewed the spectacle. Samuel Williams described how, in their famous attack on the St. Francis Indians in 1759, Rogers' Rangers used "the Indian method of slaughter and destruction." The murder of the Conestoga Indians by the Paxton Boys and the assassination of Cornstalk were well-publicized blots on the white man's integrity. The activities of Michael Cresap prior to Dunmore's War properly horrified Jefferson; Doddridge believed the whites entirely responsible for that conflict.[29]

The white man did not let the bald accusation of his imitative

28. Seaver, *Life of Mary Jemison,* chap. 8.

29. Beverley, *History and Present State of Virginia,* ed. Wright, 54; Stith, *History of First Discovery of Virginia,* 208–211, 217; Douglas Edward Leach, *Flintlock and Tomahawk: New England in King Philip's War* (New York, 1958), 212; Colden, *History of the Five Indian Nations,* 135–137; Williams, *History of Vermont,* 2d ed., I, 431; Franklin, "A Narrative of the Late Massacres in Lancaster County," Smyth, ed., *Writings of Franklin,* IV, 289–314; Jefferson, *Notes on Virginia,* ed. Peden, app. 4; Doddridge, *Notes, on Settlement and Indian Wars,* 227.

savagery stand unchallenged. After all, the Indian had started it all; let the blame be placed at the point of origin. Some, like Franklin, went a step further and sought a scapegoat to alleviate the white man's guilt. He blamed the murder of the Moravian Indians at Gnadenhutten on the British king. "It is he who has furnished the Savages with Hatchets and Scalping Knives, and engages them to fall upon our defenceless Farmers, and murder them with their Wives and children." In their exasperation at a long series of unpunished murders, the western settlers have killed Indians indiscriminately, but the blame must be placed on the king, that "Man in England, who happens to love blood." Should anyone wish to charge the white man with barbarism in waging war with the Indians, wrote Doddridge,

let him, if he can bear the reflection, look at helpless infancy, virgin beauty, and hoary age, dishonoured by the ghastly wounds of the tomahawk and scalping knife of the savage. Let him hear the shrieks of the victims of the Indian torture by fire, and smell the surrounding air, rendered sickening by the effluvia of their burning flesh and blood. Let him hear the yells, and view the hellish features of the surrounding circle of savage warriors, rioting in all the luxuriance of vengeance, while applying the flaming torches to the parched limbs of the sufferers, and then suppose those murdered infants, matrons, virgins and victims of torture, were his friends and relations, the wife, sister, child, or brother; what would be his feelings! After a short season of grief, he would say "I will now think only of revenge."[30]

In 1811, before the Creek War brought him south, Andrew Jackson responded to the menace of Indian attacks in the Northwest by offering to lead five hundred to a thousand Tennesseans against those "decitfull" and "unrelenting barbarians." *The blood of our murdered countrymen must be revenged.* The banditti ought to be swept from the face of the earth." And another uncompromising Indian opponent, John Sevier, in one of his classic Indian-hating outbursts, spoke of "exotic tribes . . . habituated to lecentiousness," "vagrant, lawless, debautched and immoral," who will be deterred from their "common desperate and rapicious practices" only by "sufficient conviction of being chastised." A nation not only had the right to "punish unjustifiable attacks; but may put the aggressors in such a condition as will prevent them in future from being guilty of like offences."[31]

30. Franklin to James Hutton, July 7, 1782, Smyth, ed., *Writings of Franklin*, VIII, 561–562; Doddridge, *Notes, on Settlement and Indian Wars*, 211–212.

31. Jackson to William Henry Harrison, Nov. 28, 1811, Esarey, ed., *Messages of Harrison*, I, 665; Samuel C. Williams, ed., "Executive Journal of Gov. John Sevier," East Tennessee Historical Society, *Publications*, No. 1 (1929) , 113.

The problem of savagery pointed up a basic ambiguity in the Jeffersonian approach to the Indian. The violence of frontier war seemed to afford ample excuse for the annihilation of the native population, but the very possibility of this choice hinted that civilization might not be as secure as civilized men were wont to think. The frontier must be made secure for the expansion of the settlements, but those settlements must also be protected against the subtle penetration of savage ways. Savagery and civilization must not be mixed, especially in war, one of the favorite pursuits of both white and Indian.

6

The sharp distinction between civilization and savagery took on special significance during the Revolutionary War, when the existence of the new nation hung on the outcome of the conflict. The British not only did all in their power to destroy American liberty but they enlisted the support of the savage tribes to aid them in their work. Nothing could have been better calculated to raise the ire of the new nation. The Indians weighed their own interests accurately in joining the British; hence the Americans were only practical in recommending neutrality to the tribes. But more important, the Jeffersonian conception of the division between savagery and civilization forbade the mixing of the two. It especially proscribed the use of savage warriors against a civilized enemy.

In spite of the deep feelings on the subject, there should have been no surprise in the use of native allies against other tribes or even against civilized opponents. In the century-long imperial conflict, all sides employed native auxiliaries. Incidents invariably occurred, such as Montcalm's failure to control the Indians at the capitulation of Fort William Henry, which illustrated the consequences of the policy. Yet native allies continued to take part in the white man's wars. From his long experience, John Heckewelder capsuled the inevitable consequences of setting the tribesmen against the whites:

The Indians are not fond of interfering in quarrels not their own, and will not fight with spirit for the mere sake of a livelihood which they can obtain in a more agreeable manner by hunting and their other ordinary occupations. Their passions must be excited, and that is not easily done when they themselves have not received any injury from those against whom they are desired to fight. Behold, then, the abominable course which must unavoidably be resorted to—to induce them to do what?—to lay waste the dwelling of the peaceable cultivator of the land, and murder his innocent wife and his helpless children.[32]

Most observers believed that the mere introduction of the warriors into the conflict meant acquiescence in savagery. Because war had totally different cultural connotations for white and Indian, efforts to control the tribesmen invariably failed. Thus Samuel Williams criticized General Burgoyne for using Indian allies during the Revolution. The British general did his utmost to curb the natives, but he began by exciting them. "Warriors," he told them, "go forth in the might of your valour and your cause—strike at the common enemies of Great Britain and America, disturbers of public order, peace, and happiness, destroyers of commerce, parricides of the state." At the same time, Burgoyne cautioned the Indians not to shed blood unless opposed by arms and not to molest old men, women, children, and prisoners even at the height of the conflict. He offered compensation for prisoners, not for scalps, although ("in conformity and indulgence to your customs") scalps could be taken from the dead when killed in fair opposition. Of course, he failed. "Though he might wish to restrain," commented Williams, "his letter was a proof that he had introduced the savages into the American plantations; and that it was not in his power to prevent them from carrying on the war agreeably to their ancient and well-known customs and maxims."[33]

Necessity soon drove the Americans to acquire Indian allies. Washington recommended the organization of Indian auxiliaries even while recognizing "the embarrassments they create in an army," because he believed that these liabilities would be outweighed by their services. Congress authorized him to procure four hundred Indians, but to engage them "in such way as will annoy the enemy without suffering them to injure those who are friends to the cause of America." John Adams stated the case against the Indians more clearly and conceded the necessity of using them more frankly. The Indians "conduct their Wars so entirely without Faith and Humanity" that for the British to ally with them would disgrace their cause throughout Europe, as it had the French during the Seven Years' War. "To let loose these blood Hounds to scalp Men and to butcher Women and Children is horrid." Nevertheless, whatever the expense of such "troublesome Confederates" and their

32. Heckewelder, "Account of the Indian Nations," Am. Phil. Soc., *Trans. of Hist. and Lit. Comm.*, I (1819) , 344.

33. Williams, *History of Vermont*, 2d ed., I, 399, II, 130–134, 438–439.

"cruel, bloody disposition, against any Enemy whatever," the "Extravagancies of British Barbarity in prosecuting the war" made such delicacy impractical.[34] Provided the natives could not be kept neutral, Adams favored an alliance.

As war governor of Virginia, Jefferson became immediately involved in the question of tribal alliances. He attempted to gain the natives' aid in order to keep them from the British camp, but he preferred that they stay out of the war entirely. British diplomacy, however, turned most of the tribes against the Americans. Once the Indian decision became clear, Jefferson knew exactly what course to follow. He recommended either the root-and-branch destruction of hostile tribes or a decisive effort to drive them beyond the Mississippi. The war ought to be carried into their own country; should they persist in their depredations, "nothing is more desirable than total suppression of Savage Insolence and Cruelties."[35]

In a letter to George Rogers Clark, Jefferson revealed the intensity of his feelings and the refinement to which he had brought his thinking on the subject. Of the British policy, he explained: "Notwithstanding their base example, we wish not to expose them to the inhumanities of a savage enemy. Let this reproach remain on them, but for ourselves we would not have our national character tarnished with such a practice. If indeed they strike the Indians, those will have a natural right to punish the aggressors and we none to hinder them. It will then be no act of ours. But to invite them to a participation of the war is what we would avoid by all possible means." He raised no objection to the use of friendly Indians against hostile tribes, and he even proposed to furnish them with arms and ammunition; but under no circumstances should American policy promote a savage attack on civilized people.[36]

In Jefferson's mind, no one had sinned more seriously against the sanctity of civilization than Henry Hamilton, the British governor at Detroit whom Clark had captured in 1779. Jefferson ordered him transported to Virginia, shackled, and held without trial in a

34. Entry of Mar. 4, 1778, Ford, ed., *Journals of the Continental Congress*, X, 220–221; Adams to James Warren, June 7, 1775, Edmund C. Burnett, ed., *Letters of Members of the Continental Congress* (Washington, D.C., 1921–1938), I, 114; Adams to Horatio Gates, Apr. 27, 1776, *ibid.*, 433.

35. Jefferson to George Rogers Clark, Jan. 3, 1778, Boyd, ed., *Jefferson Papers*, II, 132–133; Jefferson to George Washington, Feb. 10, 1780, *ibid.*, III, 281; Jefferson to William Preston, June 15, 1780, *ibid.*, 447–448; Jefferson to Abner Nash, Aug. 12, 1780, *ibid.*, 544–545; Jefferson to Samuel Huntington, Feb. 17, 1781, *ibid.*, IV, 639–640.

36. Jefferson to George Rogers Clark, Jan. 29, 1780, *ibid.*, III, 276.

dank Williamsburg jail in retaliation for his employment of Indians in the frontier war. Specifically, the Virginians charged Hamilton with inciting "the Indians to perpetuate their accustomed cruelties" and also with offering bounties for scalps but none for prisoners. British officers who committed "enormities" under his command, the indictment claimed, had themselves led scalping parties; their behavior had been "savage and unprecedented among civilized nations." Jefferson saw Hamilton as an unconscionable war criminal, tainted with the blood spilled by his savage agents.

> The known rule of warfare with the Indian Savages is an indiscriminate butchery of men women and children. These Savages, under this well-known character are employed by the British nation as allies in the War against the Americans. Governor Hamilton undertakes to be the conductor of the War. In the execution of that undertaking, he associates small parties of the whites under his immediate command with large parties of the Savages, and sends them to act, sometimes jointly, sometimes separately, not against our forts, or armies in the field, but the farming settlements on our frontiers. Governor Hamilton then is himself the butcher of Men Women and Children.

He could not have been more positive in expressing the deep horror felt by the white man at the violent propensities of the Indians.[37]

7

From Pontiac's uprising to the close of the Creek War in 1814, frontier conflict held a prominent place in Indian-white relations. At the same time that government agents, traders, and missionaries offered the Indians a new prospect for life in America, white set-

37. "Order of the Virginia Council Placing Henry Hamilton and Others in Irons," June 16, 1779, *ibid.*, II, 292–294; Jefferson to William Philips, July 22, 1779, *ibid.*, III, 46. Gilbert Chinard, *Thomas Jefferson: The Apostle of Americanism,* 2d ed., rev. (Ann Arbor, 1957), 111–112, contends that Jefferson considered Hamilton's actions an attack on the foundations of civilization. The usual discussion of Hamilton concerns the problem of whether he did or did not buy scalps and promote savage attacks on American noncombatants. For a defense of the Englishman, see Nelson Vance Russell, "The Indian Policy of Henry Hamilton: A Re-valuation," *The Canadian Historical Review,* XI (1930), 20–37, and Walter H. Mohr, *Federal Indian Relations: 1774–1788* (Philadelphia, 1933), 89–91. The best and most extensive account of the problem by Orville John Jaebker, "Henry Hamilton: British Soldier and Colonial Governor" (Ph.D. diss., Indiana University, 1954), 102, maintains that there is not sufficient evidence for a definite conclusion; see also John D. Barnhart, ed., *Henry Hamilton and George Rogers Clark in the American Revolution with the Unpublished Journal of Lieut. Gov. Henry Hamilton* (Crawfordsville, Ind., 1951), 35. But the scalp issue and Jefferson's undue petulence aside, the main point everyone concedes—Hamilton did employ Indians to fight British battles, and this was his primary offense.

tlers moved beyond the Alleghenies into the heart of the Indian country. The tribes fought a series of stubborn holding actions that delayed the frontier only slightly but fueled as never before the passion of many whites to see in the Indian signs of human degradation. The ferocity of the conflict in this critical period, stimulated by civilized technology and the native's declining culture, gave new life to the image of the vicious savage. Faced with the imminent collapse of his world, attacked frontally by the frontiersman and internally by the trader and the philanthropist, the Indian fought desperately to maintain his tribal integrity.

Brackenridge derived his description of the tribesmen as "animals vulgarly called Indians" from that experience.[38] The image appealed as much to the frontiersman with his immediate involvement in conflict as it did to those who constructed the more formal, public description of the Indian. This negative conception could be seen as the antithesis of noble savagism. At each point the vicious savage reversed the qualities of his noble relative. Neither was any more real than the other. But as the image of the noble savage provided the basis for the amelioration of native society, the negative conception removed all hope for its future progress. The Indian on the warpath possessed none of the virtues that made incorporation promising. Instead he seemed bent on destroying the civilized life he was supposed to imitate.

In actuality, the capacity of the Indian to violently resist the white man stemmed from his extraordinary adaptability. Through a cunning combination of wilderness proficiency, the white man's guns, and intertribal alliances arranged under the stress of civilization's advance, the Indians put up a formidable defense. Few white men could see the relationship between the profound changes taking place in tribal life and the determined attacks on the frontier. Most found it easier to interpret the frenzy of savage conflict and torture as revelatory of the diabolical force of primitivism. The vigor of tribal opposition, itself a token of the success of the civilizing process, only exacerbated the tendency to see a deep fissure between civilization and savagery.

In fact, frontier war had little direct effect on the civilizing program. Benjamin Hawkins might complain of his charges during the Creek War that "the destruction of every American is the song of the day. They have wholly neglected their crops and mostly destroyed their live animals. They are daily persevering in this mode

---

38. Brackenridge, ed., *Indian Atrocities*, 62.

of destruction."[39] For the most part, however, the civilizing effort developed after the major conflict between white and Indian east of the Mississippi had subsided. Similarly, the conception of the violent Indian spread more rapidly after he had ceased being violent, at exactly the time that the philanthropic program increased in intensity. As the philanthropists worked greater changes in tribal life, spreading malaise in the process, the conception of the savage warrior became more complex and sophisticated. Though the Indian warrior could do little to prevent the growth of civilization in the tribes, Jeffersonians persisted in using the obduracy of the violent savage to explain the failure of their program to achieve immediate success.

39. Hawkins, "Extracts of occurrences in the agency for Indian affairs," Aug. 15, 1813 (typed transcript) , Hawkins Papers, Ga. Dept. of Archives and History.

Chapter VIII

Disintegration

I

The idea of savagery attested to the great difference between primitive and civilized man; the conception of the degraded Indian demonstrated the consequences of attempting to bring the two together. Whatever factual basis existed for enthusiasm over the civilizing program came largely from the early nineteenth-century success in coaxing the southern tribes, especially the Cherokees, to take up farming. Certainly, the previous experience of Indian-white relations had been characterized as much by violence and the disruption of tribal culture as by the happy convergence of the two societies. Despite the apparent achievements of philanthropy in the South, the anticipation of ultimate success for the civilizing program was usually dulled by the failure of incorporation and the reality of the Indian's personal and frequently tribal disintegration. As a result, the civilizing venture assumed the character of a race carried on against the inexorable processes of cultural breakdown.

The Indian seemed to enjoy an insatiable appetite for the products of the white man's world. He was often contemptuous of European civilization as a whole, but he remained fascinated by the miscellaneous artifacts that European man produced. The indirect method of civilizing the tribes played on this basic weakness. Highly pleased with almost any evidence that the Indian had increased his level of civilization, Jefferson tended to think of the process as quantitative—the accumulation of an absolute amount of culture— an idea consistent with environmentalist theory. But the actual effects of the white man's culture soon became apparent. The artifacts of European civilization, although obviously increasing the efficiency of the Indian, set him adrift from his old manner of life, made him dependent on the white man, and gave him an insecure base on which to erect a new society.

The truth about the future of the tribes was always obscured by the complexity of the relations between the two societies. Some Indians thrived in their new way of life, others broke under the strain despite all efforts to save them. Native society appeared at once stubborn and resilient, facile in its ability to absorb the white man's ways, and also strangely susceptible to the disintegrating influences of an overpowering way of life. The greater the success of the civilizing plan in limited areas, the more precipitate seemed the general decline of the Indian. Believing in progress and convinced that their own society represented an important or even final stage of development, philanthropists found it difficult to perceive fully the corrosive effects of civilization on Indian society. Yet they did see that the native's declining condition resulted from contact with the white man. They attributed it to the combination of civilization's vices and diseases. Unruly frontiersmen and traders carried whiskey and their thieving ways into the wilderness, as the first settlers had brought smallpox and other diseases, to speed the disappearance of the tribes. It was the wide array of unregulated associations characteristic of the frontier that appeared to jeopardize the civilizing effort and menaced the survival of the Indian.

Some who detected the malaise in tribal society saw that, besides the communication of specific vices, the very contact between white and Indian worked subtly to undermine the native culture. Crèvecoeur spoke of "a sort of physical antipathy" between white and Indian that caused among the natives, whenever they lived in the neighborhood of Europeans, "a variety of accidents and misfortunes" from which they sank "into a singular sort of indolence and sloth." Fraud, violence, and injustice hastened the end of the Indians, but so also did the moderation and goodwill of the whites. As a very perceptive lady from New York State put it: "The very nature of even our most friendly mode of dealing with them was pernicious to their moral wellfare." William Henry Harrison contended that he could tell merely by looking at a native whether he belonged to a "Neighbouring or a more distant Tribe. The latter is generally well clothed healthy and vigorous the former half naked, filthy and enfeebled with Intoxication, and many of them without arms except a Knife which they carry for the most vilanous purposes." Responsibility still lay mainly with the white man's vices, but the stark differentiation between Indians with civilized associations and those who remained isolated tended to indict the whole of the white man's society. In his later years McKenney called to mind the "melancholy reflection" that the Indians "should be thus chafed, tribe after tribe, away," their extinction induced "by a kind of *chafing,* or *friction*—by a worrying and heart-breaking neglect on the one hand, and an impoverishing and wasting policy on the other."[1] Generalized fears of this sort fed Jefferson's nagging insistence that the movement toward civilization must be speeded lest it be overtaken by the destruction of the tribes.

This widespread agreement that native society had begun to disintegrate created a vague sense of impending misfortune that would affect both the Indian and the white man. For example, white influence had led to increased factionalism in the tribes, which philanthropists greeted with mixed reactions. Some of these groups supported the civilizing effort. They had been formed precisely because of the influence of civilization in the tribes. Yet philanthropists tended to draw a close relationship between the unity and vigor of native society and the hope of success. Tribes riven by warring parties could not be seen as integrated, primitive societies on the verge of civilization. By pressing for change, government agents and missionaries elicited from the tribes a variety of responses, some of which could be interpreted as signs of precipitate collapse rather than as evidence of imminent success. The harried philanthropist clung to the positive signs but became increasingly impressed by their negative implications.[2]

The Indians themselves supplied evidence of their decline. White observers detected a sense of defeat, a forlorn and disquieting loss of self-esteem that signaled the disappearance of the hearty and occasionally saucy aborigine of the past. Ezra Stiles noted cannily that "the New England Indians, upon the accession of the English were soon ashamed of their old religion, or rather finding it ridiculed by us and considered it idolatrous, that they concealed much from us." After their defeat at Horseshoe Bend, the faction-ridden

1. Crèvecoeur, *Letters from an American Farmer,* 142, 146; [Anne] Grant, *Memoirs of an American Lady* . . . (New York, 1809), 117–118; Esarey, ed., *Messages of Harrison,* I, 29; McKenney, *Sketches of a Tour to the Lakes,* 55; Prucha and Carmony, eds., "Memorandum of Lewis Cass," *Wis. Mag. of Hist.,* LII (1968), 39; McCoy, *Remarks on Indian Reform,* 12–13; "On the State of the Indian," *No. Am. Rev.,* XVI (1823), 34.

2. Alexander Cornells to Benjamin Hawkins, June 22, 1813, *American State Papers, Indian Affairs,* I, 846; Hawkins to David B. Mitchell, July 5, 1813, *ibid.,* 847; Hawkins to John Armstrong, July 28, 1813, *ibid.,* 850; Hawkins to Mitchell, June 21, 1813 (typed transcript), Hawkins Papers, Ga. Dept. of Archives and History; Clinton, "Private Canal Journal," in Campbell, ed., *Life of Clinton,* 187; *Panoplist,* XII (1816), 121; Emily J. Blasingham, "The Depopulation of the Illinois Indians," *Ethnohistory,* III (1956), 373; Robert F. Berkhofer, Jr., "The Political Context of a New Indian History," *Pacific Historical Review,* XL (1971), 373–380.

and spiritless Creeks began, according to the government agent, George Stiggins, "to believe in the instabilities of fortune and transitory scenes of war." They wanted nothing so much as to get out of harm's way; "their retributive spirit for retaliation and war was broke and cool, there was no consistency in anything they projected or done." Uncertain and dejected, "in a torture through the anxieties always prevalent in the days of misfortune," many made their way to safety at Pensacola. When compared with the supposedly untouched and independent aborigine, the native overwhelmed and intimidated by his contact with civilization seemed even more worthy of pity. The American Board missionaries reported that on first encounter the Cherokees would not even sit down to eat if not entirely welcome, in marked contrast with those Indians who, after living for generations close to the whites, always felt degraded.[3]

The appearance in times of stress of nativist and messianic movements among the tribes furnished convincing evidence of the beginnings of deterioration. From the Delaware prophet who inspired Pontiac to Tecumseh's movement in the War of 1812 and the conglomerate religion of Handsome Lake among the Senecas, the native tribes had been inspired by home-grown seers who announced the end of the white man's reign and the return of the unadulterated Indian world. Symptomatic of serious flaws in tribal organization, nativist movements may have been merely reactions to the disruption of the familiar and personally fulfilling life Indians had known, but they also provided positive evidence that the white man's ways had taken deep root. Tecumseh's brother proposed to drive out the white settlers, but with guns, not bows and arrows. The prophet larded his new religion with the very formulations that the missionaries had been promoting. Handsome Lake's religious views drew heavily on the evangelical enthusiasm that spread throughout upper New York in the early nineteenth century. The ambivalence in the natives' attitude demonstrated the great measure to which the integrity of their life had been compromised. Patently, the Indians could not return to the old; they could only try desperately to rebuild some of the social defenses that had protected them in the past, barriers against the intolerable

3. Entry of June 27, 1783, Dexter, ed., *Literary Diary of Ezra Stiles*, III, 76–77; Theron A. Nunez, Jr., ed., "Narrative of George Stiggins, Creek Agent, 1831–1844," *Ethnohistory*, V (1958), 298–299; Ard Hoyt *et al.* to Samuel Worcester, Dec. 21, 1818, ABC 18.3.1; Anthony F. C. Wallace, *King of the Delawares: Teedyuscung, 1700–1763* (Philadelphia, 1949), 17.

stress induced by the white man's influence and their own receptivity.[4]

Frontiersmen saw mainly the violence that accompanied the Indian reaction and opposed the prophets as a menace to the settlements. But many observers recognized the antiprogressivist implications of the Indians' return to the past. Not only did the tribesmen reject the improvements of civilization, they revealed a part of themselves that ill fitted the hopeful image of the amenable native. Some, like Albert Gallatin's correspondent and William Henry Harrison's enemy, John Badollet, perceived the positive aspects of the nativist program. Besides opposing the white man's advance, the Shawnee prophet had forbidden the consumption of alcohol and encouraged his followers to till the land, thus accomplishing "more towards civilizing them and . . . seconding the benevolent and philanthropic views of the General Government than all the Indian agents that have been or may be sent amongst them." But the positive aspects seemed incidental to the hysteria and destructiveness of tribal nativism. In general, philanthropists saw stubborn obstructionism rather than an understandable attempt to reconstitute a lost world.[5]

Ultimately, civilized men showed only a vague perception of the toll they exacted from native culture. Although the relations between the two societies set in train a wasting attrition of the tribes' vitality, reformers persisted in seeing the process as a simple transition from one mode of existence to another. Especially in the at-

4. A. Irving Hallowell, *Culture and Experience* (Philadelphia, 1955), chaps. 6, 14, 17; Ralph Linton, "Nativistic Movements," *Am. Anthro.*, N.S., XLV (1943), 230-240; Bernard Barber, "Acculturation and Messianic Movements," *American Sociological Review*, VI (1941), 663-669; Anthony F. C. Wallace, *The Death and Rebirth of the Seneca* (New York, 1970), chaps. 9, 10, 13.

5. Badollet to Gallatin, Sept. 25, 1810, Gayle Thornbrough, ed., *The Correspondence of John Badollet and Albert Gallatin, 1804-1836 (Indiana Historical Publications, XXII [Indianapolis, 1963])*, 167-168; Dorothy Libby, ed., "Thomas Forsyth to William Clark, St. Louis, December 23, 1812," *Ethnohistory*, VIII (1961), 193-194; Alexander Cornells to Benjamin Hawkins, June 22, 1813, *American State Papers, Indian Affairs*, I, 846: "The prophets are enemies to the plan of civilization, and advocates for the wild Indian mode of living." Jefferson was far too optimistic to think that the obscurantism of Tecumseh's prophet could interfere with the civilizing program. He wrote to John Adams, Apr. 20, 1812, Cappon, ed., *Adams-Jefferson Letters*, II, 299: "I concluded . . . that he was a visionary, inveloped in the clouds of their antiquities, and vainly endeavoring to lead back his brethren to the fancied beatitudes of their golden age. I thought there was little danger of his making many proselytes from the habits and comforts they had learned from the Whites to the hardships and privations of savagism, and no great harm if he did." Also Jefferson to Henry Dearborn, Aug. 12, 1807, and Aug. 28, 1807, Lipscomb and Bergh, eds., *Writings of Jefferson*, XI, 325, 342-343.

mosphere of compulsory change, the civilizing program imposed a
heavy burden of stress and anxiety on the tribal order. Many white
men recognized the signs of dissolution, which engaged their sympathies profoundly, but they saw in them evidence of the need to
hurry the process of amelioration. In consequence, philanthropy
tended to increase the level of tension instead of reducing it. The
Indian, whether he made a frenzied effort to defend what remained
of his way of life or simply increased his efficiency in this task by
adopting more of the white man's ways, compounded the irony by
becoming more dependent on civilization and hence less autonomous in his own way of life.

2

Tribal society grasped at every vestige of stability to maintain its
independence. Messianism generated a hysterical but formidable
opposition to civilization. But the more the Indians yearned nos-
talgically for the past, the more they thirsted for the conveniences
of civilization. Chided at Lancaster in 1744 that native life before
the arrival of the Europeans had been mean and squalid, Canasatego, the Onondaga chief, rose to the challenge. If the Indians
could believe their forefathers, he asserted, their life in ancient
times had many virtues: "We had then Room enough, and Plenty
of Dear which was easily caught; and tho' we had not Knives,
Hatchets, or Guns, such as we have now, yet we had Knives of
Stone, and Hatchets of Stone, and Bows and Arrows, and those
served our Uses as well then as the *English* ones do now. We are
now straitened, and sometimes in want of Deer, and liable to many
other Inconveniences since the English came among us."[6] He recognized the attractiveness of civilized ways, but he also understood
that these newfound riches would cost the Indian his independence.
His society now operated at the behest of its benefactors. The noble
Indian and even the wilderness marauder whom the whites so
feared depended equally on the artifacts of civilized existence.

Every representative of civilization brought into the wilderness
some element of a foreign environment. The missionary came with
a European world view, the government agent arrived with ideas
about order in the forest and the work habits of hunters and
warriors, the trapper and the frontiersman brought a smattering
of skills that they left behind on their inevitable departure, but
the trader introduced the tangible artifacts of European culture.
Though the Indian rejected much of what the white American

6. Boyd, ed., *Indian Treaties*, 52.

offered (religion for example) and, for a time at least, attempted to ignore the power of civilization, he accepted incontinently a rich assortment of the products of civilized technology.

The list seemed endless. Weapons and tools became necessary for the natives' everyday activities: muskets, rifles, flints, lead, bullet molds, knives, axes, tomahawks, spare parts, arrow points, kettles, awls, needles, files, scissors, combs, hoes, and nails. The Indian taste in apparel sustained a lucrative trade in waistcoats, breeches, shroud, blankets, hats, stockings with clocks, silk handkerchiefs, hose, shoes, garters, ribbons, calico, brass buttons, thread, and laces. Among the other miscellaneous items of exchange (rings, ear-bobs, war paint, especially vermilion), glass beads for wampum held a crucial place. Before the European arrival, the Indians used shells and wood for this necessary ceremonial artifact, but with the assurance of a steady supply of cheap beads, they became dependent on the white traders for an essential ingredient of their public life.[7]

Most whites fully appreciated the impact of commerce on the Indians; trade, after all, held a significant place in philanthropic planning. On his return from the West, Meriwether Lewis reported to Jefferson that the Tetons, "the vilest miscreants of the savage race . . . ever remain the pirates of the Missouri, until such measures are pursued, by our government, as will make them feel a dependence on its will for their supply of merchandize." James Adair charged that in the early years the Cherokees had been enticed into

7. An invoice with a particularly full list of gifts for the Indians may be found in William Eustis to Tench Coxe, Jan. 18, 1810, Letters Sent, Sec. War (M-15), Roll 3: 11–12; Wilbur R. Jacobs, *Diplomacy and Indian Gifts: Anglo-French Rivalry along the Ohio and Northwest Frontiers, 1748–1763* (Stanford, 1950), 12, 46–47. In their journey over the mountains and down the Columbia to the West Coast, Lewis and Clark found rich evidence of the white man's presence—numerous articles had filtered into the unexplored hinterland from the brisk trade carried on along the coast. See Thwaites, ed., *Journals of Lewis and Clark Expedition*, III, 19, 138, 166, 175–176, 194, 195, 217, 328. From information supplied by Lewis, Jefferson made a list—with wampum beads at the head—of desirable items for exchange with the Indians; Jefferson to Henry Dearborn, Feb. 14, 1807, Jackson, ed., *Letters of Lewis and Clark Expedition*, 375. Wallace, *King of the Delawares*, 162–163, cites an example of the native taste in clothes: "John [Teedyuscung's son] bought a regimental coat, a gold-laced hat with cockade, a pair of shoes, a checkered shirt, a ruffled shirt, a plain shirt for his wife, a cotton handkerchief, two pairs of breeches, a pair of buckles, a yard of scarlet shalloon for a flag, a yard and a half of half-thicks for leggings." Linton, ed., *Acculturation in Seven Indian Tribes*, 485, 505–507; William N. Fenton, "Iroquoian Culture History: A General Evaluation," in Fenton and John Gulick, eds., *Symposium on Cherokee and Iroquois Culture*, Smithsonian Institution, Bureau of American Ethnology, *Bulletin 180* (Washington, D.C., 1961), 266.

the traders' hands by low prices; having taken the bait, they lost their independence. Some years before, the wily Colonel Byrd proposed to supply the Indians with firearms "because it makes them depend entirely upon the English, not only for their Trade, but even for their subsistence."[8] In keeping with the manipulative aspects of the philanthropic ethos, the role of the trading factories and the wide distribution of civilized goods among the tribes further contributed to the natives' tributary status.

Although philanthropists had deliberately created the dependent Indian by their efforts to supply the tribes with every facility of civilized life, they persisted in holding a high opinion of the potential of the independent and self-possessed tribesman. Hence they worried constantly about the decline in native life. In reality, however, the dependent native, slightly broken in spirit from his encounter with civilization, provided a more likely candidate for a change in personality. Just as the trader served his own interests by tying the Indian to a steady supply of civilized goods, thus giving him the weakest position in the trading nexus, the humanitarian found it easier to dispense his cultural wares to natives who had lost the support of an integrated society. The traders merely exploited the tribes, leaving the wreck of a primitive culture behind; the philanthropists hoped to offer something better in return, but they also recognized the advantage of the Indian's dependent position.[9]

Of all the instruments accepted by the Indian from civilization, the gun left the deepest mark. At first he looked on it with fear and wonder. It killed with decisive power; the powder that made it work could be dangerous and required care. He thought that it would scare the game; indeed, it always seemed to the tribesman to partake of a certain civilized clumsiness. The native's bow and arrow continued to have a silent efficiency, but it could not compete in the

8. Thomas Jefferson, *Message from the President of the United States, Communicating Discoveries Made in Exploring the Missouri, Red River and Washita, by Captains Lewis and Clark* . . . (Washington, D.C., 1806), 33; Adair, *History of American Indians,* 230; W. K. Boyd, ed., *Byrd's Histories of the Dividing Line,* 116.

9. Heckewelder, "Account of the Indian Nation," Am. Phil. Soc., *Trans. of Hist. and Lit. Comm.,* I (1819), 182–183; Wainwright, *George Croghan,* 60; Wainwright, ed., "George Croghan's Journal, 1759–1763," *Pennsylvania Magazine of History and Biography,* LXXI (1947), 357. For Jefferson's notion that the Indians' acquaintance with the white man's way of life would lead to civilization, see his letter to W. C. C. Claiborne, May 24, 1803, Lipscomb and Bergh, eds., *Writings of Jefferson,* X, 394; Padover, ed., *Complete Jefferson,* 463–464, 475.

long run against the power of firearms. The Indians quickly understood the merit of this new weapon, and hence they took an important step in opening the closed tribal world to civilized influence.

Europe wanted furs, and the Indians could supply them only by using European weapons. But the efficiency of these new instruments, guns and traps, as well as the native hunter's craving for more of the artifacts that civilization furnished in return for furs, took a heavy toll of the supply of game. The tribesmen either invaded new preserves—and frequently fought other Indians for the right to do so—or they established commercial relations with distant tribes in order to supply the needed furs. The reduction in available game led to a change in diet and an increased reliance on the European for supplies of food. The gun itself required special skills for its upkeep, which very few natives acquired, and an ample supply of spare parts, which could be obtained only from the agents of civilization. Thus the Indian found himself locked into a new social and economic arrangement designed by the white man to further his own interests. Even in opposing the white man's drive for land, the Indian could hope for success only by using the enemy's weapon.[10]

The economic relationship between white and Indian worked profound changes in the native's social character. Jefferson believed that the process began with the first contact between the two societies. Enticed by "matchcoats, hatchets, and fire locks," the natives willingly surrendered their skins and went busily about the task of procuring more. William Bartram observed the same process. With Quaker providence, he noted that the Indians "wage eternal

10. William Clark records the first experience of a chief of a tribe he calls the Shalatoohs with a gun. "He was astonished and pleased to see White People. The Indians who had seen us had described to him ourselves and the effects of our gun—which he was anxious to see. He sent a young man for a beaver (there was one brought up) and asked if I would show them upon beaver. I made Collins take beaver about 40 or 50 [feet?] hold him up by tail, and I shot him in head. Chief ran up to Beaver and astonished to see hole. He wished to know if it was the noise that had killed beaver—looked at the gun, looked at me, at the party and then brought up his mule and wanted me to accept it which I declined." Jackson, ed., *Letters of Lewis and Clark Expedition*, 502. For the use of the gun in Lewis's and Clark's only serious conflict with the Indians, see Thwaites, ed., *Journals of Lewis and Clark Expedition*, V, 223–226; also, *ibid.*, I, 130, 131, III, 30, 346. See, for the natives' fear of gunpowder, Stith, *History of First Discovery of Virginia*, 96–97; Keith, *History of British Plantations*, 113–114. See also George E. Hyde, *Indians of the Woodlands*, 120, and Hyde's *Indians of the High Plains: From the Prehistoric Period to the Coming of the Europeans* (Norman, 1959), 79–80.

war against deer and bear, to procure food and clothing, and other necessaries and conveniences; which is indeed carried to an unreasonable and perhaps criminal excess, since the white people have dazzled their sense with foreign superfluities." In contrast to the usual frugality attributed to the tribesmen, David Zeisberger recognized the terrible attrition of game when native hunters slaughtered fifty to a hundred deer each fall. They no longer killed primarily for sustenance. If white critics can be believed, this new prodigality left the forest strewn with skinned carcasses fed upon by packs of wolves. In addition, the frontier settlers, living close to the Indian style, took their own share of the game. The Shawnee complained in 1802 that "at present they kill more than we do[.] They would be angry if we were to kill a cow or a hog of theirs, the little game that remains is very dear to us." DeWitt Clinton called the fur trade a "box of pandora," irresistibly attractive to the Indian but filled with evil.[11]

Many white men, therefore, understood the impossible dilemma that the fur trade imposed on the Indian. "All Traders," wrote Thomas Forsyth,

do everything in their power to keep peace and quietness among the different Indian Nations, encouraging them (by means of presents at times) to hunt for the purpose of paying their overloaded debts, The Indians exert themselves, and some years when every thing is quiet, they kill and destroy all before them. Being very successful one year in hunting and in paying a portion of their debts, they obtain of the Traders, a greater credit the next year with an expectation of making another great hunt, but having destroyed the game the year previous, they are unable to procure a sufficiency of furs to pay their debts, or to compare with the returns of the former year.[12]

This dismal cycle, repeating itself season after season, offered the tribes no comfort. Realistically, philanthropists could see the merit of introducing the Indian to the economic requirements of civilization; just as realistically, the Indian's increasingly derivative condition created an image of decline in place of the robust independence that seemed indicative of progress and imminent incorporation.

11. Jefferson, *Notes on Virginia*, ed. Peden, 54; Harper, ed., *Bartram's Travels*, 212; Hulbert and Schwarze, eds., "Zeisberger's History," Ohio Archaeol. and Hist. Soc., *Pubs.*, XIX (1910), 14, 57, 61; Speech of Black Hoof, Feb. 5, 1802, Letters Sent, Sec. War (M-15), Roll 1: 151; DeWitt Clinton, "Discourse Delivered before the New-York Historical Society," N.-Y. Hist. Soc., *Colls.*, II (1814), 59, 85.

12. "Thomas Forsyth to Lewis Cass, St. Louis, October 24, 1831," *Ethnohistory*, IV (1957), 203.

First materially and then gradually in the arts necessary for survival, the native society became helpless without the aid of civilization. Everywhere the natives were eager for new things; but they soon lost the capacity to thrive in the old way, and they often did not absorb the competence for the efficient manipulation of the white man's world. For example, the tribes usually found the services of a smith necessary. At government forts and in the mission establishments, the smith became an indispensable representative of civilization, especially for the care of the native's firearms. On their journey across the continent, Lewis and Clark served as roving ambassadors with civilization's special fund of knowledge. They repaired muskets, distributed some of the less familiar artifacts such as sewing needles, and became a great success as curers of the sick. The natives instinctively recognized the superiority of the white man's ability to manage his environment, and they showed few inhibitions in applying to him for help. Slowly both Indian and white came to realize that the more the Indian accepted help, the less he could help himself. Long before the close of the Jeffersonian period, Indian society had become a satellite of the white man's culture.[13]

3

Traders sought profits in the wilderness, and they did not usually express interest in the effects of trade on tribal society. The resultant cultural attrition was of concern to the government, the philanthropist, and the Indian himself, but not to the trader. Mrs. Grant recorded a conversation between a wilderness merchant and a potential customer that revealed the consequences of a relatively simple frontier business exchange. Said the trader: "If you will purchase from me a blanket to wrap round you, a shirt and blue shroud for under garments to yourself and your woman; and the same for leggings, this will pass the time, and save you the great labour of dressing the skins, making the thread, etc. for your clothing: which will give you more fishing and shooting, in the

13. Jacobs, *Diplomacy and Indian Gifts*, 42; Thwaites, ed., *Journals of Lewis and Clark Expedition*, III, 300, V, 21, 58. On Mar. 20, 1751, Franklin wrote to James Parker recommending that smiths be sent to live with the Indians to repair their guns. Smyth, ed., *Writings of Franklin*, III, 44–45. See also Beverley W. Bond, ed., "The Captivity of Charles Stuart, 1755–57," *Mississippi Valley Historical Review*, XIII (1926), 64. During her captivity in King Philip's War, Mary Rowlandson made her way among the Indians by sewing for them. Howard H. Peckham, *Captured by Indians: True Tales of Pioneer Survivors* (New Brunswick, N.J., 1954), 8–10.

sturgeon and bear months." Suspicious that this proposal held deep significance for the future of his people, the Indian stammered: "But the custom of my fathers." The trader insisted that customs should not be allowed to interfere with the acquisition of so many new and wonderful possessions; the Indian's innocent desire to obtain them cemented the bargain.[14]

Extraordinary perception of this sort seldom characterized the philanthropic view of trading. Instead the usual critique dwelled on the vices that the traders brought into the wilderness, although McKenney took the broader view in his defense of the government factory system. He detected the inequality in the meeting of civilized trader and primitive Indian: "Commercial intercourse ceases to reciprocate its advantages whenever either party shall yield to the other in intelligence or power. The keen and adventurous trader, skilled in the arts of deception and speculation, and who is bent on making gains, will be found oftentimes an overmatch for his less keen, and less intelligent, though *civilized* brother; but how entirely at the mercy of such must be an ignorant and powerless community of dependent savages!"[15] To correct this imbalance, the government operated trading factories and licensed independent traders. But these well-meant expedients neither raised the reputations of the traders nor solved the problem.

As James Adair remembered it, the relationship between traders and Indians had been very much better "before the Indians were corrupted by mercenary empirics." In those days, the "Indians were simple in manners . . . , a society of friendly and sagacious people," grateful for the supplies brought to them by the traders. This pleasant relationship ended abruptly in 1763 when the Royal Proclamation threw open the trade. With that change in policy, a horde of "mean reprobate peddlars" who cheated and corrupted the tribesmen entered the southern wilderness. Adair recommended tighter public control so that the current breed of traders would not "instruct the unknowing and imitating savages in many diabolical lessons of obscenity and blasphemy."[16] Adair's version of the

14. Grant, *Memoirs of an American Lady*, 122.

15. McKenney to the Senate, Dec. 27, 1821, *American State Papers, Indian Affairs*, II, 261.

16. Adair, *History of American Indians*, 230, 286, 366, 413. For Indian trade and the Proclamation of 1763, see John Richard Alden, *John Stuart and the Southern Colonial Frontier: A Study of Indian Relations, War, Trade, and Land Problems in the Southern Wilderness, 1754–1775* (Ann Arbor, 1944), 207–209. Adair believed that the Indians benefited from a regulated trade and suffered when forest commerce was thrown open. Alden, *John Stuart*, 18, emphasizes the seamy side: "In general, the traders were unscrupulous and abandoned wretches." Prucha, *American Indian Policy*, 72–73, 76, agrees with the Adair

effects of imperial policy in the 1760s carried less weight than his very positive opinions concerning the quality of the trading population.

Few critics derived their opinion of traders from the generally beneficent activities of such men as Sir William Johnson, Conrad Weiser, George Croghan, John Stuart, or Adair. The worst of the profession created its reputation. Bernard Romans exceeded all bounds by referring to the traders as "monsters in human form, the very scum and outcast of the earth . . . , more prone to savage barbarity than the savages themselves." "The villainous over reachings, chicanery, and mutual calumniations of the abandoned wretches, who reside among the savages, joined to their worse than brutish or savage way of life," retarded the civilizing process. One could hardly credit the accuracy of his views, but many observers shared them. Carver, Bartram, and Heckewelder all pointed to the nefarious reputations of these men. A memorial sent to Congress by the Missouri Baptist Association in 1818 encapsuled the often repeated indictment: "They are, generally speaking, men who have no principle but gain; and being at a distance from the restraints of civilized manners, they give full scope to their corrupt propensities. For gratifying these, they defraud the Indians of their property, corrupt their morals, debauch their manners, and consequently, increase the wretchedness of those already miserable people, and prejudice their minds against the Government, our citizens, and our manners, and lead them to have the most contemptible ideas of our civilization, and religion." DeWitt Clinton drew the pertinent conclusions. In the broadest sense, the decline of the Indians resulted from their contact with white men of all classes, including the traders, who had "contaminated their morals, destroyed their population, robbed them of their country, and deprived them of their national spirit."[17]

---

distinction. Jefferson was most insistent that all trade with the Indians be publicly controlled, though for the purpose of countering British influence he supported the interests of Astor. Jackson, ed., *Letters of Lewis and Clark Expedition*, 11; Jefferson to John Jacob Astor, Apr. 13, 1808, and to Meriwether Lewis, July 17, 1808, Lipscomb and Bergh, eds., *Writings of Jefferson*, XII, 28, 99. Benjamin Hawkins evaluated most of the 46 traders under his direction. He had a favorable opinion of 18, an unfavorable view of 13, and no opinion of the rest. Some of the less complimentary descriptions were: "A Jew of bad character," "Savannah Jack: much of a savage," "an indolent careless man," "fond of drink and much of a savage when drunk," "an Irishman, who drinks hard," "an enemy of truth," "a man of infamous character." *Letters of Hawkins*, 168–171.

17. Romans, *Concise Natural History*, 60–74; Carver, *Three Years Travels*, 141; Harper, ed., *Bartram's Travels*, 351; Heckewelder, "Account of the Indian Nations," Am. Phil. Soc., *Trans. of Hist. and Lit. Comm.*, I (1819), 7–8; Bap-

The one-sidedness of the description made the traders carry the guilt of civilization. As with the frontiersmen, they became major villains in the philanthropists' attempt to clear themselves of blame for the failure of the civilizing plan and the apparent breakdown of tribal society. Zebulon Pike described his astonishment at finding how greatly the Indians feared the whites. More than once in his explorations, Indians paddled well out of their way to avoid meeting him. "It appears evident to me that the Traders have taken great pains to impress on the minds of the Savages, an idea of our being a very vindictive, ferocious and War like people." This misapprehension, spread by the traders for their own profit, will be dispelled "when they find, that our conduct towards them is guided by magnanimity and justice; instead of operating in an injurious manner, it will have the effect of making them reverence, at the same time they fear us."[18] Pike would not forego the advantages of fear. Sufficient that he attributed its crasser applications to the traders.

Even if McKenney had succeeded in sending the traders into the Indian country armed with all the ameliorative compulsions of missionaries, the great disparity between the two societies would have persisted. The traders' vices had been no less responsible for the decline of the tribal order than the conflict between distinct cultures that possessed different conceptions of reality. Operating on the principles of supply and demand, the trader presented the Indian with a foreign world, to which he adjusted at the price of internal tension. One of Jedidiah Morse's correspondents commented on the Indian's incomprehension of the commercial nexus. "If you speak to an Indian upon the subject of their Great Father, the President, supplying them with goods from his factories, he will say at once, 'You are a *pash-i-pash-i-to* (a fool) our Great Father is certainly *no trader;* he has sent these goods to be *given* to us, as presents; and his Agents are endeavoring to cheat us, by *selling* them for our peltries.' " But condemnations of the trader's viciousness generally took no cognizance of his role as the transmitter of an alien mode of life. One of Robert Rogers's noble savages intoned a profounder truth:

---

tist memorial quoted by Prucha, *American Indian Policy,* 71; Clinton, "Discourse Delivered before the New-York Historical Society," N.-Y. Hist. Soc., *Colls.,* II (1814) , 84; Morse, *Report on Indian Affairs,* 40; Senate Document 47, 16th Congress, 1st Session, Feb. 16, 1820, ser. 26.

18. Jackson, ed., *Journals of Pike,* I, 22.

We're poison'd with the Infection of our Foes,
Their very Looks and Actions are infectious,
And in deep Silence spread Destruction round them.[19]

4

The impact of the white man's vices and the total effects of his culture on the tribes raised questions of moral intent. The white man could be blamed for debauching the natives or even for gradually overwhelming them with civilized ways, but he could not be blamed for spreading European diseases that worked a more immediate and a wider devastation among the tribes. The conviction that the Indian suffered whenever the two societies came together, whether from violence or the deterioration of internal stress, became more credible from the knowledge of the effects of European diseases. Aside from those who held that civilization would spread across the continent more quickly in the presence of fewer Indians, most whites in the Jeffersonian age regretted that new diseases had done the native population grave injury.

European diseases, such as the mysterious plague that appeared in New England in 1618, attacked the native population even before the settlers landed in great numbers. The white man's arms could never have cleared the continent for settlement as quickly as new infections devastated tribe after tribe. Before the European invasion, the North American Indians enjoyed immunity from many of the malignant disorders that had ravaged the civilized world for centuries: smallpox and measles and, very likely, tuberculosis, malaria, yellow fever, typhoid, and typhus. The various venereal infections may have originated in either Europe or America. At least it is certain that, besides the general effects of the white man's cultural penetration of the native's world, civilization brought with it a number of physical disabilities, especially smallpox, which had a disastrous impact on the Indian populations and contributed substantially to the eventual disintegration of tribal society.[20]

19. Morse, *Report on Indian Affairs*, 41, 57; James Bowdoin to Franklin, Nov. 12, 1753, Labaree *et al.*, eds., *Franklin Papers*, V, 111–112; *The Memoirs of Lieut. Henry Timberlake* . . . (London, 1765), 62–63; Harper, ed., *Bartram's Travels*, 255–258; Rogers, *Ponteach*, 224.

20. Percy Moreau Ashburn, *The Ranks of Death: A Medical History of the Conquest in America*, ed. Frank D. Ashburn (New York, 1947), *passim*; E. Wagner Stearn and Allen E. Stearn, *The Effect of Smallpox on the Destiny of the Amerindian* (Boston, 1945), 13–20; John Duffy, *Epidemics in Colonial America* (Baton Rouge, 1953), 224; Duffy, "Smallpox and the Indians in the

As a common disease among the whites and a major killer of
Indians, smallpox caused much concern and experimentation in the
centers of medical knowledge. The tribesmen seemed particularly
susceptible to it. "The Indians of America," wrote Franklin, "suffer
extreamely by this Distemper when it gets among them." In addition, Clinton and many others contended that the radical therapy
used by the native practitioners increased the death rate in the
tribes. For smallpox the natives recommended immersion in a cold
bath, after which, so the story went, the patient invariably died.[21]
Well knowing the weakness of the Indians, the English proposed
to introduce smallpox among them during Pontiac's uprising. Since
it already raged among the northwestern Indians, this early example
of germ warfare proved superfluous, but it demonstrated that civilization possessed an incomparable ally for use against its primitive
enemy.[22]

Few observers missed an opportunity to note the suffering smallpox caused among the Indians. Lawson recorded that the disease,
aggravated by the native treatment, spread unchecked among the
North Carolina Indians and that it frequently swept away whole
towns. "Neither do I know any Savages," he wrote, "that have traded
with the English but what have been great Losers by this Distemper." Adair told of the Cherokee disaster in 1738, when the
"Guineamen" from Charlestown brought smallpox into their towns
in infected goods. Within a year, they lost half their numbers. On
his travels in the Northwest, Jonathan Carver found a Fox village
of fifty lodges deserted. Half the inhabitants had been carried
off by smallpox; the rest had fled into the woods. Heckewelder reported a conversation with a chief in which the native described
the annihilation of the Nanticokes as a result of maladies contracted
from the white man. In his report of 1822, Morse emphasized the
dire effects of smallpox on the western Indians: "In 1802, it swept
off half the population from the Missouri to New Mexico, in the
region of the Pawnees, and west to the Rocky Mountains: and the
Ottawas, at L'Abre Croche, about the year 1799, lost half their
number by the same disease." Smallpox even appeared in the rela-

---

American Colonies," *Bulletin of the History of Medicine*, XXV (1951), 324–
325. For a different version, see William Christie MacLeod, *The American Indian Frontier* (London, 1928), 40.

21. Labaree *et al.*, eds., *Franklin Papers*, III, 445; Clinton, "Discourse Delivered before the New-York Historical Society," N.-Y. Hist. Soc., *Colls.*, II (1814),
87–88; also Harriss, ed., *Lawson's History of North Carolina*, 5–6.

22. Bernhard Knollenberg, "General Amherst and Germ Warfare," *MVHR*,
XLI (1954), 489–494.

tively untraveled parts of the continent. Lewis and Clark found it among the Mandans and also on the West Coast. Lewis reported in his *Journal:* "The small pox has destroyed a great number of the natives in this quarter, it prevailed about 4 years since among the Clatsops and destroy[ed] several hundred of them, four of their chiefs fell victims to its ravages. . . . I think the late ravages of the small pox may well account for the number of remains of villages which we find deserted on the river and Sea coast in this quarter."[23] The evidence abounds, consequently, that the whites fully understood the seriousness of the disease for the natives; moreover, many whites accepted a measure of responsibility for its spread.

Probably in 1837, a correspondent sent Gallatin a description of the terrible conditions among the western tribes. Smallpox had always been a frightful menace, but now, curiously, with their population thinned out, the situation seemed worse. War, famine, and all other causes of death combined could not be compared to smallpox. In 1802 three-fourths of the different tribes along the Mississippi and the Missouri had perished. Now a new generation repeated the experience. Again the sedentary Mandans bore the brunt. The scourge arrived in July, and when the writer passed in October,

the scene was horrible—the large level prairie surrounding the Village had been converted into one great grave yard, whilst hundreds of (loathsome) carcasses (which had not received the rites of sepulture), lay mouldering on the surface of the earth, emitting fetid exhalations which poisoned the surrounding atmosphere—and made it quite sickning even at the distance of several miles.

A desperate phrenzy seems to have seized the few survivors in order to escape a loathsome lingering death—put an end to their own lives—some by throwing themselves from a high rocky precipice which stands near the village, others by drowning, hanging etc.—Thirty one Mandans only were living at the time I passed their villages.

It spread thence to other tribes; few who contracted it survived. The tribal order broke down, and new leaders arose who blamed the whites and exhorted the Indians to seek revenge.

The same correspondent also reported that the Blackfeet had been decimated. Believing themselves attacked by a demon, they

23. Harriss, ed., *Lawson's History of North Carolina*, 24; Adair, *History of American Indians*, 232; Carver, *Three Years Travels*, 30; Heckewelder, "Account of the Indian Nations," Am. Phil. Soc., *Trans. of Hist. and Lit. Comm.*, I (1819), 75; Morse, *Report on Indian Affairs*, 92; Thwaites, ed., *Journals of Lewis and Clark Expedition*, I, 109–110, 220, IV, 50; Jefferson, *Message from the President*, 14, 18, 20.

sacrificed several thousand of their best horses for his appeasement. When that expedient failed, they turned out in full battle array to challenge their illusive tormenter, but he could not be found. Many then despaired and committed suicide. Gallatin's informant believed that seventeen thousand Indians had perished in the previous three months.[24]

Whatever the white man's sense of responsibility, he could do little to save the natives. Once deposited in the New World, the disease took its natural course. Even for the white man, only an immunity cultivated over generations of endemic contact could be considered effective. Without this barrier, the Indians suffered accordingly. Adair tried to save lives by moderating the severities of native medicine and by successfully instructing the Indians in the use of quarantine. Jefferson favored vaccination and sought to spread the practice among the tribes. When Little Turtle, a Miami chief, came east with a delegation in 1797, he arranged for Benjamin Rush to vaccinate the chief and his companions. He directed Lewis and Clark to carry a specimen of the "kinepox" on their expedition and to take the opportunity to show the Indians how to use it. The War Department supplied a quantity of vaccine for the Long expedition to distribute along the Missouri in 1819, though unfortunately it was ruined in an accident. The injury to the tribes, however, had already been done. Considering the state of medical knowledge at the time, no mere desire to help could have saved the Indians from smallpox.[25]

Civilization may have been recognized as the ultimate source of smallpox, but the connection seemed less obvious and more tenuous than with the various venereal disorders. These infections probably caused fewer deaths, but they were more patently social and hence more illustrative of the effects of civilization on the Indians. Syphilis, especially, carried with it melancholy connotations of moral and social disintegration.

The Jeffersonian generation did not solve the problem of the origins of the venereal diseases. With a certain relish for the justice

24. Gallatin Papers, Box 65, N.-Y. Hist. Soc. See also John Bradbury, *Travels in the Interior of America* . . . (Liverpool, 1817); Isaac McCoy, "Report on the Country Reserved for the Indians West of the Mississippi," House Doc. 172, 22d Cong., 1st Sess., Mar. 16, 1832, ser. 220.

25. Adair, *History of American Indians*, 259, 339; Edwin T. Martin, *Thomas Jefferson: Scientist* (New York, 1961), 41; Stern and Stern, *Effect of Smallpox on Amerindian*, 56–58; Corner, ed., *Autobiography of Rush*, 240–241. See also Jackson, ed., *Letters of Lewis and Clark Expedition*, 64; Thwaites, ed., "James's Account of S. H. Long's Expedition," in *Early Western Travels*, XV, 202.

of the transaction, such European writers as Raynal and Robertson maintained that the Indians transmitted them to the whites. In the New World, Lawson came to a similar conclusion. Yet the eminent medical authority of the age, Benjamin Rush, believed that venereal ailments originated with the Europeans, an opinion concurred in by Carver and Heckewelder. On one point everyone agreed: no matter what their origin, these afflictions took a heavy toll of Indian lives. Some of the most provocative evidence came from Lewis and Clark, who found traces on their expedition. The illnesses seemed especially serious in the Far West. They found them also among the Shoshonees, which caused Lewis to conclude that they were native to the country. Despite confusion over their origins, white men generally treated the presence of venereal infections among the tribes as further evidence of native decline for which civilization could be held responsible.[26]

Besides the obvious physical manifestations, Jeffersonian observers also recognized the broader consequences of the spread of venereal diseases. Of course, no one directly related the decline in native population, the reduction in the birth rate, and the increase in anxiety to the incidence of syphilis and gonorrhea among the Indians. Enough that Jeffersonians perceived dimly that these maladies generally accompanied a moral collapse in the tribes. In an exchange with Charles Willson Peale over a minor incident, Jefferson disclosed the intensity of his own feelings on the subject.

26. Raynal, *Philosophical and Political History,* trans. Justamond, II, 363; Robertson, *History of America,* II, 82–83; Harriss, ed., *Lawson's History of North Carolina,* 14–15; Rush, "Inquiry into the Natural History of Medicine among the Indians," in *Medical Inquiries,* 3d ed., I, 117; Carver, *Three Years Travels,* 257; Heckewelder, "Account of the Indian Nations," Am. Phil. Soc., *Trans. of Hist. and Lit. Comm.,* I (1819), 215, 255; Thwaites, ed., *Journals of Lewis and Clark Expedition,* I, 248, 279, II, 373, III, 186, 232, 240, IV, 16; Jackson, ed., *Letters of Lewis and Clark Expedition,* 506. For the origin of syphilis, see Samuel Eliot Morison, *Admiral of the Ocean Sea: A Life of Christopher Columbus* (Boston, 1942), II, 193–218; he contends that the disease was probably endemic among the Indians and was transmitted by them to Europe where it became epidemic. See also Wm. Allen Pusey, *The History and Epidemiology of Syphilis* (Springfield, Ill., 1933), chap. 1; Paul S. Martin *et al., Indians before Columbus: Twenty Thousand Years of North American History Revealed by Archeology* (Chicago, 1947), 267, 353; and Gerbi, *La disputa del nuevo mundo.* For the argument that syphilis originated in Europe, see Ashburn, *Ranks of Death,* chap. 11; Duffy, "Smallpox and the Indians in the American Colonies," *Bull. Hist. Med.,* XXV (1951), 325; MacLeod, *American Indian Frontier,* 40; Alfred W. Crosby, Jr., "The Early History of Syphilis: A Reappraisal," *Am. Anthro.,* N.S., LXXI (1969), 218–227. Whatever the origin, once the initial infection had begun, reinfection from either white or Indian undoubtedly took place. Thus it is easy to see why the blame was placed, quite accurately, on both sides.

Peale reported from Philadelphia that a delegation of Indians from beyond the Mississippi "had been with the women of bad fame in the lower part of the town and contracted the venereal disease." He suggested to Jefferson the importance of curing them before they returned home. Jefferson agreed to take the proper measures, but the arch obscurity of his language revealed a profound prudishness. Instead of frankly recognizing an important problem for the tribes, he seemed more concerned with guarding the precious delicacy he insisted upon in all sexual matters. Venereal diseases evoked in his mind images of moral decay about which he would speak only with reluctance and circumlocution.[27]

5

Alcohol held a special place in the history of tribal disintegration. Seemingly the most innocent of commodities, the Indian tribes paid dearly for its introduction into the New World. Without the startling finality of smallpox, it set in train the process of lingering devastation that not only wore on the physical health of the natives but attacked the very coherence of their social order. In epidemic force it ravaged tribe after tribe until the drunken, reprobate Indian became a fixture in American folklore.

John Heckewelder told a classic story that he claimed had long been cherished by the Delawares. As he described the scene, a party of white men had just landed on Manhattan Island (the name was derived from the Indian word meaning "the island where we all became intoxicated") , led by a man of impressive bearing, elaborately attired in bright red. The Indians called him the Mannitto (a sort of god) and watched intently as a servant filled his glass with an unknown substance.

He drinks—has the glass filled again, and hands it to the chief standing next to him. The chief receives it, but only smells the contents and passes it on to the next chief, who does the same. The glass or cup thus passes through the circle, without the liquor being tasted by any one, and is on the point of being returned to the red clothed Mannitto, when one of the Indians, a brave man and a great warrior, suddenly jumps up and harangues the assembly on the impropriety of returning the cup with its contents. It was handed to them by the Mannitto, that they should drink out of it, as he himself had done. To follow his example would be pleas-

27. William Bartram, "Observations on the Creek and Cherokee Indians," American Ethnological Society, *Transactions*, III (1853) , 43–44; Blasingham, "Depopulation of the Illinois Indians," *Ethnohistory*, III (1956) , 385; Peale to Jefferson, Feb. 10, 1807, and Jefferson to Peale, Feb. 13, 1807, Jackson, ed., *Letters of Lewis and Clark Expedition*, 373–374.

ing to him; but to return what he had given them might provoke his wrath, and bring destruction on them. And since the orator believed it for the good of the nation that the contents offered them should be drunk, and no one else would do it, he would drink it himself, let the consequence be what it might; it was better for one man to die, than that a whole nation should be destroyed. He then took the glass, and bidding the assembly a solemn farewell at once drank up its whole contents. Every eye was fixed on the resolute chief, to see what effect the unknown liquor would produce. He soon began to stagger, and at last fell prostrate on the ground. His companions now bemoan his fate, he falls into a sound sleep, and they think he has expired. He wakes again, jumps up and declares, that he has enjoyed the most delicious sensations, and that he never before felt himself so happy as after he had drunk the cup. He asks for more, his wish is granted; the whole assembly then imitate him and all became intoxicated.[28]

The anecdote contained an ominous portent of the Indian's later experience. Ignorant of intoxicating beverages, he approached the drink warily, but he soon took it down with eagerness and suffered its baneful effects. In addition, once presented with the liquor, he showed his perplexity in the face of civilization: he wished to please because he perceived the strength of the whites and because he feared the consequences of opposition.

In this first meeting, the brittleness of the tribal order became evident. Premonitions of insecurity and tension impressed themselves on the Indian, but he took the first of many drinks anyway, and he liked what he tasted. Soon his appetite for liquor would become inordinate. Civilized observers agreed that the Indian would drink large quantities whenever he could obtain it; that he drank compulsively for the sole purpose of getting drunk; that he lost control of his actions when he drank; and that he willingly surrendered valuable possessions to obtain liquor. Rum, whiskey, and brandy assumed major importance in trade between white and Indian and were critical factors in the decline of native society. The disintegrated Indian became preeminently the drunken Indian.[29]

28. Heckewelder, "Account of the Indian Nations," Am. Phil. Soc., *Trans. of Hist. and Lit. Soc.,* I (1819) , 56–57, 256.

29. It is generally agreed that the North American Indian had neither fermented nor distilled beverages and, therefore, no experience with the social control of drunkenness. See C. A. Browne, "The Chemical Industries of the American Aborigines," *Isis,* XXIII (1935), 410–411; Weston La Barre, "Native American Beers," *Am. Anthro.,* N.S., XL (1940) , 233. There is little information on the reasons for the compulsive drinking habits of the American Indians; Donald Horton, "The Functions of Alcohol in Primitive Societies: A Cross-Culture Study," *Quarterly Journal of Studies on Alcohol,* IV (1943–1944)', 199–320, notes that "the primary function of alcoholic beverages in all societies is the reduction of anxiety." Hallowell, "Some Psychological Characteristics of

Apart from guns and ammunition, liquor was soon the staple of the Indian trade. Though white men understood its debilitating effect on native society, the demand remained so strong that nothing effective could ever be done to stem its flow. Unlicensed traders, some of whom sold liquor exclusively, shouldered most of the blame, but no trader would survive without at some time dealing in liquor. For this reason, the government probably never possessed the means to shut off the trade until the establishment of the reservation system in the nineteenth century, and it failed to do so even then. Franklin summed up the opinion in the Jeffersonian period when he said that at best the traffic could be limited to licensed traders. Any effort to stop it completely would only enhance the position of the lawless renegades who made it their business to debauch the natives.[30]

Timothy Pickering took a realistic view. He wanted to exclude rum entirely from the trade, but he doubted that the "habits of the Indians in this respect could be . . . controuled." Liquor must be provided, though every opportunity should be taken to advise the Indians against it—not so strongly, however, as to "hazard their disgust." Only small quantities should be given to the natives while they did business at a trading post, for if they remained sober, they would be assured a fair transaction. But on their departure the

---

the Northeastern Indians," in *Culture and Experience*, 132–150, associates this general contention with what he considers the basis of the northeastern Indian's psychic structure: "The whole psychological picture is one that suggests underlying anxiety—anxiety lest one fail to maintain the standard of fortitude required no matter what the hardship one must endure; anxiety lest one give way to one's hostile impulses; anxiety lest one provoke resentment in others." Lacking previous experience with an intoxicating beverage, the Indians had no internalized guides to direct its use; but they did have in their high anxiety quotient ample reason to find the white man's liquor soothing. The already high level of anxiety was undoubtedly compounded by the insecurity attendant upon the challenge from European culture. Also note the important thesis of Craig MacAndrew and Robert Edgerton in *Drunken Comportment: A Social Explanation* (Chicago, 1969), chaps. 6 and 7, which interprets native behavior under the influence of alcohol as imitative of the white man. In this view, the Indian's first experience with liquor was neutral. It became for him the source of deviant behavior only after he perceived that it played a similar role for the white man. It remains true, however, that white men were deeply impressed by the serious consequences of drinking for the Indian.

30. Heckewelder, "Account of the Indian Nations," Am. Phil. Soc., *Trans. of Hist. and Lit. Comm.*, I (1819), 256, 261; Hulbert and Schwarze, eds., "Zeisberger's History," Ohio Archaeol. and Hist. Soc., *Pubs.*, XIX (1910), 90–91, 118–119; Smyth, ed., *Writings of Franklin*, XV, 470. Morse, *Report on Indian Affairs*, 42, favored complete suppression of the liquor traffic. Prucha, *American Indian Policy*, chap. 6.

traders should give them as much rum as they wished to buy. Similarly, Lewis Cass could see no hope of cutting the Indians off from their supply of alcohol. Their attachment to it was "probably without a parallel in all the history of man." As the government raised the penalties imposed on the trade, the Indians would merely sacrifice more in order to obtain it, thus accelerating the process of decline.[31]

Some Indians understood the consequences of heavy drinking for their people. They blamed the whites for giving them the evil fluid, and they attempted in vain to prohibit its distribution. But they could never diminish the insatiable craving of their fellow tribesmen. Neither the white man's regulations nor even the discipline of the Indian's own social authority proved capable of drying up tribal life. It seemed clear to most observers that, as long as the Indian wanted to drink, the means would be available to mollify his desire.[32]

Although everyone agreed that Indians overindulged and suffered seriously as a result, few speculated on the causes of the problem. Samuel Williams and Heckewelder attributed the Indian's unquenchable thirst to his generally bland diet, which failed to satisfy the natural human need for gustatory stimulation. Gallatin shifted the problem of blandness from the native's stomach to his mental outlook. Bored by hunting, the Indian sought some artificial stimulant to stir him from his torpor. With sharper anthropological insight, Cass attempted to connect the absence of any intoxicating drink before the white man's arrival with the inordinate taste for it that developed after, but he was vague about its actual meaning. "This remarkable abstinence, of which few examples can be found," he wrote, "has been succeeded by a melancholy reaction, equally unprecedented." Furthermore, drunkenness had always been an individual lapse; among the Indians, it affected entire tribal seg-

31. Pickering to Edward Price, Nov. 26, 1795, Letter Book, Creek Trading House (M-4); Lewis Cass, "Removal of the Indians," *No. Am. Rev.*, XXX (1830), 66.

32. Labaree *et al.*, eds., *Franklin Papers*, V, 97; Jefferson, Message to the Senate and House, Jan. 27, 1802, Richardson, ed., *Papers of the Presidents*, I, 322–323; [Charles Thomson], *An Enquiry into the Causes of the Alienation of the Delaware and Shawanese Indians from the British Interest, and into the Measures Taken for Recovering Their Friendship* (London, 1759), 23–24; Harper, ed., *Bartram's Travels*, 490–491; Jeremy Belknap and Jedidiah Morse, *Report on the Oneida, Stockbridge, and Brotherton Indians, 1796*, Indian Notes and Monographs, No. 54, Museum of the American Indian, Heye Foundation (New York, 1955), 21.

ments. White men found no experience in their own lives to explain the catastrophic consequences of drinking for the Indians.[33]

The white man recorded the natives' boozy exploits with a fascination equal to the Indians' enthusiasm in performing them. Guzzling Indians with "incredible" thirsts became common participants in all relations between the two societies. Tench Coxe, for example, had the foresight to order five hundred gallons of rum for a meeting with the Iroquois in 1794. William Henry Harrison said that he believed the six-hundred-odd warriors living on the Wabash River consumed six thousand gallons of whiskey a year. Pointing up the avidity of the native craving, Philip Freneau's favorite Indian, Tomo Cheeki, contemplated suicide while drinking apple cider, but abandoned the idea when a passing trader offered him a better drink, brandy, making life worth living once again.[34]

At the treaty of Carlisle in 1753, Benjamin Franklin witnessed a familiar incident that brought together the native affinity for alcohol and its serious consequences for his society. The commissioners insisted that the Indians remain sober until they had concluded the business of the conference. Since the tribesmen could obtain no liquor, they complied. But promptly on the afternoon that the deliberations closed, the Indians presented themselves to claim a reward for their abstemiousness:

In the Evening, hearing a great Noise among them, the Commissioners walk'd out to see what was the Matter. We found they had made a great Bonfire in the middle of the Square. They were all drunk Men and Women, quarrelling and fighting. Their dark-colour'd Bodies, half naked, seen only by the gloomy Light of the Bonfire, running after and beating one another with Firebrands, accompanied by their horrid Yellings, form'd a Scene the most resembling our Ideas of Hell that could well be imagin'd. There was no appeasing the Tumult, and we retired to our Lodging. At Midnight a Number of them came thundering at our Door, demanding more Rum; of which we took no Notice. The next Day, sensible they had misbehav'd in giving us that Disturbance, they sent three of their old Counsellors to make their Apology. The Orator acknowledg'd the Fault, but laid it upon the Rum; and then endeavour'd

33. Williams, *History of Vermont*, 158–159; Heckewelder, "Account of the Indian Nations," Am. Phil. Soc., *Trans. of Hist. and Lit. Comm.*, I (1819), 260–261; Gallatin, "Synopsis of Indian Tribes," Am. Antiq. Soc., *Archaeologia Americana*, II, 151; Cass, "Indian Treaties," *No. Am. Rev.*, XXIV (1827), 404–405; Belknap and Morse, *Report on the Onieda, Stockbridge and Brotherton Indians, 1796*, 17.

34. Romans, *Concise Natural History*, 77; Coxe to Nicholas Hoffman, July 29, 1794, Letters of Coxe (M-74), 101; Harrison to Henry Dearborn, July 15, 1801, Esarey, ed., *Messages of Harrison*, I, 29; Freneau, "The Splenetic Indian," in Marsh, ed., *Prose of Freneau*, 126–129.

to excuse the Rum, by saying, *"The great Spirit who made all things made every thing for some Use, and whatever Use he design'd any thing for that Use it should always be put to; Now, when he made Rum, he said,* LET THIS BE FOR INDIANS TO GET DRUNK WITH. *And it must be so."* And indeed if it be the Design of Providence to extirpate these Savages in order to make room for Cultivators of the Earth, it seems not improbably that Rum may be the appointed Means. It has already annihilated all the Tribes who formerly inhabited the Sea-coast.[35]

The Jeffersonian generation saw the Indian's improvidence while under the influence of alcohol as a major factor in his coming destruction. Of course, white men had never believed that the Indian took sufficient care in allocating his limited stock of goods, but he seemed to lose all conception of future necessity in his weakness for alcohol. John Lawson contended that the Indian would sell all he owned to get his full dose of the precious fluid. One of the Shawnees who captured Charles Johnston exchanged a horse worth about two hundred dollars for five gallons of whiskey. From his limited preserve of patience, Pickering burst out in exasperation: "Brant will get drunk—The Farmer's Brother will get drunk—Red Jacket will get drunk." He knew of only three chiefs who did not drink—and even they occasionally succumbed. He once gave the Farmer's Brother a shilling to redeem his coat, which the Indian had sold for a pint of whiskey. McKenney summarized the white man's recognition of the native's helplessness:

No one who has not witnessed it, can conceive the sacrifices an Indian will make for whiskey; how far he will travel, laden with the returns of his winter's hunts; how little he forsees, or regards the consequences to himself, or any body else, of his indulgence in this final poison. The awakening from his delirious dream, and finding his furs and peltries gone, and in their places a few worthless articles, unsuited in quality or quantity to screen himself and his family from the winter's cold, may distress him, and kindle his revenge for the time being, but it is forgotten whenever a new occasion happens in which he can indulge the same excess! Of all men, an Indian is the most improvident and furnishes the most painful example of a reckless disregard to the impoverishing and life-consuming effects of intemperance.[36]

Often the Indians seemed determined to enjoy an immediate and spectacular demise. Drunken tribesmen engaged in orgies of violence

35. Leonard W. Labaree *et al.*, eds., *The Autobiography of Benjamin Franklin* (New Haven, 1964), 198–199.

36. Harriss, ed., *Lawson's History of North Carolina*, 214; *A Narrative of the Incidents Attending the Capture, Detention, and Ransom of Charles Johnston* . . . (New York, 1827), 59; Pickering to Henry Knox, Aug. 10, 1791, Pickering Papers, LX, 116, Mass. Hist. Soc. (microfilm); McKenney, *Memoirs, Official and Personal*, 20.

in which they seriously incapacitated themselves and mutilated their fellows. In a spasm of mayhem, they concluded the task of self-destruction already well advanced by widespread drinking. The "dreadful carnage" that invariably accompanied Indian intoxication appeared all the worse to some whites because they knew the tranquility of native domestic life in its more sober moments. Indians readily destroyed their enemies, but it took alcohol to make them injure their friends. Then violence became a tribal event; not just a series of unfortunate incidents between individuals, but a mass fracas in which a village would set about the process of mutual immolation. "A drunken Indian and squaw act more like demons than rational human beings, and nearly a whole town in the same situation. . . . It does make many thinking men view such a scene with horror, and pity . . . when they consider the depravity of the human stability, for chiefs common men and women will wallow in filth and mire so long as they can raise the means to purchase spirits to drink[.] During such time of frenzy they will fight each other indiscriminately frequently taking each others lives."[37]

Violence on this scale could be merely portentious; it lacked the anecdotal interest of personal conflict. Ezra Stiles told an old New England tale of Indian inebriation and its consequences. "Great Grandfather of present Ninecraft [a Narraganset chief] married a Pequot of high Blood. All got drunk one night, and the King waking found his Sunk [queen] lying near another Ind. and was jealous. He took his Knife and cut three Strokes on each Cheek of his Wife in derision for Adultery and sent her home to the Pequots." Mary Jemison blamed liquor for the deaths of her three sons. The oldest, John, made a reputation as a medicine man, had a violent temper, and kept two wives. His brother Thomas long hated him and, when he drank, often tormented him for his many wives. In 1811, after a drunken quarrel, John killed his brother with a tomahawk blow. Despondent, John in turn took to liquor and the next year killed his younger brother Jesse in a drunken brawl. In

37. Smyth, *Tour in the United States*, I, 187; John D. Hunter, *Manners and Customs of Several Indian Tribes Located West of the Mississippi* . . . (Philadelphia, 1823), 46–47; Nunez, ed., "Narrative of George Stiggins," *Ethnohistory*, V (1958), 35. See also Long, *Voyages and Travels*, 49, 50, 56, 64–71, 85, 91, 93, 104, 108, 111; Heckewelder, "An Account of the Indian Nations," Am. Phil. Soc., *Trans. of Hist. and Lit. Comm.*, I (1819), 215–217, 254–257; Rogers, *Concise Account of North America*, 151–152, 209–210; Boudinot, *Star in the West*, 237–239.

1817 he was himself murdered in similar circumstances by two Indian companions.[38]

The white man's conviction, therefore, that the Indian would destroy himself through compulsive drinking rested on substantial evidence. The somewhat vague fear that the process would make its way to devastating completion reflected reality as accurately as the many recorded instances of self-destruction. Liquor attacked the basis of social control. Whole villages, including women and children, fell into chronic alcoholism, health deteriorated, and social cohesion inevitably dissolved. In Jefferson's words: "It has weakened their bodies, enervated their minds, exposed them to hunger, cold, nakedness, and poverty, kept them in perpetual broils, and reduced their population." The white man's social lubricant proved itself a poison of startling efficacy to primitive America.[39]

6

As the model for a disintegrating native society, the drunken Indian presented an unlikely candidate for civilization. "Your children are not wanting in industry," said the Miami chief Little Turtle in a speech at the War Department in 1802, "but it is the introduction of this fatal poison, which keeps them poor. Your children have not that command over themselves you have, therefore before anything can be done to advantage this evil must be remedied." Cyrus Kingsbury, though ever optimistic of the Indian's eventual acquiescence in the philanthropic plan, experienced some shaky moments with intoxicated tribesmen. By 1825 his apparent successes with the Choctaws in organizing schools and influencing the villages to adopt farming seemed dashed by their inordinate penchant for liquor. One of the towns had refrained from whiskey for three or four years, only for a reprobate chief to give "permission to his warriors to buy whiskey, get drunk, fight and kill for one month." The surrounding white settlers did an active business in purchasing Choctaw property, with the result that "poverty and wretchedness, and fighting and murder are desolating the country." And a year later the situation did not look better. "The property accumulated in preceding years, has been profusely squandered in the purchase

38. Dexter, ed., *Extracts from the Itineraries of Ezra Stiles*, 142; Seaver, *Life of Mary Jemison*, 105–111, 127–129, 136–137, 151; McCoy, *Remarks on Indian Reform*, 13, 23.

39. Padover, ed., *Complete Jefferson*, 460.

of whiskey." John Ridge spoke from intimate knowledge when he defended the progress the Cherokees had made toward civilization, but he warned: "Nations cannot be civilized unless they renounce every inducement that tends to their deterioration." Unless the tribes followed Ridge's advice, philanthropy offered little hope for transforming the Indians into imitations of the white man's better self.[40]

Unfortunately, while making his way toward civilization, the Indian seemed increasingly more besotted, certainly less healthy than his primitive brethren. By virtue of its idealistic premises, incorporation always remained short of accomplishment. But now the philanthropist could see emerging from the relationship between the two societies evidence that the Indian might never be properly civilized. All hinged upon the tribesman's acceptance of the white man's virtues. If instead he absorbed those characteristics that civilized men recognized as vices and became simultaneously more a subject of pity than respect, incorporation would be pushed further into the future. Thus the intermingling of white and Indian that should have accomplished the amelioration of the native condition proved both abrasive and destructive, and when the tribes no longer had the strength for abrasiveness, it became increasingly destructive.

The reformist mentality hesitated to accept the proposition that the immediate consequences of its program inhibited the possibilities for ultimate success. Blame for the tribes' misfortunes could always be placed, not on the fragility of their culture, but on the Indians themselves. The errant ways of some of the chiefs and the reluctance of some of the Indians to cooperate with the civilizing plan could be put down to the intrigues of selfish reactionaries with an interest in preserving the status quo. The internecine conflict that followed the aggressive introduction of civilized ways could similarly be accounted the result of the persistence of primitive life. Sufficient that the philanthropists should insist that the Indians change their ways, drive out the leadership that opposed the new progressive order, and stop clinging to the remnants of a savage existence. At base a moral movement whose principal agent was the missionary, philanthropy saw opposition as immoral. More to

40. Speech of Little Turtle, Jan. 4, 1802, Letters Sent, Sec. War (M-15), Roll 1: 141–142; Kingsbury to Thomas L. McKenney, Oct. 11, 1825, Letters Received, Off. Indian Affairs (M-234), Schools, Roll 772: 581; Kingsbury to McKenney, June 5, 1825, *ibid.*, Roll 773: 239–241; Ridge to Albert Gallatin, Mar. 10, 1826, Gallatin Papers, Box 64–3, fol. 42, N.-Y. Hist. Soc.

the point, how could a specifically moral end, the civilization of the Indian, bring in its train the misfortunes that demoralized Indian society?

Moreover, a full description of the transaction between the two societies tended to free the white man of responsibility. Certainly the willful distribution of smallpox, measles, and the venereal diseases formed no part of the philanthropic program, nor was it the secret wish of the white man's society. Disease attacked all of mankind and aroused as much sympathy for the afflicted Indian as for the white—more so since he suffered more and had obviously not been responsible for its introduction. Liquor was another question. Religious reformers typically entertained dry opinions. They believed drinking sinful for whites as well as for Indians and wanted to halt the traffic, but they recognized that the Indian's addiction made this impossible. The tribesman's determination to have the liquor shifted the responsibility; he did seem incorrigible when intoxicated. The only solution lay in sobering him up by giving him civilization in the hope that disease had not so thinned his numbers that the enterprise would be futile.

Of course, the many artifacts that the tribes received from civilization played a primary role in the decline of native culture. Since the very act of taking most of these constituted an important sign of progress, the philanthropist did not perceive the decay they caused at the root of Indian life. But the effects could be seen. No one thought the obsequious, dependent Indian a happy sight or a particularly fit subject for civilization. Yet this very Indian, receptive and infantile, willingly took what the white man offered. Dependence flowed directly from philanthropic activity, inherent in the supposition that the white man knew best what the Indian needed.

Long in developing, the conception of the disintegrating Indian assumed greater pertinence when it became clear that a formidable force in the country would refuse to accept the Indians, civilized or not, as part of the white man's world. When the frontier had advanced to the point of spilling around the native lands, state authorities, land speculators, and professional Indian haters determined that some expedient other than incorporation must be found to solve the Indian problem. Many philanthropists, their doubts increased by the mounting evidence that the civilization program required more time and that the Indian could not stand the strain of constant association with a superior and aggressive people, found in the removal policy a convenient alternative. In the vigorous and occasionally rancorous argument over removal in the 1820s, the humanitarians who favored it as a respite for the natives used the familiar figure of the declining Indian to support their position.

Chapter IX
Removal

I

The tendency of philanthropists to resort to manipulation and intimidation left them open to the charge of opportunism and even hypocrisy. By supporting removal, they seemed to furnish positive evidence not only of the shallowness of their principles but also of the frailty of their commitment to the Indian's welfare. Since philanthropy had failed to fulfill its major object, incorporation, its claim to virtue rested heavily on good intentions. Moreover, by setting an impossible goal and investing it with profound moral connotations, the philanthropists found themselves in the difficult position of adopting expedients that reflected directly on their claim to moral superiority.

By the mid-1820s, certain truths about Indian-white relations had become clear: the acceptance of civilization by the Indians did not lead necessarily to incorporation; many Indians who rejected civilization, and also many of those strongly influenced by the white man's ways, seemed to be in the throes of cultural decline; authorities in the state governments, especially Georgia, Alabama, and Mississippi, failed to appreciate the attractions of Jeffersonian philanthropy. On the basis of these realizations, a significant segment of humanitarian opinion adopted the expedient of removing the tribes beyond the Mississippi. Although the policy rested on the recognition of failure, its supporters did not conceive of it as a fundamental change in the philanthropic plan. The goal was still incorporation, but now the civilizing program would be carried on for a longer period of time and in a different location.[1]

1. The interrelation of the two policies is noted by Prucha, *American Indian Policy*, chap. 9. Most historians have maintained that the two policies were in contradiction; see Reginald Horsman, *Expansion and American Indian Policy*, *1783-1812* ([East Lansing, Mich.], 1967), 109-111, 116-117, 140; William T.

This close association between civilization and removal extended not only to the hopeful view that the apparent failure of the program in the East would soon be remedied in the West but also to the occasional cry of despair that arose from sympathetic white men at the persistence of savage violence. In 1776, for example, Jefferson recommended that the Cherokees and all the other tribes that supported the British should be driven beyond the Mississippi. "This then is the season for driving them off," he wrote, "and our Southern colonies are happily rid of every other enemy." Jefferson expressed the same view in 1813 when the Creeks attacked the frontier. After their defeat, he thought, they would "submit on the condition of removing to such new settlements beyond the Mississippi as we shall assign them." In the early stage of philanthropic disillusionment, such visceral reactions generated no positive plans for removal. But in pouring out his wrath upon the obstreperous natives, whose "ferocious barbarities justified extermination," Jefferson did anticipate one element in the later argument by stressing his disappointment that the civilizing program had not halted conflict on the frontier.[2]

To be sure, many early efforts to aid the Indians had resulted in the separation of the two societies. New Englanders established isolated praying towns in order to bring the various tribes together where they could be proselytized more conveniently. For less spiritual reasons, the British authorities in 1763 attempted to keep colonist and Indian apart by halting the frontier at the Alleghenies and later by arguing for a separate Indian state. During the Confederation period, the Congress strengthened the precedent for a separate Indian country by forbidding entrance into the area beyond state jurisdiction to settlers and unlicensed traders.[3] More generally, despite trade, diplomacy, and occasional intermarriage, Indian and white remained physically apart.

Long before the southern Indians had made any notable progress toward civilization, removal seemed to some a reasonable solution for the problems of the frontier. John Mitchell, the botanist and

Hagan, *American Indians* (Chicago, 1961), 44, 54; Mary Elizabeth Young, *Redskins, Ruffleshirts, and Rednecks: Indian Land Allotments in Alabama and Mississippi, 1830–1860* (Norman, 1961), 5–6, 9; Beaver, *Church, State, and the American Indians*, 90.

2. Jefferson to Edmund Pendleton, Aug. 13, 1776, Boyd, ed., *Jefferson Papers*, I, 494; Jefferson to David Baillie Warden, Dec. 29, 1813, Jefferson Papers, Lib. of Congress (microfilm).

3. The best study is Annie H. Abel, "Proposals for an Indian State, 1778–1878," American Historical Association, *Annual Report for 1907* (Washington, D.C., 1908), I, 87–102. Prucha, *American Indian Policy*, 31.

mapmaker, noted in 1767 that the Creeks and Choctaws formed the only obstacle to the expansion of Carolina to the Mississippi. These tribes had been engaged for some time in ruinous conflict, and Mitchell thought it would be advantageous for them to remove to Florida, where the British could supply them with farming tools. The northern Indians might at the same time be drawn into Canada.[4] In the 1790s, Timothy Pickering, perceiving the declining condition of the northern tribes, saw removal beyond the Mississippi as an alternative to extinction. Gilbert Imlay maintained in 1797 that the Indians must be civilized or else confined to a "particular district" where, he hoped, "some amelioration will take place in their savage and sanguinary dispositions." The whites would continue to press upon the eastern tribes from Ohio to Florida and compel them to live more "domestic lives" and eventually assimilate them or drive them to the western side of the Mississippi. Thus before the purchase of Louisiana and Jefferson's proposal to use it as a haven for the tribes, many observers saw removal as an easy solution to the Indian problem.[5]

2

The acquisition of Louisiana gave removal a feasibility it had not possessed before. Previous notions about keeping Indians and whites separate came close to abrogating philanthropic responsibility. In effect, they declared the Indian incorrigibly violent or at least unredeemable and proposed to drive him into the wastes beyond the Mississippi. Now the ownership of the territory by the United States and the information about the region supplied by Lewis and Clark provided ground for a new and positive policy. Jefferson weighed all the implications of the acquisition, but he considered it mainly in light of its significance for Indian-white relations.

In 1803 he held high hopes for incorporation, but he knew that it would not take place immediately. In the meantime, enclaves of native society stood in the way of the spreading white population that moved around them in disarray and occupied new land as quickly as it became available. With the acquisition of vast stretches of unused territory, the frontier would be even more attenuated and lose whatever semblance of coherence it still possessed. Jeffer-

4. [John Mitchell], *The Present State of Great Britain and North America . . .* (London, 1767), 231–232n.
5. Pickering, "Remarks on the Proposed Instructions to the Commissioners," 1793, Pickering Papers, XLIX, 29, Mass. Hist. Soc. (microfilm); Imlay, *Topographical Description*, 52, 295.

son advocated incorporation precisely because the Indian represented a disparate element in the order of nature. As long as the tribesman remained separate from civilized life and in possession of a portion of the continent destined for the white man's use, the new nation would fail to achieve the kind of ordered maturity he favored.

Thus when Jefferson drew up a constitutional amendment, ostensibly to assuage his strict-constructionist scruples over the purchase, he devoted his greatest attention to the Indians. Besides making Louisiana part of the United States, the amendment set aside the territory above the thirty-first parallel for the tribes in exchange for their eastern lands. His vision of a neatly arranged, tightly knit, and predominantly pastoral country would be changed profoundly by the addition of the western land. Yet the new territory might also be turned to good use, "condensing instead of scattering our population." If the lands were reserved for the Indians (they would be permitted to sell their land only to the government), white settlements would be forced to consolidate in the East on lands that, when held by the natives, constituted a source of friction and division. To complete the symmetry of the design, land offices would be opened to distribute the eastern territories, and the proceeds would cover the national debt, thereby further tightening the self-sufficiency and independence of the new nation.[6]

In the first years after the purchase, removal complemented the civilizing program and was applied mainly to hunters who rejected civilized ways. By persisting in their tribal habits, these Indians retarded the development of both white and Indian toward social homogenization. Their removal beyond the Mississippi cleared the way for the continuation of that process. As hunting declined in the East, many Indians made their way across the Mississippi in search of game. Some remained there, and a steady trickle followed them. The government never adopted a specific policy calling for the separation of the hunters from tribesmen inclined toward civilization, but federal officials recognized it as a desirable pro-

6. "Drafts of an Amendment to the Constitution," July 1803, Paul Leicester Ford, ed., *The Writings of Thomas Jefferson* (New York, 1892–1899), VIII, 241–249; Jefferson to Horatio Gates, July 11, 1803, *ibid.*, 262–263; Jefferson to John Dickinson, Aug. 9, 1803, *ibid.*, 262–263; Jefferson to John C. Breckenridge, Aug. 12, 1803, *ibid.*, 244n. John Sibley thought the idea of removing all the whites from west of the Mississippi "Laughable." Jefferson, of course, had suggested moving only those north of the 31st parallel. Sibley to William C. C. Claiborne, Oct. 10, 1803, Jefferson Papers.

cedure and promoted it at every opportunity. The Indians were encouraged to follow their own bent in the hope that the hunters' departure would accelerate the movement toward incorporating the natives remaining in the East.

Daniel Clark reported from Louisiana in 1803 that an increasing number of Cherokees, Choctaws, and Chickasaws traveled to Arkansas in search of better hunting. Many married into the local tribes and seemed inclined to settle permanently. Jefferson approved of such voluntary transferal and proposed to furnish the Indians generously with arms and ammunition, thus making their position in the West attractive to other emigrants. He was willing to see hunters indulged in their primitive livelihood—west of the river. Much later, in 1824, Calhoun noted the government's awareness that small parties of Cherokees, tempted by the abundance of game, had continued to find their way across the Mississippi. The Indians themselves recognized the superiority of the western regions over their old and depleted hunting grounds.[7]

Governor W. C. C. Claiborne of Orleans Territory repeated the common expectation that the interrelation between civilization and removal would work itself out in practice. As part of the southern tribes became civilized, the warrior and the hunter would withdraw "from a Country, whence the manly amusement 'the chase,' is not held in the first estimation." Though David Campbell held out little hope for removal of the Cherokees in 1804, he thought that they would eventually relinquish their lands north of the Tennessee for hunting grounds in the West. He associated this expected exchange with tribal progress toward civilization.[8] Three factors—the depletion of the game, the gradual transformation of the tribes, and the possibility of removal—formed a vague fusion in the white man's mind.

When news of internal division among the Cherokees reached Jefferson in 1808, he advised them to heal their differences and to continue progress toward civilization. But when it became clear that the disagreement went to the very heart of the problem of the natives' acceptance of the white man's ways, he modified his position. The upper towns, he recommended, should adopt separate

7. Daniel Clark, "An Account of the Indian Tribes of Louisiana," Sept. 29, 1803, Carter, ed., *Territorial Papers*, IX, 63–64; Jefferson to Claiborne, May 24, 1803, Lipscomb and Bergh, eds., *Writings of Jefferson*, X, 393–394; John C. Calhoun to James Monroe, Mar. 29, 1824, *American State Papers, Indian Affairs*, II, 461–462.

8. Claiborne to Jefferson, July 13, 1803, and Campbell to Jefferson, Jan. 1, 1804, Jefferson Papers.

ownership and come under the white man's laws, but the lower towns should be permitted to maintain the old ways. Though usually reluctant to accommodate any refusal to accept the inevitable dictates of progress, he was for once less exacting. The tribesmen of the lower towns should exchange their lands for territory in the West, where they could continue to hunt. It pleased him, he said, that so many had taken to cultivating the soil, but he did not "blame those who, having been brought up from their infancy to the pursuit of game, desire still to follow it to distant countries. I know how difficult it is for men to change the habits in which they have been raised." The hunters should send explorers to the Arkansas and White rivers to locate a place for settlement, "the higher up the better," where they would for a time be free from the intrusions of the white man, whose own settlements would begin at the mouths of the rivers. As in the past, Jefferson stressed volition. "It may be proper," his secretary of war, Henry Dearborn, wrote to the Cherokee agent Return J. Meigs, "to encourage such of them, as are not inclined to be farmers, to remove, but the act of removal should be the result of their own inclinations without being urged to the measure."[9]

The drain of Indians to the West continued, but so also did the flood of white settlement, and the native society came more and more to live in crisis. The policy makers in the government, who remained convinced that savagery should not stem the tide of civilization and that the Indian should have a part in the advance, continued to see in removal a partial remedy. The familiar themes ran through their understanding of the problem. Said William H. Crawford, speaking of the Cherokees, "they cannot much longer exist in the exercise of their savage rights and customs. They must become civilized, or they will finally . . . become extinct." Indians who had developed an attachment to property through the white man's influence would see the need for laws and efficient administration. New settlements in the West would make a valuable contribution because the "restless and indolent" part of the nation would be attracted to them by the decrease of game in the East. For the eastern Cherokees, who presumably wanted to be civilized, the alternative to removal would be the elimination of tribal land ownership and the acceptance of individual reservations. Meigs saw the

9. Jefferson to the Chiefs of the Upper Cherokees, May 4, 1808, Padover, ed., *Complete Jefferson*, 494–495; Jefferson to the Deputies of the Cherokees of the Upper and Lower Towns, Jan. 9, 1809, *ibid.*, 506–507; Dearborn to Meigs, May 5, 1808, Letters Sent, Sec. War (M-15), Roll 2: 376.

process with a finality few others accepted. He made a sharp distinction between the Indians who went West and those who remained. The latter, he said, would certainly cease to be Cherokees; "they must be incorporated, or rather blended with american citizens." Only the western Cherokees would retain their Indian character. Although he seemed to have little hope that many would stay and be transformed into white men, he clearly defined the choices open to the tribesmen.[10]

The idea of the removal of hunters persisted into the 1820s, as the tension mounted between the slow acculturation of the tribes and the steady pressure of the frontier. Even Andrew Jackson, who did not often sympathize with the Indians, said of the Choctaws in 1820 that the land they had accepted beyond the Mississippi would "have the happy effect of gradually draining the nation of all those whose habits and dispositions are inimical to industry and improvement, and whose absence will greatly facilitate the views of the Government in the civilization of those who remain." The Choctaws themselves claimed in 1825 that only small tracts of land remained to the few tribesmen left in the East and that a majority of these farmed the land and "would in time become useful citizens." They also admitted that "a large number still continue a wandering life, are wretched and degraded. These it would give us pleasure to see settled west of the Mississippi. It would be better for them and better for those who remained."[11]

But the removal of hunters did no more than supplement the program to civilize the Indians. By the 1820s many observers found it impossible to suppress any longer their doubts about the success of the program. It became widely accepted that the Indian could not, or would not, be civilized and that, even if he did accept the outward forms of civilization, he would not be admitted into the

10. Crawford to Meigs, Sept. 18, 1816, Letters Sent, Sec. War (M-15), Roll 3: 426–428; Meigs to Calhoun, Feb. 10, 1819, Letters Received, Sec. War (M-271), Roll 2: 1351–1352. See also Calhoun to Joseph McMinn, July 29, 1818, Letters Sent, Sec. War (M-15), Roll 4: 194–195; Charles Hicks to Calhoun, Feb. 8, 1818, Letters Received, Sec. War (M-271), Roll 2: 1102; Calhoun to McMinn, Dec. 29, 1919, *ibid.*, 999–1001; Cherokee Treaty, July 8, 1817, *American State Papers, Indian Affairs*, II, 129; McMinn to Cherokees, Nov. 18, 1818, *ibid.*, 485; Report of the Committee on Public Lands, Dec. 1, 1818, *ibid.*, 180–181; *Niles' Weekly Register*, XXVII (1824), 222.

11. Jackson to Thomas Hinds, Oct. 19 and 21, 1820, *American State Papers, Indian Affairs*, II, 243; Choctaw Delegation to Congress, Feb. 18, 1825, *ibid.*, 559. For a similar approach to the Delaware in the Northwest, see John Johnston to William Clark, Mar. 20, 1821, Letters Received, Sec. War (M-271), Roll 3: 898.

white man's world. In light of these changes in thinking, removal took on new significance. Instead of serving as one of the many expedients for divesting the native of his savage ways, it was in danger of becoming an alternative to that process—which it had become already for the hunting factions among the tribes. Still, for the philanthropic mind, the removal policy remained intimately related to the civilizing program, a way of gaining time for the Indian to complete the task of civilizing himself.

3

The recognition that civilization had not succeeded in changing the Indian's way of life implied an admission of powerlessness. Philanthropy rested on the white man's self-esteem, on his belief in the superiority and universal acceptability of his own way of doing things. In the potentially radical change in thinking of the 1820s, philanthropists lost their sense of control, their confidence that the Indian would make the easy transition to civilization. Instead the natives seemed to be disintegrating before the very eyes of those who wished to save them. Furthermore, the desire to transform the Indians and then to incorporate them into the white man's society ran directly contrary to the determination of the state authorities (especially in Georgia) and the western populace to resist such efforts. Even if the tribes had proved resilient enough to maintain their integrity and at the same time accomplish the transition to civilized ways, the basic lack of realism in the civilizing program would have been revealed in the opposition of the states. Philanthropists lacked the capacity to bring their program to a successful conclusion. From this perspective, removal could be considered a realistic step, but it also should have been a profound revelation of impotence.

From his position as head of the Indian office in the War Department, McKenney took the lead among philanthropists in promoting removal. He had been a prominent and sometimes uncritical supporter of the civilizing policy, but by the mid-1820s he had given up hope of success in the East. He solidified his change of opinion while touring the tribal areas in 1826 and 1827, after which he lobbied publicly in favor of removal. The preamble to the constitution of the New York Indian Board, an organization he created to further removal and for which he obtained official support, contained an explicit recognition of the dual problem facing the government and the Indian: "The situation of the scattered remains of the Aborigines of this country, involving on the one side the wrongs, the calamities, and probably extinction of an interesting race of men; and on the other side, the great perplexity of the Government of the United States, arising from its unwillingness, as well as from its want of power to interfere with the sovereignty of the States' Governments, has for a long time employed the skill of the statesman, and the benevolence of the religious community." The harmony of the United States and the cause of humanity, thought McKenney, required that a new turn be taken in dealing with the Indians.[12]

When McKenney changed his opinions, he gave to removal the same enthusiasm he had once devoted to the civilizing program. Curiously enough, however, the progress he had so often praised and encouraged among the Indians now seemed to have vanished. "Two centuries have gone round," he said, "and the remnants of these people, that remain, are more wretched than when they were a great and numerous people."[13] From the vehemence of his views, one might have supposed that the civilizing plan had utterly failed and that the very concept needed reevaluation. But McKenney never abandoned his philanthropic commitment. Despite the apocalyptic rhetoric with which he described the coming ruin of the tribes, he still believed in ultimate incorporation.

In making his case for the decline of the Indians, McKenney concentrated on the Creeks. Benjamin Hawkins had spent many years among them propagating civilization, but during the War of 1812, part of the tribe ignored his advice and attacked the frontier. Since that time the Creeks had made little progress. On his trip into the South in 1827, McKenney found them in worse condition than any of the other southern tribes. He reported to Secretary of War James Barbour that, "conscious of their own inefficiency to manage for themselves their concerns," they have become dependent on a

12. *Documents and Proceedings relating to the Formation and Progress of a Board in the City of New York, for the Emigration, Preservation, and Improvement, of the Aborigines of America* (New York, 1829), 21–22. There is no biography of McKenney; the best study is Herman J. Viola, "Thomas L. McKenney and the Administration of Indian Affairs, 1824–30" (Ph.D. diss., Indiana University, 1970). Dorothy Anne Dondore in *DAB* s.v. "McKenney, Thomas Loraine," is unfavorable and inadequate; McKenney, *Memoirs, Official and Personal*, is defensive but informative. See also Francis Paul Prucha, "Thomas L. McKenney and the New York Indian Board," *Mississippi Valley Historical Review*, XLVIII (1962), 635–655, and Prucha's *American Indian Policy*, 57–58, 225–227. Isaac McCoy became convinced of the need for removal in 1823; see Lela Barnes, "Isaac McCoy and the Treaty of 1821," *Kans. Hist. Qtly.*, V (1936), 122.

13. McKenney to Rev. Eli Baldwin, Apr. 14, 1827, Letters Sent, Off. Indian Affairs (M-21), Roll 4: 17.

group of exploiting half-breed leaders who oppose removal for their own interests. "But this is not all. They are habitually drunk. Their total abandonment to vice," he concluded, "demands that the government save them from destruction by removal to the west." McKenney took up the cry again in 1829. The Creek agent, he wrote, had been forced to purchase and distribute corn "to save thousands of them from actual starvation." "There is no sketching that can convey a clear perception of the misery and degradation in which this tribe is involved. If ever mercy pleaded, it pleads now, and beseeches the good and humane . . . to get these people to their fertile Country West of Arkansas." And in 1830, as the agitation for removal became more intense and the opposition mounted a strong campaign, he wrote that nothing could be "more degrading, than the condition of the Creeks. I never saw Human Nature in a more abject condition, or men who claimed the assistance of the Humane by such strong appeals to the general sympathy." No change took place in the basic humanitarian sentiment, save that it became more acute when combined with the prospect of the Indian's imminent destruction.[14]

McKenney used the Creeks because their condition made the most convincing case for removal. But he was no less concerned about the other tribes. The Passamaquoddies in Maine and the Seminoles in Florida, he wrote in 1830, both lived on sterile land devoid of game. The whites had humbled them, and they nurtured a sense of grievance. McKenney found the condition of the Florida Indians particularly deplorable; they had advanced not one step toward civilization. Moreover, in the Northwest, the natives continued to manifest what he called the ancient character of their race: "They catch fish—and plant patches of corn; dance, paint, hunt, fight, get drunk when they can get liquor and often starve." The Baptist missionary Isaac McCoy confirmed McKenney's opinions. "Their condition," he wrote, "is becoming more and more miserable every year. I repeat it, *they are positively perishing.*" So also did an Episcopal missionary among the Oneidas who wrote that, in their present "unhappy condition," they were "fast fading from our Land." About the Chippewas, McKenney himself noted:

14. McKenney to Barbour, Nov. 29, 1827, *ibid.,* 154; McKenney to Eli Baldwin, Oct. 8, 1829, *ibid.,* Roll 6: 104–105; McKenney to John Eaton, Mar. 22, 1830, *ibid.,* 349–351. McKenney's vehemence on the condition of the Creeks developed after his confrontation with John Ridge. See Viola, "McKenney," 227–232.

"Their extreme poverty, and the wretched and miserable condition in which they exist, I have not language to give you any adequate description."[15]

Much inclined to sentimentality, McKenney became increasingly overwrought in arguing for removal. Not only did the success of the civilizing program require removal, but the very survival of the Indian depended on it. Desperately seeking to forestall the native's impending doom and to avoid a stain upon the white man's character, he addressed a warning to Edward Everett: "While I am writing to you the paths of the wilderness are pressed by the fallen bodies of *starved* and expiring Indians!" By any account, the natives were "fast melting away," "for every winter hurries away before its blasts into eternity, and gives them its 'snows for their winding sheets,' hundreds of this very tribe [Chippewa], whose misery I have witnessed and deplored."[16] Caught up in the rhetoric of crisis, McKenney seemed to lose all sense of limitation; he now predicted the instant obliteration of the tribes.

But what of all the resources and enthusiasm poured into the civilizing program by the government and the missionary agencies? Surely McKenney could see that the breakdown and the crisis of tribal society cast some doubt on the feasibility of the philanthropic scheme. Or, more pertinently, had it not become evident that the civilizing plan itself had contributed to the dissolution of native culture? The investment ran too high in resources spent and in intellectual and emotional commitment to expect an admission of complete failure or a recognition that philanthropy yielded results different from those intended. Yet McKenney did not entirely miss the point. If he could not divine the shortcomings of his own position, he did know that something had gone wrong. Referring to previous apparently successful efforts to civilize the Indians, he cried out to Cyrus Kingsbury: "But where are they? where are those high hopes, and cheering prospects, even more bright, but not more illusive than are those which you now entertain in regard to the Choctaws? All vanished." Compelled to recognize that the effort to civilize the Indian had accomplished little, he drew a significant

15. McKenney to John H. Eaton, Mar. 22, 1830, Letters Sent, Off. Indian Affairs (M-21), Roll 6: 349–351; McCoy, *Remarks on Indian Reform*, 12; Solomon Davis to Eaton, Nov. 4, 1829, Letters Received, Off. Indian Affairs (M-234), Schools, Roll 774: 66–67; Cass, "Removal of the Indians," *No. Am. Rev.*, XXX (1830), 113; McKenney, *Sketches of a Tour to the Lakes*, 376.

16. McKenney to Everett, Apr. 12, 1826, Letters Sent, Off. Indian Affairs (M-21), Roll 3: 25; McKenney, *Sketches of a Tour to the Lakes*, 13, 341.

conclusion: they could not be civilized "situated as they are."[17] All roads led to removal. It preserved the philanthropists from the despair that should have followed from the rhetoric of obliteration and permitted them to project their humanitarian achievement into the future. The Indian would now be civilized in the West.

McKenney's views were accepted by Lewis Cass, the knowledgeable governor of the Michigan Territory, who went deeply into the question of the failure of the civilizing program. Cass favored removal; he also supported the effort to transform the Indian, and he believed ultimately that the process should be continued in the western territories. He credited the Indians with very little progress towards private ownership and farming. Even the Cherokees, who had long been the proving ground for the philanthropic program, did not measure up. The great body of them, he maintained, lived in "helpless and hopeless poverty," and "with the same improvidence and habitual indolence, which mark the northern Indians." One could not find "upon the face of the globe, a more wretched race than the Cherokees. . . . Many of them exhibit spectacles as disgusting as they are degrading." Perhaps some few had adopted the white man's ways, but these were largely mixed bloods and their immediate connections, who were not nearly numerous enough to affect his general conviction that the Indians had not become civilized. In fact, he observed, some of the more outrageous manifestations of savagery had occurred since the supposed transformation.[18]

Cass questioned neither the philanthropic program nor the qualifications of those who conducted it. "There seems," he wrote, "to be some insurmountable obstacle in the habits or temperament of the Indians, which has heretofore prevented, and yet prevents, the success of these labors." "It is difficult to conceive that any branch of the human family can be less provident in arrangement, less frugal in enjoyment, less industrious in acquiring, more implacable in their resentments, more ungovernable in their passions, with fewer principles to guide them, with fewer obligations to restrain them, and with less knowledge to improve and instruct them." The Indians

17. McKenney to Kingsbury, Mar. 8, 1830, Letters Sent, Off. Indian Affairs (M-21), Roll 6: 315–316. See also McKenney to Eaton, Mar. 22, 1820, *ibid.*, 351; McKenney to John Forsyth, Apr. 1, 1830, *ibid.*, 361–362; McKenney, *Memoirs, Official and Personal*, I, 240–241, 332; and Kingsbury to Choctaws, Oct. 24, 1825, Letters Received, Off. Indian Affairs (M-234), Schools, Roll 772: 585–586.
18. Cass, "Removal of the Indians," *No. Am. Rev.*, XXX (1830), 71, 94–95. See also Prucha and Carmony, eds., "Memorandum of Lewis Cass," *Wis. Mag. of Hist.*, LII (1968), 35–50.

seemed to have taken no part in the common meliorative processes of human existence. "If they have not receded," he wrote, "they certainly have not advanced." Of all those won over to removal in the crisis of the 1820s, Cass alone sought a basic explanation for the failure of philanthropy. If McKenney saw the failure of the civilizing program as no more than a delay in the process of improvement that would be continued in the West, Cass came close to doubting the very possibility of native progress. Considering the extremity to which some reformers carried their crisis rhetoric, he may have been justified in drawing his dismal conclusions.[19]

And yet Cass's position never veered sharply from the main path. He may have lacked the full measure of humanitarian sympathy— certainly he did not easily become sentimental about the Indian— but he adhered fully to the civilizing plan. Even though he did not hold the highest opinion of the natives' capacity, he thought they should be trained in farming and the value of individual ownership. And his conversion to removal arose from the same source that had impelled McKenney to change his mind: the failure in the East and the hope that the program would be continued west of the Mississippi. He believed, as did all reformers, that savagery was contrary to the natives' best interests, and he had no hesitation in drawing the necessary conclusions from that proposition.[20]

But the extraordinary circumstances that required the removal of the tribes hundreds of miles to the west in order to save them from destruction certainly reflected on the quality of the white man's civilization. "As an abstract proposition," said Senator Theodore Frelinghuysen in a speech against removal, "it implies a reproach somewhere. Our virtues certainly have not such deadly and depopulating power."[21] This very possibility forced the whites to draw a distinction between the virtues passed on by the missionaries and the vices that the tribes took over from contact with the frontier. The acceptance of removal constituted an admission that some of the white man's ways would not be good for the Indian. It revealed also that philanthropy did not speak for the whole of white society. The government had already acknowledged its inability to protect the Indian from the frontier; now the philanthropists admitted

19. Cass, "Removal of the Indians," *No. Am. Rev.*, XXX (1830), 69, 73; Cass, "Indian Treaties," *ibid.*, XXIV (1827), 391.

20. Cass, "Removal of the Indians," *ibid.*, XXX (1830), 109–121.

21. *Speeches on the Passage of the Bill for the Removal of the Indians, Delivered in the Congress of the United States, April and May 1830* (Boston, 1830), 25.

their own impotence to control the flow of civilized ways, some good and some bad, without isolating the Indian in the West.

McKenney's explanation of the deleterious effects of the white man's ways on the Indian was at once more subtle than the vision of the primitive Indian suffering the consequences of his attraction for civilized vices and more naive in its conception of the native's ability at self-evaluation. The Indian, he argued, fell into decline when he observed the superiority of civilization and hence recognized his own degradation. He pined away in humiliation because his white neighbor seemed so well off and he could see so little prospect for his own improvement. Indeed, as the Indian's condition improved, he became even more sensitive to the differences that distinguished his own achievements from those he saw in the civilized world. In the same breath that he described the primitive ignorance of the native, McKenney assumed that he would suffer from anxiety for his failure to duplicate civilized life. Removal would permit the tribesman to continue the process of melioration without this constant reminder of his inferiority.[22]

The overall philanthropic argument was more plausible. It may have ignored much of the real progress made by the Indians and it may have been too willing to believe that all benevolence was for their greater good, but it did recognize the truth of tribal disintegration, and it did realize how little the government could or would do to hold back the frontier. By the late 1820s, Georgia's insistence on its right to the Indian lands became the critical factor. The breakdown of native society had been in process for some time; it was recognized as crucial only when the state made its demands. The philanthropists had not contrived the argument merely to cover the failure of their program and the land avarice of the frontier. They believed it sincerely, but not so insistently until Georgia asserted its rights.

4

In a compact signed in 1802 to settle the Yazoo controversy, the federal government sanctioned Georgia's claim to the Indian lands within its borders. The Jefferson administration agreed to extinguish the Indian title as soon as it could be done peaceably and on

22. McKenney to James Barbour, Nov. 15, 1855, Letters Sent, Off. Indian Affairs (M-21), Roll 2: 236–237; McKenney to Barbour, Dec. 13, 1825, *ibid.*, 305–306; McKenney to Hon. Hemon Lincoln, Sept. 28, 1829, *ibid.*, Roll 6: 97–98; McKenney to Rev. Eli Baldwin, Oct. 23, 1829, *ibid.*, 134; McCoy, *Remarks on Indian Reform*, 12.

reasonable terms. In the two decades after the agreement, Georgia often pressed for its fulfillment; by the 1820s the state's demands became insistent and occasionally shrill. Though not in its origin directly connected with removal, the compact became the crux of the Georgia position when the dispute flared in the 1820s. Removal pleased the Georgians by opening new land, settling the Indian problem, and fully complying with the 1802 compact. It satisfied the philanthropists by promising to save the Indians from the Georgians.[23]

The humanitarian position rested on a delicate balance of right and hoped-for reality. In the long run, when the Indian gave up his tribal possessions, he would hold land individually, as civilized man held it. This would become the reality. But as a matter of right, the Indian could not be dispossessed arbitrarily. He should occupy the land until he either sold it voluntarily or lost it in war.[24] The areas of tension in the position soon became evident. The Indians never gave the land up quickly enough to pacify the white man's hunger for it. Unable to satisfy Georgia if it kept strictly within the bounds of the natives' rights, the government became more manipulative in dealing with the tribes. Still, it maintained the fiction of partial sovereignty by purchasing tribal lands and repeatedly asserting that the Indians need not sell unless they wanted to. Supposedly, as the natives moved closer to civilization, they would gradually give up their territory—which happened up to a point. The tribes surrendered the land because the white man brought sufficient pressure to compel them to do so, not because, as they acquired civilization, they saw the need to forsake their primitive rights. The rule was clear enough: the more savage the Indians, the more easily they might be disgorged of their landed possessions; and the more civilized, the more stubbornly they held on to them. "It cannot be doubted," wrote Calhoun, "that much of the difficulty of acquiring

23. For Monroe's message proposing removal together with the compact of 1802, see Sen. Doc. 63, 18th Cong., 1st Sess., ser. 91. Ulrich B. Phillips, *Georgia and State Rights: A Study of the Political History of Georgia . . .* (Washington, D.C., 1902), 34–35; Annie Heloise Abel, "The History of Events Resulting in Indian Consolidation West of the Mississippi River," Am. Hist. Assoc., *Annual Report for the Year 1906* (Washington, D.C., 1908), I, 323.

24. Jefferson, "Jefferson's Observations on Demeunier's Manuscript," Boyd, ed., *Jefferson Papers*, X, 44; Jefferson to Henry Knox, Aug. 26, 1790, *ibid.*, XVII, 430–431; Notes, Feb. 26, 1773, "The Anas," Lipscomb and Bergh, eds., *Writings of Jefferson*, I, 340–341; Jefferson to Knox, Aug. 10, 1791, *ibid.*, VIII, 226–227; Notes of a Conversation with George Hammond, June 3, 1792, *ibid.*, XVII, 328–329. See also Washburn, "Moral and Legal Justifications for Dispossessing the Indians," in Smith, ed., *Seventeenth-Century America*, 25–29; Prucha, *American Indian Policy*, 139–144.

additional cessions from the Cherokee nation, and other southern tribes, results from their growing civilization and knowledge, by which they have learned to place a higher value upon their lands than more rude and savage tribes."[25] As the natives became more civilized, they became more conscious of their tribal identity. In effect, they combined the white man's concept of national sovereignty with their familial loyalties. Philanthropic policy called for the transferal of the tribal lands, but in actuality it generated the opposite results.

Georgia refused to tolerate the existence of tribal lands within its borders, but the state also rejected the federal government's plan for incorporation and individual ownership of land by Indians. Governor George M. Troup saw no hope in uniting the two societies. At best, public opinion in the state would concede the Indians "a middle station, between the negro and the white man; and that, as long as they survived this degradation, without the possibility of attaining the elevation of the latter, they would gradually sink to the condition of the former—a point of degeneracy below which they could not fall; it is likely, before they reached this, their wretchedness would find relief in broken hearts." Only removal would "afford no pretext for the intrusions or annoyances of the white man."[26] An argument first formulated to save tribal society from internal breakdown became, from the pen of the Georgia governor, a means of asserting state sovereignty and of condoning frontier aggression.

The immediate problem arose in 1827 when the Cherokees adopted a constitution similar to the federal document and Georgia responded by extending state laws over the Indian country. The Cherokee action forced the state's hand, though in light of Georgia's views on the presence of Indians within her borders, it was probably a welcome provocation.[27] The main question centered on tribal sovereignty. Indians had always been dealt with in at least the forms of independence. As they became more civilized, they understood more clearly the importance of such forms and insisted upon them more tenaciously. The fiction of native sovereignty had a way of becoming more real as the native became less Indian, but the

---

25. Calhoun to James Monroe, Mar. 29, 1824, *American State Papers, Indian Affairs*, II, 462.

26. Troup to Calhoun, Feb. 28, 1824, *ibid.*, 475–476.

27. John H. Eaton to Cherokee Delegation, Apr. 18, 1829, Letters Sent, Off. Indian Affairs (M-21), Roll 5: 410. See also McKenney to Eli Baldwin, Oct. 28, 1829, *ibid.*, Roll 6: 140; John Forsyth, *Register of Debates in Congress*, 21st Cong., 1st Sess., pp. 332–333 (Apr. 15, 1830).

idea meant little until the Cherokees put it into official phrases that the Georgians interpreted as an unmistakable challenge to their own exaggerated political pretensions.[28]

The Cherokees may have been imprudent in announcing their independence, but in reality their action grew directly out of the partial success of the philanthropic program. Progress toward the goal of replacing the tribal organization with the white man's system of individualism and admission into the state political structure strengthened the tribesman's sense of Indianness. His parochial loyalties were transformed into an allegiance to a new quasi-political, racial organization with the primary function of defense against the white man. With tension increasing between federal and state power over other issues, the southern states reacted sharply to this action by the federal government's native clients. In 1820 Calhoun had established the principle that the Indians could not remain as an independent people within the confines of the white man's society. A sovereign entity of the sort the Cherokees had in mind, surrounded by another equally independent power, would be "incompatible with our system." Secretary of War John Eaton repeated Calhoun's warning. The Indians had always relied on the power of the federal government for aid and patronage, but now they had stepped beyond their usual dependent status and created a new area of conflict between the federal government and the states. Eaton told the Cherokees that they had overreached their mark and could not expect the federal authorities to back them if it would lead to open conflict with the states.[29]

Cass went further than anyone else in stripping the argument of humanitarian sentiment. He could see no point in maintaining even the fiction of Indian independence. "There is no mercy in suffering these Indians to believe, that their pretensions can be established and their independent government supported." He found such delicacy intolerable. "We have long passed," he con-

---

28. Malone, *Cherokees of the Old South,* 84.

29. McKenney to Barbour, Nov. 29, 1827, Letters Sent, Off. Indian Affairs (M-21), Roll 4: 156; Calhoun to Henry Clay, Jan. 15, 1820, *American State Papers, Indian Affairs,* II, 201; Calhoun to Cherokee Delegation, *ibid.,* 473; Eaton to Cherokee Delegation, Apr. 18, 1829, Letters Sent, Off. Indian Affairs (M-21), Roll 5: 410. In the debate over removal, Sen. Asher Robbins of Rhode Island noted the irony of the argument against the Cherokee constitution. It was impossible to accuse the Indians of savagery and degradation and at the same time to condemn them for establishing an independent state. "Ill fated Indians! barbarism and attempts at civilization are alike fatal to your rights; but attempts at civilization are more fatal of the two." *Register of Debates in Congress,* 21st Cong., 1st Sess., pp. 376–377.

tinued, "the period of abstract rights." Even though the government claimed a "perfect" jurisdiction over the tribes, it should always be guided by circumstances. And circumstances, above all, now dictated that the Indians must be subordinate and that they certainly must not be permitted to erect a sovereign power in opposition to the white man's authority. "A just regard for the safety of both requires that we should govern and they obey."[30]

In contrast, the opposition to removal, originating largely from the American Board of Commissioners for Foreign Missions, upheld the legitimacy of Indian sovereignty. As Cass judged the relative rights of Indian and white by concrete circumstances, Jeremiah Evarts, the secretary of the American Board, and Theodore Frelinghuysen insisted on a full implementation of natural rights. Since the Indians existed as a people and had occupied the continent before the white men left Europe, the settlement of America in no way affected the original sovereignty of the tribes. Carrying the argument further, they contended that civilized man had an obligation to protect the Indian tribes in their sovereignty. The differences between the two societies that so much concerned Cass and McKenney in no way mitigated the imperatives of natural justice.[31]

In practice, Cass's opinion seemed much less humanitarian than the position held by Evarts and the American Board, although both sides acknowledged the basic proposition that the Indian should accept civilization as a gift. Cass merely supplied an alternative, should the process not work out as expected. With ruthless objectivity, he saw the impasse in Indian-white relations and sought to break it with removal. He would have required the tribesmen to accept their subordinate condition, pack their belongings, and move west, all in the name of preserving the Indians. Evarts saw in this hypocrisy and evil intentions; Cass meant it as the only hope for continuing the program of civilizing the tribes. The justification

30. Cass, "Removal of the Indians," *No. Am. Rev.*, XXX (1830), 83, 88, 93–94, 112. There was also something a little insensitive about Cass's realism: "What has a Cherokee to fear from the operation of the laws of Georgia? If he has advanced in knowledge and improvement, as many sanguine persons believe and represent, he will find these laws more just, better administered, and far more equal in their operation, than the *regulations* which the chiefs have established and are enforcing. What Indian has ever been injured by the laws of any state?" *Ibid.*, 102.

31. [Jeremiah Evarts], *Essays on the Present Crisis in the Condition of the American Indians* . . . (Boston, 1829), 8, 10, 14–15, 21, 85. The arguments in Congress against removal were similarly abstract: see particularly Theodore Frelinghuysen in the Senate, Apr. 7, 1830, *Speeches on the Passage of the Bill for the Removal of the Indians*, 5–6.

of removal rested on the observations of McKenney and Cass himself that the program had not changed the Indians. On this point, neither side was so much wrong as irrelevant. Many Indians had altered their way of life, and many had not. But even those who had did not thereby make their way into American society. Evarts by implication came to the point of upholding the native right to live a life separate from the white man's world. He did not abandon the desire to civilize the Indian and to end that process with incorporation, but in rejecting removal he defended the rights of the southern tribal organizations to an independent and sovereign existence. Cass held to the original philanthropic intention: the Indians should become civilized and should forsake the tribal order as a preliminary step to incorporation. And he went further in asserting that this process could not be completed in the East because neither the missionaries nor the federal government possessed the power to protect the tribes against the frontiersmen and the state authorities.

The absolutism of the position taken by Evarts conformed to the missionaries' highly moralistic attitude toward the Indians. The heavy responsibility of Christianizing and civilizing the aborigine made it difficult for the missionary mind to tolerate both the indecisiveness of cultural change and the moral ambiguity necessarily associated with any public policy affecting the conflict of culture. Evarts skirted such ambiguity by basing his criticism of removal on the white man's moral obligations. The native's natural right to his land, the oft-repeated treaty guarantees given by the government, and the white man's proclivity for demanding more land than he needed, Evarts judged by the strictest moral standard. And of course, the missionary mentality was acutely sensitive to the obloquy that would cling to white America's reputation should the Indian finally disappear. But Evarts and the philanthropic opposition to removal did more than uphold a high moral standard. They utterly denied the importance of circumstances—the distribution of power among the federal government, the states, the Indians, and themselves. Reasoning from a set of abstract suppositions about Indian rights and their own moral obligations, they insisted on a policy that left the Indians exposed to overwhelming forces. They counted the weakness of the tribes not as evidence to support a change in policy but as a measure of the white man's guilt in destroying a helpless people.[32]

32. [Evarts], *Essays on the Present Crisis*, 4, 5, 16, 73, 90–91.

5

In the period after the War of 1812, the American Board missionaries voiced disapproval of removal, though not as strongly as they
would in the 1820s and 1830s. Cyrus Kingsbury wrote from the
Cherokee mission in 1816 that he should "blush" for his country if
the government removed Indians, even though it might be for their
own good. Samuel Worcester, the board secretary, informed the
men in the field that all precautions should be taken to keep out
of the dispute. No sign should be given that the board disagreed
with government policy. The missionaries themselves reported that
they thought removal would retard progress toward civilization,
but they agreed to remain aloof and not become partisans in the
growing controversy. Since the government did not yet press the
policy seriously, the missionaries found it easy to avoid the issue.[33]

Even in the crisis before removal, Evarts did not immediately
express his positive and moralistic opposition. McKenney believed
for a time, indeed, that he would find support for removal in
the missionary party. Those who had been instrumental in carrying into effect the government's program could be expected to support removal if, as McKenney believed, it afforded the only possibility for preserving the Indians and continuing the civilizing
process. In particular, McKenney wrote to Evarts in 1827 hoping to
draw him into the propaganda movement he had organized as the
New York Board.[34] Except for the important defection of Evarts
and the American Board, a strong contingent of missionaries did,
in fact, support removal. Isaac McCoy, the Baptist missionary in
the Northwest, became one of the earliest and most persistent advocates of removal and also of an independent Indian state. Other
Baptists and especially the Methodists supported the policy. Evarts
himself wrote in the summer of 1827 that he did not think removal
would succeed but he thought it should be "fairly tried." In the
next year he noted that he feared for the result, but he also conceded that "many real friends of the Indians" supported removal.
In part this early ambivalence stemmed from calculation. Above

33. Kingsbury to Worcester, Nov. 28, 1816, ABC 18.3.1.III: 6; Worcester to
Kingsbury, Jan. 30, 1818, ABC 1.01.III: 13; Worcester to Calhoun, Feb. 6, 1818,
ABC 1.01.III: 22; Worcester to John M. Peck, Nov. 19, 1818, ABC 1.01.III:
103–104; Ard Hoyt *et al.* to Worcester, July 15, 1818, ABC 18.3.1: 112. Later
the missionaries did not find it so easy to avoid controversy, and the government came to see them as a menace to government policy. See Report of Secretary of War Peter B. Porter, Nov. 24, 1828, Sen. Doc. 1, 20th Cong., 2d Sess.,
ser. 181, p. 22.

34. McKenney to Evarts, Mar. 23, 1827, ABC 18.3.3.I: 14; McKenney to
James Barbour, Dec. 1, 1827, Letters Sent, Off. Indian Affairs (M-21), Roll
4: 160.

all, the missionaries wanted to continue their efforts among the Indians, even if need be in the West. Their opposition congealed only after the government seemed determined to push removal as a final solution, no matter what the consequences.[35]

For all McKenney's practicality, his belief in the righteousness of his policy led him to adopt a moral absolutism similar to that used by Evarts and the missionaries. If the Indians did not remove and the consequences turned out as McKenney predicted, then the blame must rest with those who believed that the tribes could be protected and civilized in the East. "Their doom will be sealed— pardon me—but it is true—by those—not designedly I know—who claim to be their friends!" The intensity of the commitment on both sides of the removal controversy reflected the basic moral content of philanthropy. By advocating removal, McKenney may well have profoundly changed the immediate prospects of the civilizing plan but he believed himself impelled by the same humanitarian spirit from which the original design of incorporation had been formed.[36]

In his immediate justification of removal, McKenney carefully related it to the civilizing plan by citing the need to carry on the program. Writing from the Cherokee country in 1816, Kingsbury demonstrated that he too understood the connection. He believed that removal would "give them longer time to become civilized, before their toes are trod upon, as they say, by the Whites." Some of the Indians who planned to remove announced their intentions to transport to the West the civilized skills they had been taught in their native land. McKenney saw the interrelation in the difficulties encountered by Choctaw youths who returned from the academy in Kentucky to find no employment for their newly acquired skills among the less civilized tribesmen. He recommended that they be granted land in the West, where they could hope to retain the civilized ways learned in schools. Allowing for some special pleading, a

35. Berkhofer, *Salvation and the Savage*, 101–106; McKenney to Peter B. Porter, Oct. 6, 1828, Letters Sent, Off. Indian Affairs (M-21), Roll 5: 148; Evarts to W. F. Vail[l], Aug. 17, 1827, ABC 1.01.VII: 381; Evarts to W. N. Hudson, July 17, 1828, ABC 1.01.VIII: 423; Kingsbury to Evarts, May 6, 1830, ABC 18.3.4.III: 45; D. S. Butrick to Evarts, Mar. 26, 1829, ABC 18.3.1.IV: 34; Isaac McCoy to Lewis Cass, June 23, 1823, Isaac McCoy Papers (microfilm), Kans. State Hist. Soc., Topeka; McCoy to Luther Rice, July 10, 1823, *ibid.*; McCoy, "Thoughts respecting the Indian Territory," MS, Aug. 6, 1828, *ibid.*; McKenney to Peter B. Porter, Oct. 6, 1828, Letters Sent, Off. Indian Affairs (M-21), Roll 5: 148; Evarts to W. F. Vail[l], Aug. 17, 1827, ABC 1.01.VII: 381; Evarts to W. N. Hudson, July 17, 1828, ABC 1.01.VIII: 423; Kingsbury to Evarts, May 6, 1830, ABC 18.3.4.III: 45.

36. McKenney to Kingsbury, Mar. 8, 1830, Letters Sent, Off. Indian Affairs (M-21), Roll 6: 315; McKenney to Col. Stone, June 11, 1830, *ibid.*, 478–479.

plausible relation could be drawn between civilization and removal.[37]

The major practical argument against removal struck at precisely
the contention that it would complement or allow for the continuation of the civilizing program. In many of the missionary reports
that described the improvements in native life, the West stood for
the wilderness, the antithesis of civilization where these gains would
be abandoned and the tribes would return to savagery.[38] More pertinently, the opposition maintained that the constant agitation over
removal, on and off for more than two decades, worked subtly
against the native's progress. As a Wyandot chief said in 1812, he
did not see the point in helping the Indians and expecting progress
toward civilization if the whites intended to turn the tribes off
their lands within fifty years. In the crisis of the 1820s, Lee Compere, a supporter of removal, spoke eloquently against the dilatori-
ness of the government's policy. He contrasted the recent decline of
the Creeks to the many advances they had made in the past. Now
they were victimized by the confusion of the time. Even with a deep
attachment for their lands, they felt so insecure that they would
make no permanent improvements.[39] Merely the threat of removal
induced a loss of will among the tribesmen.

To compound the Indians' fears, the Georgians made it clear that
they considered any effort to improve the land a threat to state
sovereignty. They looked forward to removal, and they realized
that, as the Indians acted more like whites, as they housed themselves and dressed like whites, and as they took their livelihood
from the earth, it would be more difficult to be rid of them. Not

37. Kingsbury to Worcester, Oct. 15, 1816, ABC 18.3.1.III: 1; John Jolly to
Calhoun, Jan. 28, 1818, Letters Received, Sec. War (M-271), Roll 2: 618-620;
Lucius Bolles to Peter B. Porter, Nov. 4, 1828, Letters Received, Off. Indian
Affairs (M-234), Schools, Roll 773: 924; McKenney to Porter, Nov. 28, 1828,
Letters Sent, Off. Indian Affairs (M-21), Roll 5: 209-211; *Missionary Herald*,
XXVI (1830), 253.

38. Thomas Wistar to William Eustis, Dec. 19, 1811, Letters Received, Sec.
War (M-271), Roll 1: 778-779; Cephas Washburn to Barbour, Oct. 1, 1825,
Letters Received, Off. Indian Affairs (M-234), Schools, Roll 772: 748; *Niles'
Weekly Register*, XXXII (1827), 227-228; Kingsbury to Evarts, May 28, 1830,
ABC 18.3.4.III: 46. Sen. John Forsyth of Georgia admitted as much in his reply
to Theodore Frelinghuysen in the removal debate: *Register of Debates in Con-
gress*, 21st Cong., 1st Sess., pp. 327-328.

39. Wyandots to President and Congress, Feb. 5, 1812, *American State Papers,
Indian Affairs*, I, 795; Compere to Barbour, Sept. 2, 1825, Letters Received, Off.
Indian Affairs (M-234), Schools, Roll 772: 456; Compere to Barbour, Sept. 10,
1827, *ibid.*, Roll 773: 948-950; McKenney, *Sketches of a Tour to the Lakes*,
70-71; Isaac McCoy, *History of Baptist Indian Missions: embracing Remarks
on the Former and Present Condition of the Aboriginal Tribes* . . . (Washington, D.C., 1840), 196-197.

only would the tribesmen be less likely to go voluntarily—the erection of an Indian state made this clear—but it would be more difficult to justify moving them. Ultimately, removal rested on the assumption that the Indian remained a savage. Georgians claimed that the new Cherokee political order had been created by half-blood leaders who exploited the more primitive majority of the tribes. Thus Governor Troup, knowing the relationship between the Indians' progress toward civilization and removal, insisted in 1824 that the Cherokee either cease all improvement or leave immediately.[40]

In many ways, the philanthropic argument corresponded to the position taken by the southern state governments. McKenney derived his evidence for the failure of the civilizing effort from his visits to the Indian country, but he had also heard the same position expressed by the Georgians. He agreed with them on the illegitimacy of the Indian state and on the role of half bloods in stirring up trouble among the tribes. This mixed-blood leadership became a special hate for him and a convenient excuse for the wreck of his policy. But McKenney and most other humanitarian observers—both those who favored and those who opposed removal —saved their deepest spleen for the frontiersmen, in whose interests the state authorities were deeply implicated. Intruders on Indian lands, in their ungovernable haste to push the frontier west, created the crisis of Indian-white relations and became the real villains of the piece.[41]

6

The activities of frontiersmen and settlers brought up once again the question of the white savage and the violence so closely associated with life in the wilderness and so inimical to the progress of civilization. Although the movement of the frontier and the civi-

40. Kingsbury to Worcester, Dec. 11, 1817, ABC 18.3.1.III: 101; George M. Troup to Calhoun, Apr. 24, 1824, *American State Papers, Indian Affairs*, II, 736; Troup to John Forsyth, Apr. 6, 1825, *ibid.*, 776. See also Adams, ed., *Memoirs of John Quincy Adams*, VI, 272; Thomas C. Stuart to Barbour, Sept. 11, 1826, Letters Received, Off. Indian Affairs, (M-234), Schools, Roll 773: 471-472; McKenney to Barbour, Dec. 27, 1826, Letters Sent, Off. Indian Affairs (M-21), Roll 3: 273-285.

41. McKenney to David Folsom and Greenwood Leflore, Dec. 13, 1827, Letters Sent, Off. Indian Affairs (M-21), Roll 4: 178; McKenney to Barbour, Mar. 24, 1828, *ibid.*, 354-363; McKenney to Eaton, Oct. 16, 1829, *ibid.*, Roll 6: 122; McKenney to Eli Baldwin, Oct. 23, 1829, *ibid.*, 133; Adams, ed., *Memoirs of John Quincy Adams*, VII, 370-371. See also William Clark *et al.* to Barbour, Nov. 19, 1826, *American State Papers, Indian Affairs*, II, 709; Clark to Barbour, Nov. 16, 1826, *ibid.*, 717; Clark to Barbour, Nov. 2, 1826, *ibid.*, 718; Prucha, *American Indian Policy*, chap. 7.

lizing or displacement of the Indian remained the ultimate object of philanthropy, the actual process often seemed disappointing. The worst representatives of the white man's society went into the wilderness first, fought with the natives, learned to hate them, and gave the impression of utter incompatibility between the white man's world and the Indian's world. Sporadically, the government tried to keep the two sides apart, often punished offenders among the whites, and encouraged the tribes to keep their own people in check, all to no avail. The philanthropists faced the ironic prospect of seeing their program disrupted by the spread of settlement, a movement that derived its energy from the same progressive initiative that impelled the civilizing plan.

For all the confidence that accompanied the white man's conquest of the continent, doubts had long existed about those who led it. It often seemed that a relaxation of social discipline must first take place before the area of civilization could be enlarged. "These Wretches set shame at naught," wrote the governor of West Florida in 1765 of the colonists then being sent to him, "and let loose the Bonds of a whole Society." Sir William Johnson spent much of his energy on the northern frontier attempting to establish settled relations between the whites and the Indians. He believed that the "lower order of people" was determined to upset his plans by stealing the Indians' lands and goods and by generally spreading havoc that interfered with the tranquility necessary for trade. He learned from William Franklin that "some of the worst People in every Colony reside on the Frontiers" and would have much preferred that the Indians keep their distance from them. Benjamin Franklin agreed with Johnson's evaluation of the frontiersmen, having learned of the white man's wrath against the Indians at first hand from the activities of the Paxton Boys. Most often the white man blamed frontier violence on the Indian, but still the frontiersmen shared the guilt. Return J. Meigs defined their real offense: "Those people," he wrote in 1815, "fly from regular society to live without restraint and avoid all the duties of good citizens which they owe to the community—and if suffered to increase may in time become dangerous malecontents."[42]

42. George Johnstone to John Pownall, Feb. 19, 1765, West Florida Transcripts, Governor's Correspondence, Alabama Department of Archives and History, Montgomery; William Franklin to Sir William Johnson, Apr. 15, 1766, James Sullivan, Alexander C. Flick, and Albert B. Corey, eds., *The Papers of Sir William Johnson* (Albany, 1921–1962), XII, 72–73; Johnson to Joseph Galloway, *ibid.*, XII, 422; Franklin to Johnson, Sept. 12, 1766, Smyth, ed., *Writings of Franklin*, IV, 462; Franklin to Samuel Elbert, Dec. 16, 1787, *ibid.*, IX, 626; Return J. Meigs to Louis Winston, Jan. 12, 1815, Carter, ed., *Territorial Papers*, VI, 492.

As a consequence of his failure to heed the necessary restraints of society and his tendency to fall into conflict with his red neighbors, the frontiersman often became an Indian hater. The constant danger of the frontier, according to Andrew Ellicott, required "brave, enterprising, and warlike" men, but these characteristics, "when not checked by education, and a correct mode of the thinking, degenerates into ferocity." Said Timothy Pickering to the Iroquois with uncharacteristic understatement: "There are some white men who do not love you." The depth of this frontier passion shocked men who should have been no strangers to war and violence. William Henry Harrison noted with dismay that a great many frontier inhabitants "consider the murdering of Indians in the highest degree meritorious." But the fears went even deeper; frontiersmen threatened to destroy the natives. Hence many whites felt the sting of Alexander McGillivray's gibe when he referred to "those who think that Indians are only animals fit to be exterminated." Philanthropists knew the bitterness of the frontier, and they knew that hatred of some whites for the tribesmen could put an end to all hope of a union between the two societies.[43]

Philanthropic sympathies fluctuated from white to Indian, though it often required a greater exercise of objectivity to see the Indian's side. Timothy Barnard, for example, reported from intimate experience on the frontier that "what the savages doe must be deemed savage cruilty [*sic*] but the white people are in some cases a good deael in fault." More to the point, many found it easier to damn both sides, to stress the incompatibility of native and white society on the frontier. In his report to Congress in 1787, Henry Knox expressed the position that held true in the succeeding years of Indian-white relations. As he put it: "The deep rooted prejudices, and malignity of heart, and conduct reciprocally entertained and practiced on all occasions by the Whites and Savages

43. Andrew Ellicott, *The Journal of Andrew Ellicott* . . . (Philadelphia, 1803), 25; Speech of Pickering to Council of the Six Nations, July 4, 1791, Pickering Papers, XL, 80–80A; William Henry Harrison to Henry Dearborn, July 15, 1801, Esarey, ed., *Messages of Harrison*, I, 25; Winthrop Sargent to Judge Putnam, Oct. 6, 1794, Carter, ed., *Territorial Papers*, III, 425; Alexander Mc-Gillivray to Thomas Pinckney, Feb. 26, 1789, *American State Papers, Indian Affairs*, I, 20; "Brainerd Journal," June 24, 1818, *Missionary Herald*, XVII (1821), 7. Travelers often brought up the frontier attitude: Smyth, *Tour in the United States*, I, 345–346; Weld, *Travels through the States*, 362, 371. The gulf between the philanthropic spirit and Indian hating can be seen in Du Ponceau's accusation that Cass was "strongly imbued with the *border-spirit*," the evidence being that "he will not allow that there is any interest in the forms or construction of the Indian languages." Peter S. Du Ponceau to Albert Gallatin, Apr. 18, 1826, Gallatin Papers, Box 31, fol. 37. See also Pearce, *Savages of America*, 225–226.

will ever prevent their being good neighbours. The one side anxiously defend their lands which the other avariciously claim. With minds previously inflamed the slightest offence occasions death, revenge follows which knows no bounds. The flames of a merciless war are thus lighted up which involve the innocent and helpless with the guilty. Either one or the other party must remove to a greater distance, or Government must keep both in awe by a strong hand, and compel them to be moderate and just."[44] At this early point, Knox's prescription for governmental action to establish order on the frontier went much beyond what would later be thought feasible, but he had defined the basic division in frontier life. Perhaps more important, with no more than an inkling of the significance of his proposal, he had pointed to the possibility of removal.

By the time Jefferson became president, all the efforts made by the government to protect the tribes from intruders seemed doomed to failure. The frontier could not be controlled. Threats to use the courts or to send in troops, instructions to agents to clear the native lands, all came to nothing. Even granting the Indian the right to kill the settlers' cattle or drive the animals out of the tribal territory did not stop the avalanche of intruders. Tribal leaders petitioned the government, appealed to state authorities and to the intruders themselves, and attempted to curb the belligerence of their own younger tribesmen. Nothing helped; the white man kept coming.[45]

As a consequence, humanitarians and politicians became increasingly intimidated by the frontier. It represented a force whose object they ultimately approved but whose efforts at immediate realization they saw as a threat to their own designs. "Will the American Congress," John Sevier announced, "cramp and refuse to the Western Americans the great natural advantages Providence has designated for, and placed before them?" Surely not in any ultimate sense, but the westerners carried on their part in the movement of civilization without attention to good order and without the slightest bow to the need for saving the natives. William H.

44. Timothy Barnard to Edward Telfair, July 7, 1793, Barnard Papers, Ga. Dept. of Archives and History; Henry Knox, Report of the Secretary of War to Congress, July 10, 1787, Carter, ed., *Territorial Papers*, II, 31.

45. Henry Dearborn to Benjamin Hawkins, June 28, 1805, Letters Sent, Sec. War (M-15), Roll 2: 88; William Eustis to James Neileg, Nov. 17, 1809, *ibid.*, Roll 3: 9; Eustis to Return J. Meigs, May 4, 1810, *ibid.*, 23; A. J. Dallas to Graham, July 14, 1815, *ibid.*, 244; John C. Calhoun to Meigs, Jan. 31, 1820, *ibid.*, Roll 4: 359; Calhoun to Andrew Jackson, Oct. 14, 1820, *ibid.*, Roll 5: 22; Calhoun to Meigs, June 26, 1822, *ibid.*, 291–292.

Crawford tried to stem the disorderly spread of whites over every area obtained from the Indians by proposing in 1816 to refuse for the present further cessions from the tribes. He had no qualms about finally obtaining the Indian lands, but he did not see how the orderly occupation of the continent and the civilizing of the Indians would be advanced by giving over national policy to the initiative of the frontiersmen. The Indians themselves complained of the "constant and habitual" intrusions on their lands. They could not go into the woods to hunt without finding the white man's cattle roaming unattended and salt logs left for the animals by their owners. "It is impossible for the government," James Barbour told the Creeks in 1827, "for any long time to prevent, or for your people, with their present habits, and scattered as they are, to successfully resist" the spread of the whites. Years before, Washington had made clear the impotence of the government, no matter how well disposed, to bring the frontier under control. In 1796 he ordered that a line between the United States and the Cherokees should be drawn and clearly marked. "The Indians urge this; The Law requires it; and it ought to be done; but I believe scarcely any thing short of a Chinese Wall, or a line of Troops will restrain Land Jobbers, and the Incroachment of Settlers, upon the Indian Territory."[46]

This sense of inevitability in Indian-white relations had always been part of philanthropic thought. The very idea that the Indian must be civilized engendered a deep-seated feeling that failure would bring catastrophy. Hence all the forces that militated against the success of the civilizing program—the persistence of the Indian's culture, the breakdown of the tribal order, the resistence of the states—contributed to the doubt that the relationship between Indian and white would come out well. The frontiersman, moreover, because his activities meshed with the problem of savage violence,

46. John Sevier to Andrew Jackson *et al.*, Nov. 26, 1797, Williams, ed., "Journal of Sevier," *East Tenn. Hist. Soc., Pubs.,* No. 3 (1931), 161; William H. Crawford to William Clark *et al.*, May 7, 1816, *American State Papers, Indian Affairs,* II, 97; Tuskegee Tustunnuggie to Benjamin Hawkins, Dec. 21, 1808, Hawkins Papers, Ga. Dept. of Archives and Hist.; Chiefs of the Lower Towns (Creeks) to Hawkins, Mar. 14, 1809, *ibid.;* Hoboheilthlee Micco to the President, May 15, 1811, Letters Rec., Sec. War (M-271), Roll 1: 554–557; James Barbour to Little Prince, June 23, 1827, Letters Sent, Off. Indian Affairs (M-21), Roll 4: 80–81. The Cherokees appointed rangers to watch for the settlers' cattle. *Cherokee Phoenix* (New Echota, Ga.), May 14, 1828. George Washington to Timothy Pickering, July 1, 1796, John C. Fitzpatrick, ed., *The Writings of George Washington from the Original Manuscript Sources, 1745–1799* (Washington, D.C., 1931–1944), XXV, 112.

because he seemed so positively committed to thwarting the plan for civilization, and also because he represented another aspect of the development of civilized life on the continent, caused philanthropists a special twinge of anxiety.

7

As a means of saving the Indian from the frontier, removal could be no more than a negative reaction. It told the philanthropists nothing about the actual process of removal, nor did it contribute any substance to their understanding of the position tribal society had then reached in its progress toward civilization. Since the government and many of the missionaries intended removal to be an extension of the civilizing process, the removal of individuals in order to separate the Indian from tribal loyalties seemed expedient. In fact, however, the government transported the Indians to the West with their tribal organizations intact. Hence removal merely testified to the failure to dissolve the tribal ties and create autonomous, individual Indians ready for incorporation. The threat of the frontier impelled philanthropists to resort to removal, but so also did their perception that the Indian retained his tribal identity.

The government probably had no alternative to the removal of tribal entities, but it did not favor this procedure. Early in the development of the civilizing program, Dearborn had proposed the removal of the Cherokees as a nation. Calhoun encouraged a discontented faction of the same tribe to move west in order to preserve its tribal identity. Nevertheless, philanthropy had no real interest in preserving the tribes for their own sake. The government and the missionary organizations often made use of them, but ultimately they sought the end of the tribal system.[47]

A compromise, represented in its purity by McCoy's proposal of an Indian state, called for the consolidation of all the Indians in the West. Though it supposed the dissolution of the tribal organization, it conceded something of a pan-Indianism that reflected the intermediate state of native organization. Calhoun described it as "a system, by which the Government, without destroying their independence, would gradually unite the several tribes under a simple but enlightened system of government formed on the principles of

47. Dearborn to Return J. Meigs, Mar. 25, 1808, Letters Sent, Sec. War (M-15), Roll 2: 364; Calhoun to Joseph McMinn, July 29, 1818, *ibid.*, Roll 4: 192–193; Calhoun to John Ross *et al.*, Jan. 30, 1824, *ibid.*, Roll 6: 37; George Graham to Lewis Cass *et al.*, Oct. 17, 1817, *ibid.*, Roll 5: 85–86; Calhoun to Red Jacket, Mar. 14, 1823, *ibid.*, Roll 6: 405–406.

our own" and from which they would eventually make the transition to civilized society. But Evarts asked realistically: "What sort of community is to be formed here? Indians of different tribes, speaking different languages, in different states of civilization, are to be crowded together under one government."[48] He spelled out the most telling argument against removal by showing that any hoped-for arrangement of Indian life in the West, save some version of the traditional tribal organization, would be necessarily contrived. Certainly, one of the major consequences of Indian-white relations had been the creation of a vague consciousness of Indian identity as opposed to the parochial loyalty to the tribe or familial band. But as events demonstrated, only the tribal bond proved strong enough to sustain the native in his new home.

Jedidiah Morse's plan for organizing the natives into "Education Families" held greater promise of realization, not only because it had achieved some success in the East but also because it rested upon the traditional basis of Indian society. Though his scheme did not explicitly prescribe removal, he intended it to accomplish the same ends. At minimum it accepted the need to separate the Indian from the white man in order to eventually make him more like the white man. And it also had the merit of drawing on Morse's personal observation of the civilizing process. By salvaging tribal remnants that would probably not have lost much from removal, he might have contributed much to their future through a renovation of the traditional social arrangement.[49]

But since the long-run object of philanthropy remained the incorporation of detribalized Indians, the removal of individuals seemed more likely to produce the desired result. And removal tended naturally in that direction. Although the small groups that migrated to the West gathered into familial bands, the transferal divided the traditional tribal organization, caused friction within the leadership, and added to the stress already prevalent in the Indian world. James Barbour in his report of 1826, after abandoning hope that the Indians would be incorporated while still in the East, proposed that the very process of removal should be made to

48. McCoy, *Remarks on Indian Reform*, 30–32, 35–37; McCoy, *History of Baptist Indian Missions*, 40; Calhoun to Monroe, Jan. 24, 1825, *American State Papers, Indian Affairs*, II, 544; [Evarts], *Essays on the Present Crisis*, 96–100; Stephen Van Rensselaer to Congress, Mar. 3, 1824, *American State Papers, Indian Affairs*, II, 447.

49. Morse, *Report on Indian Affairs*, 78–79, 82–83, 311–312; Abel, "History of Events Resulting in Indian Consolidation West of the Mississippi," *Am. Hist. Assoc., Annual Report for 1906*, I, 298–304.

contribute to the rise of individualism among the natives. Thus removal became more than a response to the failure of the civilizing plan; it became part of the intricate process of transforming the Indian into a white man. The optimism of the philanthropists found a way of turning even failure to its own purpose.[50]

The government had long tried to promote detribalization by inducing individual Indians to accept 640-acre reservations in the East. By refusing the new owners the right of alienation, this plan protected the natives against exploitation at the same time that it established the principle of individual responsibility. The major obstacle, besides the internal contradiction and the usual over-confidence, was the refusal of the state authorities to permit individual land ownership by Indians. In the treaties with the Cherokees in 1817 and 1819, the government attempted seriously to implement the reservation policy while encouraging those who refused to accept a grant of land to remove, but it finally backed down in the face of state opposition. The government's determination to distribute individual reservations measured its confidence in the success of the civilizing program, but it also showed that not even the government possessed sufficient power to incorporate the Indians. How many might have accepted reservations and then lived as white farmers could not be determined. The whites refused to accept them, and the Indians themselves developed a new loyalty to the tribal state. The reservation system failed both as the consummation of the civilizing policy and as the complement of removal.[51]

50. Barbour to John Cocke, Feb. 3, 1826, *American State Papers, Indian Affairs*, II, 647–649; Return J. Meigs to William H. Crawford, Nov. 8, 1816, *ibid.*, 116; Calhoun to Cherokee Delegation, Feb. 11, 1819, Letters Sent, Sec. War (M-15), Roll 4: 247; McKenney to Cocke, Jan. 23, 1827, Letters Sent, Off. Indian Affairs (M-21), Roll 3: 328–329; P. G. Randolph to Hugh Montgomery, June 18, 1830, *ibid.*, Roll 6: 487.

51. Cherokee Treaty, July 8, 1817, *American State Papers, Indian Affairs*, II, 130; George Graham to Lewis Cass, Mar. 23, 1817, Letters Sent, Sec. War (M-15), Roll 4: 22; Graham to Andrew Jackson *et al.*, May 10, 1817, *ibid.*, Roll 4: 38; Graham to Cass, July 30, 1817, *ibid.*, 62; Graham to Meigs, Aug. 9, 1817, *ibid.*, 71–72; Calhoun to William Wirt, July 20, 1820, *ibid.*, 474; Calhoun to John Floyd *et al.*, June 15, 1822, *ibid.*, Roll 5: 282; Calhoun to Lewis McLane, Mar. 25, 1824, Letters Sent, Off. Indian Affairs (M-21), Roll 1: 7; Joseph McMinn to Calhoun, Nov. 29, 1818, Letters Received, Sec. War (M-271), Roll 2: 1300; Calhoun to Jackson, Aug. 21, 1820, Letters Sent, Sec. War (M-15), Roll 5: 9; Calhoun to William Ward, Mar. 27, 1821, *ibid.*, 72; "Report of a Select Committee of the House of Representatives," Jan. 7, 1822, *American State Papers, Indian Affairs*, II, 259–260; McKenney to James Barbour, Nov. 29, 1827, Letters Sent, Off. Indian Affairs (M-21), Roll 4: 155; Eaton to John Crowell, Mar. 27, 1829, *ibid.*, Roll 5: 372–373. For the failure of the reservation system after formal removal, see Young, *Redskins, Ruffleshirts, and Rednecks*.

In yet another way, removal seemed unlikely to aid in civilizing the tribesmen. Morse believed that it would make those Indians who had adopted civilized ways regress and that it would fix in their primitive condition those who had made little progress. The Indians themselves saw the point clearly. "We are not yet civilized enough to become citizens of the United States," said the Cherokees, "nor do we wish to be compelled to remove to a country so much against our inclination and will, where we would, in the course of a few years, return to the same savage state of life that we were in before the United States, our white brothers, extended their fostering care towards us, and brought us out of a savage state into a state similar to theirs." The argument repeated the white man's notion that the wilderness equaled savagery. An abundance of uncultivated land, from which a livelihood could be taken without labor, would necessarily lead to indolence. Ironically, the Indian, in being saved from destruction in the East, would be exposed to a more dangerous environment in the West. Besides contending with vast stretches of untouched land, the savage Indians already on the land would have to be pacified, a task that would retard the rise of civilization.[52]

Yet removal weathered all these criticisms because it was a panacea. Its success depended on future contingencies: the Indian must be allowed a period free from the pressure of the frontier, and the civilizing program must move west with the tribes. Should these expectations be fulfilled, the inconvenience of removal and the crisis of Indian-white relations would have been only incidental to the long-run accomplishment. McKenney, for example, genuinely believed that removal would offer the Indian safety. For all his lack of illusions, Cass asserted that the previous failure to raise a permanent barrier to protect the natives did not mean that they would not have security for the future. By the time the whites

52. Morse, *Report on Indian Affairs*, 83; Cyrus Kingsbury, "Annual Report of the Choctaw Schools," Oct. 1829, ABC 18.3.4.III: 41; William Coody to Jeremiah Evarts, Mar. 19, 1830, ABC 18.3.1.IV: 368; Cherokees to Indian Commissioners, July 2, 1817, *American State Papers, Indian Affairs*, II, 143; Path Killer to Crawford, 1817, Letters Received, Sec. War (M-271), Roll 2: 10–11; "Report of the Prudential Committee," *Panoplist*, XV (1819), 551–552; Lewis Cass to William Clark, Mar. 2, 1821, Letters Received, Sec. War (M-271), Roll 3: 903; John Ross *et al.* to Senate, Apr. 16, 1824, *American State Papers, Indian Affairs*, II, 502. See also Cass to Calhoun, Sept. 30, 1819, Carter, ed., *Territorial Papers*, X, 865; Stockbridge Indians to Society for Propagating the Gospel among Indians, Sept. 6, 1827, ABC 13.I: 40; William Wirt to James Kent, Oct. 8, 1830, James Kent Papers, VI, Lib. of Congress (photocopy, Papers of John Marshall, Institute of Early American History and Culture, Williamsburg, Va.).

reached the White and Arkansas rivers, the Indians would have "acquired new habits, which would cause our intercourse to be without danger to them and without pain to us, or they would have either crossed the Rocky Mountains or disappeared." This new success would be achieved by the same means already tried in the East. "Nor should these people be left to roam at large, after arriving in the Country West of the Mississippi," wrote McKenney. "There they should have houses and fields, and workshops; Schools and teachers; a Government, and laws formed expressly for their use—and the future should never be permitted to become to them the source of that calamity which has characterized the past." Philanthropists learned nothing from their failures; optimism remained strong, more so now that the crisis had been left behind.[53]

8

This persistence of the humanitarian expectation that Indian-white relations would end happily with the eventual coalescing of the two societies raised serious questions about the sincerity of the philanthropic advocates of removal. A policy so demonstrably painful to the Indians and one supported also by men with no interest in the native's welfare could not be easily reconciled with benevolence. Furthermore, a substantial part of the philanthropic interest opposed the policy and predicted the most dire consequences from it. How then could such palpable wrongheadedness masquerade under the guise of goodwill? In part the answer was clear enough: removal made the best of a bad situation. Its supporters presented a good case for it on the ground that the alternatives would be worse. If the Indian did not remove, he would endure any one of a number of disastrous consequences. If he refused to accept the blessings of civilization, he would find nothing to replace his old mode of life and would disintegrate personally. Or, even if he did accept the forms of civilized life, he faced the prospect of being despoiled by the frontiersmen or by the new state governments that had no enthusiasm for the incorporation of reformed savages within their jurisdiction. Yet the argument in its favor did not conceive of removal as a plausible solution to a virtually impossible problem. For the most part, the optimism that clung to the civilizing program

53. Cass, "Removal of the Indians," *No. Am. Rev.*, XXX (1830), 109; McKenney to Peter B. Porter, Dec. 1, 1828, Letters Sent, Off. Indian Affairs (M-21), Roll 5: 214–215; McKenney to H. L. White, Feb. 26, 1830, *ibid.*, Roll 6: 293.

also made removal a desirable stage in the Indian's emergence from savagery.

Perhaps philanthropists deluded themselves by using removal unconsciously or covertly to mask the futility of their progressive principles. Even so, removal had the virtue of postponing the final verdict on the impracticality of the civilizing program and of eliminating the Indian from competition for the continent without the bloody necessity of openly destroying him. Still, such men as McKenney, Cass, and Calhoun did not adopt the policy lightly. For the better part of a decade, both sides offered extensive criticisms and justifications of removal. Out of this discussion emerged a realistic appraisal of the Indians' position in the East and of some of the likely consequences of removal. Those who argued for removal recognized that it would work hardships on the natives, but they promoted it only as a last resort, and in the 1820s, at least, they refused to impose it by force.[54] Surely the breadth and intensity of the discussion belies the charge of hypocrisy.

Nevertheless, it remained true that humanitarian policy coincided with the intentions of the frontier, which wanted only to be rid of the Indians. Ironically, philanthropists resorted to removal because they understood the evil designs of the frontier, but in doing so they became tainted precisely with those nefarious purposes they wished to avoid. The undisciplined movement of the frontier and the self-serving as well as selfless desire of the philanthropists to impose their manner of life on the Indian represented alike an expanding and overbearing civilization. If the philanthropists drew on a different source for their agreement with the state authorities, they pursued the same policy. All wanted the obliteration of savagery, and removal served that purpose.

54. See Monroe's message proposing removal, Sen. Doc. 63, 18th Cong., 1st Sess., Apr. 2, 1824, ser. 91, pp. 3–4.

Conclusion

       The Indian survived. Incorporation presupposed a total change in his way of life, but the tribesman never took more than a small step at a time in the direction of civilization. Even though the aggregate of those steps constituted a serious impairment of the character of tribal life, the tribes still remained, invigorated by the very process that was to spell their destruction. Because the tribesmen never quite lost their perception of themselves as Indians, the humanitarian plan could never be said to have achieved its purpose. Even when most of the outward signs signaled an end to tribal culture and the beginnings of civilized life, the Indians did not seem quite ready to make the transition into unity with the white man's society. Incorporation could take place only when the last vestiges of Indian ways had been erased, a change that would occur only if the tribal society died the physical death that beset individual Indians. Native society could be transformed, but it could not become extinct.

    Indian life endured not only because the government and the missionaries failed to accomplish their purpose but because they did all that they could to protect the tribesmen from the assault of the frontier. Left to their own devices, the settlers with their overwhelming power might have succeeded in breaking up the tribal order and scattering the native people before them. The fate of the northeastern tribes, each in its turn worn down by war and contacts with the whites, supplied unmistakable evidence of what lay in store for the southern Indians. Governmental policy in the Jeffersonian period called for the protection of the remaining tribes as a prerequisite for their reception of civilization. And this meant protection from the destructive influences of the frontier. Philanthropic goodwill could be effective in civilizing the Indians only if it succeeded in preserving them from the impact of the frontier.

Yet this tendency of government and missionary to side with the tribes against the western populace was more illusion than reality. Humanitarian distaste for frontier behavior stemmed, not from any desire to preserve the wilderness, but from an opinion that such behavior was more imitative of savage existence than of the restraint and decorum taught by civilization. Tribal life could derive no comfort from philanthropic solicitude. The civilizing plan was as well designed for the elimination of tribalism as the advance of the frontier was inimical to the life of the Indian. Ultimately, hating Indians could not be differentiated from hating Indianness. If the frontiersman adopted the direct method of murdering Indians, humanitarians were only more circumspect in demanding cultural suicide of the tribes.

This basic unity of civilization in its relation to the native peoples was only dimly perceived in the Jeffersonian period. Most humanitarians saw their own activities as a way of preserving the Indians and as something distinct in its effects from the results of conflict on the frontier. One critic, in reviewing Jedidiah Morse's *Report to the Secretary of War of the United States, on Indian Affairs* in the *North American Review,* went beyond this comforting interpretation. Referring to the desire to save the remaining eastern Indians, he asserted:

We lament that they have vanished: we would take measures to preserve the present stock. But what is it we would preserve? Their language? that first great bond and symbol of national identity, curious as many of their languages are in their structure, and perhaps the only historical monument of their ancient emigrations, affinities, and fortunes? Would we preserve these? O no. It is recommended at once, to hasten these into oblivion. Dr. Morse, in his appendix, expressly says, "as fast as possible, let Indians forget their own languages, in which nothing is written, and nothing of course can be preserved, and learn ours, which will at once open to them the whole field of useful knowledge." Is it their mode of life, tenure of property in common, their manners, that which makes them in all externals to be what they are: is it these, which we deplore as lost, and would fix and perpetuate where they still exist? No. The whole drift of Dr. Morse's speculations on the subject is to gather the Indians all into convenient settlements, wean them from the chase, teach them individually to hold a farm in fee, and plough and dig it. Is it their national faith, the religion of their fathers, their traditions, that we would cherish and perpetuate among them? Far from it. Their religious conceptions are notoriously of the grossest and most degrading kind, their traditions mere bloody recollections of prisoners scalped and tomahawked. Is there any thing left then that we wish in fact to preserve? Nothing in the last analysis, but the copper color; and why a civilized, christianized person, speaking our language, subsisting by regular labor, is any better for being copper colored, we cannot see. But some will not leave even this. Dr. Morse quotes a respectable Frenchman, who strongly recommends intermarriages, and is evidently not unfriendly himself to the suggestion; and the advantages are that it will ameliorate the manners of the natives, and *the offspring be nearly white*. All this may be very well, but what becomes in the meantime of the Indians. The very efficacy of this course is to hasten their disappearance.[1]

The ironies were rich. Ultimately, the white man's sympathy was more deadly than his animosity. Philanthropy had in mind the disappearance of an entire race.

Although philanthropists condemned the unbridled behavior of the western settlers, they continued to instill in the native population values similar to those celebrated on the frontier. The sources of order that the native derived from the tribe would be replaced by evangelical religion and secular individualism. Separation of the Indian's person from tribal discipline was the essential step in the civilizing process. In order to tame what he interpreted as the savage impulse, the missionary set the native free of his customary way of life. The Indian did not thence behave differently, not only because he never completely severed his ties with the old order but also because the missionary taught positive virtues of self-control. Yet the fact remained that the philanthropists could not quite disown the success of the frontier even if they found it frequently an obstacle to their own plans.

For similar reasons, the white man's governmental authorities could never muster the will to impose order in the West. Without military force or a bureaucratic structure capable of enforcing humanitarian policies, they could not protect the Indian. Reluctantly, the federal government and an important segment of the humanitarian interest were forced to agree that the frontier white man's time had come. For all of his defects, the settler represented civilization, and the Indian must either join him or retire to the West.

Neither environmentalism nor noble savagism supplied the Jeffersonian era with the means for explaining the actual consequences of Indian-white relations. Why, for example, after the combined impact of the frontier and the philanthropic program, did the Indians change their ways only partially? Why did many natives, instead of thriving on the riches provided by civilized men, fall into

1. *No. Am. Rev.*, XVI (1823), 39-40.

decline? Why did many Indians reject the white man's good offices and elect to defend the tribal order? And why, finally, despite the considerable success of the civilizing effort, did incorporation fail to take place? None of these questions could be answered satisfactorily within the definitions of Jeffersonian thought. All of them testified to the limitations that the persistence of culture imposed on any attempt at social transformation. Environmentalism described the process of change mechanically, with explicit rules of procedure and clearly defined stages of growth. And it left no doubt about the outcome: the Indian would eventually become like the white man. The paradisaic formula invested the outcome with cosmic necessity. Both of these conceptions derived from a priori and unhistorical definitions of human existence; neither accounted for the devastating and paradoxical effects of the white man's society on tribal culture.

In so far as the Jeffersonian observer recognized many of the actual consequences of Indian-white relations, he was justified in attributing them to such impersonal forces as war, disease, and the mysterious chemistry of liquor among the native peoples. All of this heightened the original sympathy that characterized the humanitarian plan. It became as important to save the Indian from vice as it had been to save him from his savage self. Indeed, it was much easier to pity the passive and suffering native than it had ever been to sympathize with the savage warrior or the stubborn pupil. Despite the growing evidence that the civilizing program would not fulfill its promise, philanthropists could propose only more of the same, albeit in a different location. Philanthropy remained true to its principles and even more sympathetic to the plight of the native tribes. "It is impossible," wrote Tocqueville, "to destroy men with more respect to the laws of humanity."[2]

2. Alexis de Tocqueville, *Democracy in America*, eds. J. P. Mayer and Max Lerner (New York, 1966), 312.

Note on Sources

In describing the relationship between ideas and policy, this study relies mainly on publicly articulated conceptions of the Indian in the Jeffersonian era. Hence it makes use of the extensive published literature in books and articles dealing with the Indian and his relationship with civilization. Natural history, travel accounts, and captivity narratives supply the major definitions of tribal life in the Jeffersonian period. Official government materials and the records of missionaries to the tribes provide the basis for associating ideas with specific policies. Personal papers have been used with caution. Much valuable information can be found in private correspondence, but it must be treated in light of the formal conceptions of the native peoples that were critical in the establishment of national policy. In fact, the two sources are not in opposition. One often finds a greater frankness in private correspondence, perhaps more signs of flagging sympathy, but the Jeffersonian generation believed privately what it said publicly.

Thomas Jefferson's views are in print largely in the foundation work of the period, *Notes on the State of Virginia,* ed. William Peden (Chapel Hill, 1955), and in the various editions of his writings: Julian P. Boyd, ed., *The Papers of Thomas Jefferson,* 17 vols. to date (Princeton, 1950–), Paul Leicester Ford, ed., *The Writings of Thomas Jefferson,* 10 vols. (New York, 1892–1899), and Andrew A. Lipscomb and Albert Ellery Bergh, eds., *The Writings of Thomas Jefferson,* 20 vols. (Washington, D.C., 1903–1904). A convenient collection of Jefferson's Indian speeches is in Saul K. Padover, ed., *The Complete Jefferson* . . . (New York, 1943), and his correspondence with John Adams may be consulted in the two-volume edition by Lester J. Cappon, *The Adams-Jefferson Letters: The Complete Correspondence Between Thomas Jefferson and*

Abigail and John Adams (Chapel Hill, 1959). For letters not printed in any of these sources, I used the microfilm version of the Jefferson Papers in the Library of Congress and the Coolidge Collection in the Massachusetts Historical Society, Boston, both available at the Alderman Library of the University of Virginia, Charlottesville.

Washington's views are contained in John C. Fitzpatrick, ed., *The Writings of George Washington from the Original Manuscript Sources, 1745–1799,* 39 vols. (Washington, D.C., 1931–1944), and in C. W. Butterfield, ed., *Washington-Irvine Correspondence: The Official Letters which Passed between Washington and Brig.-Gen. William Irvine and between Irvine and Others concerning Military Affairs in the West from 1781 and 1783* (Madison, 1882). The stereotyped opinions of Franklin are easily consulted in Leonard W. Labaree *et al.,* eds., *The Papers of Benjamin Franklin,* 15 vols. to date (New Haven, 1959–), and in the same editors' *The Autobiography of Benjamin Franklin* (New Haven, 1964). The older version of *The Writings of Benjamin Franklin,* 10 vols. (New York, 1905–1907) was edited by Albert H. Smyth. Julian P. Boyd, ed., *Indian Treaties Printed by Benjamin Franklin, 1736–1762* (Philadelphia, 1938), remains an extraordinary example of how white men who actually knew Indians conceived of them in the traditional formulas. Franklin Bowditch Dexter has edited *The Literary Diary of Ezra Stiles . . . ,* 3 vols. (New York, 1901) and *Extracts from the Itineraries and Other Miscellanies of Ezra Stiles . . .* (New Haven, 1916). *The Autobiography of Benjamin Rush . . .* (Princeton, 1948), edited by George W. Corner, and the *Letters of Benjamin Rush* (Princeton, 1951), edited by L. H. Butterfield, throw light on the opinions of the Philadelphia doctor. Donald Jackson's collection of *Letters of the Lewis and Clark Expedition, with Related Documents, 1783–1854* (Urbana, 1962) supplements Reuben Gold Thwaites, ed., *Original Journals of the Lewis and Clark Expedition, 1804–1806,* 8 vols. (New York, 1904–1905). Jackson's edition of *The Journals of Zebulon Montgomery Pike, with Letters and Related Documents,* 2 vols. (Norman, 1966) is also useful. Material on the frontier point of view can be found in William Henry Smith, ed., *The St. Clair Papers . . . ,* 2 vols. (Cincinnati, 1882); Samuel C. Williams, ed., "The Executive Journal of Gov. John Sevier," East Tennessee Historical Society, *Publications,* Nos. 1–4 (1929–1932); Gayle Thornbrough, ed., *The Correspondence of John Badollet and Albert Gallatin, 1804–1836, Indiana Historical Publications,* XXII (Indianapolis, 1963); and

Logan Esarey, ed., *Messages and Letters of William Henry Harrison*, in the Governors' Messages and Papers Series, *Indiana Historical Collections*, VII, IX (Indianapolis, 1922). Charles Francis Adams, ed., *Memoirs of John Quincy Adams, Comprising Portions of His Diary from 1795 to 1848*, 12 vols. (Philadelphia, 1874–1877), contains occasional but pertinent references. Thomas L. McKenney justifies himself in *Memoirs, Official and Personal; with Sketches of Travels among the Northern and Southern Indians*, 2 vols. (New York, 1846) and *Sketches of a Tour to the Lakes, of the character and customs of the Chippeway Indians, and of incidents connected with the Treaty of Fond du Lac* (Baltimore, 1827).

The richest source of material on Indian affairs can be found in the Records of the Bureau of Indian Affairs (Record Group 75), National Archives, which may be obtained on microfilm. There are letters and reports here by virtually every prominent person (and many more not so prominent) concerned with Indian-white relations in the Jeffersonian period. Dearborn, Coxe, Harrison, Calhoun, Crawford, Barbour, Hawkins, Meigs, Clark, Cass, and McKenney are some whose opinions are recorded in these documents. They form the basis for the examination of public policy contained in this book. The two volumes on *Indian Affairs* in the series of *American State Papers. Documents, Legislative and Executive . . .* (Washington, D.C., 1832–1861) are an extraordinarily well-chosen selection of government material. Clarence E. Carter, ed., *The Territorial Papers of the United States*, 24 vols. (Washington, D.C., 1934–   ) and James D. Richardson, ed., *A Compilation of the Messages and Papers of the Presidents, 1789–1902*, 10 vols. (Washington, D.C., 1913) provide added governmental material on Indian affairs. For the Revolutionary War and Confederation periods, Worthington C. Ford *et al.*, eds., *Journals of the Continental Congress, 1774–1789*, 34 vols. (Washington, D.C., 1904–1937), The Papers of the Continental Congress, 1774–1789, available on microfilm, and Edmund C. Burnett, ed., *Letters of Members of the Continental Congress*, 8 vols. (Washington, D.C., 1921–1938) are the basic sources. *Speeches on the Passage of the Bill for the Removal of the Indians, Delivered in the Congress of the United States, April and May, 1830* (Boston, 1830) is a convenient collection of the speeches against the removal bill. The entire debate can be followed in *Register of Debates in Congress*, 21st Congress, 1st Session, 305*ff* and 580*ff*. Reports on Indian affairs can be consulted in the serial set of congressional documents. Much of this material, however, duplicates letters and reports in the National Archives.

Of the vast array of archival material available for the investigation of Indian-white relations, I found the following collections useful for the understanding of philanthropic attitudes toward the Indians. The American Board of Commissioners for Foreign Missions Papers in the Houghton Library, Harvard University, Cambridge, Mass., is the single most important source. The American Board was the major philanthropic instrument in the later years of the Jeffersonian era, and its archives contain letters and reports from such important figures as Samuel A. Worcester, Jeremiah Evarts, Cyrus Kingsbury, and Elias Cornelius. The Vaill Collection, Yale University Library, New Haven, Conn., which I read on microfilm, proved revealing for the Gold-Boudinot marriage. Two Moravian missionaries left sophisticated accounts of their knowledge of the natives: John Heckewelder, "An Account of the History, Manners, and Customs, of the Indian Nations, who Once Inhabited Pennsylvania and the Neighbouring States," American Philosophical Society, *Transactions of the Historical and Literary Committee*, I (1819), 1–348, and Archer Butler Hulbert and William Nathaniel Schwarze, eds., "David Zeisberger's History of the Northern American Indians," Ohio Archaeological and Historical Society, *Publications*, XIX (1910), 1–189. The career of the Baptist missionary Isaac McCoy may be traced in Lela Barnes, ed., "Journal of Isaac McCoy . . . ," *Kansas Historical Quarterly*, V (1936), 227–277, 339–337. McCoy's papers (microfilm) are in the Kansas State Historical Society, Topeka.

The papers of Benjamin Hawkins, both manuscripts and the large collection of transcripts brought together by Louise F. Hays, in the Georgia Department of Archives and History, Atlanta, contain much information on the early effort to civilize the Cherokees. Published Hawkins material can be found in the *Letters of Benjamin Hawkins, 1796–1806*, Georgia Historical Society, *Collections*, IX (Savannah, 1916), and in his "A Sketch of the Creek Country, in the Years 1798 and 1799," in the same *Collections*, III (Savannah, 1848). Also in the Georgia Department of Archives and History, the Timothy Barnard Papers (manuscripts and transcripts) and a small collection of Return J. Meigs material offer a glimpse of frontier life, as do the Georgia Governor's Letter Books. The Albert Gallatin Papers in the New-York Historical Society, especially boxes 64 through 67 containing his Indian vocabularies, testify to the basic connection between scholarly interest in the tribes and benevolence. Gallatin wrote a summary of his views of the Indians in his "A Synopsis of the Indian Tribes within the United

States East of the Rocky Mountains, and in the British and Russian Possessions in North America," American Antiquarian Society, *Archaeologia Americana* (*Transactions and Collections*, II [Worcester, Mass., 1836]) , 7–422. The miscellaneous DeWitt Clinton manuscripts also in the New-York Historical Society reveal a similar scholarly and philanthropic interest. I used microfilm of the Timothy Pickering Papers in the Massachusetts Historical Society, edited by Frederick S. Allis and Roy Bartolomei. They reveal a man of broad interest and intelligence and of deep sympathy for the Indians. Volumes 59 through 62 contain the bulk of the Indian material. The sources available in the American Philosophical Society were easily accessible through John F. Freeman, comp., *A Guide to Manuscripts Relating to the American Indian in the Library of the American Philosophical Society* (Philadelphia, 1966) , which is Volume LXV of the society's Memoirs. The Miscellaneous Manuscripts Collection there holds the remnants of Jefferson's Indian vocabularies and much material referring to the tribes. Letters by Peter S. Du Ponceau and Caspar Wistar were valuable for information on tribal ethnology.

Titles

BOOKS:

Acosta, Joseph D. *The Natural & Moral History of the Indies,* ed. Clements R. Markham. 2 vols. London, 1880.

Adair, James. *The History of the American Indians.* . . . London, 1775.

Affecting History of the Dreadful Distresses of Frederick Manheim's Family. . . . Exeter, N.H., 1793.

Ashe, Thomas. *Travels in America.* . . . London, 1809.

Atwater, Caleb. *Description of the Antiquities Discovered in the State of Ohio and Other Western States.* . . . [Circleville, Ohio], 1820.

Barton, Benjamin Smith. *New Views of the Origin of the Tribes and Nations of America.* Philadelphia, 1797.

Bartram, William. *The Travels of William Bartram: Naturalist's Edition,* ed. Francis Harper. New Haven, 1958.

Belknap, Jeremy. *A Discourse, Intended to Commemorate the Discovery of America by Christopher Columbus.* . . . Boston, 1792.

Belknap, Jeremy, and Jedidiah Morse. *Report on the Oneida, Stockbridge, and Brotherton Indians, 1796.* Indian Notes and Monographs, No. 54, Museum of the American Indian, Heye Foundation. New York, 1955.

Beverley, Robert. *The History and Present State of Virginia,* ed. Louis B. Wright. Chapel Hill, 1947.

Bleeker, Ann Eliza. *The History of Maria Kittle.* Hartford, 1797.

Boudinot, Elias. *A Star in the West; or, A Humble Attempt to discover the long lost Ten Tribes of Israel.* . . . Trenton, 1816.

Brackenridge, H. H. *Indian Atrocities. Narratives of the Perils and Sufferings of Dr. Knight and John Slover, among the Indians, during the Revolutionary War.* . . . Cincinnati, 1867.

Brackenridge, H. M. *Views of Louisiana; Together with a Journal of a Voyage up the Missouri River, in 1811.* Ann Arbor, 1966; orig. publ. Pittsburgh, 1814.

Bradbury, John. *Travels in the Interior of America.* . . . Ann Arbor, 1966; orig. publ. Liverpool, 1817.

Bristed, John. *The Resources of the United States of America.* . . . New York, 1818.

Bryan, Daniel. *The Mountain Muse: Comprising the Adventures of Daniel Boone; and the Power of Virtuous and Refined Beauty.* Harrisonburg, Va., 1813.

Buffon, [George Louis Leclerc], Count de. *Natural History, General and Particular . . .* , trans. William Smellie. 3d ed. 9 vols. London, 1791.

[Burke, Edmund]. *An Account of the European Settlements in America. . . .* New ed. London, 1766.

Byrd, William. *William Byrd's Histories of the Dividing Line Betwixt Virginia and North Carolina*, ed. William K. Boyd. Raleigh, 1929.

Campbell, William W. *The Life and Writings of De Witt Clinton.* New York, 1849.

Carver, Jonathan. *Three Years Travels Through the Interior Parts of North-America. . . .* Philadelphia, 1796.

Catesby, Mark. *The Natural History of Carolina, Florida, and the Bahama Islands. . . .* 2 vols. London, 1771.

Charlevoix, Pierre François Xavier de. *Journal of a Voyage to North America*, ed. Louise Phelps Kellogg. 2 vols. Chicago, 1923; orig. publ. London, 1761.

[Cheever, George B.]. *The Removal of the Indians. An Article from the American Monthly Magazine. . . .* Boston, 1830.

Clinton, DeWitt. *A Memoir on the Antiquities of the Western Parts of the State of New-York.* Albany, 1818.

Colden, Cadwallader. *The History of the Five Indian Nations Depending on the Province of New-York in America.* London, 1747.

Crèvecoeur, Michel-Guillaume St. Jean de. *Crèvecoeur's Eighteenth-Century Travels in Pennsylvania & New York*, ed. and trans. Percy G. Adams. [Lexington, Ky.], 1961.

————. *Journey into Northern Pennsylvania and the State of New York*, trans. Clarissa Spencer Bostelmann. Ann Arbor, 1964.

————. *Letters from an American Farmer.* New York, 1904; orig. publ. London, 1782.

————. *Sketches of Eighteenth Century America: More "Letters from an American Farmer,"* eds. Henri L. Bourdin, Ralph H. Gabriel, and Stanley T. Williams. New Haven, 1925.

Documents and Proceedings relating to the Formation and Progress of a Board in the City of New York, for the Emigration, Preservation, and Improvement, of the Aborigines of America. New York, 1829.

Doddridge, Joseph. *Notes, on the Settlement and Indian Wars, of the Western Parts of Virginia & Pennsylvania. . . .* Wellsburgh, Va., 1824.

Drake, Samuel G. *Indian Captivities or Life in the Wigwam. . . .* Auburn, [N.Y.], 1852.

Ellicott, Andrew. *The Journal of Andrew Ellicott. . . .* Philadelphia, 1803.

Elliot, James. *The Poetical and Miscellaneous Works of James Elliot. . . .* Greenfield, Mass., 1798.

[Evarts, Jeremiah]. *Essays on the Present Crisis in the Condition of the American Indians. . . .* Boston, 1829.

Ferguson, Adam. *An Essay on the History of Civil Society. . . .* 8th ed. Philadelphia, 1819.

Filson, John. *The Discovery, Settlement and Present State of Kentucke: and An Essay towards the Topography, and Natural History of that important Country. . . .* Wilmington, 1784.

Flint, Timothy. *Indian Wars of the West.* . . . Cincinnati, 1833.

————. *Recollections of the Last Ten Years.* . . . New York, 1968; orig. publ. Boston, 1826.

Force, Peter, ed. *American Archives.* . . . Washington, D.C., 1837–1853.

Foster, Augustus John. *Jeffersonian America* . . . , ed. Richard Beale Davis. San Marino, Calif., 1954.

Freneau, Philip. *The Last Poems of Philip Freneau,* ed. Lewis Leary. New Brunswick, N.J., 1945.

————. *The Poems of Philip Freneau: Poet of the Revolution,* ed. Fred Lewis Pattee. 3 vols. Princeton, 1902–1907.

————. *The Prose of Philip Freneau,* ed. Philip M. Marsh. New Brunswick, N.J., 1955.

Grant, [Anne]. *Memoirs of an American Lady.* . . . New York, 1809.

Grotius, Hugo. *On the Origin of the Native Races of America* . . . , ed. and trans. Edmund Goldsmid. Edinburgh, 1884.

Harris, Thaddeus Mason. *The Journal of a Tour into the Territory Northwest of the Alleghany Mountains.* . . . Boston, 1805.

Henry, Alexander. *Alexander Henry's Travels* . . . , ed. Milo Milton Quaife. Chicago, 1921.

Hunter, John D. *Manners and Customs of Several Indian Tribes Located West of the Mississippi.* . . . Philadelphia, 1823.

Imlay, Gilbert. *A Topographical Description of the Western Territory of North America: containing a Succinct Account of its Soil, Climate, Natural History, Population, Agriculture, Manners, and Customs.* . . . 3d ed. London, 1797.

Jackson, Halliday. *Civilization of the Indian Natives.* . . . Philadelphia, 1830.

James, Edwin. "James's Account of S. H. Long's Expedition, 1819–1820." In *Early Western Travels, 1748–1846,* ed. Reuben Gold Thwaites. XIV–XVII. Cleveland, 1905.

Janson, Charles William. *The Stranger in America: Containing Observations made during a Long Residence in that Country, on the Genius, Manners and Customs of the People of the United States.* . . . London, 1807.

Jefferson, Thomas. *Message from the President of the United States, Communicating Discoveries Made in Exploring the Missouri, Red River and Washita, by Captains Lewis and Clark.* . . . Washington, D.C., 1806.

Johnson, Sir William. *The Papers of Sir William Johnson* . . . , ed. James Sullivan. 13 vols. Albany, 1921–1962.

Johnston, Charles. *A Narrative of the Incidents Attending the Capture, Detention, and Ransom of Charles Johnston.* . . . New York, 1827.

Jones, Hugh. *The Present State of Virginia* . . . , ed. Richard L. Morton. Chapel Hill, 1956.

Kalm, Peter. *The America of 1750: Peter Kalm's Travels in North America,* ed. Adolph B. Benson. 2 vols. New York, 1937.

Kames, [Henry Home], Lord. *Essays on the Principles of Morality and Natural Religion; with other Essays concerning the proof of a Deity.* Edinburgh, 1751.

————. *Sketches of the History of Man.* 4 vols. Dublin, 1775.

Keith, William. *The History of the British Plantations in America.* . . . London, 1738.

Lawson, John. *Lawson's History of North Carolina* . . . , ed. Frances Latham Harriss. 2d ed. Richmond, 1952.

Ledyard, John. *John Ledyard's Journey through Russia and Siberia, 1787–1788* . . . , ed. Stephen D. Watrous. Madison, 1966.

————. *A Journal of Captain Cook's Last Voyage.* . . . Chicago, 1963; orig. publ. Hartford, 1783.

Locke, John. *An Essay Concerning Human Understanding.* 24th ed. London, 1823.

Long, J[ohn]. *Voyage and Travels of an Indian Interpreter and Trader.* . . . London, 1791.

Loskiel, George Henry. *History of the Mission of the United Brethren among the Indians in North America,* trans. Christian Ignatius La Trobe. London, 1794.

Loudon, Archibald, comp., *A Selection, of Some of the Most Interesting Narratives of Outrages, Committed by the Indians in Their Wars with the White People.* . . . Harrisburg, 1888.

McCoy, Isaac. *History of Baptist Indian Missions: embracing Remarks on the Former and Present Condition of the Aboriginal Tribes.* . . . Washington, D.C., 1840.

————. *Remarks on the Practicability of Indian Reform, Embracing Their Colonization.* 2d ed. New York, 1829.

McKenney, Thomas L., and James Hall. *The Indian Tribes of North America,* ed. Frederick Webb Hodge. 3 vols. Edinburgh, 1933.

Mackenzie, Alexander. *Exploring the Northwest Territory* . . . , ed. T. H. McDonald. Norman, 1966.

Mather, Cotton. *Magnalia Christi Americana; or, The Ecclesiastical History of New-England.* 2 vols. Hartford, 1820; orig. publ. London, 1702.

Miller, Samuel. *A Brief Retrospect of the Eighteenth Century.* . . . 2 vols. New York, 1803.

[Mitchell, John]. *The Present State of Great Britain and North America.* . . . London, 1767.

Moore, Clement C. *Observations upon Certain Passages in Mr. Jefferson's Notes on Virginia, which Appear to have a Tendency to Subvert Religion, and Establish a False Philosophy.* New York, 1804.

Morse, Jedidiah. *The American Universal Geography.* . . . 2 vols. Boston, 1796.

————. *The History of America.* 3d ed. Philadelphia, 1798.

————. *A Report to the Secretary of War of the United States, on Indian Affairs, Comprising a Narrative of a Tour Performed in the Summer of 1820.* . . . New Haven, 1822.

————. *Signs of the Times.* . . . Charlestown, Mass., 1810.

Moses, Montrose J., ed. *Representative American Plays by American Dramatists, 1765–1819.* New York, 1946.

Nuttall, Thomas. *A Journal of Travels into the Arkansa Territory during the Year 1819.* . . . Ann Arbor, 1966; orig. publ. Philadelphia, 1821.

Oldmixon, John. *The British Empire in America.* . . . 2 vols. London, 1708.

Page, Eugene R., ed. *Metamora & Other Plays.* Princeton, 1941.

P[auw, Cornelius] de. *Recherches philosophiques sur les Américains.* . . . 2 vols. London, 1770.

Priest, Josiah. *American Antiquities, and Discoveries in the West.* . . . 2d ed., rev. Albany, 1833.

Raynal, Guillaume Thomas François. *Histoire Philosophique et Politique, Des Établissemens & du Commerce de Européens dans les deux Indes.* 6 vols. Amsterdam, 1770.

————. *A Philosophical and Political History of the Settlements and Trade of the Europeans in the East and West Indies,* trans. J. O. Justamond. 2d ed. London, 1798.

Robertson, William. *The History of America.* 10th ed. 4 vols. London, 1803.

Rogers, Robert. *A Concise Account of North America.* . . . London, 1765.

————. *Ponteach: or The Savages of America. A Tragedy.* Chicago, 1914; orig. publ. London, 1766.

Romans, Bernard. *A Concise Natural History of East and West Florida.* . . . New York, 1775.

Rowlandson, Mary. *The Narrative of the Captivity and Restoration of Mrs. Mary Rowlandson.* . . . Boston, 1930.

Rush, Benjamin. *Essays, Literary, Moral and Philosophical.* 2d ed. Philadelphia, 1806.

————. *Medical Inquiries and Observations.* Philadelphia, 1789. Also 2d and 3d eds. 4 vols. Philadelphia, 1805, 1809.

————. *Sixteen Introductory Lectures.* . . . Philadelphia, 1811.

————. *Three Lectures upon Animal Life.* . . . Philadelphia, 1799.

Seaver, James E. *A Narrative of the Life of Mrs. Mary Jemison.* . . . New York, 1961; orig. publ. Canandaigua, N.Y., 1824.

Smith, John Augustine. "A Discourse, on the Manner in Which Peculiarities in the Anatomical Structure Affect the Moral Character. . . ." In *A Syllabus of the Lectures Delivered to the Senior Students in the College of William and Mary on Government.* Philadelphia, 1817.

Smith, Samuel Stanhope. *An Essay on the Causes of the Variety of Complexion and Figure in the Human Species.* . . . Philadelphia, 1787. 2d ed. New Brunswick, N.J., 1810.

Smyth, J. F. D. *A Tour in the United States of America.* . . . 2 vols. London, 1784.

A Statement of the Indian Relations; with a Reply to the Article in the Sixty-Sixth Number of the North American Review, on the Removal of the Indians. New York, 1830.

Stith, William. *The History of the First Discovery and Settlement of Virginia.* . . . Williamsburg, 1747.

Stoddard, Amos. *Sketches, Historical and Descriptive, of Louisiana.* Philadelphia, 1812.

[Stork, William]. *A Description of East-Florida, with a Journal, Kept by John Bartram of Philadelphia.* . . . 3d ed. London, 1769.

[Thomson, Charles]. *An Enquiry into the Causes of the Alienation of the Delaware and Shawanese Indians from the British Interest, and into the Measures Taken for Recovering Their Friendship.* London, 1759.

Timberlake, Henry. *The Memoirs of Lieut. Henry Timberlake.* . . . London, 1765.

Tocqueville, Alexis de. *Democracy in America,* eds. J. P. Mayer and Max Lerner. New York, 1966.

Urness, Carol, ed. *A Naturalist in Russia: Letters from Peter Simon Pallas to Thomas Pennant.* Minneapolis, 1967.

Weld, Isaac. *Travels through the States of North America.* . . . London, 1799.

White, Charles. *An Account of the Regular Gradation in Man.* . . . London, 1799.

White, John. *The American Drawings of John White, 1517–1590* . . . , eds. Paul Hulton and David Beers Quinn. 2 vols. London, 1964.

Williams, John. *The Redeemed Captive Returning to Zion.* . . . 6th ed. Ann Arbor, 1966; orig. publ. Boston, 1795.

Williams, Samuel. *The Natural and Civil History of Vermont.* Walpole, N.H., 1794. Also 2d ed. 2 vols. Burlington, Vt., 1809.

Williamson, Hugh. *Observations on the Climate in Different Parts of America, Compared with the Climate in Corresponding Parts of the Other Continent.* . . . New York, 1811.

Woodward, Thomas S. *Woodward's Reminiscences of the Creek, or Muscogee Indians.* . . . Tuscaloosa, Ala., 1939.

PERIODICALS AND SERIALS:

Alabama Historical Quarterly
American Academy of Arts and Sciences, *Memoirs*
American Anthropologist
American Antiquarian Society, *Archaeologia Americana (Transactions and Collections)*
American Ethnological Society, *Transactions*
American Historical Review
The American Museum
American Philosophical Society, *Transactions* and *Proceedings*
American Philosophical Society, *Transactions of the Historical and Literary Committee*
Analectic Magazine
The Annals
Annals of Nature
Cherokee Phoenix (New Echota, Ga.)
Columbian Magazine
East Tennessee Historical Society, *Publications*
Ethnohistory
Georgia Historical Society, *Collections*
Historical Society of Pennsylvania, *Memoirs*
Indiana Historical Collections
Kansas Historical Quarterly
Literary and Historical Society of New-York, *Transactions*
Miscellaneous Magazine
Missionary Herald (Panoplist)
Mississippi Valley Historical Review
Monthly Anthology and Boston Review
National Intelligencer
New-York Historical Society, *Collections*
New York Medical and Philosophical Journal and Review

New-York Review
Niles' Weekly Register
North American Review
North Carolina Historical Review
Ohio Archaeological and Historical Society, *Publications*
Pennsylvania Magazine of History and Biography
Quarterly Review
Smithsonian Contributions to Knowledge
Spirit of the Pilgrims
Western Review
William and Mary Quarterly
Wisconsin Magazine of History

Index

NINETEENTH AND TWENTIETH CENTURY.
AMERICAN HISTORY IN NORTON PAPERBACK

David Freeman Hawke *Those Tremendous Mountains: The Lewis and Clark Expedition* 30289

Thomas Wentworth Higginson *Army Life in a Black Regiment* 30157

Michael F. Holt *The Political Crisis of the 1850s* 95370

Townsend Hoopes *The Limits of Intervention* 30427

Francis Jennings *The Invasion of America: Indians, Colonialism and the Cant of Conquest* N830

Michael P. Johnson and James L. Roark *Black Masters: A Free Family of Color in the Old South* 30314

Michael P. Johnson and James L. Roark, Eds. *No Chariot Let Down: Charleston's Free People of Color on the Eve of the Civil War* 95524

George F. Kennan *Russia Leaves the War (Soviet-American Relations, 1917–1920, 1)* 30214

George F. Kennan *The Decision to Intervene (Soviet-American Relations, 1917–1920, 2)* 30217

Gabriel Kolko *Railroads and Regulation, 1877–1916* N531

Stanley I. Kutler *Privilege and Creative Destruction: The Charles River Bridge Case* N885

Walter LaFeber *Inevitable Revolutions: The United States in Central America* (Exp. Ed.) 30212

Peggy Lamson *The Glorious Failure: Black Congressman Robert Brown Elliott and the Reconstruction in South Carolina* N733

Suzanne Lebsock *The Free Women of Petersburg: Status and Culture in a Southern Town, 1784–1860* 95264

John Lynch *The Spanish-American Revolutions, 1806–1826* (2d Ed.) 95537

Richard P. McCormick *The Second American Party System: Party Formation in the Jacksonian Era* N680

William S. McFeely *Grant: A Biography* 30046

William S. McFeely *Yankee Stepfather: General O.O. Howard and the Freedmen* 00537

Robert C. McMath, Jr. *Populist Vanguard: A History of the Southern Farmers' Alliance* N869

Herbert S. Mitgang *The Man Who Rode the Tiger: The Life and Times of Judge Samuel Seabury* N922

Burl Noggle *Teapot Dome* N297

Douglass C. North *The Economic Growth of the United States, 1790–1860* N346

G.J.A. O'Toole *The Spanish War: An American Epic, 1898* 80304

Robert E. Quirk   *An Affair of Honor: Woodrow Wilson and the Occupation of Veracruz*   N390

James L. Roark   *Masters Without Slaves: Southern Planters in the Civil War and Reconstruction*   N901

Richard H. Sewell   *Ballots for Freedom: Antislavery Politics in the U.S.*   N966

Bernard W. Sheehan   *Seeds of Extinction: Jeffersonian Philanthropy and the American Indian*   N715

Kathryn Kish Sklar   *Catharine Beecher: A Study in American Domesticity*   N812

John W. Spanier   *The Truman-MacArthur Controversy and the Korean War*   N279

Sarah Stage   *Female Complaints: Lydia Pinkham and the Business of Women's Medicine*   N038

Dorothy Sterling, Ed.   *We Are Your Sisters: Black Women in the Nineteenth Century*   30252

Ida M. Tarbell   *History of the Standard Oil Company*   (David Chalmers, Ed.)   N496

George Brown Tindall   *The Disruption of the Solid South*   N663

Richard W. Van Alstyne   *The Rising American Empire*   N750

Ronald G. Walters   *The Antislavery Appeal: American Abolitionism After 1830*   95444

Thomas L. Webber   *Deep Like the Rivers: Education in the Slave Quarter Community, 1831–1865*   N998